Pro iOS 5 Augmented Reality

Kyle Roche

Apress®

Pro iOS 5 Augmented Reality

ISBN 978-1-4302-3912-3

ISBN 978-1-4302-3913-0 (eBook)

President and Publisher: Paul Manning
Lead Editor: Kate Blackham
Technical Reviewer: Yosun Chang, Peter Ma, Graham Wood
Editorial Board: Steve Anglin, Mark Beckner, Ewan Buckingham, Gary Cornell, Morgan Ertel, Jonathan Gennick, Jonathan Hassell, Robert Hutchinson, Michelle Lowman, James Markham, Matthew Moodie, Jeff Olson, Jeffrey Pepper, Douglas Pundick, Ben Renow-Clarke, Dominic Shakeshaft, Gwenan Spearing, Matt Wade, Tom Welsh
Coordinating Editor: Corbin Collins
Copy Editor: Vanessa Moore
Compositor: MacPS, LLC
Indexer: BIM Indexing & Proofreading Services
Artist: SPi Global
Cover Designer: Anna Ishchenko

Distributed to the book trade worldwide by Springer Science+Business Media, LLC., 233 Spring Street, 6th Floor, New York, NY 10013. Phone 1-800-SPRINGER, fax (201) 348-4505, e-mail orders-ny@springer-sbm.com, or visit www.springeronline.com.

For information on translations, please e-mail rights@apress.com, or visit www.apress.com.

Apress and friends of ED books may be purchased in bulk for academic, corporate, or promotional use. eBook versions and licenses are also available for most titles. For more information, reference our Special Bulk Sales–eBook Licensing web page at www.apress.com/info/bulksales.

Any source code or other supplementary materials referenced by the author in this text is available to readers at www.apress.com. For detailed information about how to locate your book's source code, go to www.apress.com/source-code/.

Contents at a Glance

Contents

About the Author

 **Kyle Roche** has been focused on emerging technologies since 2000. During his time at Appirio, he led some of the world's first and largest Google and Force.com cloud platform migrations. He is the chief architect behind RingDNA (ringdna.com) and the co-founder of 2lemetry (2lemetry.com). Mobile applications and connected electronics (M2M) are the main focus of all of Kyle's projects. Augmented reality and gaming frameworks play a large part in how these applications are visualized. Kyle studied mathematics and was on the wrestling team at the University of New Mexico. He currently lives in Denver, Colorado with his wife Jessica and their four children: Aodhan, Avery, Kelly, and Timmy. If there is ever free time outside of family life, Kyle spends it playing hockey or building iOS applications for local nonprofits. You can find him at kyleroche.com.

About the Technical Reviewers

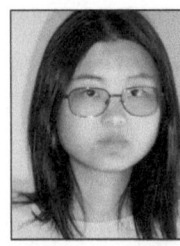

Yosun Chang has been creating apps for iOS and Android since early 2009, and is currently working on a next generation 3D and augmented reality mobile games startup called nusoy. Prior to that, since 1999 she did web development on the LAMP stack and Flash. She has also spoken at several virtual world, theater, and augmented reality conferences under her artist name of Ina Centaur. She has a graduate level background in physics and philosophy from UC San Diego and UC Berkeley. An avid reader who learned much of her coding chops from technical books like the current volume, she has taken care to read every single word of the chapters she reviewed — and vet the source. Contact her @yosunchang on Twitter.

Peter Ma has been working with web, iOS, Android, WebOS, and WP7 since 2007. He has been building projects from database design to mobile presentation. Peter has won many hackathons and developer challenges, all using native tools. He has won a TED Prize sponsored challenge and gave a TED talk about building mobile apps during TED Global2010. The mobile app Pickup Sports was the foundation for Spotvite and had over 80,000 signups. Peter is also involved in many open source projects; he has pioneered the TEDx app that helps organizers to build their own iOS and Android applications. Contact him @Nyceane on Twitter.

Graham Wood is a mobile application developer whose primary focus is the iOS platform. He has 11 years of experience in software development, with most of that time spent writing software for safety critical embedded systems for commercial aircraft. Graham holds a Bachelor of Science degree in Computer Science from the University of Minnesota. His company, Wood App Developers LLC, develops mobile applications for clients, along with its own suite of iOS applications. He can be reached at graham@woodappsllc.com or followed on Twitter at @woodappsllc.

Acknowledgments

I wrote this book in the middle of a transition between startups. We were transitioning from one company and starting two new projects. Furthermore, iOS 5 was in beta for most of the timeline. It was a very difficult time to be writing a book. It wouldn't have been possible without the support from the Apress team, led by Corbin Collins and Steve Anglin.

From a technical perspective, I want to thank my colleague Sergey Loshchilov. Sergey is a post-graduate student from Nizhny Novgorod State Technical University. He was a huge help on the OpenCV sections and the new iOS 5 APIs. Sergey is publishing a paper comparing the algorithms in the more popular AR frameworks. I'll post links to it from kyleroche.com.

On a personal note, my wife and four kids have been very supportive with the long nights and weekends it takes to get a book published. I'd like to thank them for their contribution of patience and time. I had a chance to have the kids participate in the facial recognition chapter, which was fun for both them and me.

Preface

This was a fun and interesting book to write! Augmented reality is a fascinating new field with tons of potential to reshape how we integrate technology into our everyday lives. Companies and toolkits are popping up each week trying to capture a piece of this emerging market.

The goal of this book was to provide you with a jump-start on building these types of applications. I begin by discussing the basic foundations of the app, such as the compass and accelerometer, and move on to more advanced ideas behind image processing.

This book is intended for experienced iOS developers. You should have moderate experience with Xcode and objective-C. I use third-party frameworks and some of the new iOS5 APIs to show you how to build augmented reality applications for location, social, and gaming purposes. You can download the source code for this book from the book's page on Apress.com, or check out www.apress.com/source-code/.

Chapter 1

Introduction

Welcome to *Pro iOS 5 Augmented Reality*. Augmented reality (AR) has existed in sci-fi movies for decades, is used in the military for head-up displays (HUDs), and until recently, has been a thing of the future. With the upswing in mobile applications since the introduction of the iPhone and the Android operating system, applications such as Layar (www.layar.com), Metaio's Junaio (www.junaio.com), and Wikitude (www.wikitude.com) have put augmented reality in the hands of the everyday consumer. In this book, I'll walk you through how to create your own augmented reality applications for iOS.

Time magazine named augmented reality among the top-ten technology trends for 2010. *Time* barely scratched the surface on the potential applications of AR. They selected a few vendor application platforms, such as Layar, and also discussed some more day-to-day applications, such as that employed by the United States Postal Service (USPS).

Augmented Reality in the Real and Cyber World

The USPS introduced an augmented reality application to its web site in 2010. If you've ever mailed something from the post office, you can attest to the fact that quickly selecting a box that fits your needs without holding up the line is a near impossible task. Either you're stuck wasting a lot of space with a bigger box or you're holding up the 20 people behind you while you jam all your items into the box that *almost* fits everything. The USPS took a shot at making this easier, without requiring you to leave your home or office. Basically, you go to the USPS web site (www.prioritymail.com) and use the Virtual Box Simulator and your webcam to try out different box sizes before you head out for the post office. It works like this:

Print out a special icon (the USPS eagle) so the simulator knows where to put the hologram of the virtual box. See Figure 1–1.

1. Make sure your webcam is enabled.

2. Launch the Virtual Box Simulator. Put the printed image in the view of the webcam and the simulator puts a hologram of different options for shipping containers around the image. See Figure 1–2.

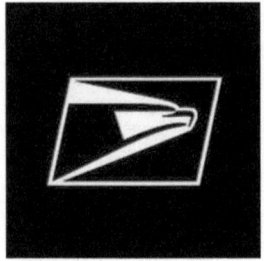

Figure 1–1. *This eagle icon is printed and used by the USPS to augment your camera's view with a simulated shipping container.*

There are a few basic principles to follow when creating icons or markers for recognition. For traditional markers, you want high-contrast objects that carry a certain uniqueness and aren't found in common scenarios. In fact, random images are often more effective. Also, you want to use images that have a certain rotation and aren't symmetrical either horizontally or vertically. This helps the AR program recognize orientation and adjust accordingly. The USPS marker is a good example of these principles.

Figure 1–2. *The hologram is overlaying the printed icon.*

Notice in Figure 1–2 that the simulator allows you to adjust transparency, move your to-be-shipped item on different angles and rotations, and experience exactly which shipping container you need to ship your materials. The USPS uses the marker and some sort of recognition algorithm to find it in the live camera view, track its orientation, and augment the picture with the current box you've selected.

Pop Culture

There are hundreds of other applications for AR in advertising, real estate, the automotive industry, and especially in consumer spending. Although statistics suggest that well over half the population of the United States has tried online shopping, the revenue accounts for only eight percent of consumer spending, according to Wikipedia. Obviously, there are various theories as to why the traction hasn't taken more market share. Among them are the basic concerns about privacy and security online, but there are equally as many theories on the lack of physical interaction accounting for an unknown product. In some cases, such as with clothing, you just need to see and feel what you're buying.

Sometime in late 2010, we started seeing multiple AR experiences penetrate the retail market. Growing up in the late '70s, I recall Jane Jetson trying out new hairstyles with the push of a button, or Luke Skywalker listening to the brief about the approach methods for the Death Star over a holographic 3D display. This type of experience is now available for consumers. From trying on new clothing and accessories, to finding out where your grocer's apples are grown, consider some of these recent examples:

- *Lego's Digital Box:* An in-store kiosk by Lego lets a child hold up the box set he or she is considering in front of a camera on the kiosk, which then overlays the fully constructed set right on top of the box. The child can move it around, turn it over, and get a feel for whether this is the set they really want to put on their Christmas list.

- *Zugara:* Zugara uses its Magic Mirror, which lets an online shopper stand in front of a webcam and try on different clothing styles, without the aid of a mouse or keyboard. In addition to overlaying the clothes from the online catalog, Zugara overlays controls in the camera's view so that the user can use gestures to interact with menu options or share their new outfit over their social network.

- *FoodTracer:* This project by Giuseppe Costana uses image recognition in AR to give grocery shoppers more information about the food they are buying. Simply wave a smartphone's camera in front of the grocer's shelf and information becomes available.

There are obvious advantages and appeals to the interactive experience. However, also consider some of the supplemental values of AR. The back end of most of these applications lives on the cloud. Image-recognition algorithms and the camera's interpretation itself are primarily running on the device, but advertising data, contextual information, location directories, and other dynamic content linked to the AR view can be loaded from the cloud and in a centralized location where updates are seamless and the applications can always remain current.

Gaming and Location-Based AR

Retail and in-store kiosks are not the only places that AR is becoming a trend. Social networks, location-based services, and gaming are leveraging AR as well. Imagine using your camera to interact with the real world in a gaming scenario. I recently saw a demo at a conference in which 3D models of zombies were rendered in the AR view of an iPhone and the user could shoot them by just tapping on the screen. It has spawned a secondary market for accessories like the iPhone gun, covered on www.augmentedplanet.com. This rifle-sized accessory mounts your iPhone to the scope, so you can have a realistic experience of shooting 3D zombies in an AR fashion.

In this book, we'll cover the basics for creating your own AR game. We'll look at various approaches to this project, including some available SDKs to speed your time to market.

Getting Your House in Order

There are a few steps you'll need to take to make sure everything on your machine is ready to go for iOS programming. In this book, we'll be using Xcode 4.2 only, and we'll be storing all our projects on GitHub. Xcode shipped with native Git integration for source-code management, so we'll be taking advantage of that to make things easier and save setup time.

Signing Up for GitHub

If you already have a GitHub account, you can skip this section. If not, you're going to need one to download the assets and starting points for each chapter. Open a browser to www.github.com and click the big **Signup** button in the middle of the page, as shown in Figure 1–3.

Plans, Pricing and Signup
Unlimited public repositories are **free!**

Figure 1–3. *The Signup button is easy to find on GitHub.*

For this book, we're going to be accessing the Git repositories that I've already set up for each chapter; and, if you're into sharing, we'll be posting any variations back for fellow readers. With that in mind, we really only need the "Free for open source" account type. Click the **Create a free account** button and fill out your information.

Accessing GitHub from Your Machine

If you've used GitHub before, you may skip this section, which is for users who have not yet created an SSH key for use with GitHub.

There are a few ways to access GitHub's remote repositories from your machine. We'll be using SSH access, which means we'll need to generate a token and post it to GitHub. Open Terminal (**Applications ➤ Utilities ➤ Terminal**) from your Mac. Take a look at Listing 1–1. Follow this same pattern in your Terminal window. I'll explain the steps next.

Listing 1–1. *Create Your SSH Key on Your Mac*

```
Kyle-Roches-MacBook-Pro-2:~ kyleroche$ cd ~/.ssh
Kyle-Roches-MacBook-Pro-2:.ssh kyleroche$ ls
known_hosts
Kyle-Roches-MacBook-Pro-2:.ssh kyleroche$ ssh-keygen -t rsa -C "kyle@isidorey.com"
Generating public/private rsa key pair.
Enter file in which to save the key (/Users/kyleroche/.ssh/id_rsa):
Enter passphrase (empty for no passphrase): [enter a passphrase here]
Enter same passphrase again: [enter your passphrase again]
Your identification has been saved in /Users/kyleroche/.ssh/id_rsa.
Your public key has been saved in /Users/kyleroche/.ssh/id_rsa.pub.
The key fingerprint is:
26:9d:3a:82:fe:r9:gf:ba:39:30:6b:98:16:fe:3b:2c kyle@isidorey.com
The key's randomart image is:
+--[ RSA 2048]----+
|                 |
|                 |
|                 |
| .       . . 4   |
|. . . ..N        |
|.  o ..+r        |
| .. ...-|=.      |
|  ..+.-E.o       |
|    +.==0000     |
+-----------------+
Kyle-Roches-MacBook-Pro-2:.ssh kyleroche$ ls
id_rsa          id_rsa.pub      known_hosts
```

The directory listing commands might have different results if you have existing keys already. In this case, you probably want to back up your key directory, just to be safe. First, we're going to use the ssh-keygen utility to create a public/private rsa key pair. The utility will ask us for a passphrase. This is optional, but passphrases do increase security. Passwords, as most of us realize, aren't all that secure on their own. Generating a key pair without a passphrase is equivalent to saving your passwords in a plain-text file on your machine. Anyone who gains access can now use your key. If you're lazy and concerned about typing it in every time, don't fret. Keychain (since we're all on a Mac) will allow you to store it after the first time you use this key pair.

So, we have a key pair. It's stored in the newly created id_rsa.pub file you see in your directory listing. Open this file in your favorite plain-text editor and copy all of its contents. It's important that you copy everything, even the headers.

Return to Github, which should be open to your account in your browser. Open your **Account Settings** page from the top-left navigation menu. Then open the subtab on the left-hand side called **SSH Public Keys**. You should see something similar to Figure 1–4.

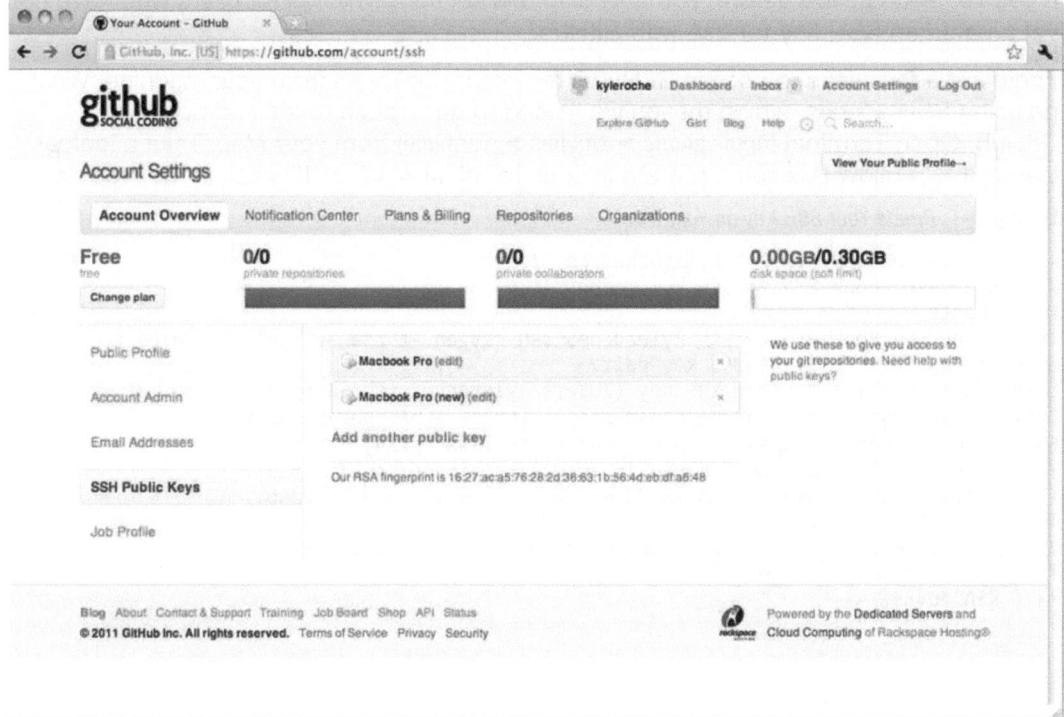

Figure 1–4. *Open the SSH Public Keys dialog on GitHub.*

Find the **Add another public key** link in the middle of the page. That will open a dialog where you will paste the contents of the id_rsa.pub file we just created. That's it! You're now set up in GitHub and your machine can access your repositories using SSH.

Because we'll be using SSH access in this book, let's quickly set up our default preferences before we move on.

We need to configure our local Git client to use the credentials that we received when signing up for GitHub. First, run the following commands from Listing 1–2 in your Terminal window to set some global flags for Git. This, in combination with your SSH keys, will authenticate your Git client to the remote repository.

Listing 1–2. *Create Your SSH Key on Your Mac*

```
Kyle-Roches-MacBook-Pro-2: kyleroche$ git config --global user.name "Kyle Roche"
Kyle-Roches-MacBook-Pro-2: kyleroche$ git config --global user.email "kyle@isidorey.com"
```

Setting Up Xcode 4.2 and Your Developer Account

If you have Xcode 4.2 already set up, you may skip this section.

To publish an app to the App Store, you need Xcode and an Apple Developer account. We can take care of both of these steps at the same time. Open your browser to `http://developer.apple.com/programs/register/` and click the **Get Started** button in the header. There are a few paths to follow here. If you want to use an existing Apple ID, you can fill that in and continue along. See Figure 1–5. Alternatively, you can create a new ID for iOS development. That might not seem reasonable, but there are a few pitfalls with using one account.

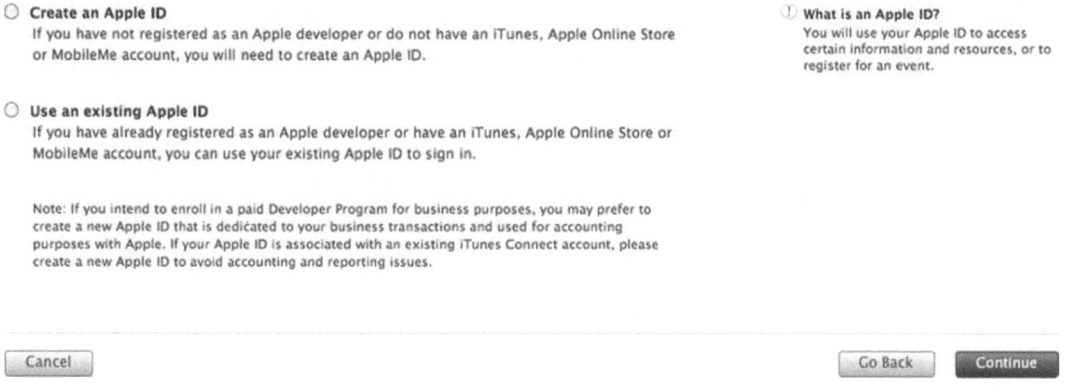

Do you have an existing Apple ID you would like to use?

○ **Create an Apple ID**
    If you have not registered as an Apple developer or do not have an iTunes, Apple Online Store
    or MobileMe account, you will need to create an Apple ID.

○ **Use an existing Apple ID**
    If you have already registered as an Apple developer or have an iTunes, Apple Online Store or
    MobileMe account, you can use your existing Apple ID to sign in.

    Note: If you intend to enroll in a paid Developer Program for business purposes, you may prefer to
    create a new Apple ID that is dedicated to your business transactions and used for accounting
    purposes with Apple. If your Apple ID is associated with an existing iTunes Connect account, please
    create a new Apple ID to avoid accounting and reporting issues.

⚠ **What is an Apple ID?**
You will use your Apple ID to access
certain information and resources, or to
register for an event.

[Cancel]   [Go Back] [Continue]

Figure 1–5. *Use existing Apple ID or create a new one?*

> **NOTE:** Choosing whether to consolidate your Apple IDs or create a second one depends on your intent in regards to publishing your apps in the future. Apple has a restriction on which publishing type you can link to an account. There are two ways to publish applications: through the App Store and through Apple's Enterprise Distribution program. An Apple ID cannot be tied to both publishing methods. Make sure you decide which ID will be responsible for which method of publishing, if you are going to cover both scenarios.

If you just want to use your account to develop and debug, then use an existing account. It's probably the simpliest path. After you are registered, log in to the **iOS Dev Center**. Find the link for **Downloads**. At the time of this writing, there are only two choices: **Download Xcode 4.2** and a series of links around iAd Producer 1.1. Download Xcode 4.2 to your machine. The download is fairly large. This is one of the drawbacks of Xcode. Each upgraded version, which have started coming more frequently since iOS, requires a new full download of the IDE.

We now have our IDE and our source control strategy set up. Let's connect the two and make sure we're ready to get started.

Linking an Xcode Project to GitHub

Return to GitHub in your browser. Click on **Dashboard** in the top-left navigation bar and find the **New Repository** button. For **Project Name** I'm going to use iOS_AR_Ch1_Introduction. Feel free to choose your own name, or if you're an experienced GitHub user, you can fork my repository from https://github.com/kyleroche. See Figure 1–6 for the options I've chosen.

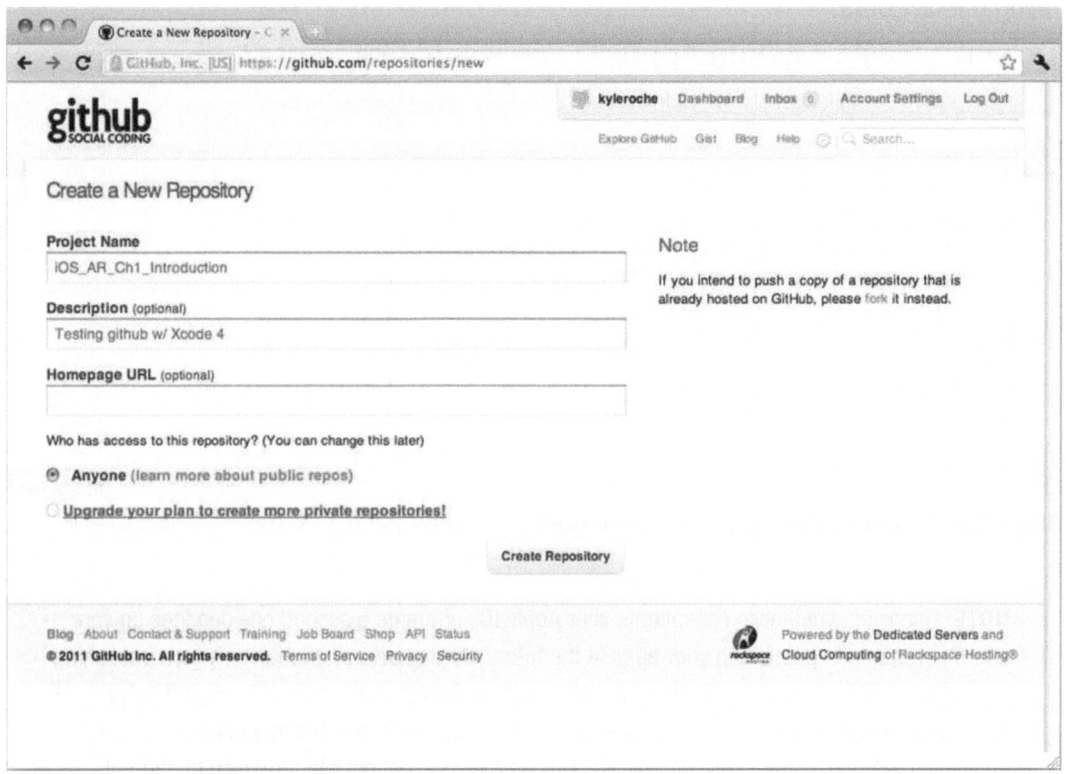

Figure 1–6. *Create a new repository at GitHub.*

Next, take note of your repository's SSH URL. You will see it in the header of the confirmation page. It will be in a form similar to git@github.com:kyleroche/ iOS_AR_Ch1_Introduction.git. You are going to need this in the next step.

Launch Xcode on your local machine. In the **Welcome to Xcode** dialog box that launches on startup, you should have an option on the left side called **Connect to a Repository**. Click this option and enter the SSH URL for your GitHub repository. See Figure 1–7 for my configuration.

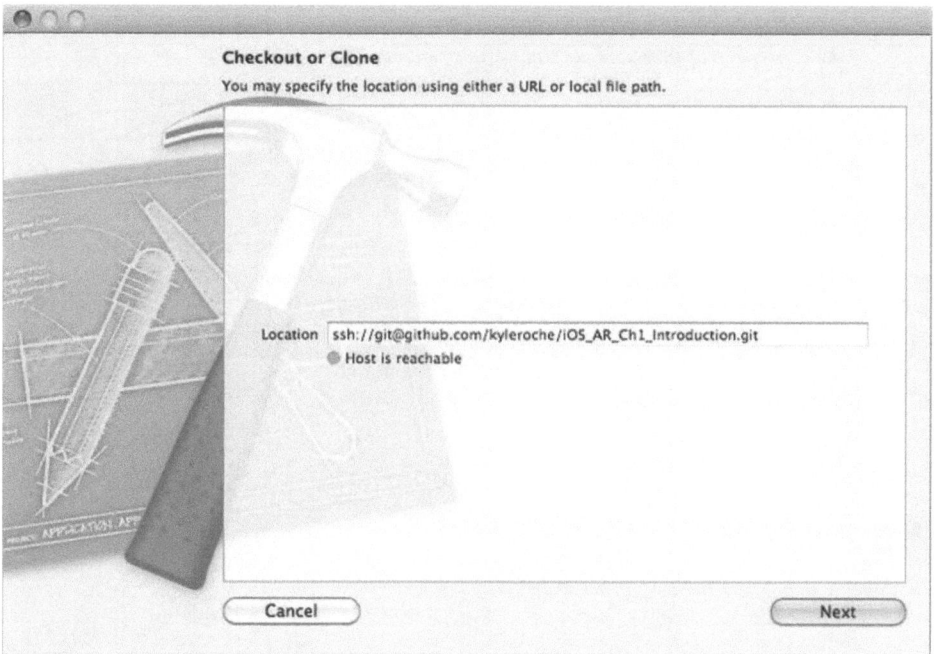

Figure 1–7. *Clone your GitHub repository for local access.*

Xcode validates your location and the ability to clone the repository. Wait a few moments until your indicator is green and the message states **Host is reachable**, then click **Next**.

You are presented with a prompt to name your new project. I am using the same name as my GitHub repository, iOS_AR_Ch1_Introduction, for simplicity. Make sure that **Type** is set to **Git** and click **Clone**.

Next, choose a location for your local repository and click **Next**.

NOTE: At the time of this writing, Xcode 4.2 still has a few bugs in regards to using Git. The first of them should have manifested itself in this last step. If your version still has issues, you will get an error similar to that shown in Figure 1–8. If this is the case, simply click **Try Again**, select the same location, choose **Replace** and everything should be fine.

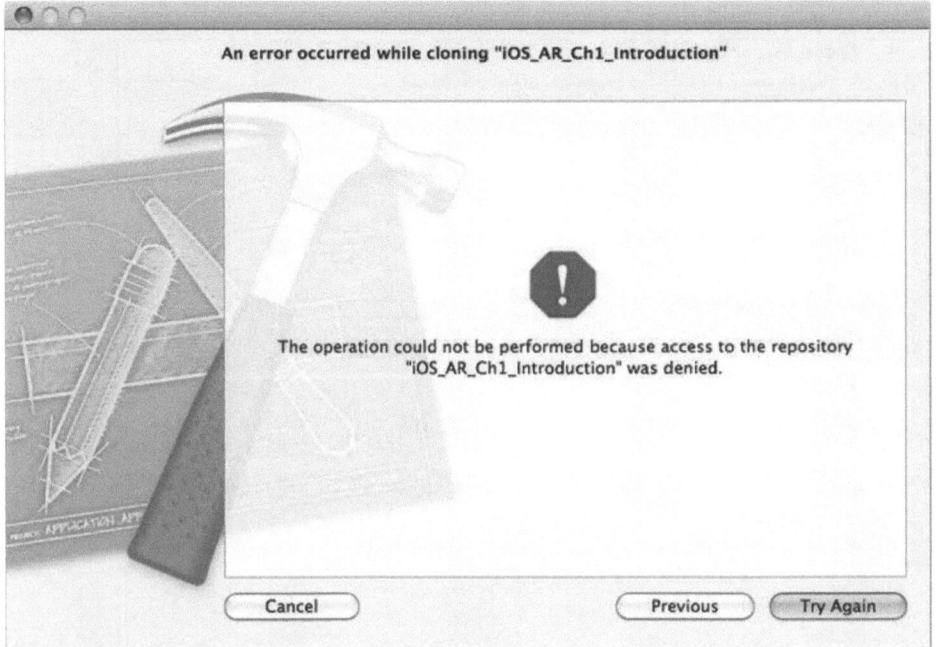

Figure 1–8. *A defect in early releases of Xcode 4.2 threw invalid errors. Simply click Try Again and it goes away.*

Creating Our Xcode Project

From Xcode's **Welcome to Xcode** screen, select **Create a New Xcode Project**. We're not going to be doing much coding in this project, so the template type isn't all that important. I'm going to select a Windows-based application template for simplicity. The next screen has a few more important options. You are now being asked for your **Product Name**. This is used as a suffix to your fully qualified **Bundle Identifier**. This is where things will start to diverge a bit. Unless you're involved in team-based development, this option will be unique to your machine. I'm going to, again, use the same name as my GitHub repository to make things easy. My options are shown in Figure 1–9.

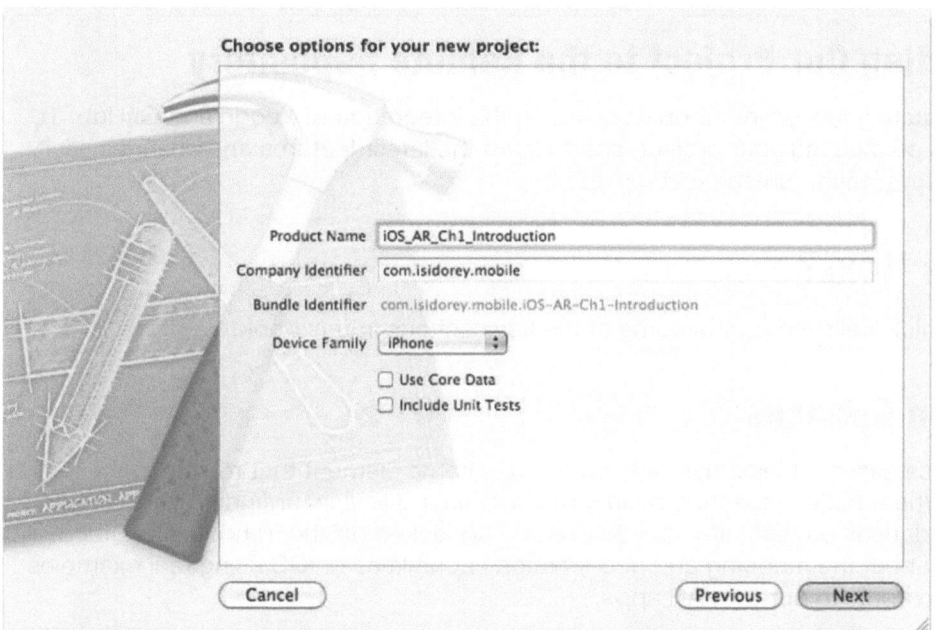

Figure 1–9. *Choose your new project options.*

Your **Company Identifier** is going to be different as well. Until we discuss distributing applications either over the App Store or over the Enterprise Distribution options, the **Company Identifier** can be a reverse DNS format. Click **Next** when you have everything filled out.

You are finally prompted to find a local location for this project. Make sure that you select the same directory as you did for cloning the GitHub repository. Also, make sure that **Create local git repository for this project** is *not* selected, as shown in Figure 1–10.

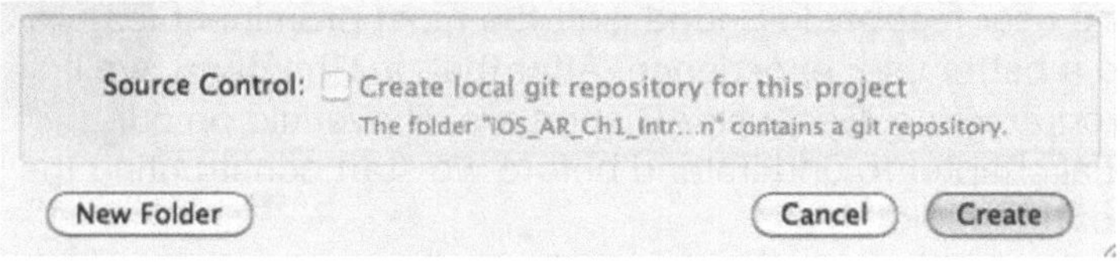

Figure 1–10. *Do not create a local Git repository.*

Great! We just created our first project. Only a few more steps and we'll be able to start updating code on GitHub. The following steps can probably be completed in various orders. I'm following this path because I find it easier. As Xcode 4.2 matures, I'm sure we'll see some improvements on the GUI-based functionality.

Connecting Our Project to the Remote Repository

There are quite a few online tutorials covering the integration of Xcode and GitHub. To get started connecting your project, and to learn the latest features and changes, visit http://help.github.com/mac-set-up-git/.

What's Next?

Here's a quick walk-through of some of the key sections in this book.

Location Services

Most AR use cases, at least the early ones, have some element that relates to the user's location. Whether it's presenting nearby restaurants in AR view or finding your friends recommendations on night life, location-based AR kicked off the trend. In Chapter 3, we'll learn about the mapping and geo-location capabilities of iOS using real examples that we can apply to our own AR apps.

Sensor Programming

Creating an AR application requires quite a bit of integration with the native sensors on the iPhone or iPad. Sensors include the accelerometer, the digital compass, and the gyroscope. In Chapter 4, I'll introduce you to sensor development with small projects demonstrating the key features we'll reuse in our AR applications.

Lights, Camera, Action . . .

In Chapter 5, I cover sound and user feedback. Sound isn't the most prominent feature in AR apps, but it does lead to a better user experience. After that, in Chapter 6, we'll dive into camera and video programming. Because AR apps are all overlaid on our camera view, this is an essential chapter to understand before we start constructing the larger AR projects at the end of the book.

Gaming Frameworks

I choose to use Cocos2D to demonstrate AR gaming capabilities. In Chapter 7, you'll get a primer on Cocos2D's essentials and we'll follow that up with a real application in Chapter 8.

Third-Party Frameworks

In Chapter 9, I talk about a few third-party frameworks that make marker-based augmented reality application development easier. We follow that up with a real example, then move on to more complicated frameworks, such as OpenCV (Open Computer Vision), which is an open source library for things such as facial or complex-object recognition. Facial recognition on the device itself has some limitations. Mostly, these limitations are related to hardware capabilities. We'll discuss a few more creative ways to supplement facial recognition using publicly available APIs.

Summary

I hope you learn much from this book. AR is such a new concept in mobile apps and has endless possibilities. The developer community is just beginning to scratch the surface of possibilities. I hope this book gives you a jump-start on your own journey into the AR world.

Let's get started by reviewing some of our application layout options and frameworks for putting together our own AR applications. In the next chapter, we'll discuss the hardware we'll be using in this book and the major features of the different models.

Chapter 2

Hardware Comparison

Every mobile developer worries about hardware compatibility. However, the main benefit of developing for Apple's iOS line is standardization among hardware. True, there are different evolutions of the devices, but there is only one vendor: Apple! With other mobile operating systems, you have to worry about OEM vendors and their unlimited variations of hardware configurations. Let's take a look under the hood of the more recent iOS devices.

Out with the Old

We're going to be using both the iPhone and the iPad for our sample projects. However, whenever the code is completely portable between platforms, we'll be coding for only the iPhone. Figure 2–1 illustrates the physical dimensions of the iPhone 4.

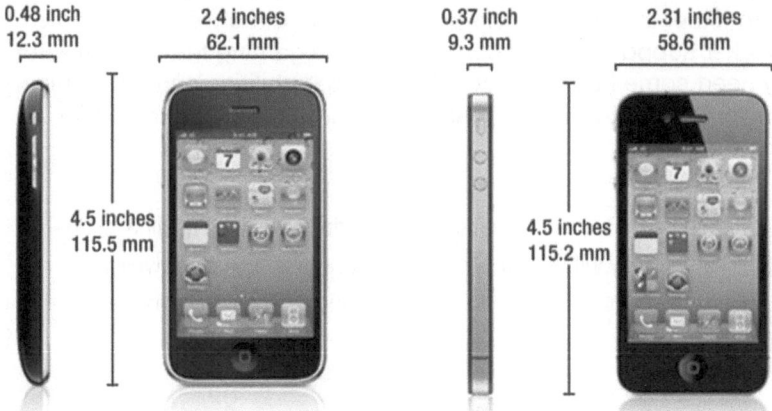

Figure 2–1. *Here we see the physical dimensions of the iPhone 4.*

The iPad hasn't been on the market as long as the iPhone, but has no less traction for its purpose. In this book, we're only going to use the iPad 2 for our examples. There are a few reasons for this. Most important, the iPad (first-generation) is missing a front-facing camera, and we're going to work on some facial recognition programming later in this book. Figure 2–2 shows the physical characteristics of the iPad 2.

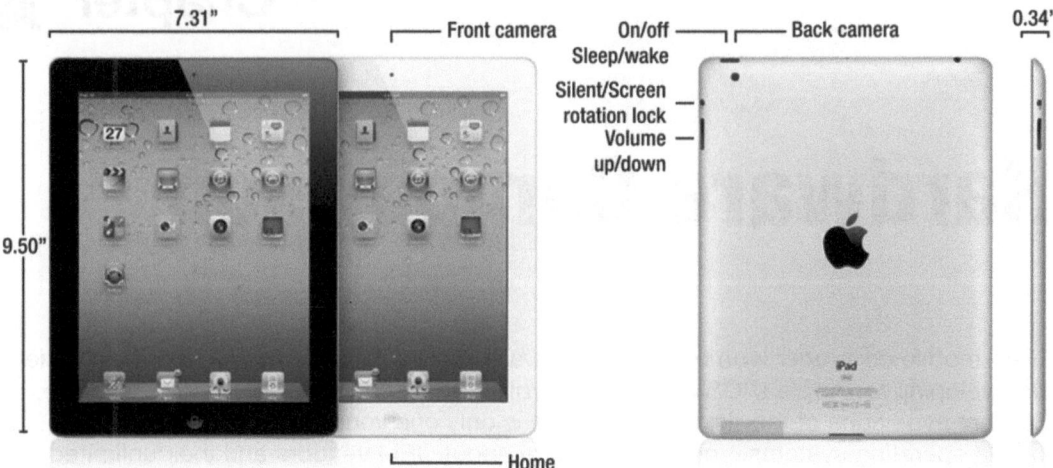

Figure 2–2. *Here we see the physical characteristics of the iPad 2.*

Hardware Components

Instead of just Listing out the hardware specs for each of these devices, let's take a minute to discuss what an augmented-reality application might require. First, and most obviously, the device would need a camera. Most augmented-reality use cases have some sort of requirement for location and direction, so a GPS and a compass would be useful. It might be useful to either listen for sound or output sound, so we should look for a microphone and speaker support. We'll incorporate some gaming features into our samples, so we probably need some hardware acceleration capabilities and a graphics toolkit. Let's translate this to Apple's terminology and walk through how to check for these various hardware components.

> **NOTE:** As we look at the different hardware components of the iOS devices, I'll be posting some small code snippets. In this chapter, they will be out of context of a sample project. However, if you want to follow along, all the code in this chapter is in the following GitHub repository:
>
> https://github.com/kyleroche

Camera Support

The camera has come a long way since Apple launched the iPhone 3GS. It still leaves a lot to be desired when compared to some other hardware models that make their differentiation around the camera, but it'll more than suffice for our purposes.

There are two ways to build augmented-reality applications over the video capabilities of the phone. First, you can actively inspect the video capture for elements, recognizable objects, and so forth. Or, you can use the video capture as the background for your application, while completely ignoring the contents. We see this approach quite a bit in augmented-reality browsers because of the heavy processing involved with constantly inspecting the video capture. In this book, we'll walk through samples of both of these approaches.

Table 2–1 details the specifics about the camera and video capability of the hardware we'll be using in this book.

Table 2–1. *Camera Details for iPhone 3GS, iPhone 4, and iPad 2*

	iPhone 3GS	iPhone 4	iPad 2
Back Camera Video	VGA, 30 frames per second with audio	HD (720p), 30 frames per second with audio	HD (720p), 30 frames per second with audio
Front Camera Video	—	VGA, 30 frames per second with audio	VGA, 30 frames per second with audio
Back Still Camera	3-megapixel still camera	5-megapixel still camera	HD still camera with 5x digital zoom
Flash	—	LED flash	—

Detecting the Camera

We can programmatically detect what camera is available on our device by using the UIImagePickerController class. There is a method called isSourceTypeAvailable we can use to determine whether the camera we want to use is available on this device. Listing 2–1 shows an example of how to use the isSourceTypeAvailable method.

Listing 2–1. *Checking for a Camera, Then for a Front-Facing Camera*

```
BOOL cameraAvailable = [UIImagePickerController
isSourceTypeAvailable:UIImagePickerControllerSourceTypeCamera];
    BOOL frontCameraAvailable = [UIImagePickerController
isSourceTypeAvailable:UIImagePickerControllerCameraDeviceFront];

    if (cameraAvailable) {
        UIAlertView *alert = [[UIAlertView alloc] initWithTitle:@"Camera"
                                             message:@"Camera Available"
                                             delegate:self
                                      cancelButtonTitle:@"OK"
                                      otherButtonTitles:nil, nil];
        [alert show];
        [alert release];
    } else {
```

```objc
        UIAlertView *alert = [[UIAlertView alloc] initWithTitle:@"Camera"
                                              message:@"Camera NOT Available"
                                              delegate:self
                                      cancelButtonTitle:@"OK"
                                      otherButtonTitles:nil, nil];
        [alert show];
        [alert release];
    }

    if (frontCameraAvailable) {
        UIAlertView *alert = [[UIAlertView alloc] initWithTitle:@"Camera"
                                              message:@"Front Camera
Available"

                                              delegate:self
                                      cancelButtonTitle:@"OK"
                                      otherButtonTitles:nil, nil];
        [alert show];
        [alert release];
    } else {
        UIAlertView *alert = [[UIAlertView alloc] initWithTitle:@"Camera"
                                              message:@"Front Camera NOT
Available"

                                              delegate:self
                                      cancelButtonTitle:@"OK"
                                      otherButtonTitles:nil, nil];
        [alert show];
        [alert release];
    }
```

This code block will demonstrate the results in a quick UIAlertView pop-up. Actually, you'll get two pop-ups from this example. You can see in the first few lines of Listing 2–1 where we are checking for the existence of UIImagePickerControllerSourceTypeCamera to see whether the camera is available. We next check for the existence of the front-facing camera using the UIImagePickerControllerCameraDeviceFront parameter. The isSourceTypeAvailable method returns a BOOL value. We use that in our if/else statements, and display the appropriate UIAlertView for each check.

Now, why would we have to check for a camera when we're only using iPhone 3GS, iPhone 4, and the iPad 2? Don't they all have cameras? Yes, they do all have cameras. However, we'll be coding in Xcode using the simulators, as well. Unlike some other mobile operating systems' IDEs, Xcode simulators do not have camera support.

Take a look at Figure 2–3. Both of these screenshots were taken from an iPhone 4 device running the previous sample code block. Since both of the if/else blocks execute in the code block, we get two UIAlertView dialogs. As you can see from the dialogs, both checks returned True, meaning the camera and the front-facing camera are available to use.

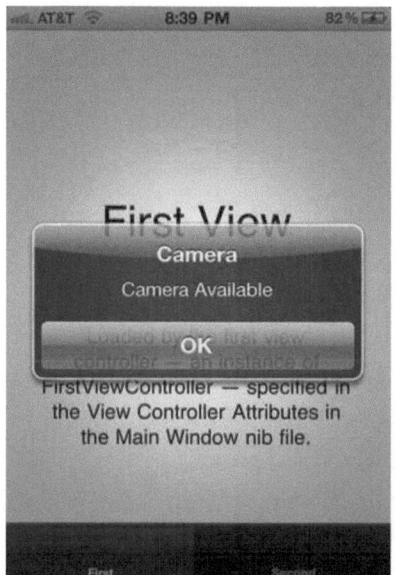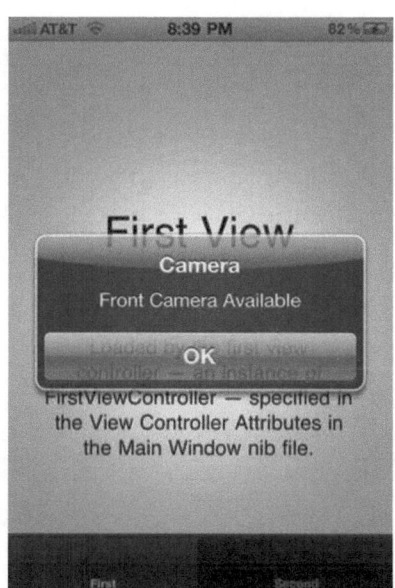

Figure 2–3. *We check for the camera (left), and then for a front-facing camera (right) on an iPhone 4 gives these results.*

To demonstrate that these functions actually do check for the availability of the camera, I ran the same code on the iPhone 4.3 Simulator from Xcode. The resulting dialogs were the opposite, as you can see in Figure 2–4.

There are a few other options we could have used to check for the camera. Technically, our first check is looking for any camera to be available. We could have used UIImagePickerControllerCameraDeviceRear as our source type argument and checked specifically for the rear-facing camera. Or, we could have checked a few options for the current flash setting on the device. This one is a bit different. Either we have to check specifically for the mode we are looking to validate, such as UIImagePickerControllerCameraFlashModeOn, or we can use the isFlashAvailableForCameraDevice method.

We'll talk more about how to use the camera to capture images and video in Chapter 8.

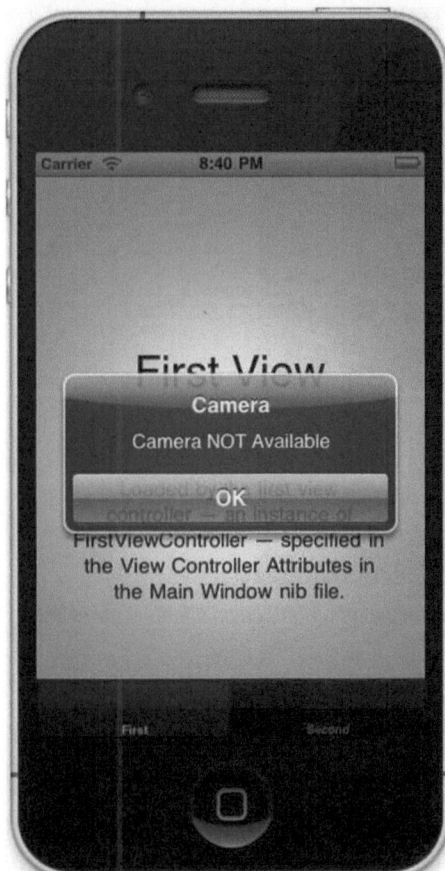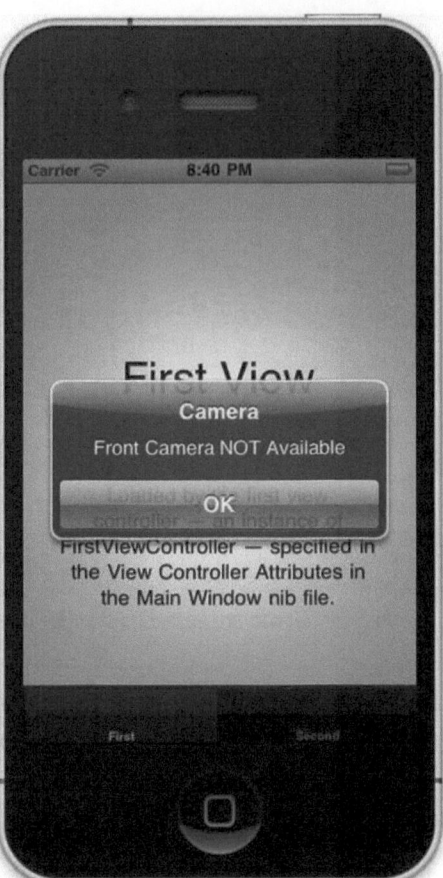

Figure 2–4. *We check for the camera (left), and then for a front-facing camera (right) on the iPhone 4.3 Simulator.*

Detecting Location Capabilities

iOS provides the Core Location Framework for interacting with location-based services and hardware on the device. Unfortunately, the Core Location Framework doesn't provide any way to detect the presence of GPS. Instead, you should enforce these hardware requirements on the application itself (see "Enforcing Hardware Requirements," later in this chapter).

Now, to be clear, you can still check whether location services are enabled. Even though location services are available in every version of iOS, there are still cases in which they might not be available to your application. For example:

- The user can disable location services in the Settings application.
- The user can deny location services for a specific application.
- The device might be in airplane mode and unable to power up the necessary hardware.

For these reasons, you should always call the `locationServicesEnabled` class method of `CLLocationManager` before attempting to use any location services. If the user has disabled these services on purpose, the automated prompt that is presented when you try to use location services might not be a welcomed feature of your application.

There are two methods available for determining the user's location:

- The Standard Location Service is a configurable, general-purpose solution, which all versions of iOS support.

- The Significant-Change Location Service offers a low-power location service for devices with cellular radios. This service, which is available only in iOS 4.0 and later, can wake up an application that is suspended or is not running.

We will discuss in detail how to start and use location services in Chapter 4.

Digital Compass

We discussed that augmented-reality applications might also benefit from a directional heading. In fact, this would be a requirement for any location-based AR application or you wouldn't be able to determine which direction the user was facing. Checking for the magnetometer (digital compass) is fairly straightforward. Before you can use the Core Location Framework, there are two steps you must take to prepare your project.

First, you must link your application binary with the Core Location library. Click on your project name in the **Project Navigator** of Xcode. Switch your view to the **Build Phases** tab of your application's target. There is a section called **Link Binary With Libraries**. Expand this section and click on the + button to add a new library. In Figure 2–5, you can see the Core Location Framework that we are adding to our project.

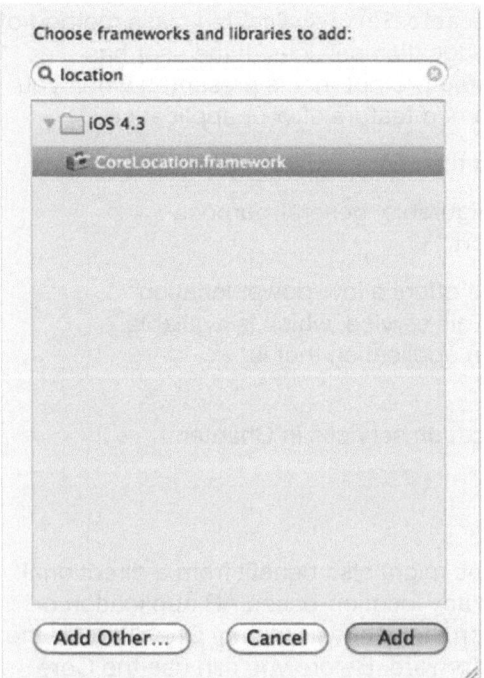

Figure 2–5. *We add the Core Location Framework to our application binary.*

Second, be sure you add the `import` statement from Listing 2–2 to your header file.

Listing 2–2. *Import the Core Location Framework*

```
#import <CoreLocation/CoreLocation.h>
```

After you've added the Core Location Framework, you can add Listing 2–3 to the code snippet from Listing 2–1 to detect the presence of the magnetometer. All this code belongs in the `.m` file. Notice that we are using the `headingAvailable` class method, and not the property. The property was deprecated recently, and the class method is the preferred way to detect whether the heading is available.

In the example posted on GitHub, I keep all this code in the `viewDidLoad` method to make sure it runs when the view is presented.

Listing 2–3. *Check for the Magnetometer*

```
BOOL magnetometerAvailable = [CLLocationManager headingAvailable];
    if (magnetometerAvailable) {
        UIAlertView *alert = [[UIAlertView alloc] initWithTitle:@"Magnetometer"
                                                        message:@"Magnetometer
Available"

                                                       delegate:self
                                              cancelButtonTitle:@"OK"
                                              otherButtonTitles:nil, nil];

        [alert show];
        [alert release];
    } else {
```

```
        UIAlertView *alert = [[UIAlertView alloc] initWithTitle:@"Magnetometer"
                                                        message:@"Magnetometer NOT
Available"
                                                       delegate:self
                                               cancelButtonTitle:@"OK"
                                               otherButtonTitles:nil, nil];

        [alert show];
        [alert release];
    }
```

Like the camera, the magnetometer is another hardware component that is not available on the simulator. Figure 2–6 illustrates the code from Listing 2–3 running on the iPhone 4.3 simulator.

If you run this same code block is against the physical iPhone device or iPad, you'll get the opposite message.

Keep in mind that you can still use hardware requirements to stop the application from launching on a particular device if the magnetometer is not available. See the section "Enforcing Hardware Requirements" for more details and instructions on that topic. We're going to cover more advanced usage of the digital compass in Chapter 7.

Figure 2–6. *We check for the magnetometer on the iPhone 4.3 simulator*

Wired for Sound

Checking for audio capabilities works in the same way as checking for other components. Checking for sound requires the AVFoundation Framework. Link this framework to your application binary the same way we linked the Core Location Framework earlier in this chapter. Next, add the appropriate import statement to your header file, as shown in Listing 2–4.

Listing 2–4. *Add the Import Statement*

```
#import <AVFoundation/AVFoundation.h>
```

Finally, switch to the .m file and uncomment the viewDidLoad method. Or, if you're adding this to the same file as the checks for location services and the magnetometer, you can simply append the code from Listing 2–5.

Listing 2–5. *Import the AVFoundation Framework*

```
AVAudioSession *audioSession = [AVAudioSession sharedInstance];
BOOL audioAvailable = audioSession.inputIsAvailable;

    if (audioAvailable) {
        UIAlertView *alert = [[UIAlertView alloc] initWithTitle:@"Audio"
                                                        message:@"Audio Available"
                                                       delegate:self
                                              cancelButtonTitle:@"OK"
                                              otherButtonTitles:nil, nil];
        [alert show];
        [alert release];
    } else {
        UIAlertView *alert = [[UIAlertView alloc] initWithTitle:@"Audio"
                                                        message:@"Audio NOT Available"
                                                       delegate:self
                                              cancelButtonTitle:@"OK"
                                              otherButtonTitles:nil, nil];
        [alert show];
        [alert release];
    }
```

Checking for Video Capabilities

We've verified that most of the components we'll need to build an augmented-reality application are present on the device. However, having a camera available doesn't necessarily mean it will function for video capture. And, after all, the video capture is what makes the augmented-reality application so appealing.

Checking for video capability of the camera is a bit more complicated than simply checking for the camera's existence. To do this, we have to add the Mobile Core Services Framework to our project. Follow the same pattern we used to add the Core Location Framework to the project when we checked for the existence of the magnetometer, but instead add the framework called MobileCoreServices.framework. In your header file, add the code from Listing 2–6 after the other import statements. Then, add the code from Listing 2–7 just above the @end.

Listing 2–6. *Import the Mobile Core Services Framework*

```
#import <MobileCoreServices/UTCoreTypes.h>
```

Listing 2–7. *Declare the isVideoCameraAvailable Method*

```
- (BOOL) isVideoCameraAvailable;
```

In Listing 2-7, we are declaring a method signature so we can use a helper function to check for video. Switch to the .m file of your class and add the following helper function from Listing 2-8.

Listing 2–8. *Add the Helper Function to the .m File*

```
- (BOOL) isVideoCameraAvailable
{
    UIImagePickerController *picker = [[UIImagePickerController alloc] init];
    NSArray *sourceTypes = [UIImagePickerController
availableMediaTypesForSourceType:picker.sourceType];
    [picker release];

    if (![sourceTypes containsObject:(NSString *)kUTTypeMovie]){

        return NO;
    }

    return YES;
}
```

In this code block, we are simply checking for all available media source types then inspecting that array to see whether it contains an object of type NSString with the value kUTTypeMovie. If we find this value, then video is supported on the device's camera. Now that this method is declared and available to our class, we can follow the same pattern we used to check for other components. Add the code from Listing 2–9 after the checks for camera support.

Listing 2–9. *Call the New Helper Function to Check for Video Support*

```
if ([self isVideoCameraAvailable]) {
    UIAlertView *alert = [[UIAlertView alloc] initWithTitle:@"Video"
                                                    message:@"Video Available"
                                                   delegate:self
                                          cancelButtonTitle:@"OK"
                                          otherButtonTitles:nil, nil];
    [alert show];
    [alert release];
} else {
    UIAlertView *alert = [[UIAlertView alloc] initWithTitle:@"Video"
                                                    message:@"Video NOT Available"
                                                   delegate:self
                                          cancelButtonTitle:@"OK"
                                          otherButtonTitles:nil, nil];
    [alert show];
    [alert release];
}
```

As you would expect (because we've already determined there is no camera on the simulator), you won't find video support on the simulator either.

Acceleration and Gyroscope

There are many use cases like virtual fitting rooms or the post office example I referred to in Chapter 1 that leverage augmented-reality features with a fixed-positional camera. However, in most mobile use cases, the user will have the ability to move the device, change orientation, or move around to interact with the application. To respond to the user's movement, we'll need some combination of data from the gyroscope and accelerometer. Before we start validating their existence on the device, let's spend a minute on the difference between the two components.

The accelerometer measures across three axes to gauge the orientation of a stationary platform relative to the earth's surface. If the device is accelerating in only one particular direction, it would be indistinguishable from the acceleration being provided by the earth's gravitational pull. The trouble with this measurement alone is that it doesn't provide enough information to maintain a particular orientation.

The gyroscope, which was introduced in the iPhone 4, complements the accelerometer in that it has the capability to measure rate of rotation around an axis. Using the same example, the gyroscope could measure the constant state of rotation around an axis and report when the rotation halts or changes. Typically, the gyroscope works across six axes. The iPhone 4 ships with a three-axis gyroscope.

In short, the gyroscope measures and maintains orientation, and the accelerometer measures vibration. We'll see where and when to use these components in later chapters. First, let's take a look at how to detect their existence in our own applications.

Checking for the existence of the gyroscope requires the addition of another framework. In this case, we're going to need to add the Core Motion Framework to our application. Link the framework to the application binary, as we did with the previous frameworks in this chapter. Next, open the header file in which you'd like to check for the existence of the gyroscope. Add the code from Listing 2–10 to the header file under the last `import` statement.

Listing 2–10. *Import the Core Motion Framework*

```
#import <CoreMotion/CoreMotion.h>
```

Next, add the code from Listing 2–11 just above the @end in the header file to declare our new helper method.

Listing 2–11. *Declare Our Helper Method*

```
- (BOOL) isGyroscopeAvailable;
```

Next, we're going to build our helper function so we can reference it in an `if/else` statement just like we did for our other hardware checks. Copy the code from Listing 2–12 into the `.m` file for this class.

Listing 2–12. *Our Helper Method Checks Whether the Gyroscope Is Available*

```
- (BOOL) isGyroscopeAvailable
{
#ifdef __IPHONE_4_0
    CMMotionManager *motionManager = [[CMMotionManager alloc] init];
    BOOL gyroscopeAvailable = motionManager.gyroAvailable;
    [motionManager release];
    return gyroscopeAvailable;
#else
    return NO;
#endif
}
```

We are using the gyroAvailable property of the CMMotionManager class to check for the existence of the gyroscope. Note that we are wrapping this in a check for the __IPHONE_4_0 macro. Because the gyroscope wasn't available in versions prior to the iPhone 4, we don't need to check for it.

Finally, we need to call this new method in our viewDidLoad method alongside our other validations. Add the code from Listing 2–13 just below the check for the video camera.

Listing 2–13. *Call the Gyroscope Helper Method*

```
if ([self isGyroscopeAvailable]) {
        UIAlertView *alert = [[UIAlertView alloc] initWithTitle:@"Gyroscope"
                                                   message:@"Gyroscope Available"
                                                  delegate:self
                                         cancelButtonTitle:@"OK"
                                         otherButtonTitles:nil, nil];
        [alert show];
        [alert release];
    } else {
        UIAlertView *alert = [[UIAlertView alloc] initWithTitle:@"Gyroscope"
                                                   message:@"Gyroscope NOT
Available"
                                                  delegate:self
                                         cancelButtonTitle:@"OK"
                                         otherButtonTitles:nil, nil];
        [alert show];
        [alert release];
    }
```

As you probably guessed by now, the gyroscope isn't available on the simulator. So, if you want to test it out, you need to deploy the application to your device.

Enforcing Hardware Requirements

In your application, it's always important to check for the required hardware before attempting to use it, but you could also stop the application from launching if it doesn't meet your hardware requirements. Configuring your application's Info.plist file does this for you. The Info.plist file is a standard component of all the iOS templates. Xcode 4.2 templates generate this file under the Supporting Files directory in your project. It will be named **ProjectName**-Info.plist, where ProjectName is the name of your Xcode project.

To add hardware requirements to your application, you first need to add another key to the `Info.plist` file. If the file is open in Xcode, you can select **Add Row** from the right-click context menu. Xcode 4.2 uses the description for selecting a new key, so look for **Required device capabilities**. This key is an array of values corresponding to the various hardware components of the iOS devices. For example, you can add the `telephony` key to require the Phone application or the `front-facing-camera` to require a front-facing camera on the device.

Using hardware requirements can be touchy, and has some implications when submitting to the App Store. You want to make sure that you require any components that you are going to use, but not to the point where you restrict your device options. In the sample project on GitHub (see the note at the beginning of this chapter), I added hardware requirements for `wifi` and `still-camera` so you can have a working example.

Table 2–2 lists the other various keys that are available for the `UIRequiredDeviceCapabilities` key (e.g., **Required device capabilities**).

Table 2–2. *Dictionary Keys for the UIRequiredDeviceCapabilities Key*

Key	Description
telephony	Checks for the presence of the Phone application. You can also use this feature to open URLs with the `tel` scheme.
wifi	Checks for the Wi-Fi networking features of the device.
sms	Checks for the presence of the Messages application. You can also use this feature to open URLs with the `sms` scheme.
still-camera	Checks for the presence of a camera on the device.
auto-focus-camera	Checks for the auto-focus capabilities in the device's still camera. This is mostly used for applications that support Macro photography or applications that require sharper image processing.
front-facing-camera	Checks for the presence of the front-facing camera.
camera-flash	Checks for the presence of a camera flash for taking pictures or shooting video.
video-camera	Checks for the presence of a camera with video capabilities on the device.
accelerometer	Checks for the presence of the accelerometer on the device. Applications that use the Core Motion Framework to receive accelerometer events can use this. You do not need this if your application is detecting only orientation changes.

Key	Description
gyroscope	Checks for the presence of the gyroscope. Applications can use the Core Motion Framework to retrieve information from the gyroscope hardware.
location-services	Checks for the ability to retrieve the device's current location using Core Location Framework. This refers to general location only. Use the gps key if you need GPS-level accuracy.
gps	Checks for the presence of GPS (or AGPS) hardware for tracking locations. If you use this key, you should also check for the location-services key. Use this for more accurate levels of tracking than location-services (via Wi-Fi or cell radios) can provide.
magnetometer	Checks for the magnetometer (digital compass) hardware. Use this to receive heading-related events through the Core Location Framework.
gamekit	Forces/prohibits use of Game Center in iOS 4.1 and later applications.
microphone	Checks for the built-in microphone or accessories that provide a microphone.
opengles-1/opengles-2	Forces/prohibits use of OpenGL ES1.1 and OpenGL ES2.0 interfaces.
armv6/armv7	Checks whether the application was compiled with armv6/armv7 instruction set.
peer-peer	Checks for peer-to-peer connectivity over Bluetooth support (iOS 3.1 or later).

Summary

In this chapter, we reviewed the commonly used hardware components of an augmented-reality application. We also walked through the steps necessary to detect this hardware on a device and even restrict the application from launching if the prerequisites aren't met. In the next few chapters, we'll be diving into how to use each of these components and get information from the hardware. This will all build up to us coding a fully functional augmented-reality application of our own.

In the next chapter, we'll start with the views and layouts available to us within iOS, and the ones that we'll be using for our sample applications.

Chapter 3

Using Location Services

Although this book is essentially about augmented reality, programming maps and location services make up a lot of the fundamental aspects needed for a successful AR application. In this chapter, we will look at the mapping capabilities of iOS and some advanced techniques to integrate these services within your AR application.

If you were just too excited to move ahead and skipped Chapter 2, I would recommend that you go back and take a quick peek at the section called "Detecting Location Capabilities." It covers how to make sure location services are available and how to prevent your app from attempting to access services that the user might have disabled. If you're ready to dive in, let's get started.

You Are Here

Let's start with an example. First, open Xcode and create a **New Project**. Select **Tab Bar Application** for your template and name your project iOS_AR_Ch3_LocationServices. Make sure the **Device Family** is set to **iPhone**. Everything we will cover in this chapter can easily be reused in your iPad applications. So, to keep things simple, we'll be using only the iPhone in this chapter.

This step is optional. I created a local Git repository with this Xcode project. From my Terminal, I navigated to the new project's directory and ran the commands shown in Listing 3–1. The finished project for this chapter is available at github.com/kyleroche.

Listing 3–1. *Connect the Local Repository to GitHub*

```
Kyle-Roches-MacBook-Pro-2:iOS_AR_Ch3_LocationServices kyleroche$ git remote add origin
git@github.com:kyleroche/iOS_AR_Ch3_LocationServices.git
Kyle-Roches-MacBook-Pro-2:iOS_AR_Ch3_LocationServices kyleroche$ git push -u origin master
Counting objects: 19, done.
Delta compression using up to 8 threads.
Compressing objects: 100% (17/17), done.
Writing objects: 100% (19/19), 10.78 KiB, done.
Total 19 (delta 5), reused 0 (delta 0)
To git@github.com:kyleroche/iOS_AR_Ch3_LocationServices.git
 * [new branch]      master -> master
Branch master set up to track remote branch master from origin.
```

We selected a **Tab Bar Application**, so we can continue to build on the concepts in this chapter without overwriting them too extensively as we progress. Let's start by opening the FirstViewController.h file in Xcode. We're going to declare a few of the outlets we'll need to structure this demo. Open the FirstViewController.h file in Xcode and add the code from Listing 3–2 inside the @interface block.

Listing 3–2. *Declare the UITextView in the Interface*

```
UITextView *locationTextView;
```

Now, just before the @end of the header, add the code from Listing 3–3.

Listing 3–3. *Add the Property to the Class*

```
@property (nonatomic, retain) IBOutlet UITextView *locationTextView;
```

We will use this UITextView outlet to print out the information from the location services we will be reviewing. Before we can use this outlet, we have to synthesize it and release it in our .m file. Switch to FirstViewController.m in Xcode and add the lines from Listing 3–4 that are in **bold**.

Listing 3–4. *Synthesize and Release the UILabel*

```
#import "FirstViewController.h"

@implementation FirstViewController
@synthesize locationTextView; // synthesize *locationTextView

/*
// Implement viewDidLoad to do additional setup after loading the view, typically from a
nib.
- (void)viewDidLoad
{

    [super viewDidLoad];
}
*/

-
(BOOL)shouldAutorotateToInterfaceOrientation:(UIInterfaceOrientation)interfaceOrientatio
n
{
    // Return YES for supported orientations
    return (interfaceOrientation == UIInterfaceOrientationPortrait);
}


- (void)didReceiveMemoryWarning
{
    // Releases the view if it doesn't have a superview.
    [super didReceiveMemoryWarning];

    // Release any cached data, images, etc. that aren't in use.
}


- (void)viewDidUnload
{
```

```
    [super viewDidUnload];

    // Release any retained subviews of the main view.
    // e.g. self.myOutlet = nil;
}

- (void)dealloc
{
    [locationTextView release];  // release the UITextView
    locationTextView = nil; // good practice to set to nil after release
    [super dealloc];
}
@end
```

You might notice that I released the variable, then also set it equal to nil. In most cases, this is a good practice for memory management. This book isn't focused on those topics, but we'll point out some details appropriate to augmented reality and memory management as they come up. Augmented-reality applications use a lot of delegates in classes, and memory management is an important aspect of structuring AR applications correctly.

Now that we've defined a UITextView that we can use for textual updates, let's create the component in our XIB file. Click FirstView.xib in the **Project Navigator** in Xcode to open the design view. You should see something similar to that shown in Figure 3–1.

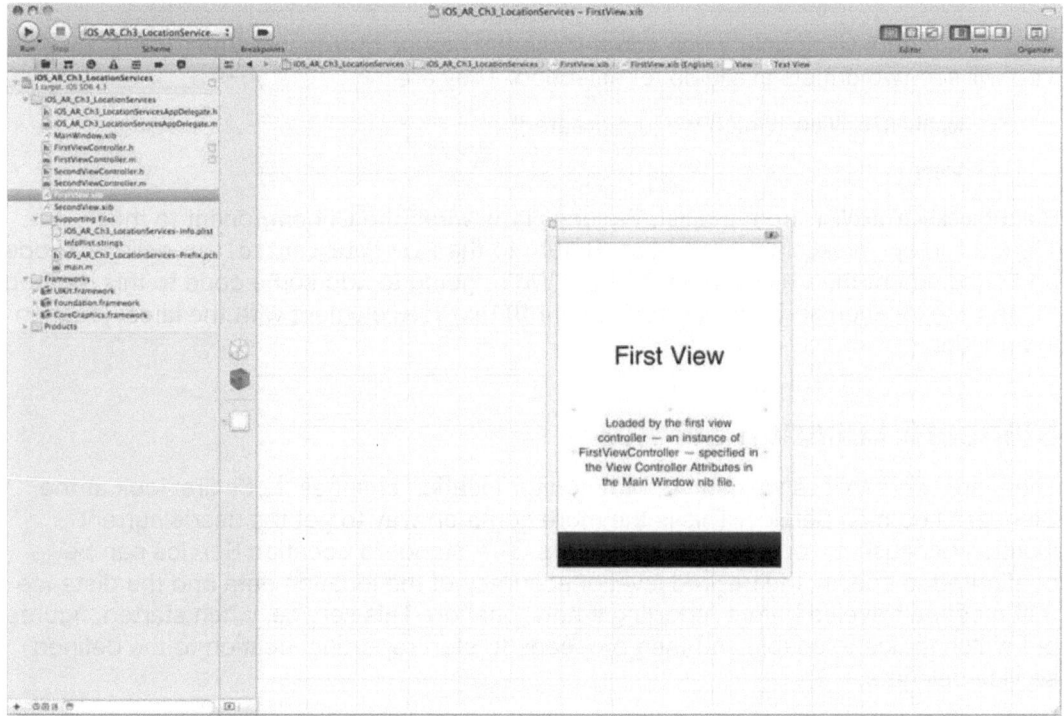

Figure 3–1. *Open the FirstView.xib in design view.*

You'll notice there are already a few components on the layout. This is why we choose to add a UITextView. We're going to simply use one of the components that are already present. On the left side of the design window, there is an icon of a translucent cube. While pressing the Ctrl key, click and drag from that icon to the UITextView outlet on the iPhone screen. Refer to Figure 3–2 for reference.

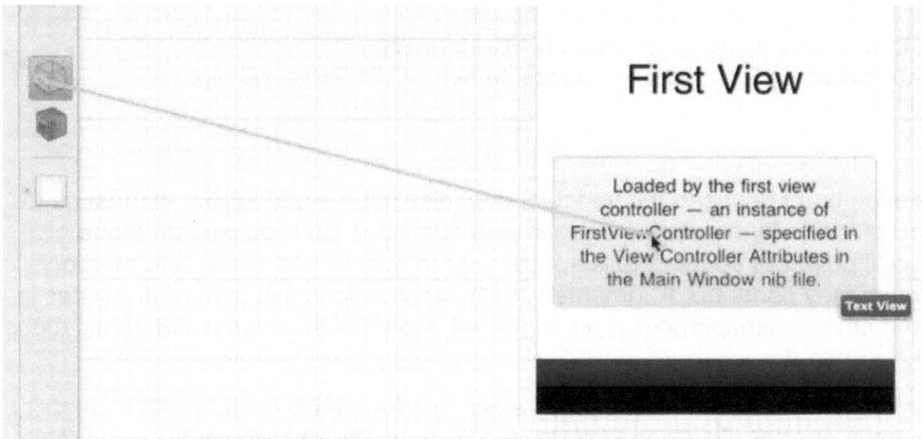

Figure 3–2. *Press Ctrl and drag from File's Owner icon to the UITextView.*

A context menu will appear when you release the mouse button over the UITextView. You will see two outlets available for selection. They are

- **locationTextView** (which we just created)
- **View**

Select **locationTextView** from the list. We have now wired the UI component to the IBOutlet in our ViewController class. Return to the FirstViewController.m file in Xcode and uncomment the viewDidLoad method. We're going to add some code to this method to start the location services and update our UITextView element with the latest location information.

Standard Location Service

There are two services we can start to monitor location changes. Let's first look at the Standard Location Service. This is the more common way to get the user's current location because it works on all iOS devices. The Standard Location Service can be configured to specify the desired level of accuracy of the location data and the distance that must be traveled before reporting a new location. This service, when started, figures out which radios to enable and then proceeds to start reporting location to the defined service delegate.

Before we can start the Standard Location Service, we need to add the Core Location Framework to our project. If you didn't skip Chapter 2, you might find this to be redundant. In Xcode, click on the name of the project in the **Project Navigator** and then

navigate to the **Build Phases** tab. Expand the section titled **Link Binary With Libraries** and add
the Core Location Framework to the project. See Figure 3–3 for reference.

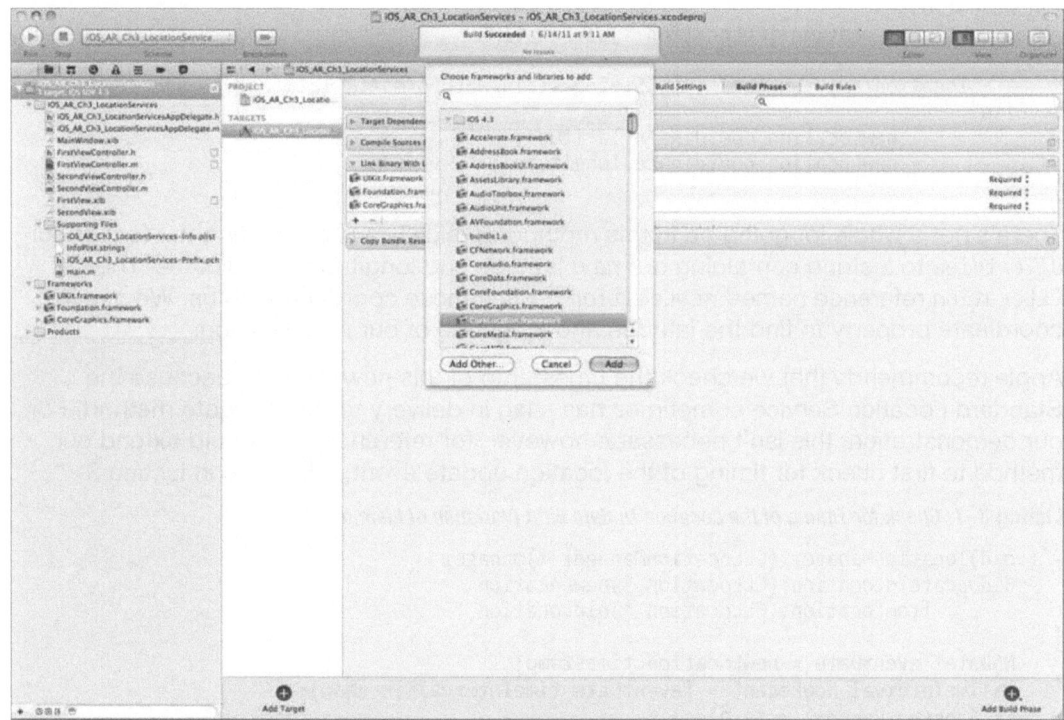

Figure 3–3. *Add the Core Location Framework to the project.*

Return to the FirstViewController.h file. Import the Core Location Framework to the
header file and declare that this class conforms to the CLLocationManagerDelegate
protocol. Your header file should now look like Listing 3–5.

Listing 3–5. *New Header File for FirstViewController*

```
#import <UIKit/UIKit.h>
#import <CoreLocation/CoreLocation.h>

@interface FirstViewController : UIViewController <CLLocationManagerDelegate> {
    UITextView *locationTextView;
}

@property (nonatomic, retain) IBOutlet UITextView *locationTextView;
@end
```

The CLLocationManagerDelegate protocol sends information to its delegate's
locationManager:didUpdateToLocation:fromLocation: method. If there's an error calling
this method, the delegate will call the locationManager:didFailWithError: method.
Switch back to the FirstViewController.m file. Add the method shown in Listing 3–6 to
your class.

Listing 3–6. *Delegate Method for CLLocationManagerDelegate*

```
- (void)locationManager:(CLLocationManager *)manager didUpdateToLocation:(CLLocation
*)newLocation
          fromLocation:(CLLocation *)oldLocation
{
        locationTextView.text = [NSString stringWithFormat:@"latitude %+.6f, longitude
%+.6f\n",
                newLocation.coordinate.latitude,
                newLocation.coordinate.longitude];
}
```

There's not a whole lot going on in this method. Basically, we are setting the text of our UITextView to a string containing our new latitude and longitude coordinates. The CLLocation reference named newLocation passes these coordinates to us. We use its coordinate property to find the latitude and longitude of our new location.

Apple recommends that we check the timestamp of this new location because the Standard Location Service sometimes has a lag in delivery to the delegate method. For our demonstration, this isn't necessary; however, for reference, you could extend our method to first check for timing of the location update event, as shown in Listing 3–7.

Listing 3–7. *Check for Timing of the Location Update First (Variation of Listing 3–5)*

```
- (void)locationManager:(CLLocationManager *)manager
    didUpdateToLocation:(CLLocation *)newLocation
          fromLocation:(CLLocation *)oldLocation
{
    NSDate* eventDate = newLocation.timestamp;
    NSTimeInterval howRecent = [eventDate timeIntervalSinceNow];
    if (abs(howRecent) < 15.0)
    {
        locationTextView.text = [NSString stringWithFormat:@"latitude %+.6f, longitude
%+.6f\n",
                newLocation.coordinate.latitude,
                newLocation.coordinate.longitude];
    } else {
        locationTextView.text = @"Update was old";
        // you'd probably just do nothing here and ignore the event
    }
}
```

So our listener is in place to receive location updates. Let's go ahead and start the service. Switch to the header file (FirstViewController.h) and add the following code from Listing 3–8 just above the @end.

Listing 3–8. *Declare the Method to Start the Location Service*

```
- (void)startStandardUpdates;
```

Now switch back to the .m file and add the method from Listing 3–9.

Listing 3–9. *The startStandardUpdates Method*

```
- (void)startStandardUpdates
{
    CLLocationManager *locationManager = [[CLLocationManager alloc] init];
    locationManager.delegate = self;
```

```
locationManager.desiredAccuracy = kCLLocationAccuracyKilometer;
locationManager.distanceFilter = 500;

[locationManager startUpdatingLocation];
}
```

There are a few important aspects to this method. First, after we declare our CLLocationManager object, we set the delegate to self. This would throw a warning if we hadn't declared this class as a CLLocationManagerDelegate back in Listing 3–5. Next, we set a few configuration options so the Standard Location Service knows when we want to receive updates. We set our desired accuracy to kilometers and tell the location manager to update its delegate when a change of more than 500 kilometers has been detected.

Finally, add the code marked in bold from Listing 3–10 to start the service in your viewDidLoad: method, right before [super viewDidLoad];.

Listing 3–10. *New viewDidLoad Method*

```
- (void)viewDidLoad
{
    [self startStandardUpdates];
    [super viewDidLoad];
}
```

We're now ready to test our demo program. In the top left of Xcode there is a drop-down menu called **Scheme**. Make sure you have your iPhone 4.3 simulator selected and click the **Run** button to the far left. The simulator will launch and will automatically open to our demo application.

You should immediately be presented with a modal dialog like the one shown in Figure 3–4, asking permissions to check your location.

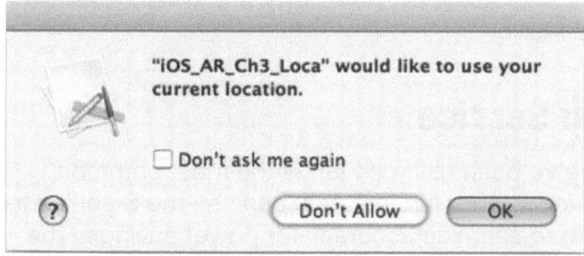

Figure 3–4. *Allow your application to use Location Services to determine your location.*

If you want to keep this dialog from reappearing, select **Don't ask me again**. Either way, make sure you click **OK** or the demo app won't function properly. Figure 3–5 illustrates the running application. You can see that the UITextView is now populated with the string we built that includes our latitude and longitude.

Figure 3–5. *Run the demonstration on the iPhone simulator.*

Significant-Change Location Service

The Standard Location Service, which we've been using so far, is the most common way of getting the device's location. However, after iOS 4.0, you can use the Significant-Change Location Service if you would like to sacrifice accuracy for power savings. The Significant-Change Location Service is accurate enough for the majority of applications. It uses the device's cellular radio instead of the GPS radio to determine location, which allows the device to manage power usage more aggressively. The Significant-Change Location Service is also capable of waking a suspended application in order to deliver new coordinates.

Once you've determined which location service best fits your application's needs, the coding difference is fairly basic. Add the method from Listing 3–11 to FirstViewController.m to start the Significant-Change Location Service.

Listing 3–11. *Start the Significant-Change Location Service*

```
- (void)startSignificantChangeUpdates
{
    CLLocationManager *locationManager = [[CLLocationManager alloc] init];
    locationManager.delegate = self;
    [locationManager startMonitoringSignificantLocationChanges];
}
```

Because we nominated this class as a CLLocationManagerDelegate and we set the delegate property of the CLLocationManager to self, running this method instead of the one we added from Listing 3–9 should result in the same screen in the simulator (so, we think anyway). Add the code from Listing 3–12 to your header file and change the viewDidLoad method as shown in Listing 3–13.

Listing 3–12. *Declare the New Method in FirstViewController.h*

```
- (void)startSignificantChangeUpdates;
```

Listing 3–13. *The New viewDidLoad Method Calls the Significant-Change Location Service*

```
- (void)viewDidLoad
{
    // [self startStandardUpdates];
    [self startSignificantChangeUpdates];
    [super viewDidLoad];
}
```

If you start the simulator and run our new version, you'll notice something a bit different. Namely, nothing happens. The UITextView never changes. If you were to deploy this to a physical device, the results would change as your position changed. Don't worry about this just yet. In the next section, "Geographic Region Monitoring," I'll introduce a new way to test your location in the simulator.

Geographic Region Monitoring Service

In some cases, monitoring a precise location doesn't exactly solve the problem. Instead, we just want to know if, or when, we are close to a certain coordinate. iOS provides a set of features for a Region Monitoring Service. It works, in most ways, just like the other location services. It provides a few key delegate methods that need to be handled to appropriately react to changes in region. We will be using the didEnterRegion: and didExitRegion: delegate methods to demonstrate the functionality.

The code in this example will work just fine on a physical device. However, to demonstrate this with a simulator, I'm going to show it on the iOS 5 simulator running Xcode 4.2 beta. Xcode 4.2 introduced a way to simulate location changes in the debugger, which will illustrate our demonstration nicely. Start by adding the method from Listing 3–14 to FirstViewController.m.

Listing 3–14. *Add New Methods in FirstViewController.m*

```
- (void)startRegionMonitoring
{
    NSLog(@"Starting region monitoring");
    CLLocationManager *locationManager = [[CLLocationManager alloc] init];
```

```
    locationManager.delegate = self;

    CLLocationCoordinate2D coord = CLLocationCoordinate2DMake(37.787359, -122.408227);
    CLRegion *region = [[CLRegion alloc] initCircularRegionWithCenter:coord
radius:1000.0 identifier:@"San Francisco"];

    [locationManager startMonitoringForRegion:region
desiredAccuracy:kCLLocationAccuracyKilometer];
}
```

The code looks very similar to our other methods of tracking location except for the last line, which starts the Region Monitoring Service. We created a CLLocationCoordinate2D with GPS coordinates in San Francisco. The reason I selected San Francisco is that it is one of the preloaded GPS coordinates found in Xcode 4.2 beta, as shown in Figure 3–6.

Don't forget to declare your new method in the header file. Add the code from Listing 3–15 to FirstViewController.h, just above the @end.

Listing 3–15. *Declare the New Method in FirstViewController.h*

```
- (void)startRegionMonitoring;
```

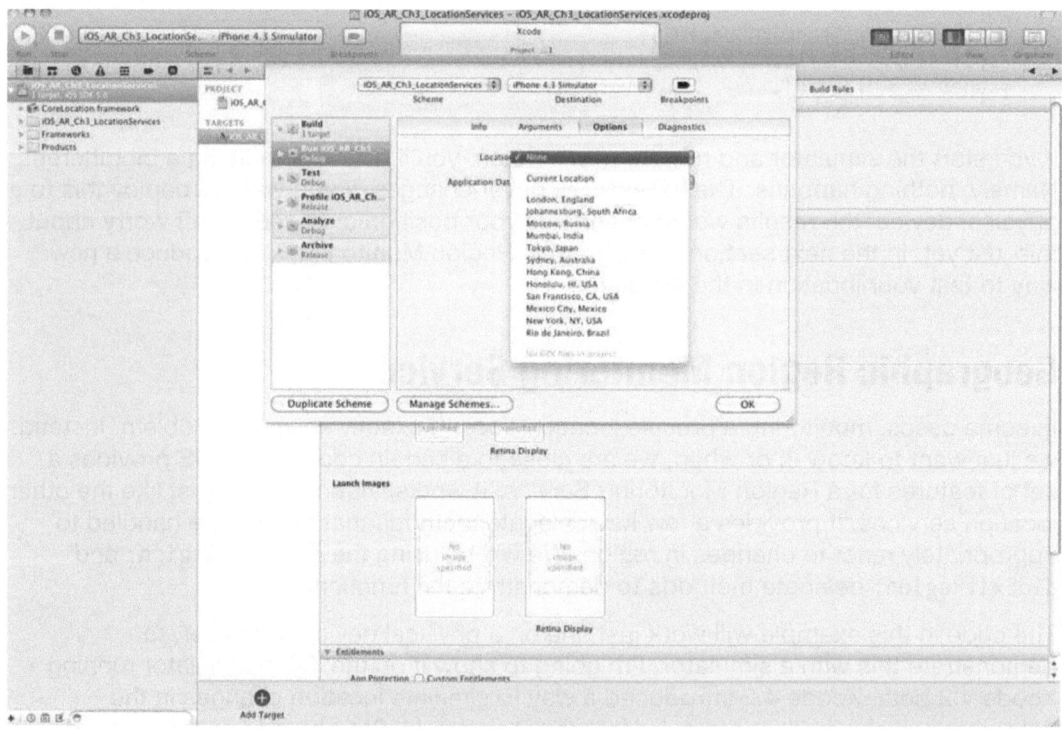

Figure 3–6. *Choose preloaded GPS coordinates in Xcode 4.2 beta.*

Now that the Region Monitoring Service is started, we need to handle the delegate methods that are called when a user enters or exits the region we are monitoring. Add the methods from Listing 3–16 to FirstViewController.m.

Listing 3–16. *Declare New Methods in FirstViewController.m*

```
- (void)locationManager:(CLLocationManager *)manager didEnterRegion:(CLRegion *)region {
    UIAlertView *alert = [[UIAlertView alloc] initWithTitle:@"Region Alert"
                                                message:@"You entered the region"
                                                delegate:self
                                    cancelButtonTitle:@"OK"
                                    otherButtonTitles:nil, nil];
    [alert show];
    [alert release];
}

- (void)locationManager:(CLLocationManager *)manager didExitRegion:(CLRegion *)region {
    UIAlertView *alert = [[UIAlertView alloc] initWithTitle:@"Region Alert"
                                                message:@"You exited the region"
                                                delegate:self
                                    cancelButtonTitle:@"OK"
                                    otherButtonTitles:nil, nil];
    [alert show];
    [alert release];
}
```

The final step to test out the Region Monitoring Service is to call the startRegionMonitoring method we just created. In Chapter 2, we discussed how to check for existing services and supported hardware prior to using them. We should do the same thing in this scenario. CLLocationManager provides a way of checking for both the availability of the Region Monitoring Service and whether the service is actually enabled. Update your viewDidLoad: method as shown in Listing 3–17.

Listing 3–17. *New viewDidLoad Method*

```
- (void)viewDidLoad
{
    [self startStandardUpdates];
    //[self startSignificantChangeUpdates];

    if ([CLLocationManager regionMonitoringAvailable]) { // check is service is
available
        [self startRegionMonitoring];
    }  // else do something
    [super viewDidLoad];
}
```

Our new method starts the Standard Location Service and the Region Monitoring Service. When you run this in the new Xcode 4.2 debugger, you'll be presented with a slightly different permissions dialog asking to use your device's location. This was another update to iOS 5's simulator. You can see an example of the new permissions dialog in Figure 3–7.

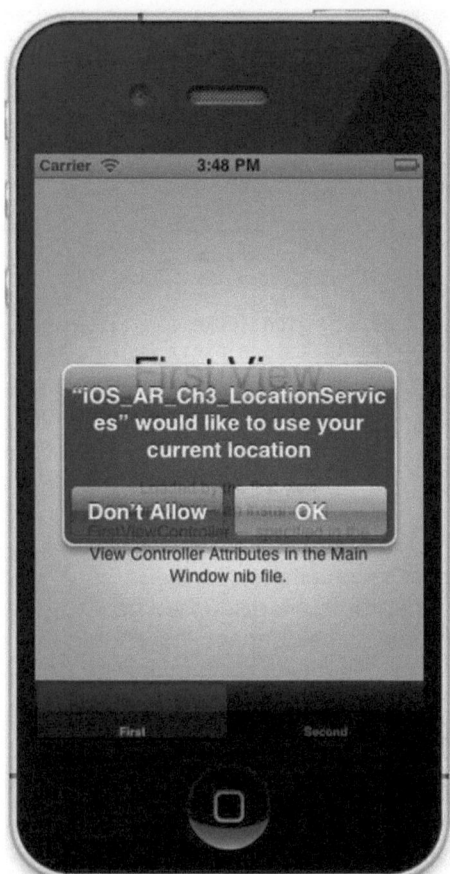

Figure 3–7. *Allow permissions from the new iOS 5 authorization dialog.*

Clicking **OK** in the dialog to load the view and start our services.

Another new feature of Xcode 4.2 is the ability to alter the simulator's location while the application is running. In the **Console** window of Xcode, you'll see a new drop-down menu for location, as shown in Figure 3–8.

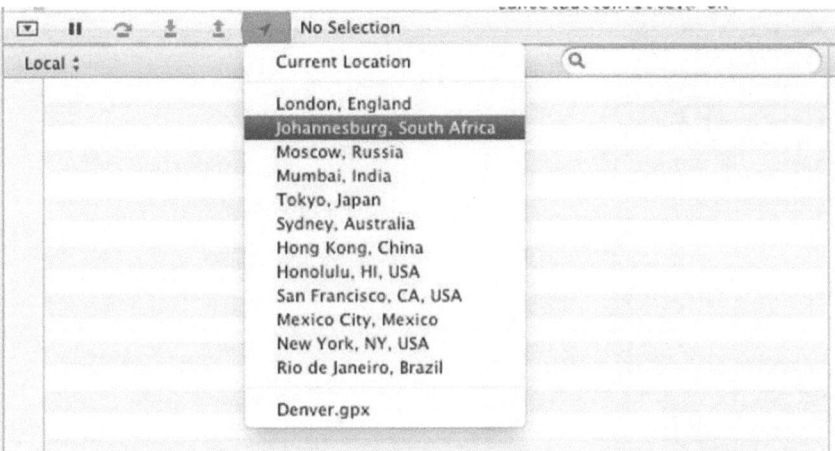

Figure 3–8. *Use the new Xcode 4.2 beta location simulator in debugger.*

When we initialized our Region Monitoring Service, we started it around a coordinate in San Francisco. So, to test our code we'll need to enter and exit that region. If you have Xcode 4.2 installed, use the pull-down menu in the debugger to select **San Francisco, CA, USA** as your location. The simulator changes its coordinates in the background; the Standard Location Service picks up the change and reports it to our delegate method. In addition, we have entered the defined region so our didEnterRegion: method fires as well. You will see something similar to what is shown in Figure 3–9.

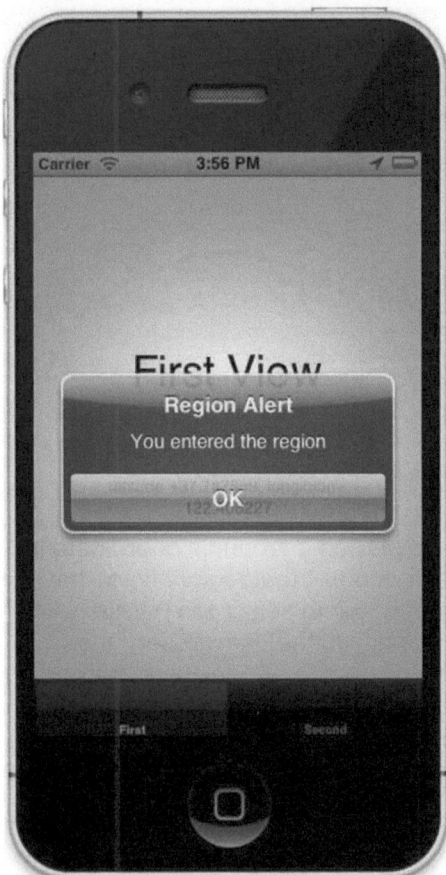

Figure 3–9. *The didEnterRegion: method fires.*

We can also use the debugger to test the didExitRegion: method. Change your location to anywhere except San Francisco, CA, USA, and you'll trigger the other delegate method as shown in Figure 3–10.

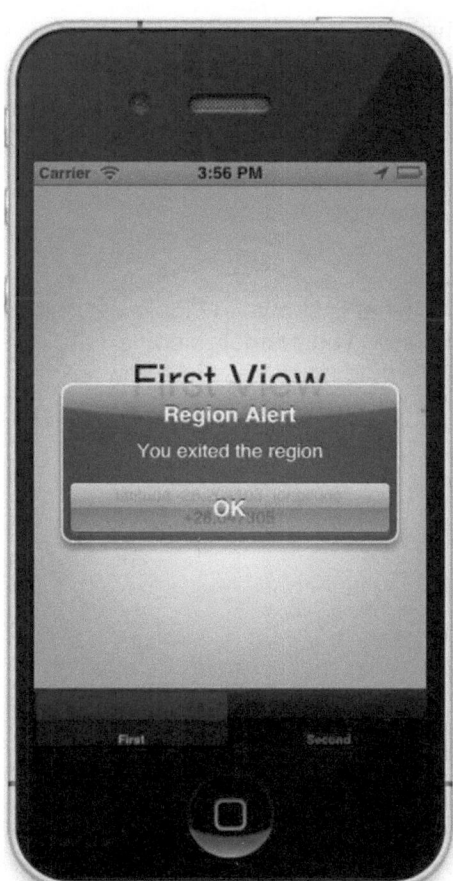

Figure 3–10. *The didExitRegion: method fires.*

So far, we have looked at the different location services to monitor the device's locations and set up some alerting options for when the device enters or exits a geographic region. Visualizing coordinates of interest in augmented-reality applications also requires that we know the distance from our device to certain coordinates of interest. To do this, let's make a quick change to our didUpdateToLocation: method that we defined earlier in this chapter. Update the method as shown in Listing 3–18.

Listing 3–18. *New didUpdateToLocation Method*

```
- (void)locationManager:(CLLocationManager *)manager
    didUpdateToLocation:(CLLocation *)newLocation
          fromLocation:(CLLocation *)oldLocation
{
    NSDate* eventDate = newLocation.timestamp;
    NSTimeInterval howRecent = [eventDate timeIntervalSinceNow];
    if (abs(howRecent) < 15.0)
    {
        //locationTextView.text = [NSString stringWithFormat:@"latitude %+.6f, longitude
%+.6f\n",
```

```
    //                              newLocation.coordinate.latitude,
    //                              newLocation.coordinate.longitude];

    CLLocationDistance dist = [newLocation distanceFromLocation:oldLocation] / 1000;
    locationTextView.text = [NSString stringWithFormat:@"distance %5.1f traveled"];
    } else {
        locationTextView.text = @"Update was old";
        // you'd probably just do nothing here and ignore the event
    }
}
```

In Xcode 4's simulator, you'll get something similar to what is shown in Figure 3–11. If you are using Xcode 4.2 beta and iOS 5 on your simulator, you can force some interesting distances. Another way to test this feature would be to pass in a new CLLocation coordinate instead of oldLocation.

Figure 3–11. *Check the distance between updates.*

Altitude

In augmented reality, checking altitude can help make sure that the angle of the camera is appropriate for the view that you are presenting to the user. Getting the altitude of the device starts with the same process as the location. Apple recommends that we check for the availability of the altitude reading, and then try to get it from the GPS or cellular radio. To determine whether the device is capable of providing altitude, at this time, use the code from Listing 3–19.

Listing 3–19. *Check Whether Altitude Is Available*

```
If (signbit(newLocation.verticalAccuracy)) {
        // get the altitude
}
```

There are a few pitfalls to altitude readings. First, older iPhones (original and iPhone 3Gs) are drastically less accurate. In some reference materials, it is noted that they are nearly ten times more inaccurate than the iPhone 4. Second, as we saw with our location services examples earlier in this chapter, Core Location updates only when the device moves a certain distance (nonvertical). So, we need to either force the GPS to reset or have the user tell us when they've changed altitudes automatically. To check for the GPS reading, add the code from Listing 3–20.

Listing 3–20. *Check the GPS Reading*

```
locationTextView.text = [NSString stringWithFormat:@"%6.2f m. ", newLocation.altitude];
```

Typically, even on newer devices, the altitude reading isn't accurate enough. There are a few other methods and publicly available web services that you can use to determine the altitude based on GPS coordinates. We'll revisit this topic in our examples in the later chapters. Before we move on to visualizing the location information on a map, let's review the classes we have been using in this chapter. Their most used methods and properties are listed in Table 3–1.

Table 3–1. *Review of Methods and Properties of Core Location*

Method/Property Name		Description
`CLLocationManager`		
`delegate`	property	Defines an object that will respond to `CLLocationManagerDelegate`
`desiredAccuracy`	property	Sets the desired accuracy as a `CLLocationAccuracy` object
`distanceFilter`	property	Defines how much lateral movement must occur to cause a location update event
`location`	property	The most recent location

Method/Property Name		Description
`CLLocationManagerDelegate`		
`locationManager:didUpdateToLocation:` `fromLocation:`	method	Delegate method that reports when an update event occurs
`locationManager:didFailWithError:`	method	Delegate method that reports when update event fails to occur
`CLLocation`		
`altitude`	property	Specifies height of the location in meters
`coordinate`	property	Returns the location as a `CLLocationCoordinate2D` variable
`timestamp`	property	Specifies `NSDate` of when location was measured

Viewing on the Map

We've explored the different methods of gathering the user's location. Let's take a look at how to render those on a map. In augmented-reality applications, using the map isn't typically required. However, it adds good debugging and visualization to testing of coordinates and locations we are using for our AR applications. We'll cover it in this chapter, so you'll have it available in your toolbox.

Let's start by setting up the SecondViewController class in our demo project. This is the second tab in the tab view template. If you've followed the chapter so far, it should still be unused. Open SecondViewController.h and make sure to declare the IBOutlet for the MKMapView, as shown in Listing 3–21.

Listing 3–21. *Declare the MKMapView IBOutlet*

```
#import <UIKit/UIKit.h>
#import <MapKit/MapKit.h>

@interface SecondViewController : UIViewController <MKMapViewDelegate>{
    IBOutlet MKMapView *mapView;
}

@property (nonatomic, retain) IBOutlet MKMapView *mapView;
@end
```

The code shown in bold in Listing 3–21 is what we added to the default template class. First, we import the Mapkit.h header file. We also nominate our class to be an MKMapViewDelegate. This will allow this class to handle the messages and updates from the MKMapView.

Next, open SecondViewController.m and synthesize your new property. Also, don't forget to release it when you're finished with it. Add the code from Listing 3–22 to SecondViewController.m.

Listing 3–22. *Synthesize and Release mapView*

```
@synthesize mapView;

- (void)dealloc
{
    [mapView release];
    mapView = nil;
    [super dealloc];
}
```

Open SecondView.xib in Xcode and remove the UITextView and UITextLabel that were there by default. Drag the **Map View** from the **Object Library** over the view and pause to let it autoscale to fill the space available. Next, press Ctrl and click and drag a line from the cube (File's Owner icon) on the left-hand side of the editor to the new MKMapView. You should see a context menu similar to that shown in Figure 3–12. Select our **mapView** property in the menu.

Figure 3–12. *Configure our MKMapView.*

Centering the Map and Setting the Displayed Region

Returning to SecondView.m, we are going to start by uncommenting the viewDidLoad: method and adding the code from Listing 3–23.

Listing 3–23. *Start a New Thread for Setting Up the Map*

```
- (void)viewDidLoad
{
    mapView.delegate=self;
    [self.view addSubview:mapView];

    [NSThread detachNewThreadSelector:@selector(displayMap) toTarget:self
withObject:nil];
    [super viewDidLoad];
}
```

First, we set the delegate of the MKMapView to self. Recall that we already nominated this class as an MKMapViewDelegate. Finally, instead of just loading up the map right here in the viewDidLoad: method, we detached a new thread for the setup. This is overkill for this sample, but it's a good introduction to threading, which we'll need later for the AR sample applications. Our thread calls a method, displayMap, which we have not yet created. Add the code from Listing 3–24 under the viewDidLoad: method to create this method.

Listing 3–24. *Create New displayMap Method*

```
- (void)displayMap {
    NSAutoreleasePool *pool = [[NSAutoreleasePool alloc] init];

    CLLocationCoordinate2D coords;
    coords.latitude = 37.33188;
    coords.longitude = -122.029497;
    MKCoordinateSpan span = MKCoordinateSpanMake(0.002389, 0.005681);
    MKCoordinateRegion region = MKCoordinateRegionMake(coords, span);
    [mapView setRegion:region animated:YES];

    [pool drain];
}
```

There are a few things to discuss in this method. First, let's run it and see what happens. Figure 3–13 illustrates this application running in the iPhone simulator. Ignore the preceding code in bold for now, as we'll get back to that later. We started by manually creating a CLLocationCoordinate2D and setting the latitude and longitude to Apple's HQ. After we set the coordinates, we created an MKCoordinateSpan to set the delta of the latitude and longitude in the display. Finally, we used the new coordinates and the span we created to set up our MKCoordinateRegion.

We used the MKMapView's setRegion method in this example to set up the defaults for our map. There are a few other options we could have added here for additional customization. You can set the mapType property, which we'll look at next, and also use the zoomEnabled and scrollEnabled methods to dictate whether the user can zoom and scroll the map.

For experimentation, comment out the code in bold and rerun the application. Your Xcode console will quickly fill up with warning messages about having no thread pool in place and that your application is **Just Leaking**. Because we have this method running on a new thread, we are required to set up a new NSAutoReleasePool to handle memory management on our new thread.

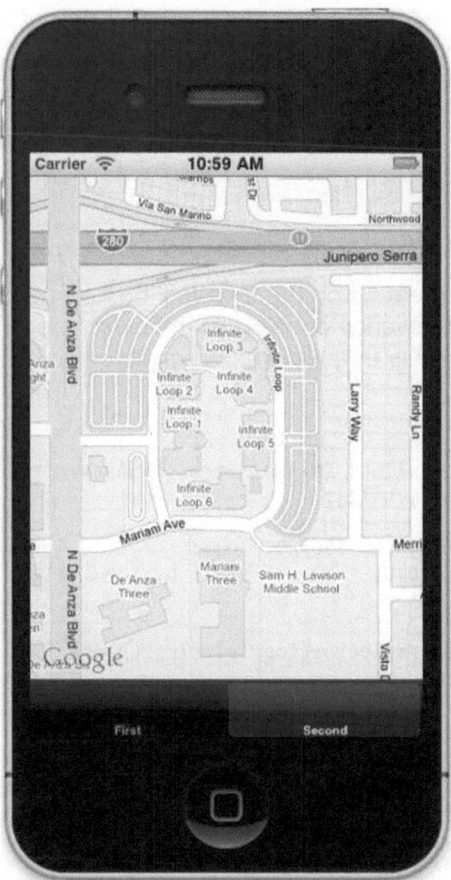

Figure 3–13. *The simulator displays Apple HQ on a map (leaking or not, it looks the same).*

The NSAutoreleasePool class is used to support the reference-counted memory system. The iOS templates (we are using the tab view template) create an autorelease pool in the main.m file under the **Supporting Files** directory. These autorelease pools contain objects that have received an autorelease message. When you drain the pool, as we did in our last line of the new viewDidLoad, the NSAutoReleasePool sends a release message to each of these objects. Because we're not on that main thread any longer, any autoreleased objects would not get their release message if we didn't create this pool. Hence, we'd be leaking memory potentially, which results in the warning messages in the console.

Changing the Map Type

I mentioned in the last section, that the mapType property was available to change the type of map we are displaying. Return to SecondViewController.h and declare a new IBOutlet, as shown in Listing 3–25.

Listing 3–25. *Declare the UISegmentedControl*

```
@interface SecondViewController : UIViewController <MKMapViewDelegate>{
    IBOutlet MKMapView *mapView;
    UISegmentedControl *buttonBarSegmentedControl;
}

@property (nonatomic, retain) IBOutlet MKMapView *mapView;
@property (nonatomic, retain) IBOutlet UISegmentedControl *buttonBarSegmentedControl;
```

Instead of adding this to the XIB file manually, let's create it on the fly. We'll be doing similar things in our augmented-reality application to overlay controls to the user's view. Add the method from Listing 3–26 under the displayMap that we created earlier.

Listing 3–26. *Create the UISegmentedControl to Change Map Type*

```
- (void)setupSegmentedControl {
    buttonBarSegmentedControl = [[UISegmentedControl alloc] initWithItems:[NSArray
arrayWithObjects:@"Standard", @"Satellite", @"Hybrid", nil]];

    [buttonBarSegmentedControl setFrame:CGRectMake(30, 50, 280-30, 30)];
    buttonBarSegmentedControl.selectedSegmentIndex = 0.0;        // start by showing the
normal picker

    [buttonBarSegmentedControl addTarget:self action:@selector(toggleToolBarChange:)
forControlEvents:UIControlEventValueChanged];

    buttonBarSegmentedControl.segmentedControlStyle = UIScrollViewIndicatorStyleWhite;
    buttonBarSegmentedControl.backgroundColor = [UIColor clearColor];
    buttonBarSegmentedControl.tintColor = [UIColor blackColor];
    [buttonBarSegmentedControl setAlpha:0.8];

    [self.view addSubview:buttonBarSegmentedControl];
}
```

This method needs to be declared in the header file as well. Make sure you do that before you run the application.

This method starts by initializing the UISegmentedControl with items from a new array. We are using three strings for our menu options: Standard, Satellite, and Hybrid. These correspond to the different options for the MKMapView.mapType property.

Next, we call the CGRectMake method to set up the area in our view for the segmented control. Segmented controls work similarly to buttons in iOS. We need to be able to add a target and respond to the events raised appropriately. The code in bold in Listing 3–27 sets the target to self and the action to a new method called toggleToolBarChange. We'll create this method next. Finally, in the setupSegmentedControl method, we set up some basic preferences for the control. We set the style, background color, and tint for the control. This is all optional, obviously, but I wanted to demonstrate some options that might match the default styling of the tab bar template that we've been using in this chapter. If we didn't set these options, the control would appear blue by default.

I mentioned that our action was set to a new method called `toggleToolBarChange`. The code for this method is in Listing 3–27. Add this to the class.

Listing 3–27. *Handle the Action of the UISegmentedControl*

```
- (void)toggleToolBarChange:(id)sender
{
        UISegmentedControl *segControl = sender;

        switch (segControl.selectedSegmentIndex)
        {
                case 0: // Map
                {
                        [mapView setMapType:MKMapTypeStandard];
                        break;
                }
                case 1: // Satellite
                {
                        [mapView setMapType:MKMapTypeSatellite];
                        break;
                }
                case 2: // Hybrid
                {
                        [mapView setMapType:MKMapTypeHybrid];
                        break;
                }
        }
}
```

The final step before we can test this new control is to call the `setupSegmentedControl` method from the `viewDidLoad` method. Right after you detached the new thread to set up the map, add the code from Listing 3–28.

Listing 3–28. *Call setupSegmentedControl*

```
[self setupSegmentedControl];
```

You're now ready to test out the new functionality. Run the code we've put together in the iPhone simulator. Switch to the second tab and experiment with the segmented control buttons. Figure 3–14 shows the simulator running the map with the satellite map type selected.

Figure 3–14. *The satellite map type is selected.*

So, we've added a map to the view, we've learned how to center it based on static location coordinates, and we dynamically added a UISegmentedControl to the view to switch map types on the fly.

Next, let's take a look at adding annotations to the map. Annotations provide a way to mark specific locations. In much the same way that they work on Google Maps or Bing, you can add pop-up displays to show the user more contextual information. The icons themselves can be customized, as well as the actions to which they respond.

Adding Annotations to the Map

To set up an annotation, we are going to use a new class that will hold the customization properties of the annotation. Right-click somewhere in your **Project Navigator** and select **New File** from the context menu. Under the **Cocoa Touch** category, select the **Objective-C class** template. Leave the class as a subclass of NSObject and name the new class MapAnnotation. Annotations on maps have a few main characteristics. They are title, subtitle, and coordinate. We're going to add the properties for these characteristics to our new class and provide some methods to set them from our map class. First, add the declarations from Listing 3–29 to MapAnnotation.h.

Listing 3–29. *MapAnnotation.h Changes*

```
#import <Foundation/Foundation.h>
#import <MapKit/MapKit.h>

@interface MapAnnotation : NSObject<MKAnnotation> {
    CLLocationCoordinate2D coordinate;
    NSString *subtitletext;
    NSString *titletext;
}
@property (nonatomic, readonly) CLLocationCoordinate2D coordinate;
@property (readwrite, retain) NSString *titletext;
@property (readwrite, retain) NSString *subtitletext;
-(id)initWithCoordinate:(CLLocationCoordinate2D) coordinate;
- (NSString *)subtitle;
- (NSString *)title;
-(void)setTitle:(NSString*)strTitle;
-(void)setSubTitle:(NSString*)strSubTitle;

@end
```

Again, we start by importing MapKit.h. We declare the properties for our initial coordinate location (where the annotation will be placed) and the title and subtitle of the annotation. We also add a few methods to the class. We have an initialization method for our coordinate, as well as a set of getters and setters for our title and subtitle.

Switch to MapAnnotation.m and add the corresponding properties and method implementations from Listing 3–30.

Listing 3–30. *MapAnnotation.m Changes*

```
@implementation MapAnnotation
@synthesize coordinate, titletext, subtitletext;

- (NSString *)subtitle{
        return subtitletext;
}
- (NSString *)title{
        return titletext;
}

-(void)setTitle:(NSString*)strTitle {
        self.titletext = strTitle;
}

-(void)setSubTitle:(NSString*)strSubTitle {
        self.subtitletext = strSubTitle;
}

-(id)initWithCoordinate:(CLLocationCoordinate2D) c{
        coordinate=c;
        return self;
}
@end
```

This class is not all that exciting. It's basic refactoring to act as a placeholder for the properties of the annotation. In SecondViewController.h add an import statement for the MapAnnotation.h header. Then, open SecondViewController.m and add the following code from Listing 3–31, just above where the setRegion method is called from within the displayMap method. Take note of the three methods from our MapAnnotation class and how they are being called.

Listing 3–31. *Create the Annotation in the displayMap Method*

```
MapAnnotation *addAnnotation = [[[MapAnnotation alloc] initWithCoordinate:coords]
retain];
[addAnnotation setTitle:@"My Annotation Title"];
[addAnnotation setSubTitle:@"this is my subtitle property"];
[mapView addAnnotation:addAnnotation];
```

First, when we create our MapAnnotation object, we call the initWithCoordinate method to set the default location of the annotation. The next two lines call the getters for our properties for title and subtitle. Finally, we add the annotation to the MKMapView.

Go ahead and run this in the simulator. Switch to the second tab and you'll see the map view and a red annotation on Apple HQ (the same coordinates we centered the map on earlier). If you click the annotation, you'll see something similar to Figure 3–15.

You'll see that both the title and the subtitle have been populated and the annotation is showing in the correct coordinates. There are plenty of options available to customize our annotation. For example, what about animating our annotation and changing its color? To customize the appearance of the annotation we would use another delegate method called viewForAnnotation. This method is called when an annotation is created and gives you the opportunity to customize that particular view with a reusable object reference. Add the method from Listing 3–32 to the class to handle the delegate method.

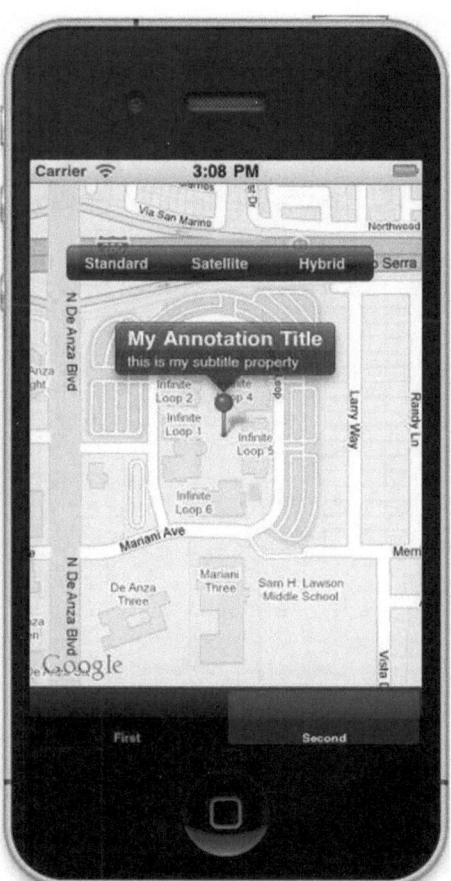

Figure 3–15. *The default annotation shows the populated title and subtitle.*

Listing 3–32. *Handle the viewForAnnotation Delegate Method*

```
- (MKAnnotationView *) mapView:(MKMapView *)mapView viewForAnnotation:(id
<MKAnnotation>) annotation{
    MKPinAnnotationView *annView=[[MKPinAnnotationView alloc]
initWithAnnotation:annotation reuseIdentifier:@"MyPin"];
    annView.animatesDrop=TRUE;
    annView.canShowCallout = YES;
    [annView setSelected:YES];
    annView.pinColor = MKPinAnnotationColorPurple;
    annView.calloutOffset = CGPointMake(-50, 5);
    return annView;
}
```

We made a few changes to the annotation. If you run it in the simulator now, you'll see
something similar to Figure 3–16.

Figure 3–16. *The simulator now shows the customized annotation.*

The first change you'll notice when the simulator changes to the second tab is that the annotation is now animated. It drops in place in a nice friendly motion. We did this using the animatesDrop property. It's also purple now. We set the color of the annotation with the pinColor property. Finally, you'll notice the dialog is off-center. We set an offset using the calloutOffset property. This is useful when you are using custom annotation images that aren't as balanced as the default pins.

Next, let's take a quick look at how to get more information about specific coordinates.

Reverse Geocoding

Finally, we come to reverse geocoding. Reverse geocoding is the process of obtaining address or location information from the latitude and longitude values, whereas geocoding is the process of getting the latitude and longitude from an address. iOS provides a class to make reverse geocoding easy on the developer. Let's extend our current example and log some actual information about the coordinate we have been using.

We're going to use a class called MKReverseGeocoder. There are a few properties and methods of this class on which we should concentrate. They are shown in Table 3–2. However, before we use any of these, we need to nominate the SecondViewController class as an MKReverseGeocoderDelegate. This is important, or the reverse geocoding will appear to do nothing.

Table 3–2. *Methods and Properties of the MKReverseGeocoder Class*

Method/Property	Type	Description
delegate	property	Specifies the delegate for messages from geocoder (errors and location information)
coordinate	property	The coordinate for which to obtain location information
querying	property	Boolean variable to indicate whether geocoder is currently processing location data
start: / cancel:	methods	Starts and cancels the request; if request completes naturally, it fires one of the two delegate methods

To keep things simple and not refactor our whole example, let's reverse geocode the address of the coordinate we've been using thus far. Find the toggleToolBarChange method and change the method to reflect what is shown in Listing 3–33. We are using this method because we want to initiate the reverse geocoding from a user action to demonstrate the feature. This method is called when you click on the segmented button, so it will serve our purpose.

Listing 3–33. *The Updated toggleToolBarChange Method Calls Reverse Geocoder*

```
...
case 1: // Satellite
{
            CLLocationCoordinate2D coords;
            coords.latitude = 37.33188;
            coords.longitude = -122.029497;

            MKReverseGeocoder *geoCoder = [[MKReverseGeocoder alloc]
initWithCoordinate:coords];
            [geoCoder setDelegate:self];
            [geoCoder start];
      [mapView setMapType:MKMapTypeSatellite];
      break;
}
...
```

First, we're a bit sloppy and repeat the code for the CLLocationCoordinate2D. In any real application, this would either be derived or set at a higher scope. After we create our coordinate again, we initialize the MKReverseGeocoder with that same coordinate. This is required to use the reverse geocoding class. We then set the delegate to self. Finally, we start the geocoding process.

As you would expect, because we set our class as an MKReverseGeocoderDelegate, there are a few more methods that the delegate implementation requires. Refer to Listing 3–34 and add the delegate methods to SecondViewController.m.

Listing 3–34. *MKReverseGeocoderDelegate Methods*

```
- (void)reverseGeocoder:(MKReverseGeocoder *)geocoder didFindPlacemark:(MKPlacemark
*)placemark {
    NSLog(@"return %@", placemark.addressDictionary);
}
- (void)reverseGeocoder:(MKReverseGeocoder *)geocoder didFailWithError:(NSError *)error
{
    NSLog(@"fail %@", error);
}
```

The key piece of code here is bolded. The MKPlacemark object is returned to the delegate method if any information is found on the specified coordinate. Figure 3–17 shows the output in the Xcode console.

```
All Output :                                                    ( Clear ) (⬜ ⬛ ⬜)
GNU gdb 6.3.50-20050815 (Apple version gdb-1518) (Sat Feb 12 02:52:12 UTC 2011)
Copyright 2004 Free Software Foundation, Inc.
GDB is free software, covered by the GNU General Public License, and you are
welcome to change it and/or distribute copies of it under certain conditions.
Type "show copying" to see the conditions.
There is absolutely no warranty for GDB.  Type "show warranty" for details.
This GDB was configured as "x86_64-apple-darwin".sharedlibrary apply-load-rules all
Attaching to process 4080.
2011-06-29 21:19:45.913 iOS_AR_Ch3_LocationServices[4080:207] return {
    City = Cupertino;
    Country = "United States";
    CountryCode = US;
    FormattedAddressLines =      (
        "10700 S De Anza Blvd",
        "Cupertino, CA 95014",
        USA
    );
    State = California;
    Street = "10700 S De Anza Blvd";
    SubThoroughfare = 10700;
    Thoroughfare = "S De Anza Blvd";
    ZIP = 95014;
}
```

Figure 3–17. *The Xcode console shows the reverse geocoding output.*

Summary

We covered a lot of ground in this chapter on location services. We started by looking at the various options available for tracking a location, such as the Standard Location Service, the Significant-Change Location Service, the Geographic Region Monitoring Service, and determining altitude. We looked at how to visualize location services on a map and how to determine contextual information from reverse geocoding that location.

There were a few subtle lessons in this chapter as well. For example, we introduced basic threading, which we'll continue to expand on in later examples; and dynamic overlays, which we'll be using in more of a HUD (head-up display) fashion in our augmented-reality chapters.

We're building the tools that we'll need to fully construct our AR applications. Next, we'll explore iOS sensor programming by working with the gyroscope and the accelerometer.

iOS Sensors

Augmented-reality programming requires the use of multiple hardware components to build an effective application. Most of these components are commonly referred to as sensors. Sensors, such as the gyroscope and accelerometer, help us figure out the device's orientation and change in position while the application is running. Since we'll be programming in AR, we'll be overlaying our application on the real-life view of the device's camera. This makes it so much more important that we track orientation so we can keep the application oriented in a realistic way.

Orientation Sensors

The accelerometer and gyroscope are used for similar purposes, but there is a subtle difference between the two, and most applications rely on the combination of both readings for maximum effectiveness. Let's take a look at the differences and similarities between the two components.

Let's start with the accelerometer. The three-axis accelerometer in the iPhone 4 gauges the orientation of the device relative to the Earth's surface. If the device happens to be in free fall or has a constant acceleration in a particular direction, the acceleration returns zero (or should return zero) because it would be indistinguishable from the acceleration being provided by the Earth's gravitational pull.

The gyroscope has the capability of measuring the rate of rotation around a particular axis. Rotation is something an accelerometer does not measure, which is why flight computers cannot rely on an accelerometer alone, but need a gyroscope as well to keep an aircraft from rolling.

An easy way to think of the difference between these components is that the gyroscope helps measure orientation, and an accelerometer measures vibration. Using this as a basis, the gyroscope can provide an angular rate (or rotation), whereas the accelerometer can measure only linear acceleration (over all three axes).

Let's start by looking at each of these components and how to use them, then move on to combining the two for better measurements. For this chapter, we're going to use the Tab Bar application template again to keep our number of sample applications to a minimum. Create a new project using the Tab Bar application template with iPhone as your target device in Xcode. Call the new project **iOS_AR_Ch4_Sensors**, or download the completed code for this chapter from github.com/kyleroche/Professional_iOS_AugmentedReality or from the Source Code/Download area of the Apress web site (www.apress.com).

Using the Accelerometer

Let's start with the accelerometer. In Xcode, open the `FirstViewController.h` file and update it, as shown in Listing 4–1.

Listing 4–1. *Updated FirstViewController.h*

```
#import <UIKit/UIKit.h>

@interface FirstViewController : UIViewController {
    UIAccelerometer *accelerometer;

    UILabel *xLabel;
    UILabel *yLabel;
    UILabel *zLabel;

    UIProgressView *xProgressView;
    UIProgressView *yProgressView;
    UIProgressView *zProgressView;
}

@property (nonatomic, retain) UIAccelerometer *accelerometer;

@property (nonatomic, retain) IBOutlet UILabel *xLabel;
@property (nonatomic, retain) IBOutlet UILabel *yLabel;
@property (nonatomic, retain) IBOutlet UILabel *zLabel;

@property (nonatomic, retain) IBOutlet UIProgressView *xProgressView;
@property (nonatomic, retain) IBOutlet UIProgressView *yProgressView;
@property (nonatomic, retain) IBOutlet UIProgressView *zProgressView;

@end
```

Let's get our `FirstViewController.m` file up to date, and then walk through the new code step by step. Switch to `FirstViewController.m` in Xcode and add the code from Listing 4–2.

Listing 4–2. *Updated FirstViewController.m*

```
// after implementation
@synthesize xLabel, yLabel, zLabel, xProgressView, yProgressView, zProgressView,
accelerometer;
// replace existing dealloc from auto-gen code
- (void)dealloc
{
    [xLabel release];
    xLabel = nil;
    [yLabel release];
    yLabel = nil;
    [zLabel release];
```

```
        zLabel = nil;
        [xProgressView release];
        xProgressView = nil;
        [yProgressView release];
        yProgressView = nil;
        [zProgressView release];
        zProgressView = nil;
        [accelerometer release];
        accelerometer = nil;
        [super dealloc];
}
```

Starting at the top, we declare a few UI elements that we'll use to display real-time readings from the accelerometer. We are going to be using three labels and three progress bars, each associated with one axis of the accelerometer. Figure 4–1 shows the X, Y, and Z coordinate axes.

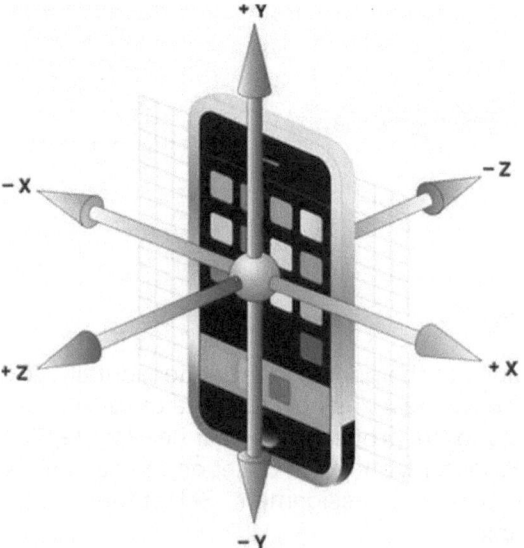

Figure 4–1. *The accelerometer uses X, Y, and Z coordinate axes.*

Open FirstView.xib in Xcode. Add the labels and the progress bar elements to the interface canvas. You should see something similar to what is shown in Figure 4–2.

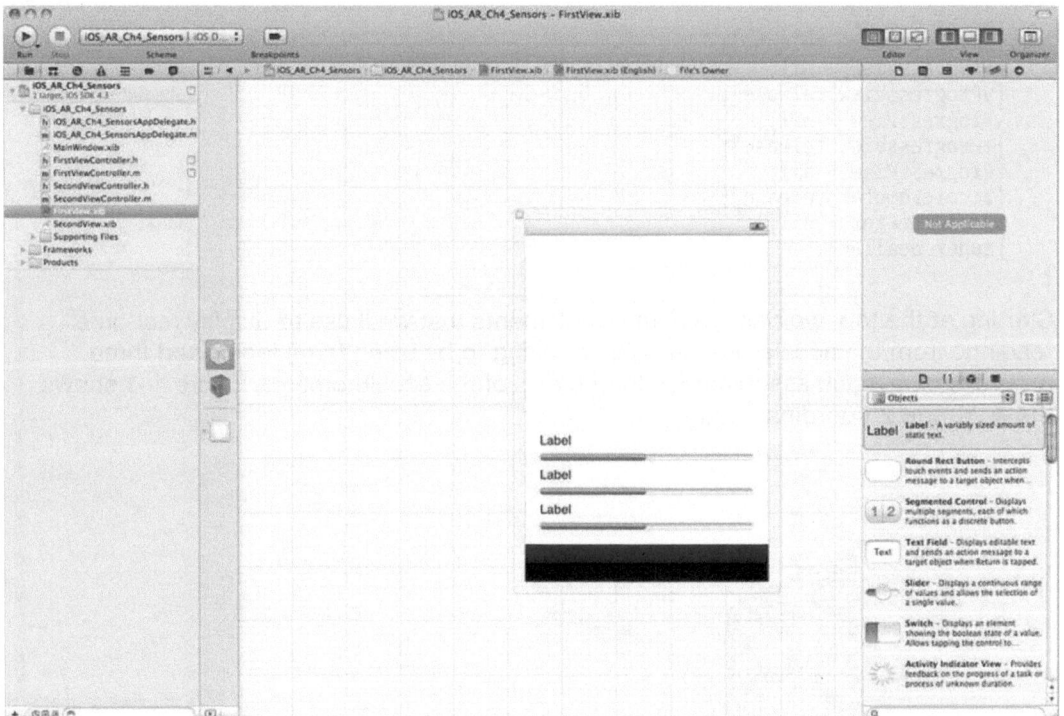

Figure 4–2. *Set up the XIB file for the accelerometer readings.*

For simplicity, let's assign the three sets of values to the outlets in order horizontally. X will be at the top, and Z at the bottom. Because Xcode 4.2 is new to some of us, we'll review this one more time. To assign the outlets to the properties in your header file, press the Ctrl key while dragging from the **File's Owner** icon to the outlet on the canvas. A pop-up dialog will display, showing eligible properties for assignment. Select the appropriate outlet. Figure 4–3 shows an example.

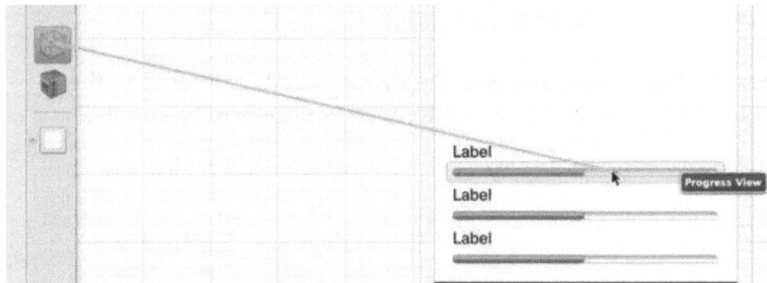

Figure 4–3. *Link the IBOutlet to the properties in FirstViewController.h.*

Repeat the process for each of the UILabel outlets and UIProgressView components.

We access the accelerometer through the UIAccelerometer class. This class uses the same delegate pattern we were using in Chapter 3 for location services. This class uses a shared UIAccelerometer singleton and is not directly accessed. Because of this, you'll notice a slight change in how we handle memory in these examples (more specifically, how we handle the subscription to the hardware messages).

The UIAccelerometerDelegate Class

Before we can start monitoring the accelerometer for updates, we must nominate this class as a UIAccelerometerDelegate. Update FirstViewController.h accordingly. Switch back to FirstViewController.m and add the method from Listing 4–3.

Listing 4–3. *Delegate Method for UIAccelerometerDelegate Class*

```
- (void)accelerometer:(UIAccelerometer *)accelerometer didAccelerate:(UIAcceleration
*)acceleration {
    xLabel.text = [NSString stringWithFormat:@"%@%f", @"X: ", acceleration.x];
    yLabel.text = [NSString stringWithFormat:@"%@%f", @"Y: ", acceleration.y];
    zLabel.text = [NSString stringWithFormat:@"%@%f", @"Z: ", acceleration.z];

    xProgressView.progress = ABS(acceleration.x);
    yProgressView.progress = ABS(acceleration.y);
    zProgressView.progress = ABS(acceleration.z);
}
```

The didAccelerate method of the delegate class is called every time the accelerometer measures new values within range of its update interval. Let's walk through the code. The first set of methods format an NSString value for the text properties of the three UILabels. It is the acceleration value of each particular axis that will populate this string value. The second block of code sets the value of the UIProgressView outlets based on the same values. You'll notice that we're also setting the values to the absolute value (ABS) of the measurement. This is because a progress bar can't display a negative value. If there's a negative measurement, you'll see it on the UILabel.

Before we can run the project, we have to set up the update interval of the accelerometer and assign it a delegate. As I mentioned earlier, the UIAccelerometer class is a singleton class. We need to create a reference to the sharedAccelerometer object to start receiving measurements. Uncomment the viewDidLoad method and adjust it, as shown in Listing 4–4.

Listing 4–4. *New viewDidLoad Method*

```
- (void)viewDidLoad
{
    accelerometer = [UIAccelerometer sharedAccelerometer];
    accelerometer.updateInterval = .5;
    accelerometer.delegate = self;

    [super viewDidLoad];
}
```

The first line in this method assigns our UIAccelerometer object to the sharedAccelerometer object. Next, you choose the updateInterval, which is in seconds. I have .5 (twice per second) selected. Feel free to adjust this and experiment with the response times. Finally, we set the `delegate` to `self` so we can receive the measurements.

Make sure you have a physical device connected and selected in the Scheme drop-down in Xcode. Run the project on your device. You should see something similar to what is shown in Figure 4–4.

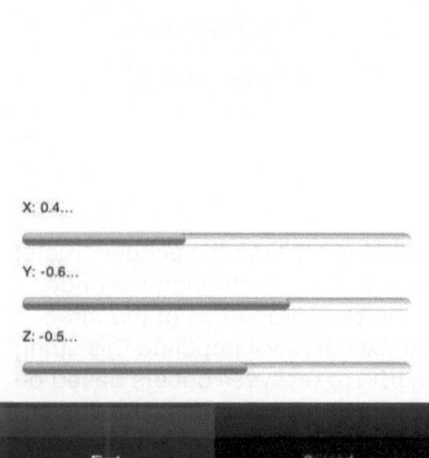

Figure 4–4. *Obtain X, Y, and Z measurements of UIAccelerometer.*

As you are testing the application, try a few different scenarios. Try to force the device downward to watch for quick changes on an axis. Try to set the device on its side horizontally, which should increase the X-axis in full (either negative or positive, depending on which side). Next, stand the device upright vertically. The Y-axis should now have a full measurement, while the other readings move toward zero. Lay the device flat with the screen facing upward. You should see the Z-axis nearing 1.0 as the other two axis measurements approach zero. Get to know the orientation of the device. We'll need to coordinate these types of readings into our applications later in the book.

Shake Detection

You can use the accelerometer to measure action from the user as well. Some popular iOS applications on the App Store, such as Facebook, use shake detection for refresh actions. Other native apps, such as messaging, use shake detection as a method for the user to cancel an action.

Return to the didAccelerate delegate method of FirstViewController.m and add the code from Listing 4–5 to the bottom of that method.

Listing 4–5. *Add to didAccelerate Delegate Method*

```
double const kThreshold = 2.0; // 2Gs is typical to measure shaking
    if (   ABS(acceleration.x) > kThreshold
        || ABS(acceleration.y) > kThreshold
        || ABS(acceleration.z) > kThreshold) {
        // if shake is detected across any axis
        NSLog(@"Shake Detected!"); // Log it!
    }
```

First, we are defining a constant to serve as a threshold for shake detection. If any axis measures vibration greater than 2Gs, the method will log our message to the console. Run the updated project on your device and shake the device when the application starts. In the Xcode console, you should see something similar to what is shown in Figure 4–5.

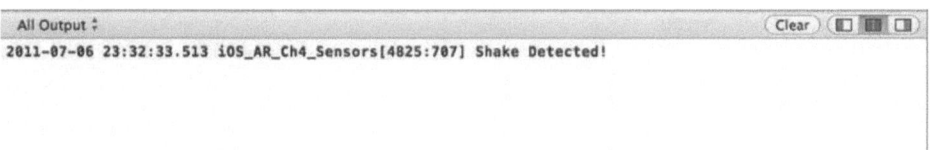

Figure 4–5. *Detect a shake from the user.*

In Chapter 5, we'll discuss sound and user feedback, and show you how to force the device to vibrate. This chapter is focused on gathering sensor data.

Low-Pass Filtering

One of the techniques we'll be using in the examples is called low-pass filtering. Basically, as we receive accelerometer data, we remove everything except gravity readings. This will help us keep the orientation of 3D objects we're putting in the AR view. Listing 4–6 shows sample code that sets up a low-pass filter.

We'll cover this subject in more detail when we get to 3D objects and augmented reality.

Listing 4–6. *Setting Up a Low-Pass Filter*

```
accel[0] = acceleration.x * kFilteringFactor + accel[0] * (1.0 - kFilteringFactor);
accel[1] = acceleration.y * kFilteringFactor + accel[1] * (1.0 - kFilteringFactor);
accel[2] = acceleration.z * kFilteringFactor + accel[2] * (1.0 - kFilteringFactor);
```

Using the Gyroscope

The gyroscope is actually a bit easier to read. There's no need to set up a delegate class or methods to handle updates. After you start the gyroscope, you can simply request the measurements through the CMMotionManager class. This class acts as a gateway to the device's hardware.

Let's use the second tab in our demo project to measure the gyroscope. Open Xcode, select SecondView.xib and set up the canvas as shown in Figure 4–6. We'll be visualizing the gyroscope based on its three attitude attributes. These are roll, pitch, and yaw.

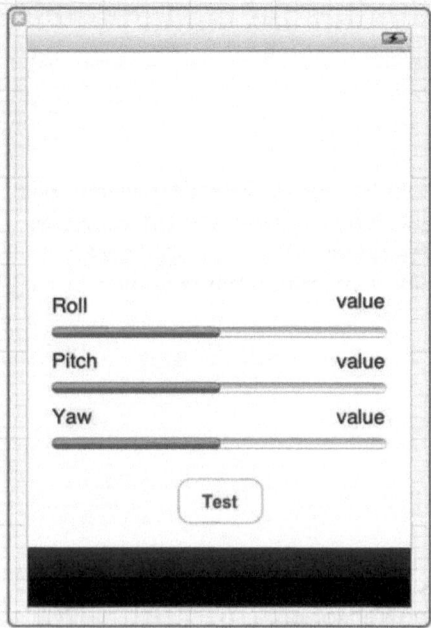

Figure 4–6. *Set up the canvas for monitoring the gyroscope.*

Before we start connecting these outlets, we must add a new framework to our project. Interacting with the gyroscope requires the Core Motion Framework. Add that to the project by selecting the project name in your Xcode **Project Navigator** and adding the framework in the **Link Binary With Libraries** section of the **Build Phases** tab of your application's target. Open SecondViewController.h and add the properties we'll need to send information to the IBOutlets we just created. Use the code from Listing 4–7 as a reference.

Listing 4–7. *New SecondViewController.h*

```
#import <UIKit/UIKit.h>
#import <CoreMotion/CoreMotion.h>

@interface SecondViewController : UIViewController {
    CMMotionManager *motionManager;

    UILabel *rollLabel;
    UILabel *pitchLabel;
    UILabel *yawLabel;

    UIProgressView *rollProgressView;
    UIProgressView *pitchProgressView;
    UIProgressView *yawProgressView;
```

```
}

@property (nonatomic, retain) CMMotionManager *motionManager;

@property (nonatomic, retain) IBOutlet UILabel *rollLabel;
@property (nonatomic, retain) IBOutlet UILabel *pitchLabel;
@property (nonatomic, retain) IBOutlet UILabel *yawLabel;

@property (nonatomic, retain) IBOutlet UIProgressView *rollProgressView;
@property (nonatomic, retain) IBOutlet UIProgressView *pitchProgressView;
@property (nonatomic, retain) IBOutlet UIProgressView *yawProgressView;

- (IBAction)readGyroscope;

@end
```

Let's walk through this code quickly, before we get too far ahead. From the top, you'll see our import statement for the Core Motion Framework, which we just added to our application. Next, in the interface block, you'll notice we aren't nominating this class as any sort of delegate, as we did with the accelerometer. The gyroscope class acts as an interface gateway to the hardware sensors. It doesn't report to a delegate method like the accelerometer class.

The UILabel and UIProgressBar properties should come as no surprise. They are the same as those used in our accelerometer example. However, we have a new property in this sample. CMMotionManager is the class that we will be using to interface to the gyroscope.

Finally, we declare an IBAction method for our button. Instead of sitting on a delegate method (as we did with the accelerometer), we'll be manually invoking a method to query the current measurements of the gyroscope.

Switch to SecondViewController.m in Xcode and synthesize our new properties; don't forget to update your dealloc method to release the properties and set them to nil, as shown in Listing 4–8.

Listing 4–8. *Synthesize and Release the New Properties*

```
// after @implementation
@synthesize motionManager;
@synthesize rollLabel, rollProgressView, pitchLabel, pitchProgressView, yawLabel,
yawProgressView;

// new dealloc
- (void)dealloc
{
    [motionManager release];
    motionManager = nil;
    [rollLabel release];
    rollLabel = nil;
    [rollProgressView release];
    rollProgressView = nil;
    [pitchLabel release];
    pitchLabel = nil;
    [pitchProgressView release];
```

```
        pitchProgressView = nil;
        [yawLabel release];
        yawLabel = nil;
        [yawProgressView release];
        yawProgressView = nil;
        [super dealloc];
}
```

Uncomment the viewDidLoad method and update it, as shown in Listing 4–9.

Listing 4–9. *Uncomment and Update the viewDidLoad Method*

```
- (void)viewDidLoad
{
    self.motionManager = [[[CMMotionManager alloc] init] autorelease];
    motionManager.deviceMotionUpdateInterval = 1.0/60.0;
    if (motionManager.isDeviceMotionAvailable) {
        [motionManager startDeviceMotionUpdates];
    }
    [super viewDidLoad];
}
```

First, we set the motionManager property to a new instance of the CMMotionManager class. Next, we set an interval for updates. Finally, we start updates if the motion manager is available. If you recall from Chapter 2 where we validated the availability of sensors, this will look familiar. If you skipped Chapter 2, just be aware that it's good practice to validate that the sensor is actually available before trying to access it.

Attitude

Before we update the UI with our values, let's just log them to the console and make sure we're able to access the hardware successfully. Add the IBAction method we declared in our header by copying the code from Listing 4–10 to SecondViewController.m.

Listing 4–10. *Add the IBAction Method—readGyroscope*

```
- (void)readGyroscope {
    CMDeviceMotion *currentDeviceMotion = motionManager.deviceMotion;
    CMAttitude *currentAttitude = currentDeviceMotion.attitude;

    NSLog(@"Attitude: %@", currentAttitude);
}
```

This method creates a CMDeviceMotion object, and reads the CMAttitude value from the gyroscope. Switch to SecondView.xib and set the UIButton's IBAction to the readGyroscope method. The CMAttitude reading has a collection of key parameters (see Table 4–1) that we'll be using in our sample applications later in the book.

Table 4–1. *CMAttitude Properties*

Property Name	Description
pitch	The pitch of the device in radians. A pitch is a rotation around a lateral axis that passes through the device from side to side.
quaternion	Returns a quaternion representing the device's attitude.
roll	The roll of the device in radians. A roll is a rotation around a longitudinal axis that passes through the device from its top to bottom.
yaw	The yaw of the device in radians. A yaw is a rotation around an axis that runs vertically through the device. It is perpendicular to the body of the device, with its origin at the center of gravity and directed toward the bottom of the device.

Run the application on a physical device. Navigate to the second tab and click the Test button. Rotate the device in different directions and continue to test the values. In the Xcode console, you should see log output resembling Listing 4–11.

Listing 4–11. *NSLog Output from Logging Attitude of Device*

```
2011-07-08 20:38:31.955 iOS_AR_Ch4_Sensors[6144:707] Attitude: Pitch: -41.931169, Roll:
-57.704060, Yaw: -177.801492 @ 0.000000
2011-07-08 20:38:33.572 iOS_AR_Ch4_Sensors[6144:707] Attitude: Pitch: -17.880685, Roll:
-62.436956, Yaw: 167.555800 @ 0.000000
2011-07-08 20:38:49.238 iOS_AR_Ch4_Sensors[6144:707] Attitude: Pitch: 28.940916, Roll:
11.359928, Yaw: -45.087161 @ 0.000000
```

The Attitude is the combination of Pitch, Roll, and Yaw for the device. If we were to access these properties individually, you would get the separate values in radians. Typically, we'll have to convert these to degrees for basic augmented-reality purposes, such as knowing the viewing angle and rotation of the device. Add the code from Listing 4–12 to the end of the readGyroscope method.

Listing 4–12. *Add to End of readGyroscope Method*

```
rollLabel.text = [NSString stringWithFormat:@"ROLL: %f", currentAttitude.roll];
rollProgressView.progress = ABS(currentAttitude.roll);
pitchLabel.text = [NSString stringWithFormat:@"PITCH: %f", currentAttitude.pitch];
pitchProgressView.progress = ABS(currentAttitude.pitch);
yawLabel.text = [NSString stringWithFormat:@"YAW: %f", currentAttitude.yaw];
yawProgressView.progress = ABS(currentAttitude.yaw);
```

The code block we just added should look familiar. We are just setting the visible values in our UI elements for quick debugging. Run the application. You should see something similar to what we see in Figure 4–7.

You can see that the values that were shown in the Xcode console aren't exactly matching up with what we're seeing on the screen. The formatting is the same but we're now looking at the radian measurement for rotation on each individual axis.

Before we get to our examples later in the book, we'll talk about a framework called cocos2D. We'll be using the framework for animation and 2D gaming features. cocos2D provides some very simple functions to convert radians to degrees.

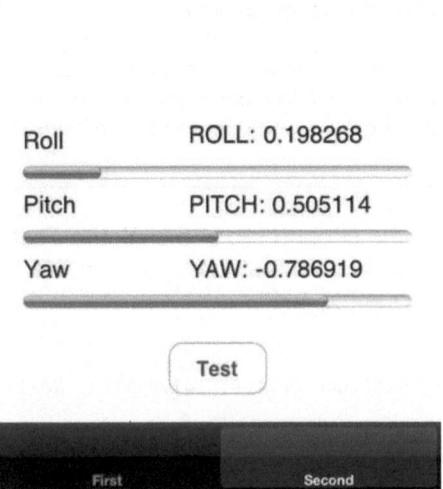

Figure 4–7. *Read gyro data from CMMotionManager.*

The motion manager blends the accelerometer and gyroscope data together automatically. One of the readings that is missing from this approach is the rate of rotation. Let's put together a quick sample to demonstrate how to gather this metric and coordinate it to an element in our UI. This will be a common task in augmented-reality programming. In most cases, when the phone is rotated, you will want to keep items that you've overlaid on the view in the correct orientation.

Rate of Rotation

Open `SecondView.xib` in Xcode. Add a `UIImageView` object above the content we already have on the view. Assign an image to the element that is more horizontally oriented. The GitHub repository for this chapter has an image of a fighter jet included, which you may use. Define the `UIImageView` in your header file and synthesize/release the object in the implementation file. Add the code from Listing 4–13 to the bottom of the `readGyroscope` method.

Listing 4–13. *Add to End of readGyroscope Method*

```
float rotation;
    float rate = motionManager.gyroData.rotationRate.z;
        if (fabs(rate) > .2) {
```

```
            float direction = rate > 0 ? 1 : -1;
            rotation += direction * M_PI/90.0;
            imageView.transform = CGAffineTransformMakeRotation(rotation);
            NSLog(@"Rotation: %f", rotation);
        }
```

This method will use the gyroData property of our motion manager to get the rotation rate of the Z-axis. There is a new function in use now to rotate the image according to the rotation of the Z-axis. We'll look more at various approaches to this type of task in our in-depth examples later in the book. Of course, we haven't started actually monitoring the gyroscope, so we need to set that up before we'll see any useful results. Update your viewDidLoad method as shown in Listing 4–14.

Listing 4–14. *Updated viewDidLoad Method*

```
- (void)viewDidLoad
{
    self.motionManager = [[[CMMotionManager alloc] init] autorelease];
    motionManager.deviceMotionUpdateInterval = 1.0/60.0;

    if (motionManager.isDeviceMotionAvailable) {
        [motionManager startDeviceMotionUpdates];
        [motionManager startGyroUpdates];
    }
    [super viewDidLoad];
}
```

Before we get too far from this point, it is important to note that this code does not stop listening to the gyroscope readings. It's important to implement a routine to start and stop monitoring sensor readings appropriately.

Go ahead and run the project. You'll find it a bit difficult to test. We are looking to validate that if we increase the rate of rotation significantly enough respective to the Z-axis that the image will rotate to the same angle as the Z-axis when we press the Test button. The main difficulty here is that we have to press the button and move the device around at the same time, which results in only minor changes in rate of rotation, as shown in Figure 4–8.

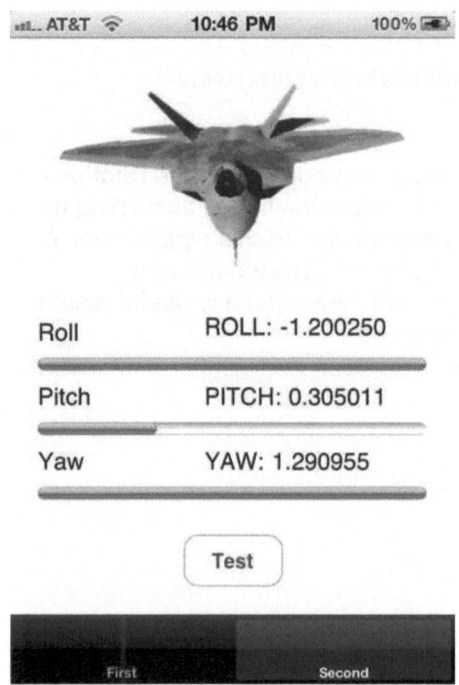

Figure 4–8. *Test the manual readings of gyro data (notice a slight rolling effect of the image).*

Instead of manually retrieving the readings in response to the click of the button, we could use the NSTimer class to set up an interval and call back to another method.

Refactor the code block from Listing 4–13 into a new method, as shown in Listing 4–15.

Listing 4–15. *Refactored Code Showing New Method—doGyroUpdate*

```
-(void)doGyroUpdate {
    float rotation;
    float rate = motionManager.gyroData.rotationRate.z;
    if (fabs(rate) > .2) {
        float direction = rate > 0 ? 1 : -1;
        rotation += direction * M_PI/90.0;
        imageView.transform = CGAffineTransformMakeRotation(rotation);
         NSLog(@"Rotation: %f", rotation);
    }
}
```

After you start listening to gyro events, create an NSTimer to call our new method. First, declare the NSTimer in your header. I'm calling mine timer. Create the timer in the viewDidLoad method. Your code should look something like Listing 4–16. Again, we're not really cleaning up after ourselves in this example because our goal is to read the data. This application has no UI flow.

Listing 4–16. *Set Up the NSTimer*

```
timer = [NSTimer scheduledTimerWithTimeInterval:1/30.0
                target:self
                selector:@selector(doGyroUpdate)
```

```
userInfo:nil
repeats:YES];
```

If you run the project again, you'll see a lot more output in the console, as well as a smoother response to rotations on the device. The gyro class is updating subsecond and we're rotating our image in conjunction with those readings.

Magnetometer

The magnetometer is the sensor that measures the strength of the magnetic field surrounding the device. Assuming that there are no strong magnetic fields next to the device, this reading will correlate to the ambient magnetic field of the Earth, which allows us to then use the readings for determining our heading. The heading of the device is its geomagnetic orientation of the device from the North Pole. Apple points out in its developer documentation, as do most other reference materials on this subject, that the geomagnetic heading and the true heading, with respect to the geographic North Pole, may vary greatly depending on your location.

We measure the geomagnetic heading of the device much like we measured the gyroscope or accelerometer readings. Let's extend our project to also display our heading.

In Xcode, add a new UIViewController class to the project. Name it headingViewController and make sure you create it with an XIB file interface building. I used Google Image Search to find a noncopyrighted image of a compass. It's included in the project on GitHub and is available from the Source Code/Download area at the Apress web site (www.apress.com). If you substitute your own image, make sure that North is centered at the top of the image. We will be rotating this image based on the device's heading, so we want to start with an angle of 0 degrees from the vertical axis to make things as simple as possible. After you have your image, add it to the project in Xcode.

Magnetometer Availability

As we discussed in Chapter 3, the CLLocationManager requires the user to enable location updates to function properly. The location manager is also capable of returning both the true and the magnetic heading of the device. However, the true heading of the device is available only if the user has location updates enabled. Magnetic heading updates, however, are always available regardless of the user's preference for location updates. This is because heading on its own does not compromise the user's privacy and, therefore, doesn't require approval.

In short, you do not need to check for availability of the magnetometer before using it, as we did with other sensors.

Calibration

Because we have a strong possibility of two readings, there are functions in iOS that allow us to calibrate the device to determine the difference between the magnetic heading and the true heading. CLLocationManager defines a delegate method named locationManagerShouldDisplayHeadingCalibration. This method overlays an orientation image instructing the user to rotate the device in a figure-8 pattern until the location manager can distinguish between any local magnetic fields and the Earth's magnetic field. The location manager uses the true heading as reference.

Let's See Where We're Headed

Open headingViewController.xib in interface builder. Add a UIImage outlet and two UILabel outlets. You can see how the sample interface is set up in Figure 4–9.

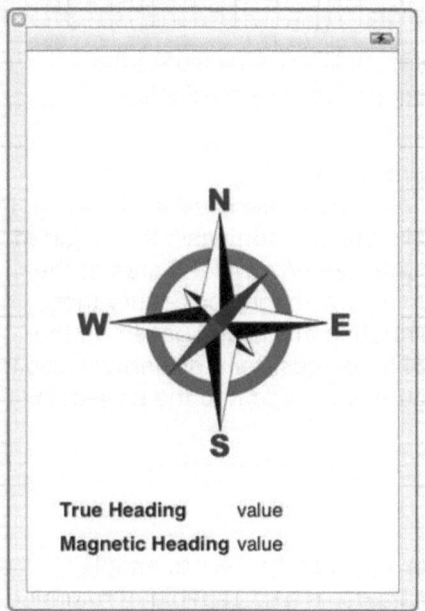

Figure 4–9. *Here is the setup of the magnetometer interface (headingViewController.xib).*

Open headingViewController.h in your assistant editor and press the Ctrl key while dragging the UIImage and the set of UILabels from interface builder to the interface file, as shown in Figure 4–10.

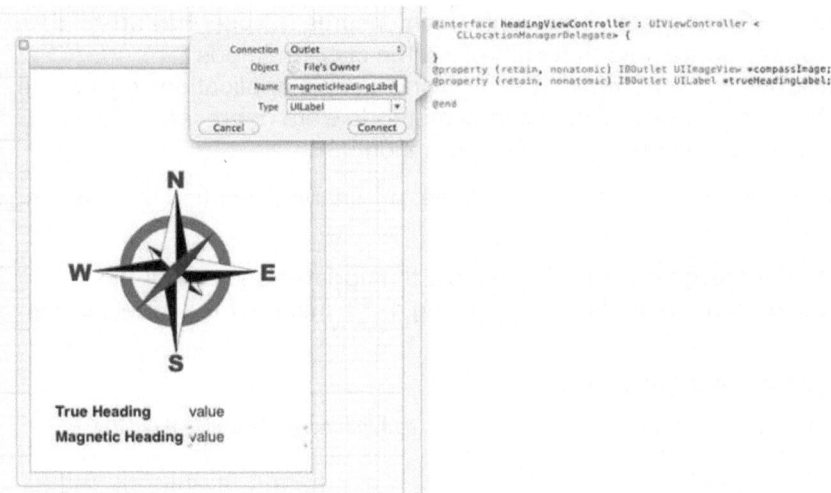

Figure 4–10. *Here are the setup properties for the IBOutlets.*

Make sure you import the <CoreLocation/CoreLocation.h> header and nominate headingViewController as a CLLocationManagerDelegate.

After you complete that, switch to headingViewController.m in Xcode. Update the viewDidLoad method with the code from Listing 4–17.

Listing 4–17. *New viewDidLoad Method*

```
- (void)viewDidLoad
{
    [super viewDidLoad];
    // Do any additional setup after loading the view from its nib.

    CLLocationManager *locationManager = [[CLLocationManager alloc] init];
    locationManager.delegate = self;
    locationManager.headingFilter = 5;
    if ([CLLocationManager locationServicesEnabled] && [CLLocationManager
headingAvailable]) {
        [locationManager startUpdatingHeading];
        [locationManager startUpdatingLocation];
    } else {
        NSLog(@"Error starting location updates");
    }
}
```

Let's walk through this a bit before moving forward. First, we set up our CLLocationManager instance. This should look familiar to what we did in Chapter 3. We set the delegate to self, as expected, but then we introduced a new attribute. The headingFilter attribute defines the threshold of change required to update the delegate methods. We set this value to 5 (degrees), so the location manager will update the delegate only on a change greater than 5 degrees in heading.

I mentioned already that you don't need to check for the availability of the magnetometer. So, why did I include a check in viewDidLoad? Heading information is available only in iPhone 3Gs and later. This verification ensures the user has up-to-date hardware. Also, it is important to note that I am using the class methods locationServicesEnabled and headingAvailable. Many sample applications online use the instance methods for this check. The instance methods were deprecated in iOS 4. Make sure you use the class methods for your application.

Finally, once we've verified the readings are available, we enabled location and heading updates.

Next, we have to add the delegate method to handle the updates and reflect the changes in our interface. Add the method from Listing 4–18, just after the viewDidLoad method.

Listing 4–18. *The didUpdateHeading Delegate Method*

```
- (void)locationManager:(CLLocationManager *)manager didUpdateHeading:(CLHeading
*)newHeading {
    if (newHeading.headingAccuracy > 0) {
        float magneticHeading = newHeading.magneticHeading;
        float trueHeading = newHeading.trueHeading;

        magneticHeadingLabel.text = [NSString stringWithFormat:@"%f", magneticHeading];
        trueHeadingLabel.text = [NSString stringWithFormat:@"%f", trueHeading];

        float heading = -1.0f * M_PI * newHeading.magneticHeading / 180.0f;
        compassImage.transform = CGAffineTransformMakeRotation(heading);
    }
}
```

You can see that we are first checking the value of headingAccuracy before we do anything else. If location updates are not enabled, the value of headingAccuracy will be set to -1. Checking for a value greater than zero ensures we have proper readings from both the magnetometer and the location manager. We are simply setting both UILabels to the values from the readings so you can see the slight difference between them, and then we're rotating the image. We are using the CGAffineTransformMakeRotation method to rotate the image. We are multiplying by the negative constant, then by pi before dividing by 180. We use 180 because the heading is always in relation to the top of the device regardless of orientation. We'll discuss this next.

Run the project on a physical device. You will see results similar to those shown in Figure 4–11.

True Heading   321.946106
Magnetic Heading 313.125000

Figure 4–11. *Retrieve both the true and magnetic heading values.*

Handling Changes in Orientation

While you're running the sample application, test what happens when the device is in landscape mode. You should see that North corresponds to the top of the device, not the top of the visible screen. If you put the device in landscape mode without changing your heading, the device will report the heading to your left or right side (depending on which way you reoriented). We can fix this with a quick addition to our class.

Open headingViewController.xib in interface builder. Add another UILabel IBOutlet to the interface. Name the property orientationLabel and add it to headingViewController.h, as we did with the other outlets. Declare the methods shown in Listing 4–19 in the interface file.

Listing 4–19. *Helper Methods*

```
- (float)heading:(float)heading fromOrientation:(UIDeviceOrientation) orientation;
- (NSString *)stringFromOrientation:(UIDeviceOrientation) orientation;
```

Switch to headingViewController.m and add the two methods shown in Listing 4–20.

Listing 4–20. *Methods to Get Degrees Based on Orientation*

```
- (float)heading:(float)heading fromOrientation:(UIDeviceOrientation)orientation {
    float correctedHeading = heading;

    switch (orientation) {
        case UIDeviceOrientationPortrait:
```

```
                    break;
            case UIDeviceOrientationPortraitUpsideDown:
                correctedHeading = heading + 180.0f;
                break;
            case UIDeviceOrientationLandscapeLeft:
                correctedHeading = heading + 90.0f;
                break;
            case UIDeviceOrientationLandscapeRight:
                correctedHeading = heading - 90.0f;
                break;
            default:
                break;
        }
    while ( heading > 360.0f ) {
        correctedHeading = heading - 360;
    }
    return correctedHeading;
}

- (NSString *)stringFromOrientation:(UIDeviceOrientation) orientation {
    NSString *orientationString;
    switch (orientation) {
        case UIDeviceOrientationPortrait:
            orientationString = @"Portrait";
            break;
        case UIDeviceOrientationPortraitUpsideDown:
            orientationString = @"Portrait Upside Down";
            break;
        case UIDeviceOrientationLandscapeLeft:
            orientationString = @"Landscape Left";
            break;
        case UIDeviceOrientationLandscapeRight:
            orientationString = @"Landscape Right";
            break;
        case UIDeviceOrientationFaceUp:
            orientationString = @"Face Up";
            break;
        case UIDeviceOrientationFaceDown:
            orientationString = @"Face Down";
            break;
        case UIDeviceOrientationUnknown:
            orientationString = @"Unknown";
            break;
        default:
            orientationString = @"Not Known";
            break;
    }
    return orientationString;
}
```

The first method adjusts the heading based on the orientation of the device. This is a fairly basic correction. You could get more complicated and precise using the gyroscope in conjunction with the orientation. For the purposes of this example, we are assuming that the device is rotated in full portrait or landscape mode, so we are correcting by factors of 90 degrees.

The second method builds a human-readable string from the device's orientation. I found this function in a few online articles. I'm not sure to whom credit is due for this function, but it was very useful.

We have to make an adjustment to the didUpdateHeading delegate method, and then we can test out our corrected sample application. Update the didUpdateHeading method with the code from Listing 4–21.

Listing 4–21. *New didUpdateHeading Method*

```
- (void)locationManager:(CLLocationManager *)manager didUpdateHeading:(CLHeading
*)newHeading {
    if (newHeading.headingAccuracy > 0) {
        //float magneticHeading = newHeading.magneticHeading;
        //float trueHeading = newHeading.trueHeading;
        UIDevice *device = [UIDevice currentDevice];
        orientationLabel.text = [self stringFromOrientation:device.orientation];

        float magneticHeading = [self heading:newHeading.magneticHeading
fromOrientation:device.orientation];
        float trueHeading = [self heading:newHeading.trueHeading
fromOrientation:device.orientation];

        magneticHeadingLabel.text = [NSString stringWithFormat:@"%f", magneticHeading];
        trueHeadingLabel.text = [NSString stringWithFormat:@"%f", trueHeading];

        float heading = -1.0f * M_PI * newHeading.magneticHeading / 180.0f;
        compassImage.transform = CGAffineTransformMakeRotation(heading);
    }
}
```

Let's walk through the bold block of code. First, we're setting up an instance of UIDevice that represents the user's actual phone. We then use our helper method to build a human-readable string and set the value or our orientation label. Next, we use the helper method to calculate the corrected heading values based on the device's orientation. The rest of the method remains the same.

Run the project on your physical device. Figures 4–12 and 4–13 show the results. Pay close attention to the orientation label. You will see that that heading is corrected in landscape mode.

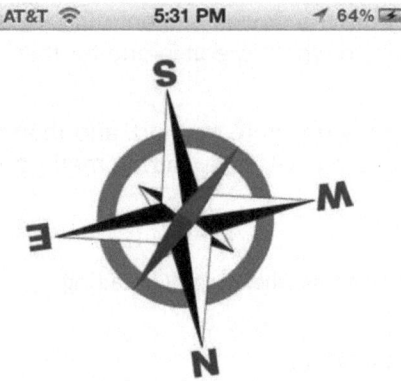

True Heading   196.881668

Magnetic Heading 188.060501

Portrait

Figure 4–12. *Display the headings in portrait mode.*

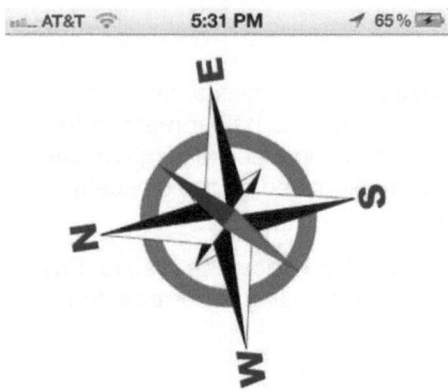

True Heading   196.881668

Magnetic Heading 188.060501

Landscape Left

Figure 4–13. *Display the headings in landscape mode.*

Summary

We did a lot of work accessing various sensors in this chapter. This might seem a bit low level or off subject as you walk through it, but it'll come in very handy as we start to build our own AR apps.

We discussed the accelerometer and the gyroscope and their conjunction with the Core Motion Framework. Then, we covered the magnetometer, and put together an example application that keeps us oriented. We're slowly completing our toolbox with everything we need to build our own AR application.

Next, in Chapter 5, we will be looking sound and user feedback.

Sound and User Feedback

Silent movies still have nostalgic value and are a key part of the history of entertainment. However, silent video games or silent interactive applications don't seem to fit in that category. A user experience needs to be engaging. Accessibility options can help make sure all users experience the same level of interaction. In this chapter, we'll talk about adding effects to events and active feedback, such as vibrations, to your applications.

Audio Data Formats

Let's start with the basics. There are a ton of options available for sound in iOS. We'll talk about the different formats first and their subtle differences, then we'll discuss how to convert from one to another. Take a look at Table 5–1, which outlines the different supported formats.

Table 5–1. *Audio Data Formats Supported by iOS*

Data Format	Description
AAC	This stands for "Advanced Audio Coding." It is designed to replace MP3, with better compression, especially at lower bit rates.
HE-AAC	This is a superset of AAC, in which the HE stands for "High Efficiency." It is optimized for low bit rate audio (e.g., streaming audio).
AMR	This stands for "Adaptive Multi-Rate." This format is optimized for speech and has very low bit rates.
ALAC	Also known as "Apple Lossless," this encoding compresses the audio data without losing quality. Compression is about 40–60 percent.
iLBC	This is good for speech and VOIP audio.
IMA4	This format gives you 4:1 compression on 16-bit audio files.

Data Format	Description
Linear PCM	PCM stands for "Pulse Code Modulation." This format converts analog sound data into digital format. This format is uncompressed, which means it'll play the fastest, but take up the most space.
MP3	This is the most popular format listed here. MP3 is a digital encoding format that compresses data by discarding some of it. This is called "lossy" compression, and is an industry standard format.

So, Which Data Format Is for Me?

This question unfortunately has the answer of "it depends." Your use case really drives which sound format best fits your application. For example, if space is not an issue, you can use linear PCM. It'll be the fastest way to play your audio and it won't impact CPU performance while it's playing (because it's not also working on uncompressing the files). However, if space is an issue, you might want to use AAC for background music or larger files to benefit from compression, and use IMA4 for sound effects and small files to gain from its advantages on 16-bit files.

What About File Formats?

The data format is one thing, but where and how do we store these files? iOS supports many different file formats including MPEG-1 (.mp3), MPEG-2 (.aac), AIFF, WAVE, and CAF. CAF is the preferred format on iOS because it can contain any of the data formats we listed in Table 5–1.

Bit Rates and Quality

The scenario in which the audio will be playing determines the quality needed for that particular event. For example, speech applications have very different sound requirements than an app that broadcasts symphony orchestra performances.

Quality can be tweaked using a variable called bit rate for the audio files. The bit rate is the number of bytes per second that a file uses. Only a few of the formats mentioned in Table 5–1 support configuration of bit rate. Table 5–2 illustrates some common bit rates.

Table 5–2. *Common Bit Rate Configurations Used in Applications*

Bit Rate	Description
32 kbit/s	AM-quality audio
64 kbit/s	Podcast-quality audio
96 kbit/s	FM-quality audio

Bit Rate	Description
128 kbit/s	Most common MP3 bit rate
192 kbit/s	Digital-quality radio
500 kbit/s	Lossless audio

Sample Rates

The sample rate for audio defines the number of samples per unit of time. Typically, this is measured in samples per inverse second, or what is more commonly described as a rate in hertz. The inverse of a sampling frequency, in case you aren't aware, is the sampling interval, or time, between the samples.

Some common sample rates are described in Table 5–3.

Table 5–3. *Common Sample Rates and Their Use Cases*

Sample Rate	Common Use Cases
8,000 Hz	Telephones, walkie-talkies, intercoms, wireless microphones
11,025 Hz	Lower quality PCM, MP3
32,000 Hz	MiniDV camcorders
44,100 Hz	Audio CD quality (also the most common sample rate for iOS)
48,000 Hz	Audio sample rate for professional video recorders
192,000 Hz	DVD audio

Converting Audio for Use in iOS

You can download samples from various places all over the Internet. Sites such as audiomicro.com and soundsnap.com offer royalty free samples for all kinds of sound categories. There are creative commons licensed sounds available at freesound.org, as well. In most cases, the formats that these samples are available in probably won't be exactly what you're looking for to enhance your application. So, you should get used to the tools that are available to help you convert some of these media formats.

Let's walk through three typical activities around testing media files. First, we'll get information about the file we're considering using, then we'll convert the file to another format, and finally, we'll test and play the file.

The sample code from this chapter is available on GitHub at https://github.com/kyleroche/Professional_iOS_AugmentedReality. If you don't have sample audio files on your local machine, you can follow along with the samples in the Xcode project on GitHub.

Getting Information on Media Files

There is a utility in Mac OS X called afinfo. This tool is available from the Terminal. Listing 5–1 shows the output of this command after I passed it the sample file, which is available in this chapter's GitHub repository.

Listing 5–1. *afinfo waterfall.caf*

```
Kyle-Roches-MacBook-Pro-2:iOS_AR_Ch5_SoundUserFeedback kyleroche$ afinfo waterfall.caf
File:           waterfall.caf
File type ID:   caff
Data format:      1 ch, 44100 Hz, 'lpcm' (0x0000000C) 16-bit little-endian signed
integer
                  no channel layout.
estimated duration: 1.950204 sec
audio bytes: 172008
audio packets: 86004
audio 86004 valid frames + 0 priming + 0 remainder = 86004
bit rate: 705600 bits per second
packet size upper bound: 2
audio data file offset: 4096
optimized
source bit depth: I16
sound check:
    approximate duration in seconds            1.95
----
```

The key parts of the output are highlighted in bold. One of these falls under the caption Data format. This is the same sample rate we mentioned earlier. 44100 Hz is commonly used for CD-quality audio and is recommended for use in iOS applications. Next, the **bit rate** is highlighted. This isn't specifically one of the rates per second that we mentioned, but it falls in the range of standard audio quality. Finally, on the last line, **afinfo** returns the **approximate duration in seconds**. This is important if you're using the sound for gaming, or in a timeline-oriented fashion.

Experiment for a bit with **afinfo**. I ran it against my iTunes library to see the different samplings of older music I imported versus newer stuff downloaded from iTunes. Listing 5–2 shows an example of the output from a download song.

Listing 5–2. *afinfo Results from iTunes Files*

```
Kyle-Roches-MacBook-Pro-2:Ukulele Songs kyleroche$ afinfo 10\ You\'re\ True.m4a
File:           10 You're True.m4a
File type ID:   m4af
Data format:      2 ch, 44100 Hz, 'aac ' (0x00000000) 0 bits/channel, 0 bytes/packet,
1024 frames/packet, 0 bytes/frame
Channel layout: Stereo (L R)
estimated duration: 203.333333 sec
audio bytes: 6491497
audio packets: 8759
audio 8967000 valid frames + 2112 priming + 104 remainder = 8969216
bit rate: 255340 bits per second
```

```
packet size upper bound: 1197
audio data file offset: 594724
optimized
format list:
[ 0] format:      2 ch,  44100 Hz, 'aac ' (0x00000000) 0 bits/channel, 0 bytes/packet,
1024 frames/packet, 0 bytes/frame
     Channel layout: Stereo (L R)
source bit depth: I16
sound check:
     sc ave perceived power coeff        2973 3040
     sc max perceived power coeff        16060 12146
     sc peak amplitude msec              26006 25263
     sc max perceived power msec         25263 24520
     sc peak amplitude                   32766 32766
----
```

Looking at the output, the biggest difference is the increased amount of information in the sound check section. Obviously, higher quality sound files have more available information.

We now have a tool we can use to verify the bit rates, sample rates, and formats of our media. Next, let's take a look at how to convert sound files to the appropriate formats.

Converting File Types

Let's use the same sample file from the GitHub project for initial testing. It's time to introduce a new utility called Audio File Convert, or afconvert. Audio File Convert will convert a source audio file to a new audio file with the specified file and data types. Listing 5–3 shows the usage statement for afconvert.

Listing 5–3. *afconvert Usage Statement*

```
Usage:
afconvert [option...] input_file [output_file]
    Options may appear before or after the direct arguments. If output_file
    is not specified, a name is generated programmatically and the file
    is written into the same directory as input_file.
afconvert input_file [-o output_file [option...]]...
    Output file options apply to the previous output_file. Other options
    may appear anywhere.
Help options:
    { -hf | --help-formats }
       print a list of supported file/data formats
    { -h | --help }
       print help
```

You can use **afconvert** to switch file formats, media formats, or to save your file with a different bit rate. Let's experiment with bit rate and our sample file to get used to **afconvert**. Run the command shown in Listing 5–4 from the Terminal window.

Listing 5–4. *afconvert to Change Bit Rate*

```
afconvert -d aac -f 'caff' -b 32768 waterfall.caf waterfallNew.caf
```

If you check your directory, you'll notice a new file was created with the name of **waterfallNew.caf.** We used the –d option to set the data format, the –f option to set the file format, and the –b option to set the bit rate. We pass the existing file to **afconvert** first, then the destination file. If you run the afinfo utility on the new file, you'll see the difference in bit rate.

Testing Your New Sound

The last utility I want to mention is called afplay. This is another command-line utility that gives you quick access to testing your audio files. Simply pass the name of the file you wish to play and it'll play it over your default output hardware.

Playing Sound in an iOS Application

Let's take some of these files and add them to an iOS application. Again, the code for this chapter is available on GitHub, but if you're following along from scratch, create a new Tab Bar application with the iPhone as a target device.

Open **FirstView.xib** and set up the interface, as shown in Figure 5–1.

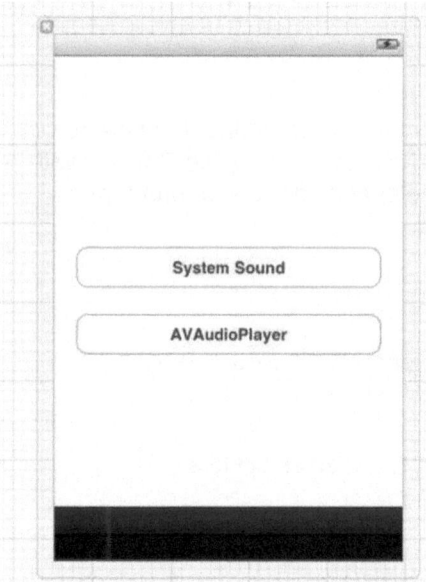

Figure 5–1. *Here we see the two UIButtons to launch the actions we'll be creating.*

We're going to demonstrate two different approaches to playing audio in the background of iOS applications. The interface is simple. Clear out the default controls and create two new UIButton elements. Use titles like those shown in Figure 5–1.

Both of the approaches we'll discuss are relatively straightforward and easy to implement. We'll cover a more advanced, gaming-centric approach in Chapter 7.

System Sound Services

System Sound Services is a great choice for playing sound effects on the device. It's designed for short sound effects, such as a button click, error beep, or a game action. Sounds played with System Sound Services are not subject to configuration using your audio session. As a result, you cannot keep the behavior of System Sound Services audio inline with other audio behavior in your application. This is the most important reason to avoid using System Sound Services for any audio apart from its intended uses. System Sound Services require that you add the AudioToolbox framework to your project.

To ensure it serves its purpose as a quick sound player, System Sound Services has some limitations. Your sound files must be

- No longer than 30 seconds in duration
- In linear PCM or IMA4 (IMA/ADPCM) format
- Packaged in a .caf, .aif, or .wav file

In addition, when you use the AudioServicesPlaySystemSound function,

- Sounds play at the current system audio volume, with no programmatic volume control available
- Sounds play immediately
- Looping and stereo positioning are unavailable
- Simultaneous playback is unavailable; you can play only one sound at a time

AVAudioPlayer Class

AVAudioPlayer is a bit more flexible, but comes with its own set of limitations. The most limiting feature of the AVAudioPlayer is its noticeable delay in queuing up and playing a file. Because of this, it's best suited for long playing, background music and use cases like that. The AVAudioPlayer requires the AVFoundation framework in your project. Using AVAudioPlayer, you can

- Play sounds of any duration
- Play sounds from files or memory buffers
- Loop sounds
- Play multiple sounds simultaneously (although not with precise synchronization)
- Control relative playback level for each sound you are playing

■ Seek to a particular point in a sound file, which supports application features such as fast forward and rewind

■ Obtain audio power data that you can use for audio level metering

Experimenting with the Multiple Audio Players

Okay, let's get to it. You have already created the interface with both of the UIButtons. After the briefing on different approaches to playing sound, the titles I used will make more sense. Before we start, we're going to require that we add to our project both of the frameworks mentioned in this section. Open the Build Phases tab of your application's target and add both the AVFoundation and AudioToolbox frameworks.

Add the code from Listing 5–5 to FirstViewController.h.

Listing 5–5. *New FirstViewController.h*

```
#import <UIKit/UIKit.h>
#import <AudioToolbox/AudioToolbox.h>
#import <AVFoundation/AVFoundation.h>

@interface FirstViewController : UIViewController <AVAudioPlayerDelegate> {
    SystemSoundID _systemSound;
    AVAudioPlayer *_audioPlayer;
}

- (IBAction)systemSoundAction;
- (IBAction)avAudioPlayerAction;

@end
```

We first import both the AudioToolbox and AVFoundation libraries to our header file. We then nominate our class as an AVAudioPlayerDelegate. We're not really building a multimedia application in this book, so I'm not going to go into this delegate and its methods too much. But, this would be something to further research if you wanted to handle events while the audio was playing.

In the interface, we declare two instance variables for our two use cases. The AVAudioPlayer requires a pointer, as we'll be creating the instance in this class. Finally, we declare two new methods to handle the click events of the UIButtons we added to our user interface.

Next, return to the **FirstView.xib** file in Xcode and hook up the two IBAction methods to our two buttons.

Switch over to **FirstViewController.m**. We're just using instance variables in this example, so we have nothing to synthesize. Add the code from Listing 5–6 to your implementation file.

Listing 5–6. *Handle the System Sound Services Method*

```
- (void)systemSoundAction {
    NSString *soundFilePath = [[NSBundle mainBundle] pathForResource:@"waterfall"
ofType:@"caf"];
```

```
        NSURL *soundFileURL = [NSURL fileURLWithPath:soundFilePath];
        AudioServicesCreateSystemSoundID((CFURLRef)soundFileURL, &_systemSound);
        AudioServicesPlaySystemSound(_systemSound);
}
- (void) avAudioPlayerAction {
    // we'll get to this next
}
```

I'm referencing the CAFF file we have in our GitHub sample project. If you have another file you'd like to use instead of the one in the sample, make sure you match the names. It is important to note that the pathForResource argument takes the core section of the file name, not the full file name. Run the project on your iOS simulator and click the System Sound Action button. You'll notice a quick (instant) response and the file will start to play.

Close down the simulator. We have a bit more work to do before we can finish the second method. Because AVAudioPlayer is better for background music, I wanted to find something more appropriate than a waterfall, as I'm not a waterfall enthusiast (not that there's anything wrong with that). The waterfall sample came from the cocos2D examples (we'll cover this in Chapter 7). Another place to get music samples is audiomicro.com and I searched their free background music samples for something a bit more appropriate.

Open your Terminal to the directory of the downloaded MP3. If you are using the MP3 in the sample, navigate to the locally cloned GitHub directory. Run the command from Listing 5–7.

Listing 5–7. *Convert the MP3 to CAFF*

```
afconvert -d aac -f 'caff' "007.mp3" backgroundMusic.caf
```

We are using the Audio File Converter to convert our MP3 file to a CAFF format that we can use in our project. It's possible to just play the MP3, but that wouldn't help us demonstrate when these utilities are useful, now would it?

Return to the FirstViewController.m file in your Xcode project. Let's fill out the rest of the avAudioPlayerAction method with the code from Listing 5–8.

Listing 5–8. *Completed avAudioPlayerAction Method*

```
- (void)avAudioPlayerAction {
    NSError *setCategoryError = nil;
        [[AVAudioSession sharedInstance] setCategory:AVAudioSessionCategoryAmbient
error:&setCategoryError];

        NSString *backgroundMusicPath = [[NSBundle mainBundle]
pathForResource:@"backgroundMusic" ofType:@"caf"];
        NSURL *backgroundMusicURL = [NSURL fileURLWithPath:backgroundMusicPath];
        NSError *error;

        _audioPlayer = [[AVAudioPlayer alloc] initWithContentsOfURL:backgroundMusicURL
error:&error];
        [_audioPlayer play];
}
```

There are many different approaches to how we could have ended this method. I chose the simplest method, which is to just play the file. You can queue the file up for playing at a later time, or start directing how to handle the file from the delegate methods.

Start the project on your iPhone simulator. Now, play both of the files. You'll notice there is a significant delay in the AVAudioPlayer method.

Playing Positional Sound

For augmented-reality applications in which the user is moving the screen around to acquire different views, it might be useful to play positional audio on occasion. You can achieve positional audio with cocos2D, as well. Instead of covering that in this chapter, and because we haven't yet introduce cocos2D, we're going to save that for Chapter 7.

User Feedback Through Vibration

There are a few nonaudible options we have available to use for providing the user with feedback. The most commonly used is the vibration effect. This is actually depressingly easy. Create a new method in your **FirstViewController** class called vibrate. Add the code from Listing 5–9.

Listing 5–9. *Completed vibrate Method*

```
- (void)vibrate {
    AudioServicesPlaySystemSound (kSystemSoundID_Vibrate);
}
```

That's it. In the sample project, I've created another button and attached this method so you could see it in a working state. If you have any trouble getting this to run, make sure your iPhone has Vibrate set to on, in the Settings panel.

Recording Sound

So far in this chapter, we've learned about the supported sound types and some of their intricacies, as well as a few approaches on how to play files in iOS applications. Next, let's take some time to understand how to record and save sound that you gather from the device.

We're going to be using the same AVFoundation framework we used in our previous example of playing audio, but now for simple audio recording. We already added the framework to our project, so you won't have to worry about that step. If you were starting with a new project, you'd need to add the framework as we did earlier.

Initializing the Audio Recorder

The first step in getting your application ready to record audio is setting up a new AVAudioRecorder object. You can manually create this object and its settings, but both the Apple documentation and most online tutorials will recommend starting with one of the other init options.

Open **SecondViewController.h** in Xcode and update it, as shown in Listing 5–10.

Listing 5–10. *New SecondViewController.h Header*

```
#import <UIKit/UIKit.h>
#import <AVFoundation/AVFoundation.h>

@interface SecondViewController : UIViewController <AVAudioRecorderDelegate,
AVAudioPlayerDelegate>{
    AVAudioRecorder *_soundRecorder;
}

- (IBAction)setupRecorder;
- (IBAction)stopRecorder;
- (IBAction)playAudioRecording;

@end
```

Walking through the code, we declared an **AVAudioRecorder** instance object, as well as three methods. In final applications, you'll probably want to consolidate some of the audio recording actions or leverage the delegate methods, but we're going to separate them here for reference. You might have noticed two other items that we've already seen a few times in this chapter. We are importing the **AVFoundation** headers and nominating this class as an **AVAudioRecorderDelegate** and an **AVAudioPlayerDelegate**.

Switch to **SecondView.xib** in Xcode and attach the IBActions to a few new UIButtons. I laid out my screen as shown in Figure 5–2. There are three UIButtons on the layout. Each of them will be wired up to their own IBAction.

I tied setupRecorder to the **Record Audio** button. Next, I tied stopRecorder to **Stop Audio**. Finally, I tied the playAudioRecording method to the **Play Recording** button.

Next, we have to implement the methods in **SecondViewController.m**.

Figure 5–2. *Here we see the screen layout for testing audio recording.*

Open **SecondViewController.m** in Xcode. We have to implement the methods we've declared. Let's start with the first method, `setupRecorder`. Add the method from Listing 5–11 to your implementation file.

Listing 5–11. *setupRecorder Method*

```
- (void)setupRecorder {
    NSString *filePath = [NSHomeDirectory()
stringByAppendingPathComponent:@"Documents/recording.caf"];
    NSDictionary *recordSettings = [[NSDictionary alloc] initWithObjectsAndKeys:
                                    [NSNumber numberWithFloat: 44100.0],
AVSampleRateKey,
                                    [NSNumber numberWithInt: kAudioFormatAppleLossless],
AVFormatIDKey,
                                    [NSNumber numberWithInt: 1], AVNumberOfChannelsKey,
                                    [NSNumber numberWithInt: AVAudioQualityMax],
AVEncoderAudioQualityKey,nil];

    _soundRecorder = [[AVAudioRecorder alloc] initWithURL:[NSURL
fileURLWithPath:filePath]
                                                                    settings:
recordSettings error: nil];
    _soundRecorder.delegate = self;
    [_soundRecorder record];
}
```

This method starts by declaring an NSString to represent the path of the file we'll be saving. Next, we set up the NSDictionary object that holds the settings for our

AVAudioRecorder. Finally, we set the delegate of the AVAudioRecorder to self, and start the recording using the record method.

Copy the next method from Listing 5–12 just after setupRecorder.

Listing 5–12. *stopRecorder Method*

```
- (void)stopRecorder {
    [_soundRecorder stop];
}
```

This method isn't too hard to follow. We're just stopping the recording.

Now, before we finish the last method, add the following method from Listing 5–13 under stopRecorder.

Listing 5–13. *Delegate Methods for AVAudioRecorder*

```
- (void)audioRecorderDidFinishRecording:(AVAudioRecorder *)recorder
successfully:(BOOL)flag {
    NSLog(@"did finish recording");
}

- (void)audioRecorderBeginInterruption:(AVAudioRecorder *)recorder {
    NSLog(@"recording was interrupted");
}

- (void)audioRecorderEndInterruption:(AVAudioRecorder *)recorder {
    NSLog(@"interruption ended... back to it");
}
```

The AVAudioRecorderDelegate that we set up earlier defines a few methods for interacting with the AVAudioRecorder. We're just logging in each of these methods so that you can see when the events fire. The only one that will fire in our set of actions is the audioRecorderDidFinishRecording method. The other two will be fun to test. If you are testing on an iPhone, you can call yourself in the middle of debugging the application; when it rings, the audioRecorderBeginInterruption method will fire. As soon as you hang up the phone, the audioRecorderEndInterruption method will fire. These events are part of the delegate interface.

We are recording our audio session and storing it to the local file systems. The final step is playing it back from local disk. Add the method shown in Listing 5–14, after the three delegate methods we just defined.

Listing 5–14. *Playing Back the File*

```
- (void)playAudioRecording {
    NSString * filePath = [NSHomeDirectory() stringByAppendingPathComponent:
@"Documents/recording.caf"];
    AVAudioPlayer *newPlayer = [[AVAudioPlayer alloc] initWithContentsOfURL: [NSURL
fileURLWithPath:filePath] error: nil];
    newPlayer.delegate = self;
    [newPlayer play];
}
```

This code should look familiar. Earlier in the chapter, we learned the same process for playing audio. We're now ready to test the application. To do this properly, you should be using a physical testing device and not the simulator. Although most of it will function on the simulator, it's still better to test sound recording from a real device.

Run the application and switch to the second tab. Start at the top and click the **Record Audio** button. Either talk into the microphone or make sure you have enough background noise to get a real sample recording. When you're done, click the **Stop Recording** button. In the console, you should see the log message, **"did finish recording"**. Finally, click **Play Recording** and you should hear your sound played back over the speakers. Make sure your phone isn't force muted.

Summary

In this chapter we learned about the different internals of iOS audio formats. We talked about bit rates and file formats, as well as which are supported and preferred in iOS. We also went through a few utilities that are available for use if you need to test a file, or convert it to another format.

In the next chapter, we're going to switch from audio to video, and start laying the groundwork for augmented-reality programming. To this point, the chapters have covered fundamental pieces of applications we'll be building. In the next chapter, we'll actually start to see things that resemble augmented-reality applications.

Chapter 6

Camera and Video Capture

Augmented reality applications typically share one common element: they are built on top of the live video feed.

In this chapter, we'll start with basic concepts of using the camera, and quickly move on to more advanced examples of video capture, and analyzing the video frame by frame.

In the later chapters, we will be using these concepts to build applications that overlay the video feed.

Quick Review

In Chapter 2, we discussed the importance of checking for the presence and the availability of a sensor or hardware component before trying to access it in your code.

You can programmatically detect what camera is available on your device using the UIImagePickerController class. There is a method called isSourceTypeAvailable that we can use to determine whether the camera we want to use is available. Listing 6–1 shows the sample method we used in Chapter 2 to detect a camera and use the front-facing camera when it is available.

Listing 6–1. *Checking for a Camera, Then a Front-Facing Camera*

```
BOOL cameraAvailable = [UIImagePickerController
isSourceTypeAvailable:UIImagePickerControllerSourceTypeCamera];
    BOOL frontCameraAvailable = [UIImagePickerController
isSourceTypeAvailable:UIImagePickerControllerCameraDeviceFront];

    if (cameraAvailable) {
        UIAlertView *alert = [[UIAlertView alloc] initWithTitle:@"Camera"
                                                message:@"Camera Available"
                                                delegate:self
                                       cancelButtonTitle:@"OK"
                                       otherButtonTitles:nil, nil];
```

```
        [alert show];
        [alert release];
    } else {
        UIAlertView *alert = [[UIAlertView alloc] initWithTitle:@"Camera"
                                                  message:@"Camera NOT Available"
                                                 delegate:self
                                        cancelButtonTitle:@"OK"
                                        otherButtonTitles:nil, nil];
        [alert show];
        [alert release];
    }

    if (frontCameraAvailable) {
        UIAlertView *alert = [[UIAlertView alloc] initWithTitle:@"Camera"
                                                  message:@"Front Camera
Available"
                                                 delegate:self
                                        cancelButtonTitle:@"OK"
                                        otherButtonTitles:nil, nil];
        [alert show];
        [alert release];
    } else {
        UIAlertView *alert = [[UIAlertView alloc] initWithTitle:@"Camera"
                                                  message:@"Front Camera NOT
Available"
                                                 delegate:self
                                        cancelButtonTitle:@"OK"
                                        otherButtonTitles:nil, nil];
        [alert show];
        [alert release];
    }
```

This code block will demonstrate the results in a quick UIAlertView pop-up. Actually, you'll get two pop-ups from this example. You can see in the first few lines of Listing 6–1 where we are checking for the existence of UIImagePickerControllerSourceTypeCamera to see whether the camera is available. We next check for the existence of the front-facing camera using the UIImagePickerControllerCameraDeviceFront parameter. The isSourceTypeAvailable method returns a BOOL value. We use that in our if/else statements, and display the appropriate UIAlertView for each check.

You will remember from Chapter 2 that the Xcode simulators do not support camera or video capture. Because of this, you must execute all examples in this chapter on a physical device.

Let's start with capturing a basic photo, before moving on to video.

Photo Capture

Capturing a photo from iOS is not a terribly difficult task programmatically. The UIImagePickerController class that we used to determine whether the camera was available provides a simple method for accessing the camera, taking a photo, and even previewing the results.

Create a new Xcode project for this chapter. I have created a project called **Ch6**, and the source is available from the Source Code/Download area of the Apress web site (www.apress.com) or can be forked from https://github.com/kyleroche/Professional_iOS_AugmentedReality. Make sure you use a tab bar application template, and your device family is set to **Universal**. My configuration screen is shown in Figure 6–1. Note that we are using Automatic Reference Counting (new to iOS 5) in this chapter, by selecting the **Use Automatic Reference Counting** check box.

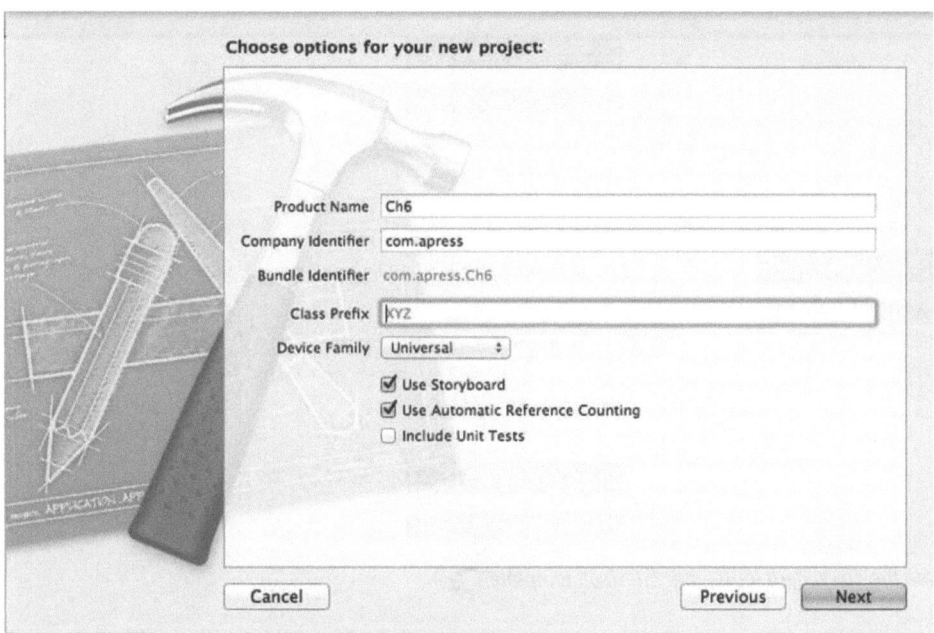

Figure 6–1. *Create the Xcode project settings for this chapter.*

Using Storyboards

We haven't discussed storyboards yet, in this book. Let's take a moment for a quick overview. Storyboards provide a consolidated XIB file for all your application views. You can still programmatically load XIB files from stand-alone interface builder classes, but you have more flexibility and time-saving opportunities using a storyboard interface. For example, Figure 6–2 shows the default storyboard for a tab bar–based interface.

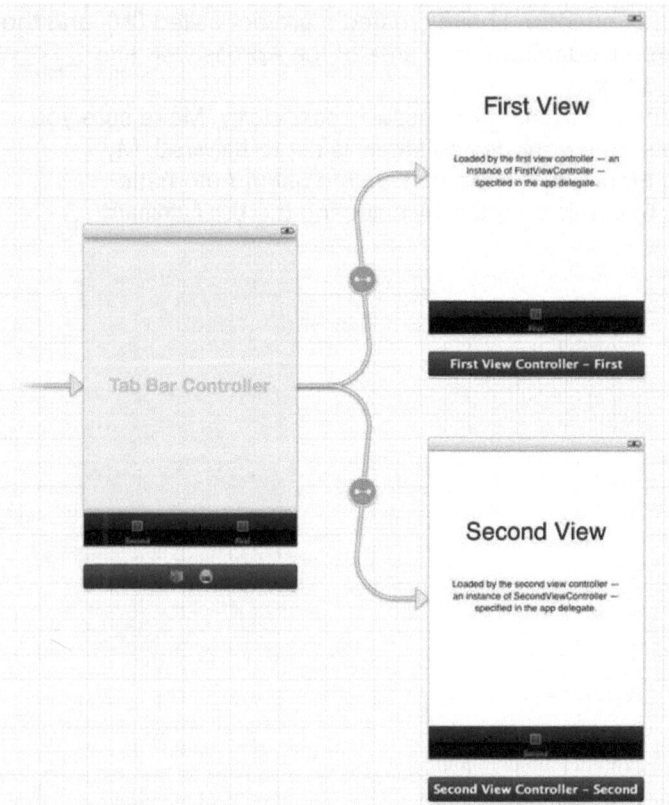

Figure 6–2. *Use the storyboard for tab bar interface template.*

Without the storyboard, there would be three separate interface files, all requiring different types of links to be integrated. With storyboards, we can get a clean look at how the application flow will present itself without switching context.

We could just reuse the layouts that are provided by default. However, so we can better understand storyboards, let's delete these and start from scratch. Delete FirstViewController.h, FirstViewController.m, SecondViewController.h, and SecondViewController.m from the Xcode project. Delete the .png files associated with each view as well.

Open both of the storyboard files. Click the FirstViewController and SecondViewController interfaces in the design window. Press Delete twice. The first time you press Delete, you are removing the class from the view. You will be left with an empty view highlighted with a blue outline. The second Delete removes the view completely. Repeat this for both view controllers.

You should be left with an empty tab bar controller in your interface builder view. Your project should be left with an AppDelegate, two storyboard files, and the Supporting Files directory. Now that we have a clean project, let's build it back up manually.

We are going to start with taking a photo and saving it to the library. So, let's add a view controller for this example and load it in a tab in our tab bar controller. Right-click the project folder and choose **New File** from the context menu. Choose **UIViewController** subclass as the template for this file. Click **Next**. On the options screen, make sure that no options are selected and name the class **PhotoViewController**. Before clicking **Next**, make sure that your option screen looks like Figure 6–3.

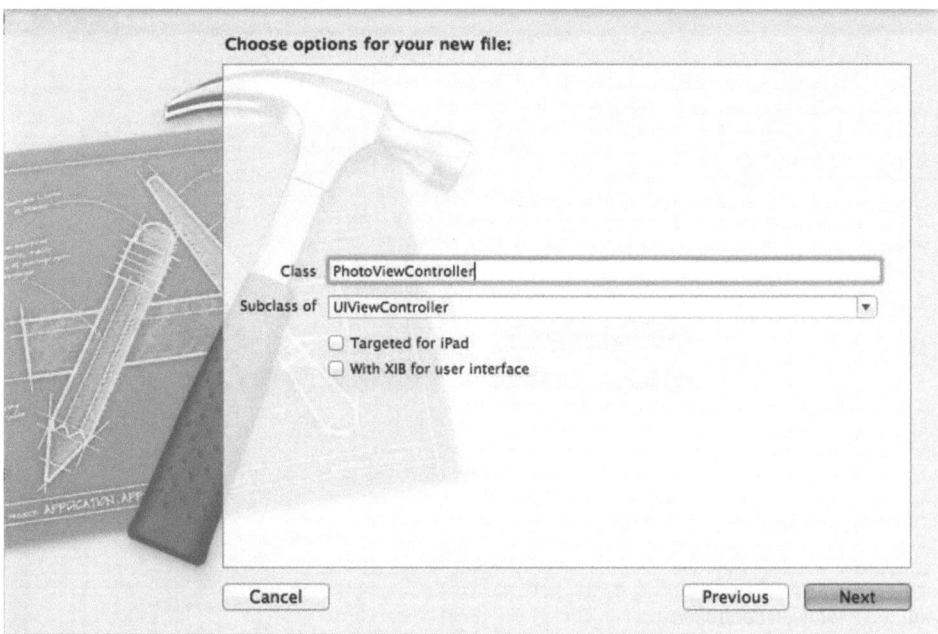

Figure 6–3. *Create the PhotoViewController class.*

From the **Objects** library, drag a **View Controller** to the interface. Click the new **View Controller** and switch to the identity inspector and change the **Custom Class** to **PhotoViewController**. The result of these three steps is shown in Figure 6–4.

Before we get too far ahead, make sure you nominate the PhotoViewController as a UINavigationControllerDelegate and a UIImagePickerControllerDelegate.

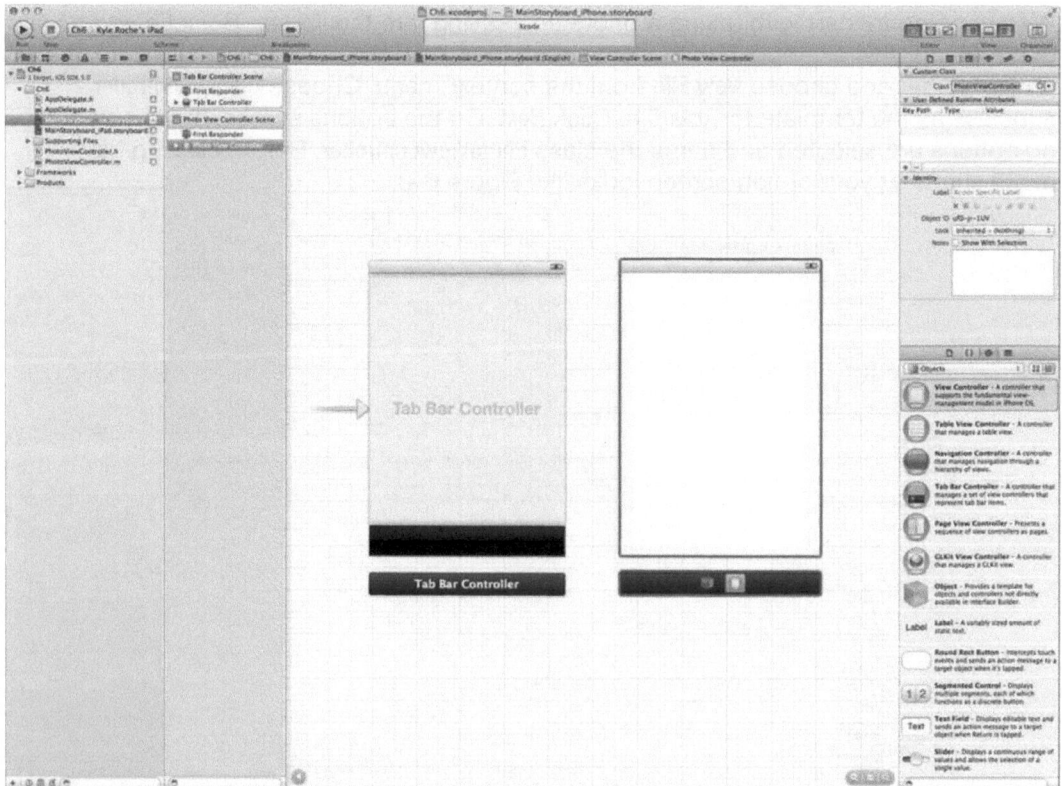

Figure 6–4. *Add the PhotoViewController.*

Right-click the **Tab Bar Controller** view in the interface builder. Under the **Storyboard Seques** category, there is an item called **Relationship – viewControllers**. Ctrl+click+drag the plus icon on the right side of this item to the **Photo View Controller** view in the interface. You will now see something similar to Figure 6–5.

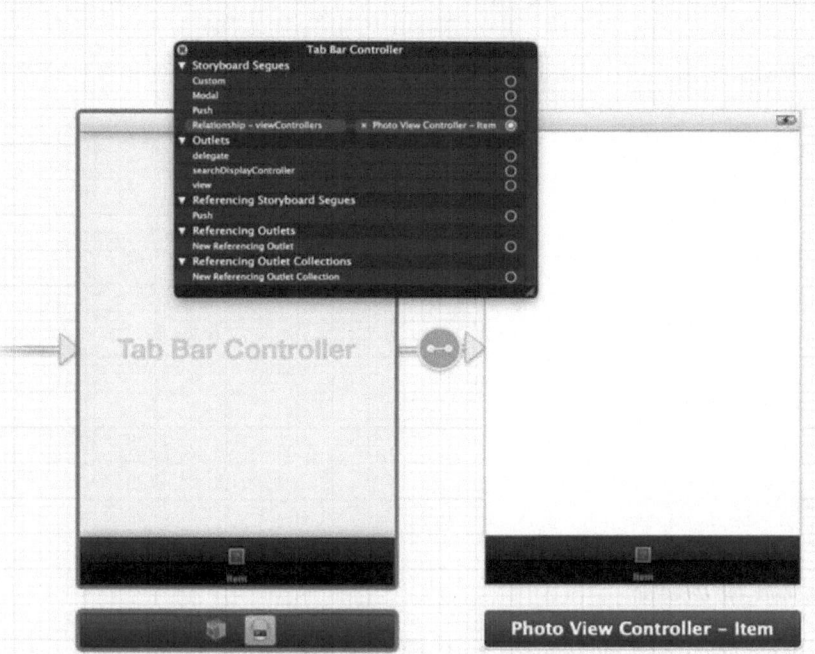

Figure 6–5. *Link the Relationship Storyboard Seque to PhotoViewController.*

Repeat this process for the iPad's storyboard, if you are using an iPad for testing, or if you truly want the app to work on both devices.

To change the name, icon, or badge associated with the tab bar item we just enabled, you need to do so in the associated view. You can no longer edit those items from the parent tab bar controller.

Next, drag a UIButton to the middle of the PhotoViewController in interface builder. Make sure the assistant editor is enabled and the PhotoViewController.h is present and Ctrl+drag the UIButton to the header file to create an action associated with this outlet. Use Figure 6–6 for reference.

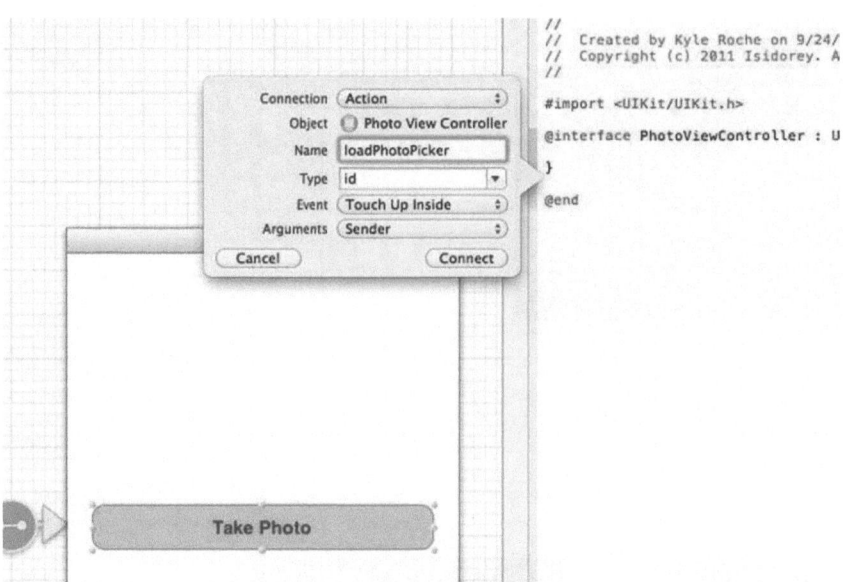

Figure 6–6. *Create an action for the UIButton.*

Name the action **loadPhotoPicker** and click **Connect**. If you are using an iPad, or you want this to be universal, you need to (once again) repeat this step in the iPad storyboard. However, connecting actions to events that are already created is a bit different. Open the iPad storyboard and add a similar UIButton to the interface. I've labeled both of my UIButton's with a Title of **Take Photo**. To connect the UIButton to an existing action, you must Ctrl+click+drag the UIButton to the view controller icon under the view in the storyboard. If that doesn't make a lot of sense reading it through, reference Figure 6–7 for some guidance.

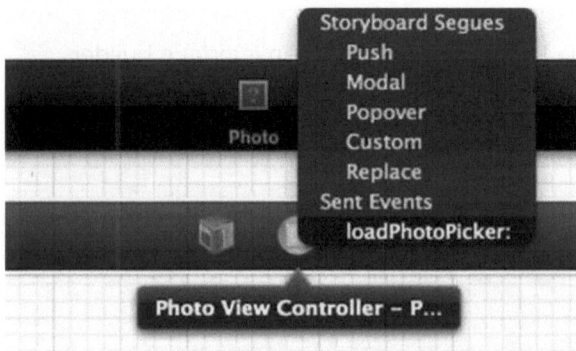

Figure 6–7. *Use this menu when connecting an outlet to an existing action.*

Well, that was quite a bit of instruction to simply connect a button, wasn't it? I wanted to go through this process in detail once, so you have it for reference when we build our more complicated examples in later chapters. Let's move on.

Using the Camera

Switch to PhotoViewController.m in Xcode. At the bottom of the file, the action method that we added in the previous steps will be empty. Expand that method as shown in Listing 6–2.

Listing 6–2. *loadPhotoPicker Method*

```
- (IBAction)loadPhotoPicker:(id)sender {
    UIImagePickerController *imagePicker = [[UIImagePickerController alloc] init];
    imagePicker.sourceType = UIImagePickerControllerSourceTypeCamera;
    // uncomment for front camera
    // imagePicker.cameraDevice = UIImagePickerControllerCameraDeviceFront;
    imagePicker.delegate = self;
    imagePicker.allowsEditing = NO;
    [self presentModalViewController:imagePicker animated:YES];
}
```

This method first creates an instance of the UIImagePickerController class. This class essentially opens the camera interface we are all used to in iOS. We set the sourceType attribute to the rear camera. If you'd prefer to set this to the front-facing camera (again, you should verify this is present first), you can uncomment the code that is commented out below this line.

Next, we set the delegate to self and disallow editing of the image picker. We then present the UIImagePickerController in a modal dialog to PhotoViewController.

If you run this now, the image picker (camera) will be displayed but nothing will be saved. Add the methods from Listing 6–3 to the implementation.

Listing 6–3. *Methods to Save the Photo Image*

```
- (void) imagePickerController:(UIImagePickerController *)picker
didFinishPickingMediaWithInfo:(NSDictionary *)info
{
    UIImage *image = [info objectForKey:@"UIImagePickerControllerOriginalImage"];

    UIImageWriteToSavedPhotosAlbum(image, self,
@selector(image:didFinishSavingWithError:contextInfo:), nil);
}

- (void)image:(UIImage *)image didFinishSavingWithError:(NSError *)error
contextInfo:(void *)contextInfo
{
    UIAlertView *alert;
    if (error) {
        alert = [[UIAlertView alloc] initWithTitle:@"Error"
                                           message:@"Unable to save image to Photo
Album."
                                          delegate:self cancelButtonTitle:@"Ok"
                                 otherButtonTitles:nil];
    } else {
        alert = [[UIAlertView alloc] initWithTitle:@"Success"
                                           message:@"Image saved to Photo Album."
                                          delegate:self cancelButtonTitle:@"Ok"
```

```
                                   otherButtonTitles:nil];
    }
    [alert show];
    [self dismissModalViewControllerAnimated:YES];
}
```

The first method is a delegate method for the UIImagePickerController class. It is fired when an image is selected from the controller. We are allocating an object for this image and sending it to the second method shown in Listing 6–3.

The second method, which was set as the selector method after saving the file, checks for an error and displays a success or failure message in a UIAlertView control. You might notice that I'm not releasing the UIAlertView instances. When we created this project, earlier in the chapter, we enabled Automatic Reference Counting. Automatic Referencing Counting (new to iOS5) forbids explicit calling of the release method.

We're ready to test the project. Start it up on either an iPhone or iPad device. Since we're using the camera, this project can't be run on the simulator.

Click the button in the middle of the interface, take a photo, and click the Use button to select that photo. You will get a UIAlertView dialog that confirms the file was saved correctly. Open the Photos application on the iPad or iPhone you used for testing. You will find the photo saved in there.

Saving Images in Different Formats

So far, we've saved an image to our photo library. What about using that image for another purpose, like object or facial recognition? We will be using images from our video buffer in our facial recognition chapters later in this book. UIKit includes a few C functions that are helpers for exporting images to files on the iOS device. The two most common formats used for export are JPEG and PNG, so let's concentrate on those first.

Open PhotoViewController.m in Xcode. Find the didFinishPickingMediaWithInfo method and add the code from Listing 6–4 at the end of the method.

Listing 6–4. *Convert and Save UIImage Object*

```
// start saving files

    NSString  *pngPath = [NSHomeDirectory()
stringByAppendingPathComponent:@"Documents/ConvertedPNG.png"];
    NSString  *jpgPath = [NSHomeDirectory()
stringByAppendingPathComponent:@"Documents/ConvertedJPEG.jpg"];

    [UIImageJPEGRepresentation(image, 1.0) writeToFile:jpgPath atomically:YES];
    [UIImagePNGRepresentation(image) writeToFile:pngPath atomically:YES];

    // optional (check for files)
    NSError *error;
    NSFileManager *fileMgr = [NSFileManager defaultManager];
    NSString *documentsDirectory = [NSHomeDirectory()
stringByAppendingPathComponent:@"Documents"];
    NSLog(@"Documents: %@", [fileMgr contentsOfDirectoryAtPath:documentsDirectory
error:&error]);
```

First, we set two strings to the full path value of what the file name will eventually become. We next use the C functions (UIImageJPEGRepresentation and UIImagePNGRepresentation) to write the files to the respective paths. We pass the image compression quality as part of the parameter set. Image compression is measured on a scale of 0.0 to 1.0. So, we are saving the image with the best quality and least compression possible.

Run the project using either physical device type. Make sure you have your console open so you can see the output. You will see something similar to Figure 6–8 after the image is saved.

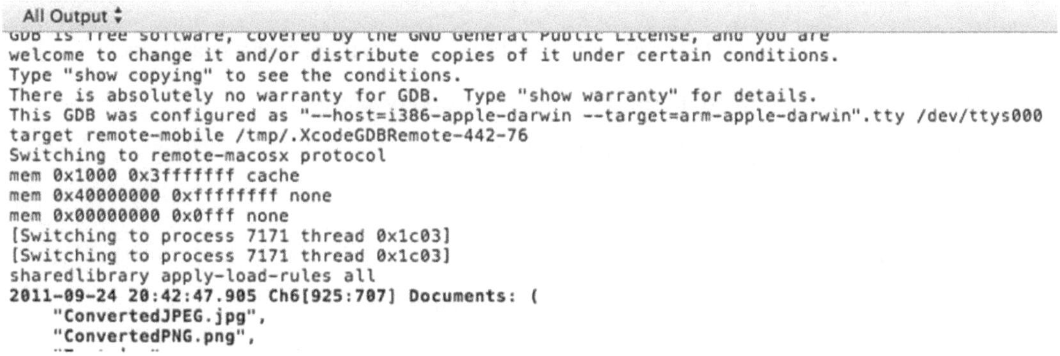

```
All Output ⬍
GDB is free software, covered by the GNU General Public License, and you are
welcome to change it and/or distribute copies of it under certain conditions.
Type "show copying" to see the conditions.
There is absolutely no warranty for GDB.  Type "show warranty" for details.
This GDB was configured as "--host=i386-apple-darwin --target=arm-apple-darwin".tty /dev/ttys000
target remote-mobile /tmp/.XcodeGDBRemote-442-76
Switching to remote-macosx protocol
mem 0x1000 0x3fffffff cache
mem 0x40000000 0xffffffff none
mem 0x00000000 0x0fff none
[Switching to process 7171 thread 0x1c03]
[Switching to process 7171 thread 0x1c03]
sharedlibrary apply-load-rules all
2011-09-24 20:42:47.905 Ch6[925:707] Documents: (
    "ConvertedJPEG.jpg",
    "ConvertedPNG.png",
```

Figure 6–8. *The image is saved, converted, and stored.*

E-mailing an Image

Maybe storing the file isn't quite enough and you'd prefer to attach it to an e-mail message. If you want to e-mail a message programmatically, you first need to import the MessageUI framework.

Click your project name in the Xcode navigator. Switch to the **Build Phases** tab and import the MessageUI framework. Next, open PhotoViewController.h in Xcode and update the interface as shown in Listing 6–5.

Listing 6–5. *Updated Interface for PhotoViewController*

```
#import <UIKit/UIKit.h>
#import <MessageUI/MessageUI.h>
#import <MessageUI/MFMailComposeViewController.h>

@interface PhotoViewController : UIViewController <UINavigationControllerDelegate,
UIImagePickerControllerDelegate, MFMailComposeViewControllerDelegate> {
}
- (IBAction)loadPhotoPicker:(id)sender;

@end
```

We imported a few headers and nominated this class as an MFMailComposeViewControllerDelegate so we can handle the event callback when the user sends the message. Add the methods from Listing 6–6 to the implementation.

Listing 6–6. *Updated Interface for PhotoViewController*

```
- (void)sendEmailMessage:(UIImage *)image
{
    NSLog(@"Sending Email");

    MFMailComposeViewController *picker = [[MFMailComposeViewController alloc] init];
    picker.mailComposeDelegate = self;

    [picker setSubject:@"iOS Augmented Reality - Chapter 6"];

    [picker setToRecipients:[NSArray arrayWithObjects:@"kyle.m.roche@gmail.com", nil]];

    NSString *emailBody = @"Hi Kyle, this stuff actually works.";

    [picker setMessageBody:emailBody isHTML:NO];

    NSData *data = UIImagePNGRepresentation(image);

    [picker addAttachmentData:data mimeType:@"image/png" fileName:@"Ch6ScreenShot"];

    [self presentModalViewController:picker animated:YES];
}

- (void)mailComposeController:(MFMailComposeViewController*)controller
didFinishWithResult:(MFMailComposeResult)result error:(NSError*)error
{
    [self dismissModalViewControllerAnimated:YES];
}
```

Let's step through each method, line by line. Let's start with the sendEmailMessage method. First we allocate an MFMailComposeViewController object and set the delegate to self so we can handle the callback events. Next, we set our Subject, ToRecipients address, and MessageBody of the e-mail. Finally, we attach the photo to the e-mail and present the drafted e-mail in a modal dialog to the user.

Next, we define another method called didFinishWithResult. This method is a delegate method for the MFMailComposeViewControllerDelegate protocol. It is called after the e-mail is actually sent by the user. When this event is fired, we are removing the modal dialog because it is no longer needed.

We're almost ready to test this code. First, we have to declare the sendEmailMessage method so we can call it from within our implementation. Add the code from Listing 6–7 after the import statements in PhotoViewController.m.

Listing 6–7. *Declare sendEmailMessage As a Private Method*

```
@interface PhotoViewController (Private)
- (void)sendEmailMessage:(UIImage *)image;
@end
```

Add a call to the sendEmailMessage method at the end of the didFinishSavingWithError method. If you try to run the code now, you will get an interesting result. Everything will appear to work as expected, but you will get an error similar to Listing 6–8 when the e-mail dialog should appear.

Listing 6–8. *Error Message*

```
2011-09-24 21:35:32.153 Ch6[1128:707] Sending Email
[Switching to process 9731 thread 0x2603]
wait_fences: failed to receive reply: 10004003
```

Not the most descriptive of errors, is it? Here's what this means. Typically, the wait_fences message indicates a running animation collided with a newly requested animation. In our case, we were just dismissing a modal dialog with the withAnimation attribute set to YES as we were trying to create a new modal dialog with the withAnimation attribute set to YES. It doesn't matter how many times you try to run that project, it will never pass that line of code successfully.

So, before testing this, we have to make a few adjustments to our previous code. Update the didFinishSavingWithError message as shown in Listing 6–9.

Listing 6–9. *Updated didFinishSavingWithError*

```
- (void)image:(UIImage *)image didFinishSavingWithError:(NSError *)error
contextInfo:(void *)contextInfo
{
    /*UIAlertView *alert;
    if (error) {
        alert = [[UIAlertView alloc] initWithTitle:@"Error"
                                           message:@"Unable to save image to Photo
Album."
                                          delegate:self cancelButtonTitle:@"Ok"
                                 otherButtonTitles:nil];
    } else {
        alert = [[UIAlertView alloc] initWithTitle:@"Success"
                                           message:@"Image saved to Photo Album."
                                          delegate:self cancelButtonTitle:@"Ok"
                                 otherButtonTitles:nil];
    }
    [alert show];*/
    [self dismissModalViewControllerAnimated:NO];

    [self sendEmailMessage:image];
}
```

You can see that the code in bold is now in a comment block. The second change that was made (also in bold) is that we have set the animated flag to NO, so that there won't be a collision. I should point out, for the more advanced readers, that there are ways around this issue. However, with heavy animations, they leave trace issues or pixilation and other complicated problems that are easily avoidable by small changes such as this change.

Figure 6–9 shows the successful execution of the project and the dialog message with the e-mail properly formatted.

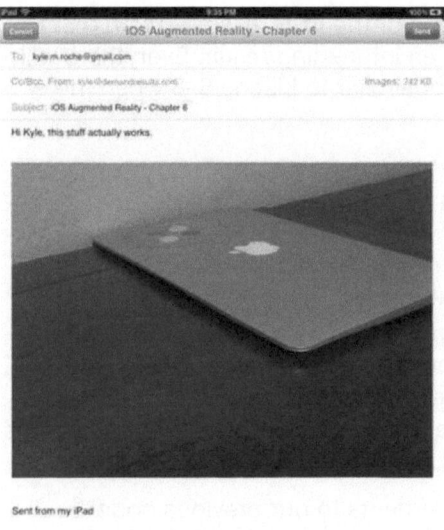

Figure 6–9. *We've now received a properly formatted e-mail.*

Video Capture

There are two main approaches to building an application on top of a video feed. First, there is the approach that does not require analyzing the frames of the video. This approach is seen in some location-based augmented reality applications, which we'll learn more about in Chapter 11. They use the heading and location classes, along with the gyroscope, to determine where to orient your AR targets. However, the video is just a gimmick. Looking at the location-based objects on top of the video gives you the feeling that it is all integrated. This approach (to save time and computing resources) is a simple matter of opening up the video preview as your base layer in the application.

Second, there is the approach that requires analyzing the video feed. This approach is seen in marker-based augmented reality applications (like we'll see in Chapter 10) and facial-recognition augmented reality applications (like we'll see in Chapter 13). Both of these applications require that each frame of video is accessible for analytics.

Building a Base on the Video Preview

In Chapter 7 we are going to discuss how to overlay a cocos2D layer on the video preview for building out augmented reality games. So, this section will be a brief introduction to some of the core concepts.

Open `PhotoViewController.m` in Xcode and find the `loadPhotoPicker` method. This method opens the `UIImagePickerController` object and allows the user to take a photo. Update that method, as shown in Listing 6–10.

Listing 6–10. *Updated loadPhotoPicker*

```
- (IBAction)loadPhotoPicker:(id)sender {
    UIImagePickerController *imagePicker = [[UIImagePickerController alloc] init];
    imagePicker.sourceType =  UIImagePickerControllerSourceTypeCamera;
    // uncomment for front camera
    //imagePicker.cameraDevice = UIImagePickerControllerCameraDeviceFront;
    imagePicker.cameraDevice = UIImagePickerControllerCameraCaptureModeVideo;
    imagePicker.showsCameraControls = NO;
    imagePicker.toolbarHidden = YES;
    imagePicker.navigationBarHidden = YES;
    imagePicker.wantsFullScreenLayout = YES;

    imagePicker.delegate = self;
    imagePicker.allowsEditing = NO;
    [self presentModalViewController:imagePicker animated:YES];
}
```

We set a few new options for the UIImagePickerController object. First, we set the
device type to the video camera. Then, we hid the camera's controls, the toolbar, and
the navigation bar. Finally, we instruct the view controller to make the
UIImagePickerController render in full-screen mode.

If you run the code, after this change, you will get something similar to Figure 6–10.

Figure 6–10. *We get a full-screen video. No controls!*

This clean video interface provides us with a perfect background for building out an
augmented reality application.

If we were to want to analyze these video frames, we would have to set up an NSTimer
and capture and save the preview screen every so often. Alternatively, we could also set
up some sort of user action that causes the image to be saved, or some sort of

programmatic loop. None of these options are ideal, and as you probably noticed from the previous examples in this chapter, saving images manually takes a second or two of the processor's time. Let's explore a better way to capture video frames for the purpose of analyzing them.

Building a Base for Frame Capture

Frame capture sessions work a bit differently. To demonstrate this, we're going to use a new class called AVCaptureSession. Let's move this into a separate tab in our example application so we can reference the differences later.

First, let's add the frameworks we will need to work with the AV Foundation Library. Add the following frameworks to your project.

- CoreVideo
- CoreMedia
- AVFoundation
- ImageIO

Next, add a new cocoa touch file using the UIViewController subclass to the project. Make sure that you are not targeting this class for iPad and you do not use an XIB file for the interface. Name the class VideoViewController.

We are going to create another tab bar item, as we did in the previous examples, and link it up to both the iPad and iPhone storyboards. Open both storyboard files and follow the same steps we did before to link them up to the tab bar. When you have finished, you should see something similar to Figure 6–11 in your iPhone storyboard.

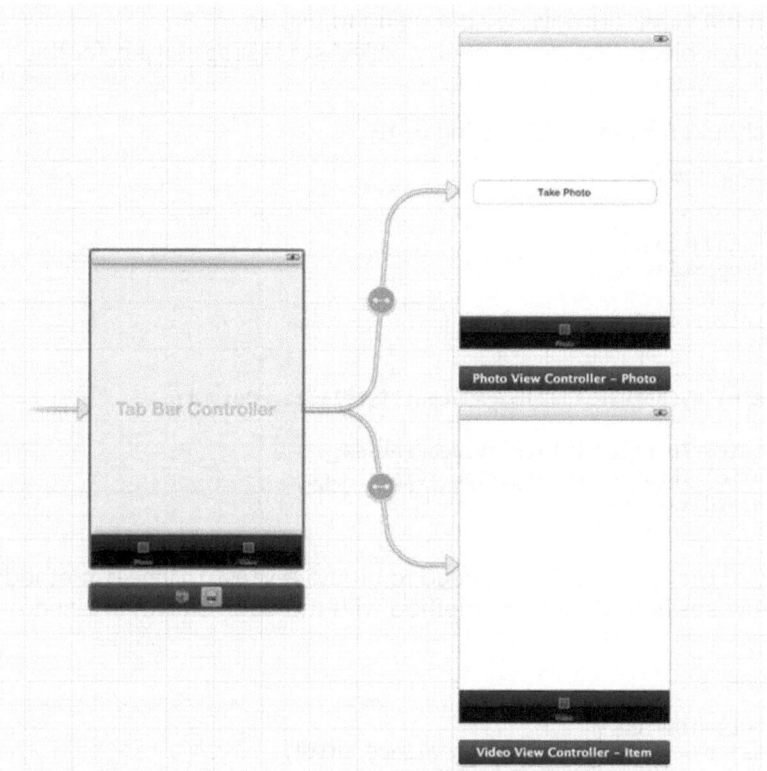

Figure 6–11. *You've added the new tab bar item to your iPhone storyboard.*

Follow the steps again for the iPad storyboard. In both of the interfaces, we are going to add a few outlets. First, add a UIView to the VideoViewController NIB. Name the UIView videoPreview. Make sure you connect the outlet to the VideoViewController header file. While VideoViewController.h is open in your assistant editor, import the AVFoundation.h and ImageIO/CGImageProperties.h headers. Your new interface file should look like Listing 6–11.

Listing 6–11. *Updated VideoViewController.h*

```
#import <UIKit/UIKit.h>
#import <AVFoundation/AVFoundation.h>
#import <ImageIO/CGImageProperties.h>

@interface VideoViewController : UIViewController {

}
@property (strong, nonatomic) IBOutlet UIView *videoPreview;
@end
```

Next, we are going to add a UIImageView outlet and a UIButton to the VideoViewController layout. Name the UIImageView videoImage and connect an action called captureScreen to the UIButton.

To save a still image from the video preview, we are going to use an AVCaptureStillImageOutput object. Create a property called stillImageOutput for this object.

VideoViewController.h should now look like Listing 6–12.

Listing 6–12. *Updated VideoViewController.h*

```
#import <UIKit/UIKit.h>
#import <AVFoundation/AVFoundation.h>
#import <ImageIO/CGImageProperties.h>

@interface VideoViewController : UIViewController {

}
@property(nonatomic, retain) AVCaptureStillImageOutput *stillImageOutput;

@property (strong, nonatomic) IBOutlet UIView *videoPreview;
@property (strong, nonatomic) IBOutlet UIImageView *videoImage;
- (IBAction)captureScreen:(id)sender;
@end
```

Switch to VideoViewController.m in Xcode. We need to create a viewDidAppear method to start the camera preview session. Create the method with the code shown in Listing 6–13.

Listing 6–13. *viewDidAppear Method*

```
- (void)viewDidAppear:(BOOL)animated {
    AVCaptureSession *session = [[AVCaptureSession alloc] init];
    session.sessionPreset = AVCaptureSessionPresetMedium;

    AVCaptureVideoPreviewLayer *captureVideoPreviewLayer = [[AVCaptureVideoPreviewLayer
alloc] initWithSession:session];
    captureVideoPreviewLayer.frame = self.videoPreview.bounds;
        [self.videoPreview.layer addSublayer:captureVideoPreviewLayer];

        AVCaptureDevice *device = [AVCaptureDevice
defaultDeviceWithMediaType:AVMediaTypeVideo];

        NSError *error = nil;
        AVCaptureDeviceInput *input = [AVCaptureDeviceInput deviceInputWithDevice:device
error:&error];
        if (!input) {
                NSLog(@"ERROR: trying to open camera: %@", error);
        }
        [session addInput:input];
        // Placeholder
        [session startRunning];
}
```

Let's walk through this a bit before moving on to testing the application. First, we create an instance of AVCaptureSession. We set our video quality to medium for this application. Next, we create an instance of AVCaptureVideoPreviewLayer. This will be used to store the real time preview of the video buffer.

Next, we set the frame to fill the size of the videoPreview UIView. We then set up our AVCaptureDevice, which we've covered in previous examples, and we check to make sure it's available.

The last few lines are very important. If you don't start your AVCaptureSession with the startRunning method, nothing will appear in your view.

You can run the application to this point. You should see your UIView filled with the camera's preview. Not all that exciting, is it? We had this already in our photo example. Let's extend this example so that our UIButton invokes a routine that captures a still image from the video buffer without affecting the live preview.

Return to VideoViewController.m in Xcode. At the end of the viewDidAppear method, we left a comment labeled // Placeholder. Find that section and replace it with the code from Listing 6–14.

Listing 6–14. *Replace the Placeholder Comment*

```
stillImageOutput = [[AVCaptureStillImageOutput alloc] init];
    NSDictionary *outputSettings = [[NSDictionary alloc] initWithObjectsAndKeys:
AVVideoCodecJPEG, AVVideoCodecKey, nil];
    [stillImageOutput setOutputSettings:outputSettings];

    [session addOutput:stillImageOutput];
```

This code has a specific purpose. It captures the still image from the camera and saves it to the AVCaptureStillImageOutput object we created earlier.

Locate the captureScreen IBAction method. Update this method with the code from Listing 6–15.

Listing 6–15. *captureScreen Method*

```
- (IBAction)captureScreen:(id)sender {
    AVCaptureConnection *videoConnection = nil;
        for (AVCaptureConnection *connection in stillImageOutput.connections)
        {
                for (AVCaptureInputPort *port in [connection inputPorts])
                {
                        if ([[port mediaType] isEqual:AVMediaTypeVideo] )
                        {
                                videoConnection = connection;
                                break;
                        }
                }
                if (videoConnection) { break; }
        }

        NSLog(@"about to request a capture from: %@", stillImageOutput);
        [stillImageOutput captureStillImageAsynchronouslyFromConnection:videoConnection
completionHandler: ^(CMSampleBufferRef imageSampleBuffer, NSError *error)
    {
                CFDictionaryRef exifAttachments = CMGetAttachment( imageSampleBuffer,
kCGImagePropertyExifDictionary, NULL);
                if (exifAttachments)
                {
            // Do something with the attachments.
```

```
                    NSLog(@"attachements: %@", exifAttachments);
                }
        else
            NSLog(@"no attachments");

        NSData *imageData = [AVCaptureStillImageOutput
jpegStillImageNSDataRepresentation:imageSampleBuffer];
        UIImage *image = [[UIImage alloc] initWithData:imageData];

        self.videoImage.image = image;
        }];
}
```

There are two main code blocks in this method. The first code block checks for the AVCaptureConnection in the AVCaptureStillImageOutput object. We verify that this is a video output and set a local reference to the AVCaptureConnection instance.

Next, we capture (asynchronously) the image from the camera. We set up an image buffer to store the image. After this, we use the ImageIO framework to capture the EXIF attachments of the image. This might be useful for setting up filters or storing values about the photo quality for other purposes.

Finally, we set the UIImageView outlet to display our captured video frame. If you run the project, you will see something similar to Figure 6–12.

Figure 6–12. *We've easily captured video evidence of wine and iced coffee.*

Our example worked perfectly. You will notice the shutter noise over the speakers when you capture a screen. This is because of how we went about grabbing the still image. In Chapter 13's example application, we'll vary this approach slightly to remove that effect.

Finally, let's take a quick look at the EXIF attachments that came with our still image. Listing 6–16 shows the output from the console.

Listing 6–16. *EXIF Attachments*

```
2011-09-25 15:46:40.751 Ch6[183:707] attachments: {
    ApertureValue = "2.526068811667588";
    BrightnessValue = "-1.04630972052318";
    ExposureMode = 0;
    ExposureProgram = 2;
    ExposureTime = "0.04166666666666666";
    FNumber = "2.4";
    Flash = 32;
    FocalLenIn35mmFilm = 32;
    FocalLength = "2.03";
    ISOSpeedRatings =     (
        800
    );
    MeteringMode = 5;
    PixelXDimension = 640;
    PixelYDimension = 480;
    SceneType = 1;
    SensingMethod = 2;
    Sharpness = 0;
    ShutterSpeedValue = "4.584985584026477";
    WhiteBalance = 0;
}
```

Summary

In this chapter, we learned about the core concepts of the video camera and its features on iOS devices. We started with basic photos. We set up a UIImageViewController object to capture pictures selected by the user. Next, we learned how to save and convert those pictures to the local file system. Finally, we sent the file over e-mail as an attachment. Along the way, we introduced storyboarding, which is new to iOS 5.

Next, we introduced video capture. This will be the main component of most of the remaining chapters in the book. We learned how to remove the camera controls and use a video preview that occupies the full-screen layout. In addition, we set up a video capture session so we could analyze the frames for purposes of marker or facial-recognition applications.

In the next chapter, we'll introduce cocos2D, which is a great framework for building games. I'll show you how to use cocos2D and the concepts from this chapter to build a foundation for your first augmented reality game.

Chapter 7

Using cocos2D for AR

We've already talked about the different use cases for augmented-reality applications. Other than the presentation of location-based information, gaming applications take a big percentage of the augmented-reality market space.

In this chapter, I'm going to introduce cocos2D for iPhone. cocos2D for iPhone is a framework for building 2D games and graphically interactive applications. It is based on the cocos2D framework, which you can read more about at www.cocos2d.org.

Overview

It is the open sourced cocos2D framework that provides the basis for cocos2D for iPhone. The original project was written in Python. Obviously, this wasn't all that useful for iOS programmers. cocos2D for iPhone is a port of this framework to Objective-C.

cocos2D has a few key characteristics, such as its ease of use, its speed and flexibility, and that it is open source. cocos2D happens to be one of the open source projects with great community support and adoption. The last, and most important, characteristic of cocos2D (if you're going to release an app, that is) is that it's approved for use on the App Store.

Installation

First, we need to get our environment set up. In this chapter, we're going to walk through setup, core concepts, and then introduce a quick augmented-reality sample application. In Chapter 8, we'll be building a full augmented-reality game with cocos2D.

Visit www.cocos2d-iphone.org/download and download the latest stable build of cocos2D for iPhone. After you've downloaded the file, double-click it in Finder to unpack the archive.

In the new directory, there is a file called cocos2D-ios.xcodeproj. This is the Xcode project for testing the cocos2D download and prerequisites. Open the project in Xcode. There should be nearly 70 targets in the project. Most of them test a specific feature of cocos2D for iPhone. Change your Scheme to point to a test target to make sure your installation has everything it needs. See Figure 7–1 for an example of how to adjust your Scheme in Xcode.

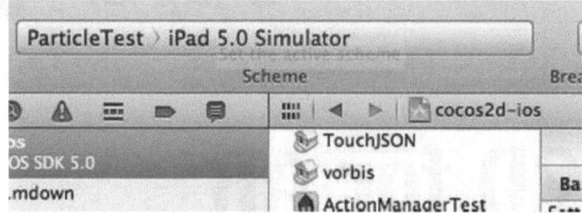

Figure 7–1. *Select ParticleTest (or another target) from the Scheme's drop-down menu.*

For good measure, step through a few of the targets and run the projects on the simulator. Most of them are a series of click-through examples that demonstrate a particular function.

Installing the Project Templates

cocos2D comes with project templates for Xcode. The download includes all the files needed to install the templates. These templates give your projects the necessary components they require and save you setup time. There are three main project templates:

- cocos2D stand-alone template
- cocos2D + box2D template
- cocos2D + chipmunk template

Before you run these scripts, make sure you have placed the unpacked directory in a location in which you are happy. Open the Terminal application and navigate to that directory. To install the templates, run the commands shown in Listing 7–1.

Listing 7–1. *Installing the Templates (Fail)*

```
cocos2d-iphone-1.0.1$ ./install-templates.sh -u
cocos2d-iphone template installer
Installing Xcode 4 cocos2d iOS template
-----------------------------------------------------

templates already installed. To force a re-install use the '-f' parameter
```

If you've already used cocos2D, you might get a message similar to the one I received (shown in Listing 7–1). If so, add the -f option as indicated in the error message. Listing 7–2 shows the results. If you have never used cocos2D before, your output should look similar to Listing 7–2 and you wouldn't have needed the -f option.

Listing 7–2. *Installing with the -f Option*

```
cocos2d-iphone-1.0.1$ ./install-templates.sh -f -u
cocos2d-iphone template installer
```

```
Installing Xcode 4 cocos2d iOS template
-----------------------------------------------------

removing old libraries: /Users/kyleroche/Library/Developer/Xcode/Templates/cocos2d/
...creating destination directory:
/Users/kyleroche/Library/Developer/Xcode/Templates/cocos2d/
...copying cocos2d files
...copying cocoslive files
...copying TouchJSON files
...copying CocosDenshion files
...copying CocosDenshionExtras files
...copying FontLabel files
...copying template files
```
[much more of this type of stuff… then…]
```
done!
```

I shortened the output of Listing 7–2 for simplicity. The installer will cycle through the various templates for Xcode 4, then finish with templates for Xcode 3, just in case you're still using both versions.

Creating a Project

Open Xcode. If you've installed the templates correctly, you should see something similar to Figure 7–2 on your launch screen.

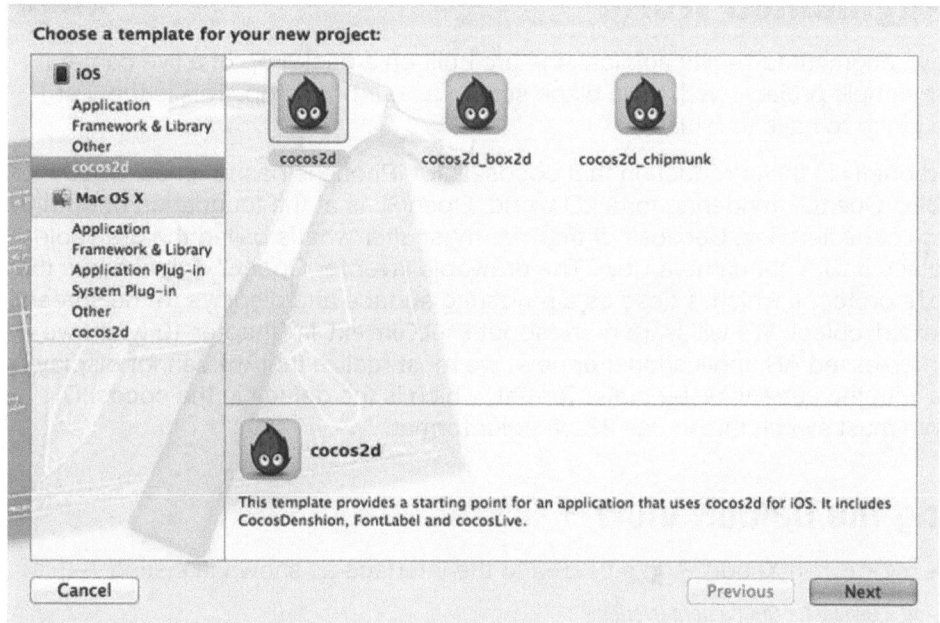

Figure 7–2. *You've successfully installed new cocos2D templates!*

Choose the cocos2D template and create a new project. Name the project **Ch7**. The code for this project is available at www.github.com/kyleroche and from the Source Code/Download area of the Apress web site (www.apress.com).

Run the project in its default form. Use either the iPad or iPhone simulator. You will get a result similar to what we see in Figure 7–3. This is the default project for all the cocos2D templates.

Figure 7–3. *Run the default project Hello World from cocos2D.*

Let's turn this Hello World into an augmented-reality Hello World application, then we'll discuss some of the features available to us in cocos2D.

Hello Augmented World

As you know, augmented-reality applications are built on a backdrop of a live camera view. In our sample project, we have a black screen as our backdrop. This is the first thing we're going to have to replace.

I mentioned briefly in the introduction that cocos2D for iPhone is based on cocos2D, which enables OpenGL rendering for a 2D world. OpenGL is at the foundation of both of these source code libraries. Because of that, we must alter what's called the drawable layer to replace it with our camera view. The drawable layer for OpenGL implements the EAGLDrawable protocol, which is used as a rendering surface and displays to the screen the EAGLContext object. We will learn more about EAGLContext in Chapter 10 when we build a marker-based AR application. For now, we must realize that we cannot display the camera with the current 16-bit buffer format, which is the default in the cocos2D template. We must switch this to use 32-bit color format.

Adjusting the Default View

Open AppDelegate.h in Xcode. Add a UIView to the interface as shown in Listing 7–3.

Listing 7–3. *Add a UIView for Our Camera Overlay*

```
UIView  *cameraView;
```

Switch to AppDelegate.m, and let's get to work. First, we have to swap the buffer to the 32-bit buffer. This should be a commented value in the cocos2D template, as this is a common change for developers to make. Find the line that looks like what is shown in Listing 7–4.

Listing 7–4. *Change the pixelFormat of the EAGLView*

```
//
// Create the EAGLView manually
//  1. Create a RGB565 format. Alternative: RGBA8
//  2. depth format of 0 bit. Use 16 or 24 bit for 3d effects, like CCPageTurnTransition
//
EAGLView *glView = [EAGLView viewWithFrame:[window bounds]
                              pixelFormat:kEAGLColorFormatRGB565        //
kEAGLColorFormatRGBA8
                              depthFormat:0];
```

You can see that the comments explain some of this. Because we cannot use the RGB565, 16-bit format for camera view, swap the value for pixelFormat with the one that is in the comment. Your code block should now look like Listing 7–5. We will leave the depthFormat at 0, as we are not working in 3D just yet.

Listing 7–5. *Change the pixelFormat*

```
EAGLView *glView = [EAGLView viewWithFrame:[window bounds]
                              pixelFormat: kEAGLColorFormatRGBA8 depthFormat:0];
```

Next, we will be adding our newly declared UIView to the screen in place of the boring black backdrop we had by default. Find the section of code shown in Listing 7–6.

Listing 7–6. *Main View Receives a SubView*

```
// make the View Controller a child of the main window
 [window addSubview: viewController.view];
```

Just below this line, add the code from Listing 7–7. I'll walk you through each line next.

Listing 7–7. *Prepare Overlay View for Camera*

```
[CCDirector sharedDirector].openGLView.backgroundColor = [UIColor clearColor];
[CCDirector sharedDirector].openGLView.opaque = NO;

glClearColor(0.0, 0.0, 0.0, 0.0);

cameraView = [[UIView alloc] initWithFrame:[[UIScreen mainScreen] bounds]];
cameraView.opaque = NO;
cameraView.backgroundColor=[UIColor clearColor];
 [window addSubview:cameraView];
```

First, we are setting the background color of the OpenGL view to clearColor. This will allow transparency so we can still write objects and text to the screen on top of our camera view. Next, we make sure this layer is not opaque (for the same purpose). We use the glClearColor method to make sure our version of "clear" is actually clear. You could adjust this a bit to make a hazy translucent layer instead of an invisible layer, which is what we're building in this chapter. The second section looks similar. We take our new UIView, stretch it to the bounds of the screen, and make it transparent as well. Finally, we are adding our new UIView to the window.

If you run the project again now, you won't see a visible difference. We haven't added anything that makes an impact yet. Let's move on.

Adding the Camera View

Just below the code we added from Listing 7–7, we are going to add the code to create the UIImagePicker and display it in camera mode. Some of this will be familiar from Chapter 6. Add the code from Listing 7–8, just below the code from Listing 7–7.

Listing 7–8. *Create the UIImagePicker and Add to the Screen*

```
UIImagePickerController *imagePicker;

@try {
        imagePicker = [[[UIImagePickerController alloc] init] autorelease];
        imagePicker.sourceType = UIImagePickerControllerSourceTypeCamera;
        imagePicker.showsCameraControls = NO;
        imagePicker.toolbarHidden = YES;
        imagePicker.navigationBarHidden = YES;
        imagePicker.wantsFullScreenLayout = YES;
}
@catch (NSException * e) {
        [imagePicker release];
        imagePicker = nil;
}
@finally {
        if(imagePicker) {
            [cameraView addSubview:[imagePicker view]];
            [cameraView release];
        }
}

 [window bringSubviewToFront:viewController.view];
```

Let's walk through this a bit, before we run the project. First, we create our UIImagePicker, set it up, and make sure the source type is set to camera so we can see the live video content. We hide the controls, the toolbar, and the navigation bar so that we get a full view of the camera.

There is one last thing to do. Switch to HelloWorldLayer.m and change the label's text and size, as shown in Listing 7–9.

Listing 7–9. *Change the Label's Text*

```
// create and initialize a Label
CCLabelTTF *label = [CCLabelTTF labelWithString:@"Hello Augmented World"
fontName:@"Marker Felt" fontSize:48];
```

Like our examples in Chapter 6, we'll have to run this on a real device because the simulator doesn't support the camera classes. Launch the project on your device. You will notice something is a bit off. Check out Figure 7–4 to see what I mean.

Figure 7–4. *Here is the camera view, but with a bit missing.*

The camera didn't cover the whole screen! There's a black bar on the edge that seems leftover from our template application. Wait, we set wantsFullScreenLayout to YES. What happened?

Scaling the Camera View

So, why do we have this strange black bar occupying part of our UI? It has to do with the difference in aspect ratio between the screen and the camera (in landscape mode). Basically, the iPhone screen now has an aspect ratio of 3:4, and the iPhone camera has an aspect ratio of 4:3. So, we need to scale the camera image to match. This explains the black bar from Figure 7–4.

To fix this, we need to scale our UIImagePicker to match the aspect ratio of the device. Return to AppDelegate.m in Xcode. Find the section of code you added from Listing 7–8, and add to it the bold lines from Listing 7–10.

Listing 7–10. *Scale the UIImagePickerController*

```
@try {
        imagePicker = [[[UIImagePickerController alloc] init] autorelease];
        imagePicker.sourceType = UIImagePickerControllerSourceTypeCamera;
        imagePicker.showsCameraControls = NO;
        imagePicker.toolbarHidden = YES;
        imagePicker.navigationBarHidden = YES;
        imagePicker.wantsFullScreenLayout = YES;
        imagePicker.cameraViewTransform =
CGAffineTransformScale(imagePicker.cameraViewTransform, 1.0, 1.3);
}
```

Run the project again. You should see that we've successfully removed the black bar and the camera is now occupying the full screen, as shown in Figure 7–5.

Figure 7–5. *No more black bar!*

cocos2D Concepts

Let's add a bit of flare to our app. At the moment, it doesn't respond to touches or do anything interesting. First, let's understand how a cocos2D application is set up.

Scenes

A scene is the foundation of a cocos2D view. Your app can have many scenes, but only one of them can be active at any given time. In our sample application, we added the camera view underneath the HelloWorldLayer scene.

Scenes are implementations of the CCScene object in cocos2D. They are independent pieces of the app's overall workflow. In typical games, there are scenes for the menus, the different levels, and the cutscenes for video content in between levels or after you've won or lost a level. Each of these CCScene objects comprises one or more layers. In our sample application, we have the clear layer with the label, and the clear layer with the UIImagePickerController.

You can use scenes for transitioning between scenes as well. These types of scenes are implementations of the CCTransitionScene object.

Director

Not surprisingly, the director handles the selection of which scene is currently active. The director is an instance of the CCDirector singleton object. It maintains, in memory, details of which scene is active and handles a stack of scenes to allow pushing of new scenes, pausing current scenes, and returning to original scenes. The CCDirectory singleton is the one who will actually change the CCScene. This singleton also initializes the OpenGL ES environment. The code in Listing 7–11, from AppDelegate.m, initializes the director from the singleton, or shared, class.

Listing 7–11. *Create Instance of Director Singleton*

```
CCDirector *director = [CCDirector sharedDirector];
```

Layers

A CCLayer has the size of the whole drawable area. It can be semitransparent (providing holes to underlying layer(s)) or fully transparent (as we have done in our application already). Layers define the appearance and behavior of a scene.

The CCLayer also defines your event handlers. When an event is propagated, it starts from the front-most layer and raises the event until some layer catches the event and accepts it. So, the farther back a layer is in the stack, the more layers have the opportunity to intercept and handle the event.

cocos2D defines a series of predefined layers that we can use in our games. It's rare to have to create your own extension or custom CCLayer class.

Adding Effects

cocos2D has tons of built-in effects and transitions we can leverage in our games. For our augmented-reality examples, we're going to use touch events to handle interaction from the user before we present any visual effects. So, we first need to learn how to handle touch events.

Handling Touch Events

There is another singleton object, CCTouchDispatcher, which sends notifications of touch events on the screen. To be able to handle touch events in our applications, we must enable touches, register the CCTouchDispatcher, and then handle the touch events themselves.

In the overview, I briefly noted that events are handled at each individual layer. They start at the front-most layer and escalate to the back-most layer until a layer accepts and handles the event.

So far, we've built our sample a bit different than a normal 2D game. We have an underlying layer (the camera view) that is always on the bottom of the stack. We used a simple layer (the label view's layer) to drive the content on the screen. In typical 2D games, you build on static graphic layers or tile-based maps. Using the live camera view for our foundation is what makes this an augmented-reality game. We will add more advanced augmented-reality concepts in the example application we will build in Chapter 8. Having said this, and understanding how touch events escalate, it makes the most sense to handle the events at our HelloWorldLayer layer.

Open HelloWorldLayer.m in Xcode and find the init method. At the bottom of the if loop, add the statement from Listing 7–12.

Listing 7–12. *Enable Touches*

```
self.isTouchEnabled = YES;
```

Next, we have to register with the CCTouchDispatcher as a layer that is accepting these types of events. Just after the init method closes, add the code from Listing 7–13.

Listing 7–13. *Register with CCTouchDispatcher*

```
- (void)registerWithTouchDispatcher {
    [[CCTouchDispatcher sharedDispatcher] addTargetedDelegate:self priority:0
swallowsTouches:YES];
}
```

We've set the delegate to self and swallowed the touch so that no other layers will respond until we've decided whether this layer can handle and accept the event. To accept the event, use the ccTouchBegan method. Just after the registerWithTouchDispatcher method, add the code from Listing 7–14.

Listing 7–14. *Accept and Handle the Event*

```
- (BOOL)ccTouchBegan:(UITouch *)touch withEvent:(UIEvent *)event {
    return YES;
}

- (void)ccTouchEnded:(UITouch *)touch withEvent:(UIEvent *)event {
    CGPoint location = [self convertTouchToNodeSpace:touch];
    NSLog(@"Touch %@: ", NSStringFromCGPoint(location));
}
```

The first method returns a YES to the dispatcher to let it know that it will accept the event, and that the dispatcher need not look further for a response. The second event reacts to the touch by logging the location of the touch on the screen. We use the NSStringFromCGPoint method to correctly cast the C struct to a string.

Run the application again on your device. Touch the screen in a few random places. In your debugger window, you should see output similar to that shown in Figure 7–6.

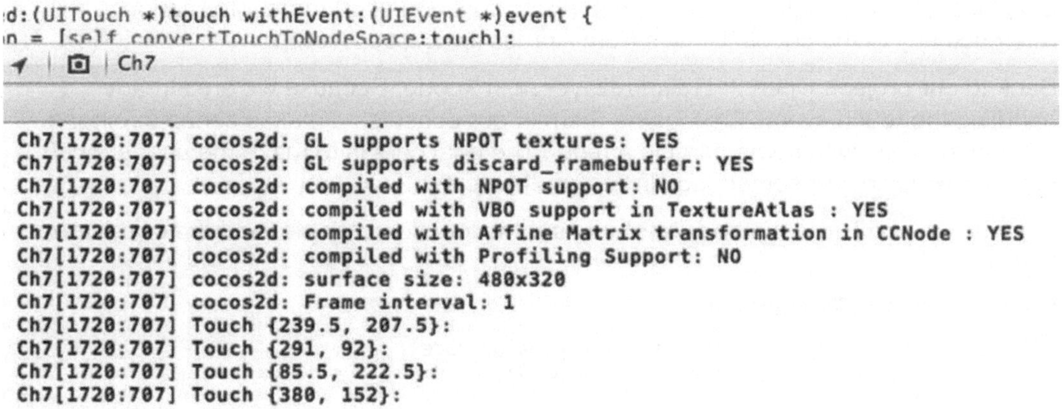

```
d:(UITouch *)touch withEvent:(UIEvent *)event {
n = [self convertTouchToNodeSpace:touch];
```

```
◄  |  ▣  |  Ch7

Ch7[1720:707] cocos2d: GL supports NPOT textures: YES
Ch7[1720:707] cocos2d: GL supports discard_framebuffer: YES
Ch7[1720:707] cocos2d: compiled with NPOT support: NO
Ch7[1720:707] cocos2d: compiled with VBO support in TextureAtlas : YES
Ch7[1720:707] cocos2d: compiled with Affine Matrix transformation in CCNode : YES
Ch7[1720:707] cocos2d: compiled with Profiling Support: NO
Ch7[1720:707] cocos2d: surface size: 480x320
Ch7[1720:707] cocos2d: Frame interval: 1
Ch7[1720:707] Touch {239.5, 207.5}:
Ch7[1720:707] Touch {291, 92}:
Ch7[1720:707] Touch {85.5, 222.5}:
Ch7[1720:707] Touch {380, 152}:
```

Figure 7–6. *We are now able to log the touch events.*

We can later use this `CGPoint` to do something a bit more exciting. Let's talk about effects briefly, then add one to our scene.

Visual Effects

cocos2D provides all kinds of graphical effects we can use in our applications, right out of the box. For example, the following list contains the types of particle emitters that are available in the cocos2D distribution:

- CCParticleFire
- CCParticleFireworks
- CCParticleSun
- CCParticleGalaxy
- CCParticleFlower
- CCParticleMeteor
- CCParticleSpiral
- CCParticleSmoke
- CCParticleExplosion
- CCParticleSnow
- CCParticleRain

There are methods of designing your own particle systems. There is a tool called Particle Designer (available at http://particledesigner.71squared.com/) that lets you create your own visual effects, and provides access to a shared library of community created effects. The tool, at the time of this writing, was under $10.

Graphical effects is not the focus of this book, so if you need more information, reference any of the cocos2D titles from Apress (www.apress.com).

Back to our project. Open HelloWorldLayer.m in Xcode. Because we are already handling the touch events (by logging them in our console), it makes sense to extend this functionality with some particle effects. The goal here is to make the user's touch start an explosion, or something similar, on the screen.

Find the ccTouchEnded method. After you set the location variable, add the code from Listing 7–15.

Listing 7–15. *Add a CCParticleSystem*

```
CCParticleSystem* emitter = [CCParticleExplosion node];
emitter.position = ccp(location.x, location.y);
emitter.life = 3.0f;
emitter.duration = 2.7f;
emitter.lifeVar = 0.1f;
emitter.totalParticles = 200;
[self addChild:emitter z:20];
```

Quickly glance back to the beginning of this section where I named the provided particle systems available in cocos2D. In line one of this code block, you'll notice we used the CCParticleExplosion class. As you're experimenting with this section, feel free to change that to any of the other types I've listed in this section.

After we declare our CCParticleSystem, we set the position to the x,y coordinates of the touch event, define the life and duration of the particle system, and set its total number of particles. Again, these are all great values to play around with and learn.

Finally, we add the CCParticleSystem to our layer. If you run the project and tap the screen, you will see something similar to what we see in Figure 7–7.

Figure 7–7. *Tap to create touch explosions!*

Adding Sound Effects

Explosions just aren't the same without sound. Don't you agree? Let's make some noise. Back in Chapter 5, we talked about adding sound to iOS applications. I introduced a few web sites where you can download free sound effects. I downloaded an MP3 and then converted it to a CAF file using the afconvert utility I showed you in Chapter 5. The sample is included in the source code on GitHub and from the Source Code/Download area of the Apress web site (www.apress.com). I called my file explosion.caf. If you use your own sound effect, make sure the names match in the following code blocks.

Open HelloWorldLayer.m in Xcode and import the SimpleAudioEngine header, as shown in Listing 7–16.

Listing 7–16. *Import SimpleAudioEngine Header*

```
#import "SimpleAudioEngine.h"
```

Next, locate the init method. Just after where we set isTouchEnabled to YES, add the code from Listing 7–17.

Listing 7–17. *Preload the Sound Effect*

```
[[SimpleAudioEngine sharedEngine] preloadEffect:@"explosion.caf"];
```

This preloads the sound effect for faster access when we need it. Finally, find the ccTouchEnded event handler. After we have added our particle effect to the layer, add the code from Listing 7–18.

Listing 7–18. *Play the Sound Effect*

```
[[SimpleAudioEngine sharedEngine] playEffect:@"explosion.caf"];
```

Run the project on your device. You should have a nice explosion sound effect on your touch events. This helps make the game a bit more fun and enjoyable for the user.

Adding a HUD Layer

In cocos2D games, the "world" is typically bigger than the view the device is currently rendering. Because of this, if you were to just render elements on the screen, it might appear slightly misaligned depending on where the scene's focus is currently. HUD (heads-up display) layers are commonly used to solve this problem. A HUD layer, is another semitransparent layer that lies on top of our action layer in our scene. In gaming, we see this quite a bit for showing scores, or lives left, and so on.

Let's add a HUD layer to our current example to count the number of explosions the user has caused. Add a new Objective-C class to the project. The class should be a subclass of NSObject. Name the class HUDLayer.mm. The .mm extension is not a typo. Using .mm for files that have a mix of Objective-C and C++ is a recommended convention. It's easier than telling the compiler to handle a single file differently and it lets future developers who read your code know that the implementation uses C++.

Open HUDLayer.h and replace it with the code shown in Listing 7–19.

Listing 7–19. *New HUDLayer.h*

```
#import "cocos2d.h"
@interface HUDLayer : CCLayer {
    CCLabelTTF *_counterLabel;
}
- (void)incrementCounter;
@end
```

We changed the subclass to CCLayer, and created a private CCLabelTTF object to hold a label on the screen. We also created an instance method called incrementCounter. The touch event will call this method to let the HUD layer know that there has been a new touch, and to increment the counter the label is displaying.

Switch to HudLayer.mm in Xcode. First, import the HelloWorldLayer header file. Next, we're going to create a local variable to hold the value of the current count and create the init method for HUDLayer. Copy the code from Listing 7-20 to HUDLayer.mm.

Listing 7–20. *Init Method for HUDLayer.mm*

```
int counter = 0;
- (id)init {
    if ((self = [super init])) {
        _counterLabel = [CCLabelTTF labelWithString:[NSString
stringWithFormat:@"Explosions: %d", counter] fontName:@"Marker Felt" fontSize:24];

        CGSize size = [[CCDirector sharedDirector] winSize];

        _counterLabel.position =  ccp( size.width * 0.85 , size.height * 0.9 );

        [self addChild: _counterLabel z:10];

    }
    return self;
}
```

The init method uses some of the code from our HelloWorldLayer class. We are simply creating a new label and adding it to the screen. In this case, we are adding it to the top right of the screen with a z-axis value of 10, so any of the explosions render behind the label.

Implement the incrementCounter method by adding the code from Listing 7–21, just after the new init method.

Listing 7–21. *The incrementCounter Method*

```
- (void)incrementCounter {
    counter++;
    _counterLabel.string = [NSString stringWithFormat:@"Explosions: %d", counter];
}
```

This method should be simple to follow. We are simply incrementing the counter, which will be stored in the HUD layer and not the game layer, and updating the label we've added to the view already.

That's it for the HUD layer. Now, we have to use it from our HelloWorldLayer layer. Switch to HelloWorldLayer.h in Xcode and start by importing the HUDLayer.h file. Next, declare a private variable called *_hud of type HUDLayer. Finally, we're going to create a new method called initWithHUD. Your new HelloWorldLayer.h file should look like Listing 7–22.

Listing 7–22. *New HelloWorldLayer.h*

```
#import "cocos2d.h"
#import "CCTouchDispatcher.h"
#import "HUDLayer.h"

// HelloWorldLayer
@interface HelloWorldLayer : CCLayer {
    HUDLayer *_hud;
}

// returns a CCScene that contains the HelloWorldLayer as the only child
+(CCScene *) scene;
- (id)initWithHUD:(HUDLayer *)hud;
@end
```

Switch to HelloWorldLayer.m and change your static scene method to look like Listing 7–23.

Listing 7–23. *New Scene Method*

```
+(CCScene *) scene
{
    CCScene *scene = [CCScene node];

    HUDLayer *hud = [HUDLayer node];
    [scene addChild:hud z:1];

    // 'layer' is an autorelease object.
    //HelloWorldLayer *layer = [HelloWorldLayer node];
    HelloWorldLayer *layer = [[[HelloWorldLayer alloc] initWithHUD:hud] autorelease];

    // add layer as a child to scene
    [scene addChild: layer];

    // return the scene
    return scene;
}
```

Let's discuss the lines in bold. First, we're declaring a new HUDLayer variable and adding it to the scene. We commented out the old init method and replaced it with a method called initWithHUD (we haven't implemented this yet, but don't worry, that's next).

Locate the init method in HelloWorldLayer.m. Change its signature from init to initWithHUD:(HUDLayer *)hud. Replace the method as shown in Listing 7–24.

Listing 7–24. *Replace init Method with This Code Block*

```
-(id) initWithHUD:(HUDLayer *)hud
{
    // always call "super" init
```

```
        // Apple recommends to re-assign "self" with the "super" return value
    if( (self=[super init])) {
        _hud = hud;
        // create and initialize a Label
        CCLabelTTF *label = [CCLabelTTF labelWithString:@"Hello Augmented World"
fontName:@"Marker Felt" fontSize:48];

        // ask director the the window size
        CGSize size = [[CCDirector sharedDirector] winSize];

        // position the label on the center of the screen
        label.position =  ccp( size.width /2 , size.height/2 );

        // add the label as a child to this Layer
         [self addChild: label];

            self.isTouchEnabled = YES;
            [[SimpleAudioEngine sharedEngine] preloadEffect:@"explosion.caf"];
    }
    return self;
}
```

Other than the method signature, we added only one line to the method. We set the private variable _hud to the new HUDLayer object we created in the static scene method.

There is one last thing to do before we test the application. Find the ccTouchEnded method and add the code from Listing 7–25, just above our NSLog statement.

Listing 7–25. *Call HUDLayer's incrementCounter Method*

```
[_hud incrementCounter];
```

That does it. Our new HUD layer should be loaded in our scene and should handle the incrementing of the current count label in the top right of the screen. Run the project on your device. The sound and particle effects should remain unchanged. However, you should see a label in the top showing the number of times you have touched the screen. Tap a few times; you should end up with something like Figure 7–8.

Figure 7–8. *You can now see the HUD layer in the top right of the screen.*

You can add more complicated HUD layers that handle user input on their own, such as buttons or selection options. We won't be covering that in this book. For more information on cocos2D or advanced gaming topics, reference any of the cocos2D titles from Apress.

Summary

In this chapter, I introduced cocos2D. We set up the sample templates and took the Hello World project from just a label to a simple augmented-reality game. We scaled the camera view to match the aspect ratio of our device in landscape mode. Then, we set up event handlers for user touch events.

Our simple game handles the touch events of the user, creates and starts a particle system for visual events, and even has explosion sound effects. We even built a separate HUD layer, independent of the gaming layer, to count metrics and display them to the user.

In the next chapter, we'll take augmented-reality gaming to the next level and work in the gyroscope to create a 360 degree first-person augmented-reality shooter game.

Chapter 8

Building a cocos2D AR Game

In this chapter, we're going to extend on what we learned in Chapter 7 and build a fully functional AR game. There are so many scenarios or possible story lines for augmented reality games. Although this plot is a little ridiculous, it'll demonstrate some important capabilities for AR gaming. We'll learn how to structure a cocos2D game with a menu and launch options. We'll also handle scoring and end game scenes. The entire game will be played on top of a camera view.

Overview

Every game starts with a story. Here's our story: Some alien pumpkins have taken over our planet. The universal police have released a special device that lets us see the pumpkins and destroy them by tapping on them through the camera. This device, of course, is our iPad or iPhone.

When the game launches, we're going to use a class new to iOS 5 called `CIDetector`. This class will be discussed in more detail in Chapter 12. All you need to know now is that it will identify faces in the camera view and allow us to overlay pumpkin images in place of people's heads. When people are found in the camera view, you will see something like Figure 8–1.

Figure 8–1. *Here is our sample pumpkin, overlaying a face.*

We should already have everything we need to start coding. In Chapter 7, we set up cocos2D and ran through a brief sample. We'll be using the same templates that we installed with cocos2D in this chapter. More precisely, we'll be using the template that includes cocos2D and the chipmunk physics library. We won't be doing too much with chipmunk in the game. We're going to use it to make our menu screen more interesting for the user.

Scoring in this game will be somewhat difficult. Since we're randomly placing pumpkins on people's faces, then blowing them up, we have to consider how quickly a pumpkin can reappear. To prevent an unwinnable game, we're going to use a static set of pumpkins. They will most likely find the same victim more than once (unless you can test this in a big crowd). After the user has cleared the whole clan of alien pumpkins, we'll let them win the game. We'll put a timer on it as well, so the aliens have a fair shot at continuing their existence.

Creating the Project

If you skipped Chapter 7, go back and make sure you follow the steps in the "Installation" section. The cocos2D framework will be absolutely required for this chapter.

Create a new project in Xcode. Make sure you choose the **cocos2d_chipmunk** template, as shown in Figure 8–2.

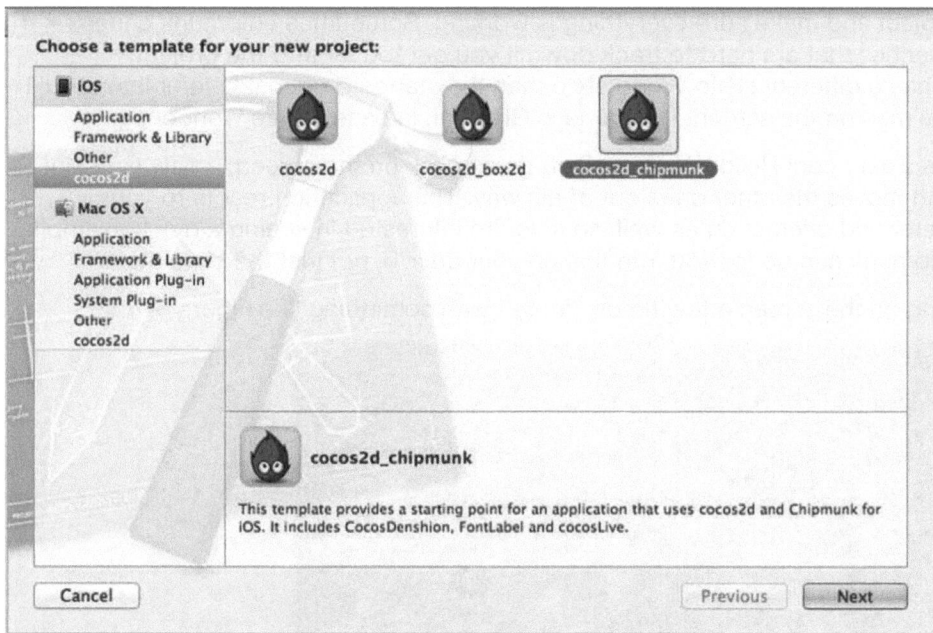

Figure 8–2. *Choose the cocos2d_chipmunk template.*

Name your project. I'm calling mine Ch8, so you can find it easily in the GitHub repository or from the Source Code/Download area at the Apress web site (www.apress.com). Make sure you set the project as a **Universal Project**. Minimize **Supported Device Orientations** to **Landscape Right** only, as shown in Figure 8–3. We are doing this to minimize the logic on pumpkin placement.

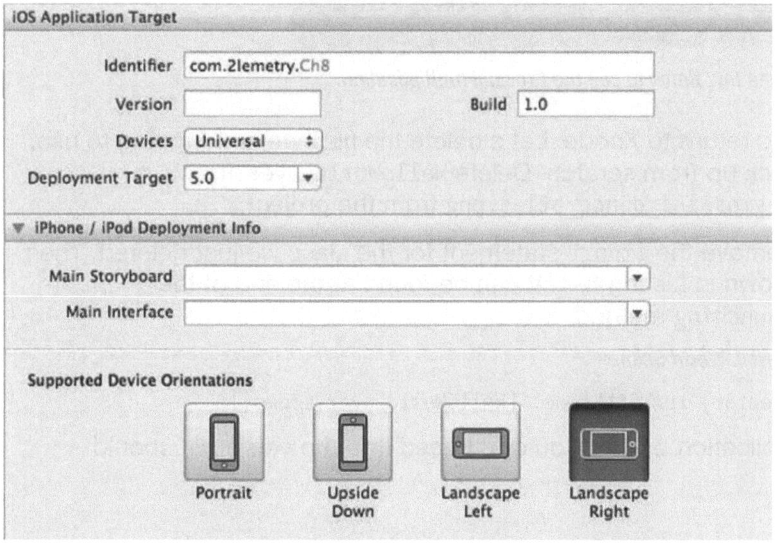

Figure 8–3. *Set the Supported Device Orientations to Landscape Right.*

Run the project and make sure everything is working. Sometimes chipmunk causes some headaches that are hard to track down if you get too far into the project. Chipmunk has a different Hello World style than the standard cocos2D template. You'll see a single man on the screen. His name is Grossini, in case you're wondering.

Now, this is a very cool Hello World project. If you click on the screen, a new Grossini appears and moves the other ones out of his way. The application reacts to your accelerometer and orientation as well, so if you're interested in seeing a quick example of what chipmunk can do for you, run this on your device, not just the simulator.

After clicking on the screen a few times, I'm left with something like Figure 8–4.

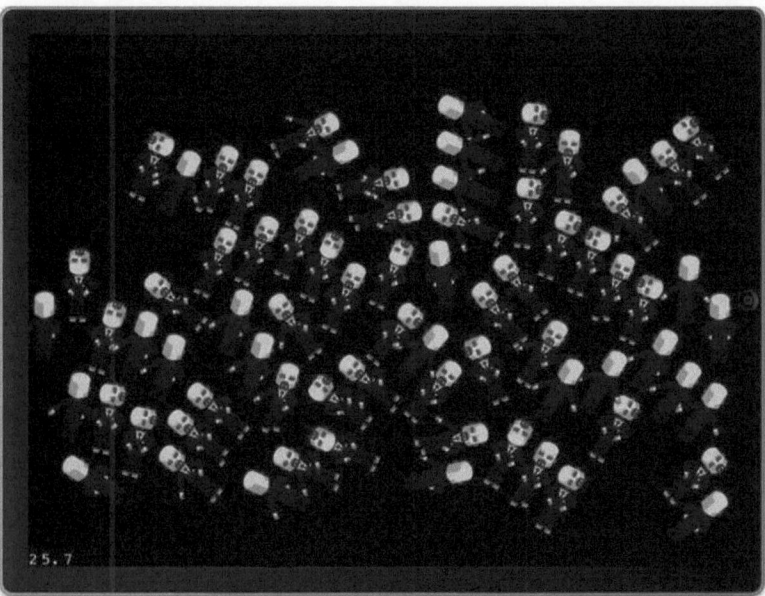

Figure 8–4. *Click on the screen a few times to see the Grossini multiplication.*

Close the application and return to Xcode. Let's delete the files we aren't going to use, and build this project back up from scratch. Delete HelloWorldLayer.h, HelloWorldLayer.m, and grossini_dance_atlas.png from the project.

Open AppDelegate.m. Remove the import statement for the class we just deleted. Then comment out the line shown in Listing 8–1. It can be found at the end of the applicationDidFinishLaunching method.

Listing 8–1. *Comment out the HelloWorld Scene*

```
//[[CCDirector sharedDirector] runWithScene: [HelloWorldLayer scene]];
```

Okay, make sure the application builds. You don't need it to run yet, but it should compile with no errors.

Camera View

Let's start by setting the camera view as our foundation layer, like we did in Chapter 7. Add the following frameworks to the project:

- CoreImage
- CoreMedia
- CoreVideo

Open AppDelegate.h in Xcode. Update the header as shown in Listing 8–2.

Listing 8–2. *New AppDelegate.h*

```
#import <UIKit/UIKit.h>
#import <AVFoundation/AVFoundation.h>

@class RootViewController;

@interface AppDelegate : NSObject <UIApplicationDelegate,
AVCaptureVideoDataOutputSampleBufferDelegate> {
    UIWindow *window;
    RootViewController *viewController;

    AVCaptureSession *_session;
    UIView *_cameraView;
    UIImageView *_imageView;
}

@property (nonatomic, retain) UIWindow *window;

@end
```

Much like we did in Chapter 7, we're setting up UIView and a UIImageView to process and display the camera view to the user. Switch over to AppDelegate.m. Add the methods from Listing 8–3 to the implementation.

Listing 8–3. *New Methods for AppDelegate.m*

```
-(AVCaptureDevice *)frontFacingCameraIfAvailable
{
    NSArray *videoDevices = [AVCaptureDevice devicesWithMediaType:AVMediaTypeVideo];
    AVCaptureDevice *captureDevice = nil;
    for (AVCaptureDevice *device in videoDevices)
    {
        if (device.position == AVCaptureDevicePositionFront)
        {
            captureDevice = device;
            break;
        }
    }

    //  couldn't find one on the front, so just get the default video device.
    if ( ! captureDevice)
    {
        captureDevice = [AVCaptureDevice defaultDeviceWithMediaType:AVMediaTypeVideo];
```

```
    }

    return captureDevice;
}

- (void)setupCaptureSession {
    NSError *error = nil;

    _session = [[AVCaptureSession alloc] init];
    _session.sessionPreset = AVCaptureSessionPresetMedium;

    //AVCaptureDevice *device = [AVCaptureDevice
defaultDeviceWithMediaType:AVMediaTypeVideo];
    AVCaptureDevice *device = [self frontFacingCameraIfAvailable]; // for debug
    AVCaptureDeviceInput *input = [AVCaptureDeviceInput deviceInputWithDevice:device
error:&error];

    if (!input) {
        NSLog(@"Some kind of error... handle it here");
    }

    [_session addInput:input];

    AVCaptureVideoDataOutput *output = [[AVCaptureVideoDataOutput alloc] init];
    [_session addOutput:output];

    dispatch_queue_t queue = dispatch_queue_create("pumpkins", NULL);
    [output setSampleBufferDelegate:self queue:queue];
    dispatch_release(queue);

    output.videoSettings =
    [NSDictionary dictionaryWithObject:
     [NSNumber numberWithInt:kCVPixelFormatType_32BGRA]
                              forKey:(id)kCVPixelBufferPixelFormatTypeKey];


    [_session startRunning];
}
```

The first method, frontFacingCameraIfAvailable, is only here for debugging purposes.
If you're not coding in a crowd, this will come in handy, so you use the front-facing
camera for testing. The lines shown in bold should swap if you're not debugging.
Meaning, either comment one or the other to force the use of a front-facing camera, if
available. Use only one of these at a time. Because I'm not coding in a crowd and
require my front-facing camera, I'll leave mine in that state.

Before we actually add the camera to the view, let's set up a menu screen using
chipmunk physics to amuse the user while they wait for the game to start.

Creating the Game Menu

Create new file using the cocos2D CCNode template, as shown in Figure 8–5.

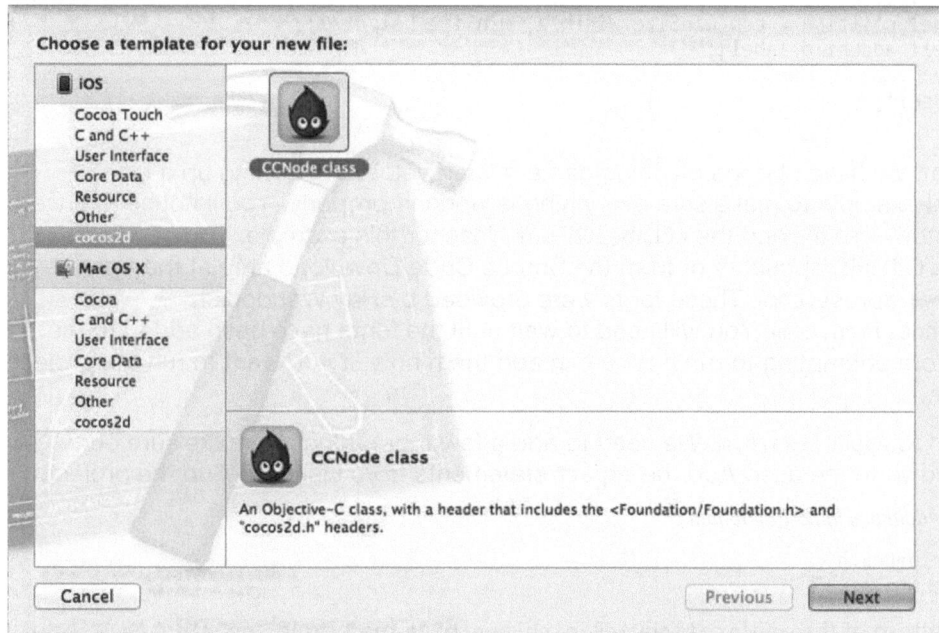

Figure 8–5. *Use the CCNode template.*

Make sure the file is a subclass of CCLayer and the name is MenuLayer.m. Open
MenuLayer.h in Xcode. Update the header to look like Listing 8–4.

Listing 8–4. *Update MenuLayer.h*

```
#import <Foundation/Foundation.h>
#import "cocos2d.h"

@interface MenuLayer : CCLayer {

}
+ (id)scene;
@end
```

Switch over to MenuLayer.m. Add the methods from Listing 8–5 to the implementation.

Listing 8–5. *Scene and init Method for MenuLayer.m*

```
+ (id)scene {
    CCScene *scene = [CCScene node];
    MenuLayer *layer = [MenuLayer node];
    [scene addChild:layer];
    return scene;
}
```

```
- (id)init {
    if ((self = [super init])) {
        CGSize winSize = [CCDirector sharedDirector].winSize;

        CCLabelBMFont *label = [CCLabelBMFont labelWithString:@"Hello, Chipmunk!"
fntFile:@"Arial.fnt"];
        label.position = ccp(winSize.width/2, winSize.height/2);
        [self addChild:label];
    }
    return self;
}
```

At this point, we haven't done anything game related yet. We're setting up a type of Hello World example to make sure everything is working properly. You'll notice that we used a custom font file and the CCLabelBMFont class for this example. You can find the code in the GitHub repository or from the Source Code/Download area at the Apress web site (www.apress.com). These fonts were provided by Ray Wenderlich (www.raywenderlich.com). You will need to wait until the fonts have been added to the project before attempting to run it. You can add them now, if you want to run the project as it stands.

Let's return to AppDelegate.m. We need to add a few more things to make sure our menu is shown to the user. Add the import statements from Listing 8–6 to the project.

Listing 8–6. *Additional import Statements*

```
#import "chipmunk.h"
#import "MenuLayer.h"
```

Find the bottom of the applicationDidFinishLaunching method in AppDelegate.m. Add the code from Listing 8–7.

Listing 8–7. *Add to the Bottom of applicationDidFinishLaunching*

```
cpInitChipmunk();
[[CCDirector sharedDirector] runWithScene: [MenuLayer scene]];
```

Go ahead and run the project on the iPad simulator. If everything was done correctly, you'll see something like Figure 8–6.

Figure 8–6. *Run the project to see "Hello, Chipmunk!"*

Okay, let's make this a bit more interesting. The idea with the menu layer is that we can give the user something to do while they are deciding whether to start a new game. Since this is a game about pumpkins, we're going to add a pumpkin to the screen that can be tossed around by touch interactions.

Artwork

For cocos2D gaming, it's best to use sprite sheets. Furthermore, it's even better if you can consolidate your images into a few sprite sheets that are optimized for space. Since this book is about augmented reality and not iOS gaming, I've created and optimized the sprite sheets for you already. They can be found in the Art directory on GitHub or from the Source Code/Download area at the Apress web site (www.apress.com). Copy the Art directory to your Xcode project before moving forward on the tutorial. You should have the following four new files:

- particleTexture.png
- PumpkinExplosion.plist
- Pumpkins.plist
- Pumpkins.png

The first two files are a particle emitter I created for this project. It will give the pumpkins the effect of an orangish dissolve when we destroy them. The second pair of files is the consolidated PNG files for the different pumpkins we'll be using. The full sprite sheet is shown in Figure 8–7.

Figure 8–7. *Use the pumpkin sprite sheet for our project.*

The pumpkins in this sprite sheet are named pumpkin#.png, where # is a number between 5 and 16. Pumpkins 1–4 had no faces, so we're just going to leave those out.

We're going to add one of these pumpkins to the menu screen and let the user throw him around a bit. Create a new file using any template. We're going to overwrite the whole thing anyway. Name the new class CPSprite.

Overwrite the header with the code from Listing 8–8.

Listing 8–8. *CPSprite.h*

```
#import "cocos2d.h"
#import "chipmunk.h"

typedef enum {
    kCollisionTypeGround = 0x1,
    kCollisionTypeCat,
    kCollisionTypeBed
} CollisionType;

@interface CPSprite : CCSprite {
    cpBody *body;
    cpShape *shape;
    cpSpace *space;
    BOOL canBeDestroyed;
}

@property (assign) cpBody *body;

- (void)update;
- (void)createBoxAtLocation:(CGPoint)location;
- (id)initWithSpace:(cpSpace *)theSpace location:(CGPoint)location
spriteFrameName:(NSString *)spriteFrameName;
- (void)destroy;

@end
```

We don't really have to worry too much about what this class is doing. We're basically setting up a wrapper for the CCSprite class, so we can more easily interact with the objects on our screen. In our case, this will help us make a pumpkin that we can toss around the screen.

Switch to CPSprite.m and replace the implementation with the code from Listing 8–9.

Listing 8–9. *CPSprite.m*

```
#import "CPSprite.h"

@implementation CPSprite
@synthesize body;

- (void)update {
    self.position = body->p;
    self.rotation = CC_RADIANS_TO_DEGREES(-1 * body->a);
}

- (void)createBoxAtLocation:(CGPoint)location {

    float mass = 1.0;
    body = cpBodyNew(mass, cpMomentForBox(mass, self.contentSize.width,
self.contentSize.height));
    body->p = location;
    body->data = self;
    cpSpaceAddBody(space, body);

    shape = cpBoxShapeNew(body, self.contentSize.width, self.contentSize.height);
    shape->e = 0.3;
    shape->u = 1.0;
    shape->data = self;
    shape->group = 1;
    cpSpaceAddShape(space, shape);

}

- (id)initWithSpace:(cpSpace *)theSpace location:(CGPoint)location
spriteFrameName:(NSString *)spriteFrameName {

    if ((self = [super initWithSpriteFrameName:spriteFrameName])) {

        space = theSpace;
        canBeDestroyed = YES;
        [self createBoxAtLocation:location];

    }
    return self;

}

- (void)destroy {

    if (!canBeDestroyed) return;

    cpSpaceRemoveBody(space, body);
    cpSpaceRemoveShape(space, shape);
```

```
        [self removeFromParentAndCleanup:YES];
}

@end
```

The implementation file sets up the properties we'll be using in our menu. For the most part, you don't have to worry too much about what is happening in this file. This file, and two others are included in the source code under the Helper Code directory. They are utility methods used to make the implementation files more easily read.

Helper Code Directory

There are four more files you need to copy from the source directory before we move forward. They are found in the Helper Code directory on GitHub or from the Source Code/Download area at the Apress web site (www.apress.com).

The files are:

- cpMouse.c
- cpMouse.h
- drawSpace.h
- drawSpace.c

Copy these files into your Xcode project. If you try to build the project, you'll get a compiler error. Click cpMouse.c in the Xcode navigator. On the right panel, open the **Identity and Type** view and set the **File Type** to **Objective-C source**, as shown in Figure 8–8.

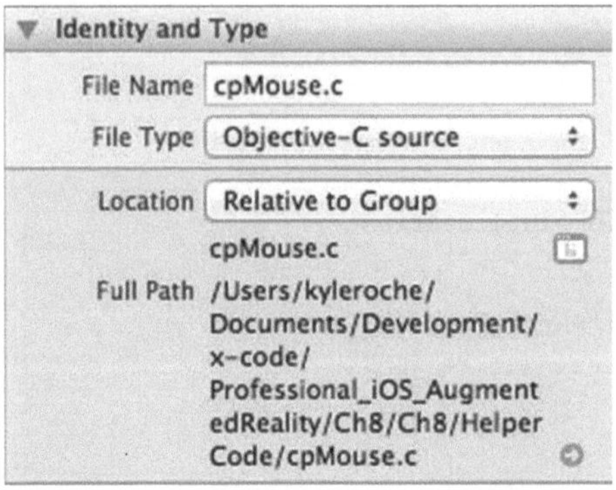

Figure 8–8. *Set the File Type of cpMouse.c.*

Repeat this process for drawSpace.c. Your project should build with no errors at this point.

Finishing the Menu Screen

Return to MenuLayer.h. Now that we have the helper classes in our project, things will be much smoother. Update the header as shown in Listing 8–10.

Listing 8–10. *Updated MenuLayer.h*

```
#import <Foundation/Foundation.h>
#import "cocos2d.h"
#import "chipmunk.h"

@interface MenuLayer : CCLayer {
    cpSpace *space;
    cpBody *ground;
}

+ (id)scene;

@end
```

After importing the chipmunk library, we declare two new private variables. First, we set up a cpSpace iVar for chipmunk. This defines the space where chipmunk will track physics actions. We then add a cpBody to the class. This will represent the bottom of our screen as sort of a floor. If we didn't have this, the pumpkin could fly off the screen in all directions. Having a ground also helps chipmunk understand gravity and friction a bit more easily.

Working with Chipmunk

Switch over to MenuLayer.m. Import the drawSpace.h header from our Helper Code class. Add the method from Listing 8–11 to the implementation.

Listing 8–11. *createSpace Method*

```
- (void)createSpace {
    space = cpSpaceNew();
    space->gravity = ccp(0, -750);
    cpSpaceResizeStaticHash(space, 400, 200);
    cpSpaceResizeActiveHash(space, 200, 200);
}
```

This method defines the space for chipmunk. We set the gravity to nothing along the X axis (no side-to-side gravity), and a fairly heavy pull for the Y axis. You can play with these values for your implementation to get the feel you are looking for. The second two lines are there to optimize chipmunk's collision detection. It divides chipmunk into grids and tells the framework to ignore objects that don't reside in the same grid. Add the method from Listing 8–12, just under the createSpace method.

Listing 8–12. *createGround Method*

```
- (void)createGround {

    CGSize winSize = [CCDirector sharedDirector].winSize;
    CGPoint lowerLeft = ccp(0, 0);
    CGPoint lowerRight = ccp(winSize.width, 0);

    ground = cpBodyNewStatic();

    float radius = 10.0;
    cpShape *groundShape = cpSegmentShapeNew(ground, lowerLeft, lowerRight, radius);
```

```
    groundShape->e = 0.5; // elasticity
    groundShape->u = 1.0; // friction

    cpSpaceAddShape(space, groundShape);
}
```

As I mentioned earlier, we're creating a ground effect so the pumpkin doesn't totally fall off the screen. We are setting up friction and elasticity, as well. If you want to have some fun with the pumpkin, you can set elasticity low and friction to 0 and get an ice-like effect. Or, you can increase elasticity and friction to get more of a trampoline effect.

Creating Objects in Chipmunk

Add the methods from Listing 8–13 to the implementation.

Listing 8–13. *createBoxAtLocation and draw (Override) Methods*

```
- (void)createBoxAtLocation:(CGPoint)location {

    float boxSize = 60.0;
    float mass = 1.0;
    cpBody *body = cpBodyNew(mass, cpMomentForBox(mass, boxSize, boxSize));
    body->p = location;
    cpSpaceAddBody(space, body);

    cpShape *shape = cpBoxShapeNew(body, boxSize, boxSize);
    shape->e = 1.0;
    shape->u = 1.0;
    cpSpaceAddShape(space, shape);

}

- (void)draw {

    drawSpaceOptions options = {
        0, // drawHash
        0, // drawBBs,
        1, // drawShapes
        4.0, // collisionPointSize
        4.0, // bodyPointSize,
        2.0 // lineThickness
    };

    drawSpace(space, &options);

}
```

The first method will be used only this once. We are going to create a few boxes and drop them on the screen to make sure chipmunk is behaving correctly. The second method enables debug draw for chipmunk. Without this, it's hard to tell what exactly you are rendering to the screen. This method will come in handy if you continue in game development. Update the init method and add a new method called update, as shown in Listing 8–14.

Listing 8–14. *New init Method and update Method*

```
- (id)init {
    if ((self = [super init])) {
        CGSize winSize = [CCDirector sharedDirector].winSize;

        [self createSpace];
        [self createGround];
        [self createBoxAtLocation:ccp(100,100)];
        [self createBoxAtLocation:ccp(200,200)];

        [self scheduleUpdate];
    }
    return self;
}

- (void)update:(ccTime)dt {
    cpSpaceStep(space, dt);
}
```

All right, things are getting more interesting. With this new, code we're setting up the chipmunk space, ground body, and creating two boxes at various coordinates. The update method steps through the changes in the chipmunk space since the last iteration. Chipmunk handles all the updates to objects in its space for you. Go ahead and run the project using the simulator to see what I mean. You should see something similar to Figure 8–9.

Figure 8–9. *Run the project to see the boxes on the screen.*

Again, not too exciting is it? Let's add what's called a *mouse joint*, so we can grab and throw the boxes. Joints are a type of constraint in chipmunk. We'll be using two types of joints in this example. We'll use the mouse joint to enable the user to grab the box, and we'll use the `cpDampedSprint` joint to make the pumpkin bounce as we toss it around.

Switch over to `MenuLayer.h` and import the `cpMouse.h` header from our Helper Code directory. Then declare a private iVar of the `cpMouse` class called `mouse`.

Add the following lines from Listing 8–15 to the `init` method, just before you run the `scheduleUpdates` method.

Listing 8–15. *Add to init Method*

```
mouse = cpMouseNew(space);
self.isTouchEnabled = YES;
```

The first line sets the new `mouse` iVar to handle mouse events in our chipmunk space. The second line enables touch events for our class.

Enabling touch events is one thing; handling them is a bit more complicated. There are two basic approaches to handling touch events in cocos2D. For this example, we're requiring only single-touch events (as opposed to multitouch events). Oddly enough, these require more code than multitouch handling. Add the code from Listing 8–16 to the implementation.

Listing 8–16. *Handle the Touch Events*

```
- (void)registerWithTouchDispatcher {
    [[CCTouchDispatcher sharedDispatcher] addTargetedDelegate:self priority:0
swallowsTouches:YES];
}

- (BOOL)ccTouchBegan:(UITouch *)touch withEvent:(UIEvent *)event {
    CGPoint touchLocation = [self convertTouchToNodeSpace:touch];
    cpMouseGrab(mouse, touchLocation, false);
    return YES;
}

- (void)ccTouchMoved:(UITouch *)touch withEvent:(UIEvent *)event {
    CGPoint touchLocation = [self convertTouchToNodeSpace:touch];
    cpMouseMove(mouse, touchLocation);
}

- (void)ccTouchEnded:(UITouch *)touch withEvent:(UIEvent *)event {
    cpMouseRelease(mouse);
}

- (void)ccTouchCancelled:(UITouch *)touch withEvent:(UIEvent *)event {
    cpMouseRelease(mouse);
}

- (void)dealloc {
    cpMouseFree(mouse);
    cpSpaceFree(space);
    [super dealloc];
}
```

This series of events lets chipmunk know that the user wants to grab any objects that collide with the touch coordinates. Chipmunk will update the position of the object until the user lets go of the touch event. At that time, gravity, friction, and any other chipmunk environmental variables will come into play and the object will settle back to a natural path. Run the project again on the simulator. You'll be able to toss the objects around the screen now. Be careful, though—you can actually toss them off the screen and you won't be able to get them back!

So, boxes on the screen weren't exactly part of our goal, were they? To make these boxes into pumpkins, we need to tie a sprite image to the box and make sure it follows it as chipmunk updates the position of the shape. And, because it's not all that useful as it stands, since the user can throw the pumpkin completely off the screen, we're going to add a groove joint to the screen for the pumpkin. Think of a groove joint like a flagpole or fixed track. The object that is tied to the joint can move along the path, but can't veer away from the pole/track.

Return to MenuLayer.h in Xcode. Update the header as shown in Listing 8–17.

Listing 8–17. *Updated MenuLayer.h*

```
#import <Foundation/Foundation.h>
#import "cocos2d.h"
#import "chipmunk.h"
#import "cpMouse.h"
#import "CPSprite.h"

@interface MenuLayer : CCLayer {
    cpSpace *space;
    cpBody *ground;
    cpMouse *mouse;

    CCSpriteBatchNode *pumpkinBatchNode;
    CPSprite *menuPumpkin1;
}

+ (id)scene;

@end
```

First, we import the CPSprite class we created earlier. This will help us easily add a pumpkin to the screen. Next, we declare a private CCSpriteBatchNode variable, as well as a CCSprite variable.

> **NOTE:** When developing games with cocos2D, it's best to use CCSpriteBatchNodes and sprite sheets to save on memory. We'll need all the memory we can get, because we'll have such a high processing requirement for facial recognition.

Creating a Spring Joint in Chipmunk

Switch over to `MenuLayer.m` and update the init method, as shown in Listing 8–18.

Listing 8–18. *Updated init Method*

```
- (id)init {
    if ((self = [super init])) {
        CGSize winSize = [CCDirector sharedDirector].winSize;

        [self createSpace];
        [self createGround];
        //[self createBoxAtLocation:ccp(100,100)];
        //[self createBoxAtLocation:ccp(200,200)];

        [self scheduleUpdate];

        mouse = cpMouseNew(space);
        self.isTouchEnabled = YES;

        [[CCSpriteFrameCache sharedSpriteFrameCache]
addSpriteFramesWithFile:@"pumpkins.plist"];
        pumpkinBatchNode = [CCSpriteBatchNode batchNodeWithFile:@"pumpkins.png"];
        [self addChild:pumpkinBatchNode];

        menuPumpkin1 = [[[CPSprite alloc] initWithSpace:space location:ccp(347, 328)
spriteFrameName:@"pumpkin15.png"] autorelease];
        [pumpkinBatchNode addChild:menuPumpkin1];

        cpConstraint *pumpkin1 = cpDampedSpringNew(menuPumpkin1.body, ground, ccp(-
100,100), ccp(250,700), 100, 5, 1);
        cpSpaceAddConstraint(space, pumpkin1);

    }
    return self;
}
```

First, we create a `CCSpriteFrameCache` with our shared sprite sheet. We are using the PLIST file I created for you, so the `CCSpriteFrameCache` knows about the contents of our sprite sheet. We'll use this again later in our action layer. Next, we set our batch node to the contents of our pumpkin PNG file.

The next two statements are a bit more interesting. We set the `CPSprite menuPumpkin1` to a new instance of `CCSprite` with a location and a default pumpkin image.

Finally, we set up a new `cpDampedSpring` constraint, using the `cpDampedSpringNew` macro, as we discussed earlier. You can play with the values I've set here, if you want. They will increase/decrease the intensity of the spring, as well as its offset. Remember, we have debug drawing enabled, so you'll be able to see the spring in action.

> **NOTE:** If you are not able to test this on an iPad, the x,y coordinates in Listing 8–18 need to be adjusted for the screen size of an iPhone. Cutting them all in half should do the trick.

Change the update method to reflect the changes in Listing 8–19.

Listing 8–19. *Updated update Method*

```
- (void)update:(ccTime)dt {
    cpSpaceStep(space, dt);
    for (CPSprite *sprite in pumpkinBatchNode.children) {
        [sprite update];
    }
}
```

This is a very small amount of code, but it has a huge impact. Try running the project with and without the code we just added. With our new code, we'll see something like Figure 8–10 when we load our game menu.

Figure 8–10. *Run the code with the updated update method to display the correct game menu.*

Notice the spring join and the box around the pumpkin. The sprite keeps up with the container when pulled by the mouse or thrown around the screen. Now, if you leave out that update block we just added, you'd get something like Figure 8–11.

As you can see, our containers are still working as expected. However, the sprite has fallen off the screen. The first thing you should take away from this exercise is that debug draw is a lifesaver. It would be a very daunting task to try to figure out exactly why that pumpkin was off the screen if we didn't have debug draw enabled. The second thing you should take away is that you must always update your scene when any changes occur. Trust chipmunk or cocos2D to take care of the details, but make sure you respect the updates.

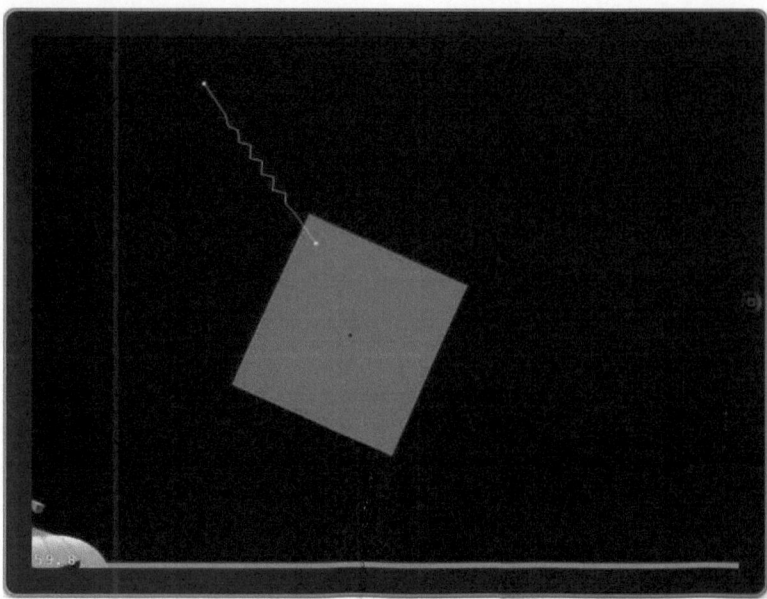

Figure 8–11. *Without the sprite update code, you will see this on the screen.*

Adding the Menu Option

This will be a basic game, but we'll still need a start game option. Before we add that to the MenuLayer, let's create a basic class so we'll know if it's working when we start the game.

Create a new file using the CCNode template again. This time call the class ActionLayer. Make sure it is a subclass of CCLayer. Open ActionLayer.h in Xcode and update it, as shown in Listing 8–20.

Listing 8–20. *Updated ActionLayer.h*

```
#import <Foundation/Foundation.h>
#import "cocos2d.h"

@interface ActionLayer : CCLayer {

}

+(CCScene *) scene;

@end
```

Just like our MenuLayer class, we're declaring the static CCScene method. This is common to cocos2D scene classes. It's what the CCDirector uses to display a new scene.

Switch over to ActionLayer.m and update the implementation, as shown in Listing 8–21.

Listing 8–21. *Updated ActionLayer.m*

```objc
#import "ActionLayer.h"

@implementation ActionLayer

+(CCScene *) scene
{
    // 'scene' is an autorelease object.
    CCScene *scene = [CCScene node];

    // 'layer' is an autorelease object.
    ActionLayer *layer = [ActionLayer node];

    // add layer as a child to scene
    [scene addChild: layer];
    // return the scene
    return scene;
}

- (id)init {
    if ((self = [super init])) {
        CGSize winSize = [CCDirector sharedDirector].winSize;

        CCLabelBMFont *label = [CCLabelBMFont labelWithString:@"Game on pumpkins!"
fntFile:@"Arial.fnt"];
        label.position = ccp(winSize.width/2, winSize.height/2);
        [self addChild:label];
    }
    return self;
}

@end
```

We'll replace most of this code later. For now, it will display a label with a little message to the pumpkins to let us know that things are in place to start loading up our game scene.

Return to MenuLayer.m. Import the new ActionLayer.h class. Find the code where we added the spring constraint to the screen. Just under that code, add the code from Listing 8–22.

Listing 8–22. *Add to the Bottom of the init Method, After the Spring Constraint*

```objc
CCLabelBMFont *newGame;
        if (UI_USER_INTERFACE_IDIOM() == UIUserInterfaceIdiomPad) {
            newGame = [CCLabelBMFont labelWithString:@"New Game" fntFile:@"Arial-
hd.fnt"];
        } else {
            newGame = [CCLabelBMFont labelWithString:@"New Game" fntFile:@"Arial.fnt"];
        }

        CCMenuItemLabel *newGameItem = [CCMenuItemLabel itemWithLabel:newGame
target:self selector:@selector(newGameTapped:)];
        newGameItem.position = ccp(winSize.width * 0.8, winSize.height * 0.3);

        CCMenu *menu = [CCMenu menuWithItems:newGameItem, nil];
        menu.position = CGPointZero;
```

```
[self addChild:menu];
```

This code block creates a cocos2D menu for the user. We're loading a font depending on the device type, then presenting the user with a single option, which is to start a new game. If the new game label is clicked, we'll fire the selector newGameTapped. This is a method we haven't yet created. Let's do that now. Add the method from Listing 8–23 to the implementation.

Listing 8–23. *newGameTapped Method*

```
- (void)newGameTapped:(id)sender {
    [[CCDirector sharedDirector] replaceScene:[CCTransitionRadialCCW
transitionWithDuration:1.0 scene:[ActionLayer node]]];
}
```

When the user taps the new game option, we're going to use a cocos2D transition to present the game in a fashionable manner. Run the project using the iPad simulator. On launch, you'll see a new menu, as shown in Figure 8–12.

Figure 8–12. *Run the project to see the new game menu.*

If you click New Game, you'll see a quick effect that enlarges the text and then there will be a screen transition to the ActionLayer as shown in Figure 8–13.

Figure 8–13. *Click New Game to transition the screen and call out the pumpkins.*

So, things are mostly in place to add the gaming logic. Let's return to the `AppDelegate` class and enable the camera support we added earlier. From this point forward, you'll have to use a physical device and not the simulator to test the project.

Enable Camera Support

Let's finish what we started for camera support and display the camera's view instead of the black background we have currently showing. Open `AppDelegate.h` in Xcode and update `AppDelegate.h`, as shown in Listing 8–24.

Listing 8–24. *Updated AppDelegate.h*

```
#import <UIKit/UIKit.h>
#import <AVFoundation/AVFoundation.h>
#import "ActionLayer.h"

@class RootViewController;

@interface AppDelegate : NSObject <UIApplicationDelegate,
AVCaptureVideoDataOutputSampleBufferDelegate> {
    UIWindow *window;
    RootViewController *viewController;

    AVCaptureSession *_session;
    UIView *_cameraView;
    UIImageView *_imageView;
    BOOL _settingImage;
}
```

```
@property (nonatomic, retain) UIWindow *window;
@property (nonatomic) BOOL isPlaying;
@property (nonatomic, retain) ActionLayer *actionLayer;
```

@end

After we import the ActionLayer.h header, we declare two new properties. First, we have a Boolean property to keep track of whether the user is playing the game. Second, we're keeping a reference to the ActionLayer for our game. This will be used to make sure that our facial recognition requests go to the active game layer only. If you were to release this game on the App Store, it might be a good idea to refactor this to another singleton class to manage state. For this purpose, we'll be fine with the approach we're taking.

Finally, we add a Boolean value to keep track of whether we are setting the image view using the camera buffer.

Switch over to AppDelegate.m. Find the declaration for EAGLView in the applicationDidFinishLaunching method. Update it as shown in Listing 8–25.

Listing 8–25. *Change the pixelFormat of the OpenGL ES View*

```
EAGLView *glView = [EAGLView viewWithFrame:[window bounds]
    pixelFormat:kEAGLColorFormatRGBA8
    depthFormat:0];
```

This should be familiar from Chapter 7. Find the line of code that calls the makeKeyAndVisible function of the window instance. Add the code from Listing 8–26, just above that function call.

Listing 8–26. *Set the Background to a Transparent View for the Camera*

```
[CCDirector sharedDirector].openGLView.backgroundColor = [UIColor clearColor];
    [CCDirector sharedDirector].openGLView.opaque = NO;

    glClearColor(0.0, 0.0, 0.0, 0.0);
    _cameraView = [[UIView alloc] initWithFrame:[[UIScreen mainScreen] bounds]];
    _cameraView.opaque = NO;
    _cameraView.backgroundColor = [UIColor clearColor];

    [window addSubview:_cameraView];

    _imageView = [[UIImageView alloc] initWithFrame:[[UIScreen mainScreen] bounds]];
    [_cameraView addSubview:_imageView];
    [window bringSubviewToFront:viewController.view];
```

Again, this code isn't new to us. We learned this method in Chapter 7. It is important to note that iOS 5 introduced a new approach to building augmented reality applications. You can essentially set the background of the OpenGL ES view to a texture showing the camera's view. However, because cocos2D is built on OpenGL, there are some version conflicts that still aren't worked out completely. This is the best approach at the time of this writing.

Before we move on to image processing, there are a few housekeeping items we've left undone. Make sure you synthesize the isPlaying property. Then, add the following code from Listing 8–27, just after you initialize the chipmunk library in the applicationDidFinishLaunching method.

Listing 8–27. *Initial Setup*

```
cpInitChipmunk(); // should exist
 [[CCDirector sharedDirector] runWithScene: [MenuLayer scene]]; // should exist
isPlaying = NO;
 [self setupCaptureSession];
```

Our AppDelegate class is already nominated as a class that implements the AVCaptureVideoDataOutputSampleBufferDelegate protocol. We haven't yet implemented any of the delegate methods. Let's add those to the AppDelegate implementation now. Add the code from Listing 8–28.

Listing 8–28. *Image-Handling Methods*

```
- (UIImage *) imageFromSampleBuffer:(CMSampleBufferRef) sampleBuffer
{
    // Get a CMSampleBuffer's Core Video image buffer for the media data
    CVImageBufferRef imageBuffer = CMSampleBufferGetImageBuffer(sampleBuffer);
    // Lock the base address of the pixel buffer
    CVPixelBufferLockBaseAddress(imageBuffer, 0);

    // Get the number of bytes per row for the pixel buffer
    void *baseAddress = CVPixelBufferGetBaseAddress(imageBuffer);

    // Get the number of bytes per row for the pixel buffer
    size_t bytesPerRow = CVPixelBufferGetBytesPerRow(imageBuffer);
    // Get the pixel buffer width and height
    size_t width = CVPixelBufferGetWidth(imageBuffer);
    size_t height = CVPixelBufferGetHeight(imageBuffer);

    // Create a device-dependent RGB color space
    CGColorSpaceRef colorSpace = CGColorSpaceCreateDeviceRGB();

    // Create a bitmap graphics context with the sample buffer data
    CGContextRef context = CGBitmapContextCreate(baseAddress, width, height, 8,
                                        bytesPerRow, colorSpace,
kCGBitmapByteOrder32Little | kCGImageAlphaPremultipliedFirst);
    // Create a Quartz image from the pixel data in the bitmap graphics context
    CGImageRef quartzImage = CGBitmapContextCreateImage(context);
    // Unlock the pixel buffer
    CVPixelBufferUnlockBaseAddress(imageBuffer,0);

    // Free up the context and color space
    CGContextRelease(context);
    CGColorSpaceRelease(colorSpace);

    // Create an image object from the Quartz image
    UIImage *image = [UIImage imageWithCGImage:quartzImage];

    // Release the Quartz image
    CGImageRelease(quartzImage);

    return (image);
}
```

```objc
- (void)captureOutput:(AVCaptureOutput *)captureOutput
didOutputSampleBuffer:(CMSampleBufferRef)sampleBuffer
fromConnection:(AVCaptureConnection *)connection
{
    UIImage *image = [self imageFromSampleBuffer:sampleBuffer];

    if(_settingImage == NO){
        _settingImage = YES;
        [NSThread detachNewThreadSelector:@selector(setImageToView:) toTarget:self
withObject:image];
    }
}

-(void)setImageToView:(UIImage*)image {
    //UIImage * capturedImage = [self rotateImage:image
orientation:UIImageOrientationRight ];
    UIImage * capturedImage = [self rotateImage:image
orientation:UIImageOrientationLeftMirrored ];
    _imageView.image = capturedImage;
    _settingImage = NO;

    if (isPlaying) {
        //NSLog(@"Playing. Send to Pumpkin layer");
        if (!actionLayer.isProcessingRequest) {
            UIImage * image = [_imageView.image retain];
            if(image!=nil){
                UIInterfaceOrientation orient =  [UIApplication
sharedApplication].statusBarOrientation;
                UIImage * rotatedImage = image;
                switch (orient) {
                    case UIInterfaceOrientationPortrait:
                        NSLog(@"Device orientation portrait");
                        rotatedImage = [self rotateImage:image orientation:
UIImageOrientationRight];
                        break;
                    case UIInterfaceOrientationPortraitUpsideDown:
                        rotatedImage = [self rotateImage:image orientation:
UIImageOrientationLeft];
                        NSLog(@"Device orientation portrait upside down");
                        break;
                    case UIInterfaceOrientationLandscapeLeft:
                        rotatedImage = [self rotateImage:image orientation:
UIImageOrientationRight];
                        NSLog(@"Device orientation landscape left");
                        break;
                    case UIInterfaceOrientationLandscapeRight:
                        rotatedImage = [self rotateImage:image orientation:
UIImageOrientationLeft];
                        NSLog(@"Device orientation landscape right");
                        break;
                };
                [actionLayer facialRecognitionRequest:rotatedImage];
            }
        }
    }
}
```

```objc
- (UIImage *) rotateImage:(UIImage*)image orientation:(UIImageOrientation) orient {
    CGImageRef imgRef = image.CGImage;
    CGAffineTransform transform = CGAffineTransformIdentity;
    //UIImageOrientation orient = image.imageOrientation;
    CGFloat scaleRatio = 1;
    CGFloat width = image.size.width;
    CGFloat height = image.size.height;
    CGSize imageSize = image.size;
    CGRect bounds = CGRectMake(0, 0, width, height);
    CGFloat boundHeight;

    switch(orient) {
        case UIImageOrientationUp:
            transform = CGAffineTransformIdentity;
            break;
        case UIImageOrientationUpMirrored:
            transform = CGAffineTransformMakeTranslation(imageSize.width, 0.0);
            transform = CGAffineTransformScale(transform, -1.0, 1.0);
            break;
        case UIImageOrientationDown:
            transform = CGAffineTransformMakeTranslation(imageSize.width,
imageSize.height);
            transform = CGAffineTransformRotate(transform, M_PI);
            break;
        case UIImageOrientationDownMirrored:
            transform = CGAffineTransformMakeTranslation(0.0, imageSize.height);
            transform = CGAffineTransformScale(transform, 1.0, -1.0);
            break;
        case UIImageOrientationLeftMirrored:
            boundHeight = bounds.size.height;
            bounds.size.height = bounds.size.width;
            bounds.size.width = boundHeight;
            transform = CGAffineTransformMakeTranslation(imageSize.height,
imageSize.height);
            transform = CGAffineTransformScale(transform, -1.0, 1.0);
            transform = CGAffineTransformRotate(transform, 3.0 * M_PI / 2.0);
            break;
        case UIImageOrientationLeft:
            boundHeight = bounds.size.height;
            bounds.size.height = bounds.size.width;
            bounds.size.width = boundHeight;
            transform = CGAffineTransformMakeTranslation(0.0, imageSize.width);
            transform = CGAffineTransformRotate(transform, 3.0 * M_PI / 2.0);
            break;
        case UIImageOrientationRightMirrored:
            boundHeight = bounds.size.height;
            bounds.size.height = bounds.size.width;
            bounds.size.width = boundHeight;
            transform = CGAffineTransformMakeScale(-1.0, 1.0);
            transform = CGAffineTransformRotate(transform, M_PI / 2.0);
            break;
        case UIImageOrientationRight:
            boundHeight = bounds.size.height;
            bounds.size.height = bounds.size.width;
            bounds.size.width = boundHeight;
            transform = CGAffineTransformMakeTranslation(imageSize.height, 0.0);
            transform = CGAffineTransformRotate(transform, M_PI / 2.0);
```

```
            break;
        default:
            [NSException raise:NSInternalInconsistencyException format:@"Invalid image
orientation"];
    }
    UIGraphicsBeginImageContext(bounds.size);
    CGContextRef context = UIGraphicsGetCurrentContext();
    if (orient == UIImageOrientationRight || orient == UIImageOrientationLeft) {
        CGContextScaleCTM(context, -scaleRatio, scaleRatio);
        CGContextTranslateCTM(context, -height, 0);
    } else {
        CGContextScaleCTM(context, scaleRatio, -scaleRatio);
        CGContextTranslateCTM(context, 0, -height);
    }
    CGContextConcatCTM(context, transform);
    CGContextDrawImage(UIGraphicsGetCurrentContext(), CGRectMake(0, 0, width, height),
imgRef);
    UIImage *imageCopy = UIGraphicsGetImageFromCurrentImageContext();
    UIGraphicsEndImageContext();

    return imageCopy;
}
```

That was our largest code block for a single addition. Most of it is code we saw back in Chapter 7. However, there is a difference in how we are handling setting the image to the screen view. When we set the image to the screen, we are also checking to see whether the action layer is busy before we send it a new image request. We haven't implemented this functionality in our action layer yet. That will be next.

Update the Private method declarations in AppDelegate.m, as shown in Listing 8–29.

Listing 8–29. *Updated Private Method Declaration*

```
@interface AppDelegate (Private)
- (void)setupCaptureSession;
- (UIImage *) rotateImage:(UIImage*)image orientation:(UIImageOrientation) orient;
@end
```

There should be two compiler errors in your AppDelegate class. They are caused by the missing property and method in the action layer. Switch over to ActionLayer.h and add the code from Listing 8–30 to the header.

Listing 8–30. *Add to ActionLayer.h*

```
@property (nonatomic) BOOL isProcessingRequest;
- (void)facialRecognitionRequest:(UIImage *)image;
```

These are the two missing elements from our AppDelegate. Switch over to ActionLayer.m. Import AppDelegate.h and synthesize the isProcessingRequest Boolean. Update the init method as shown in Listing 8–31.

Listing 8–31. *Updated init Method*

```
- (id)init {
    if ((self = [super init])) {
        isProcessingRequest = NO;
        [AppDelegate instance].actionLayer = self;
        [AppDelegate instance].isPlaying = YES;
```

```
    }
    return self;
}
```

We removed the code that created the message to the pumpkins, and added a few default variables. You'll notice this new instance method from our `AppDelegate` class shows a warning. We haven't yet implemented that static method, so disregard that for now. If you tried to compile, you would also get an error due to the missing static instance method, which we'll implement in a moment. Implement the `facialRecognitionRequest` method, as shown in Listing 8–32.

Listing 8–32. *facialRecognitionRequest Method*

```
- (void)facialRecognitionRequest:(UIImage *)image {
    NSLog(@"Image is: %f by %f", image.size.width, image.size.height);
}
```

For now, we're just going to log the event with some details to make sure we're receiving a proper image. Open `AppDelegate.h` in Xcode and declare the static method shown in Listing 8–33.

Listing 8–33. *Static instance Method for AppDelegate.h*

```
+ (AppDelegate *)instance;
```

This method is inconsequential to the goal of this project. It's more of a habit with my implementations. It provides a simple way to get the singleton representation of the `AppDelegate` without too much effort. Switch over to `AppDelegate.m` and add the method from Listing 8–34.

Listing 8–34. *Static instance Method for AppDelegate.m*

```
+ (AppDelegate *)instance {
    return (AppDelegate *)[[UIApplication sharedApplication] delegate];
}
```

While you're in the `AppDelegate.m` file, make sure you've synthesized the `actionLayer` property we set up earlier. Go ahead and run the project on a physical device (preferably an iPad 2). You will see a welcome menu, as shown in Figure 8–14.

Figure 8–14. *Run the project again to see the game menu with camera background.*

If you click the New Game menu, you can watch your debug console for updates. You should see tons of messages coming through, as illustrated in Figure 8–15.

```
▼   II   ⟳   ↧   ↥  | No Selection

All Output ⬍
2011-10-23 23:58:23.529 Ch8[5416:5c7b] Image is: 480.000000 by 360.000000
2011-10-23 23:58:23.547 Ch8[5416:1b5b] Device orientation landscape right
2011-10-23 23:58:23.549 Ch8[5416:1b5b] Image is: 480.000000 by 360.000000
2011-10-23 23:58:23.578 Ch8[5416:1b5f] Device orientation landscape right
2011-10-23 23:58:23.580 Ch8[5416:1b5f] Image is: 480.000000 by 360.000000
2011-10-23 23:58:23.627 Ch8[5416:1b67] Device orientation landscape right
2011-10-23 23:58:23.629 Ch8[5416:1b67] Image is: 480.000000 by 360.000000
2011-10-23 23:58:23.648 Ch8[5416:5c87] Device orientation landscape right
2011-10-23 23:58:23.650 Ch8[5416:5c87] Image is: 480.000000 by 360.000000
2011-10-23 23:58:23.678 Ch8[5416:5c8b] Device orientation landscape right
2011-10-23 23:58:23.679 Ch8[5416:5c8b] Image is: 480.000000 by 360.000000
2011-10-23 23:58:23.727 Ch8[5416:5c93] Device orientation landscape right
2011-10-23 23:58:23.728 Ch8[5416:5c93] Image is: 480.000000 by 360.000000
2011-10-23 23:58:23.748 Ch8[5416:1b73] Device orientation landscape right
2011-10-23 23:58:23.749 Ch8[5416:1b73] Image is: 480.000000 by 360.000000
```

Figure 8–15. *Watch the screen buffer logging messages.*

You can see that our call to the action layer is happening frequently. In fact, this would be a good area for improvement. Slowing down the processes that make it to the action layer could help our game perform more optimally.

Finishing the Action Layer

Let's think about what else we might need to make this game have some structure. We are missing the pumpkins, obviously. But, otherwise, we should implement some sort of counter to keep track of how many alien pumpkins have been eliminated. There are 12 different pumpkin images in our sprite sheet. Let's set this as a countdown-type game in which the user has to eliminate each of the 12 pumpkins before the game is over.

First, let's tackle the facial recognition problem. We're going to use a class that is new to iOS 5 called CIDetector. We'll discuss this in more detail in Chapter 12. In ActionLayer.h, add the property from Listing 8–35.

Listing 8–35. *CIDetector Property*

```
@property (nonatomic, retain) CIDetector *detector;
```

Open ActionLayer.m and synthesize the property. Inside the if block in the init method, add the code from Listing 8–36.

Listing 8–36. *Set Up the CIDetector*

```
NSDictionary *detectorOptions = [NSDictionary
dictionaryWithObjectsAndKeys:CIDetectorAccuracyLow, CIDetectorAccuracy, nil];
        self.detector = [CIDetector detectorOfType:CIDetectorTypeFace context:nil
options:detectorOptions];
```

As I mentioned, we'll discuss this class in more detail in Chapter 12. For now, you need to know that the CIDetector tracks the x,y coordinates of faces it recognizes in images. In our case, we'll be using it to track faces in the camera view. Update the facialRecognitionRequest method, as shown in Listing 8–37.

Listing 8–37. *Updated facialRecognitionRequest Method*

```
- (void)facialRecognitionRequest:(UIImage *)image {
    if (!isProcessingRequest) {
        isProcessingRequest = YES;
        NSArray *arr = [detector featuresInImage:[CIImage imageWithCGImage:[image
CGImage]]];

        if ([arr count] > 0) {
            NSLog(@"Faces found.");
        } else {
            NSLog(@"No faces found");
        }
    }
    isProcessingRequest = NO;
}
```

I know I said we'd talk about this later, but the small amount of code required to process an image for facial recognition is pretty impressive. The line in bold is really all it takes. If we find a face in the camera view, we log to the console. The same thing happens if we don't find a face.

Go ahead and run the application again on a physical device. You should see console output similar to Figure 8–16.

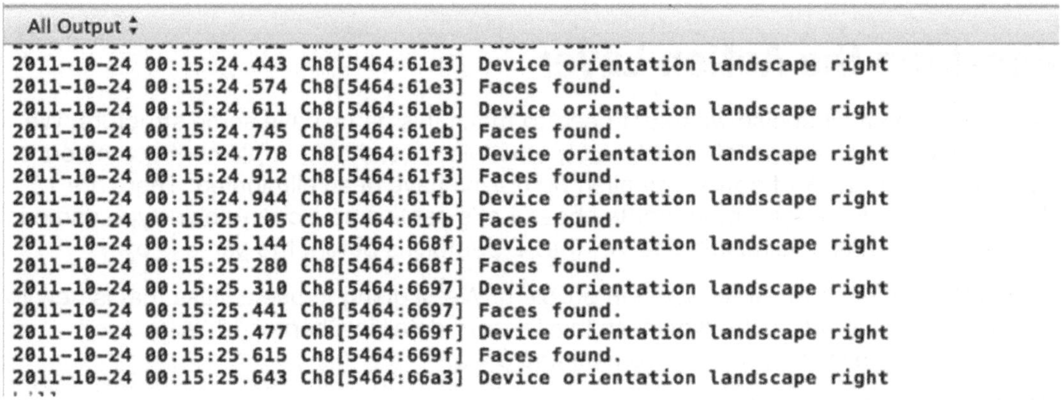

Figure 8–16. *View the screen buffer logging messages, and notice the "Faces found" messages.*

It looks like things are working. Let's add the logic to display the pumpkins on the target's face.

Here Come the Pumpkins

We're going to allow for only one alien pumpkin to be present at any given time. Basically, the first face we find is the unlucky victim of a pumpkin takeover.

To manage this, we're going to add a pumpkin to the screen and make him invisible. When we detect a face, we'll move the pumpkin to the coordinates of the face and we'll set the pumpkin back to opaque so he shows up in our camera view.

Open `ActionLayer.h`. Declare the private variables shown in Listing 8–38.

Listing 8–38. *New private Variables*

```
CCSpriteBatchNode *pumpkinBatchNode;
CCSprite *pumpkin;
int pumpkin_count;
```

These variables will be used to set up our initial pumpkin image. Like before, we'll be using a `CCSpriteBatchNode` to hold our images. The `pumpkin_count` integer will be used to track backward from 12, so we know how many alien pumpkins are left to destroy. Switch over to `ActionLayer.m`. Update the init method as shown in Listing 8–39.

Listing 8–39. *New init Method*

```
- (id)init {
    if (self = [super init]) {
        //CGSize winSize = [CCDirector sharedDirector].winSize;

        NSDictionary *detectorOptions = [NSDictionary
dictionaryWithObjectsAndKeys:CIDetectorAccuracyLow, CIDetectorAccuracy, nil];
        self.detector = [CIDetector detectorOfType:CIDetectorTypeFace context:nil
options:detectorOptions];
```

```
pumpkinBatchNode = [CCSpriteBatchNode batchNodeWithFile:@"pumpkins.png"];
[self addChild:pumpkinBatchNode];

pumpkin = [CCSprite spriteWithSpriteFrameName:@"pumpkin5.png"];
pumpkin.position = ccp(0,0);
pumpkin.opacity = 0;
[self addChild:pumpkin];

// Start the game
isProcessingRequest = NO;
pumpkin_count = 12;
[AppDelegate instance].actionLayer = self;
[AppDelegate instance].isPlaying = YES;

self.isTouchEnabled = YES;
    }
    return self;
}
```

Here, we set up our CCSpriteBatchNode with the same sprite sheet we used earlier. Then we initialize the pumpkin variable as a new CCSprite using the pumpkin5.png frame from our sprite sheet. We then set it to transparent and add it to the scene.

Make sure your project is still building without errors. There's nothing new to see yet, so it's no use running it on a device. Update the facialRecognitionRequest method, as shown in Listing 8–40.

Listing 8–40. *New facialRecognitionRequest Method*

```
- (void)facialRecognitionRequest:(UIImage *)image {
    //NSLog(@"Image is: %f by %f", image.size.width, image.size.height);

    if (!isProcessingRequest) {
        isProcessingRequest = YES;
        //NSLog(@"Detecting Faces");
        NSArray *arr = [detector featuresInImage:[CIImage imageWithCGImage:[image
CGImage]]];

        if ([arr count] > 0) {
            //NSLog(@"Faces found.");
            for (int i = 0; i < 1; i++) { //< [arr count]; i++) {
                CIFaceFeature *feature = [arr objectAtIndex:i];
                double xPosition = (feature.leftEyePosition.x +
feature.rightEyePosition.x+feature.mouthPosition.x)/(3*image.size.width) ;
                double yPosition = (feature.leftEyePosition.y +
feature.rightEyePosition.y+feature.mouthPosition.y)/(3*image.size.height);

                double dist = sqrt(pow((feature.leftEyePosition.x -
feature.rightEyePosition.x),2)+pow((feature.leftEyePosition.y -
feature.rightEyePosition.y),2))/image.size.width;

                yPosition += dist;
                CGSize size = [[CCDirector sharedDirector] winSize];
                pumpkin.opacity = 255;
                pumpkin.scale = 5*(size.width*dist)/256.0;
```

```
        [pumpkin setDisplayFrame:[[CCSpriteFrameCache sharedSpriteFrameCache]
spriteFrameByName:[NSString stringWithFormat:@"pumpkin%d.png", pumpkin_count + 4]]];
                CCMoveTo *moveAction = [CCMoveTo actionWithDuration:0
position:ccp((size.width * (xPosition)), (size.height * ((yPosition))))];
                [pumpkin runAction:moveAction];
            }
        } else {
            pumpkin.opacity = 0;
        }
    }
    isProcessingRequest = NO;
}
```

This is the most important code block of the whole game, so let's step through it slowly. First, we check to see whether a current request is in progress. If not, we run the CIDetector methods to find the faces in the camera image. If at least one face is found, we continue forward.

At this point, I'm actually hard-coding a loop of no more than one iteration. If you want to extend this game, this would be another area for improvement. Implement a randomizer in the place of this loop and chose a random pumpkin to attach to a random target in the camera view. There could be a significant amount of processing to track which user has which pumpkin on their head, but it would make for a more robust gaming experience.

Next, we triple the X and Y coordinates of the eyes that CIDetector found to better place our pumpkin on the top of the actual image on the screen, and not the image we're processing, which is smaller in ratio.

We calculate the distance using the good old Pythagorean theorem and divide it by the width of the screen. This helps us scale the image so that it fits your face as you move away from the screen. Try this yourself when you run the application. The pumpkin will follow you to and from the screen and scale appropriately.

Finally, we set the opacity back to 255 (so it's visible) and move the sprite to the location where we found the face. We're using two cocos2D macros to simplify this step. We first set the sprite frame to the pumpkin_count image (we'll get back to this in a moment), and then we use the CCMoveTo action to move the sprite to the X,Y coordinates of the face.

Run the application on a physical device. Start the game by choosing New Game from the menu options. You'll see something similar to Figure 8–17.

Figure 8–17. *Dude, I'm a pumpkin!*

I'm not sure I like being a pumpkin. Earlier, we set the ActionLayer class to be touch enabled, but we never implemented the response methods. Declare a new private variable of the CCParticleSystemQuad class called emitter in the ActionLayer.h file. Open ActionLayer.m and add the methods from Listing 8–41.

Listing 8–41. *Touch Methods*

```
- (void)registerWithTouchDispatcher {
    [[CCTouchDispatcher sharedDispatcher] addTargetedDelegate:self priority:0
swallowsTouches:YES];
}

- (BOOL)ccTouchBegan:(UITouch *)touch withEvent:(UIEvent *)event {
    return YES;
}

- (void)ccTouchEnded:(UITouch *)touch withEvent:(UIEvent *)event {
    CGPoint location = [self convertTouchToNodeSpace:touch];
    if (CGRectContainsPoint(pumpkin.boundingBox, location)) {
        pumpkin_count--;

        emitter = [CCParticleSystemQuad particleWithFile:@"PumpkinExplosion.plist"];
        emitter.position = ccp(location.x, location.y);
        [self addChild:emitter z:1];

        if (pumpkin_count == 0) {
            NSLog(@"You won");
        }
    }
    //NSLog(@"Touch %@: ", NSStringFromCGPoint(location));
}
```

Earlier in the chapter, we imported the Art directory from the sample project. I also created a particle effect using Particle Designer (from www.71squared.com) to vaporize the pumpkins.

When a pumpkin is vaporized, we want to subtract from the number of remaining pumpkins and change the pumpkin's image (so we see each pumpkin once during the game).

The code we added in Listing 8–41 starts by checking the touch location. We use the convertTouchToNodeSpace macro to get screen coordinates for the touch event. In some cocos2D games the "game world" exceeds the boundaries of the screen (e.g., tile map games like Legend of Zelda), so we need to convert this to the coordinates of the device's screen. Next, we check to see if the touch location is within the bounding box of our pumpkin. If it is, we set up our particle emitter (to add the vaporize effect), we decrement our pumpkin_count, and we refresh the scene. If you blast enough pumpkins, your console will show the "You won" message. Vaporized pumpkins should have an effect similar to Figure 8–18.

Figure 8–18. *Now, I'm a vaporized Pumpkin.*

Ending the Game

Games are no fun if they never end. We are already decrementing the pumpkin count variable when we vaporize a pumpkin. Let's add a scene to the game to handle the end game state and a restart if the user is interested.

Create a new class called EndLayer. Make sure it uses the CCNode template and is a subclass of CCLayer. Open EndLayer.h in Xcode and update the header, as shown in Figure 8–42.

Listing 8–42. *Updated EndLayer.h File*

```
#import <Foundation/Foundation.h>
#import "cocos2d.h"

@interface EndLayer : CCLayer {

}

+(CCScene *) scene;

@end
```

Looks familiar, eh? We are, again, adding the static CCScene method to our new layer. Switch over to EndLayer.m. Start by importing the ActionLayer.h file. Then, add the methods from Listing 8–43 to the implementation.

Listing 8–43. *New Methods in EndLayer.m*

```
+(CCScene *) scene
{
    // 'scene' is an autorelease object.
    CCScene *scene = [CCScene node];

    // 'layer' is an autorelease object.
    EndLayer *layer = [EndLayer node];

    // add layer as a child to scene
    [scene addChild: layer];

    // return the scene
    return scene;
}

- (id)init {

    if ((self = [super init])) {

        CGSize winSize = [CCDirector sharedDirector].winSize;

        CCLabelBMFont *titleLabel;
        if (UI_USER_INTERFACE_IDIOM() == UIUserInterfaceIdiomPad) {
            titleLabel = [CCLabelBMFont labelWithString:@"New Game" fntFile:@"Arial-
hd.fnt"];
        } else {
            titleLabel = [CCLabelBMFont labelWithString:@"New Game"
fntFile:@"Arial.fnt"];
        }

        CCMenuItemLabel *newGameItem = [CCMenuItemLabel itemWithLabel:titleLabel
target:self selector:@selector(playTapped:)];
        newGameItem.position = ccp(winSize.width * 0.8, winSize.height * 0.3);

        CCMenu *menu = [CCMenu menuWithItems:newGameItem, nil];
        menu.position = CGPointZero;

        [self addChild:menu];
```

```
    }
    return self;
}


- (void)playTapped:(id)sender {
    [[CCDirector sharedDirector] replaceScene:[CCTransitionRadialCCW
transitionWithDuration:1.0 scene:[ActionLayer scene]]];
}
```

The scene and init methods should contain no surprises. In the init method, we are setting up another game menu to allow the user to start the game over. Before we display the EndLayer scene, we need to clear some of our variables in our ActionLayer. Return to ActionLayer.m. Start by importing the EndLayer.h header.

Find the code shown in Listing 8–44. Replace it with the code from Listing 8–45.

Listing 8–44. *Find This Code . . .*

```
if (pumpkin_count == 0) {
            NSLog(@"You won");
}
```

Listing 8–45. *Replace with This . . .*

```
if (pumpkin_count == 0) {
            NSLog(@"You won");
            isProcessingRequest = YES;
            [AppDelegate instance].isPlaying = NO;
            [[CCDirector sharedDirector] replaceScene:[EndLayer scene]];
}
```

When our ActionLayer class is initialized, we set isProcessingRequest to YES. We also set the isPlaying Boolean of our AppDelegate to NO. Before we can end the game and allow the user to restart it, we have to reset our environment. After that's taken care of, we tell the CCDirector to play the EndLayer scene.

After you vaporize the dozen pumpkins, you'll be presented with a restart menu, as shown in Figure 8–19.

Figure 8–19. *All pumpkins are vaporized, and a New Game menu is presented.*

If you select the New Game menu, the game restarts in its default state (12 pumpkins left to kill).

> **NOTE:** Before you bring this game out to a party, you might want to switch it from the front-facing camera to the default video device. Also, make sure you swap back the rotation effect. CIDetector has trouble with nonvertical image processing. Also, you can remove the debug draw method from the MenuLayer to make the menu less coder-ish.

Summary

This was a really fun chapter. We started with a default cocos2D chipmunk template and built a fully functional game. We started by making the menu interesting for the user. We took a pumpkin and hooked him up to a spring constraint so we could abuse him without having him fly off the screen.

We built out the game menu to launch the action scene and start taking in facial recognition requests. We learned about sprite sheets and batch nodes and some simple methods to handle overlays, like CCMoveTo and setting the opacity of a sprite.

We introduced CIDetector, which we'll learn about in Chapter 12, to find faces so we could move our pumpkins to the right place. We finished up with some particle effects to vaporize the alien intruders and we built an end game menu.

The cocos2D framework, as we've seen in the last two chapters, makes game development so much easier than building these features from scratch in OpenGL ES.

In Chapter 9, we'll introduce some other third-party frameworks and SDKs that are available for augmented reality projects. Most of these frameworks concentrate on location-based AR or marker-based AR. We'll see a bit more gaming flavor in Chapter 13.

Third-Party Augmented Reality Toolkits

In this book, we're going to cover quite a few technologies that are available to help you with your AR development. A key part of bringing an application to market quickly is not reinventing the wheel. For AR, even though this is a new space, this still holds true. There are toolkits available to developers for marker-based applications, location-based applications, and even 3D drawing applications.

In this chapter, we'll discuss some of these tools and their strengths and weaknesses. Along the way, we'll build a few sample applications as well.

Overview

In this chapter, we're going to talk about the toolkits listed in Table 9–1.

Table 9–1. *Frameworks Covered in This Chapter*

Name	Download Location	Cost	Key Benefits
String SDK	`http://poweredbystring.com/licensing`	$0 demo or $499 for App Store release	Development time is nearly nothing
Qualcomm	`https://ar.qualcomm.at/qdevnet`	$0	Tracks partial markers for zooming
ARKit	`https://github/zac/iphonearkit`	Open Source	About 100 various GitHub forks

Each of these toolkits has a unique advantage and, in some cases, comes with some drawbacks in comparison to the other toolkits. We'll talk about each of these and look at some samples as well.

Powered by String

Let's start with the Powered by String SDK. Open your browser to http://poweredbystring.com/developers/register. You should be on the registration page; fill out the information requested.

After you've registered and signed in, go to http://poweredbystring.com/licensing and download the Demo version of the toolkit. You'll be asked for some more information, then taken to a screen that looks like Figure 9–1.

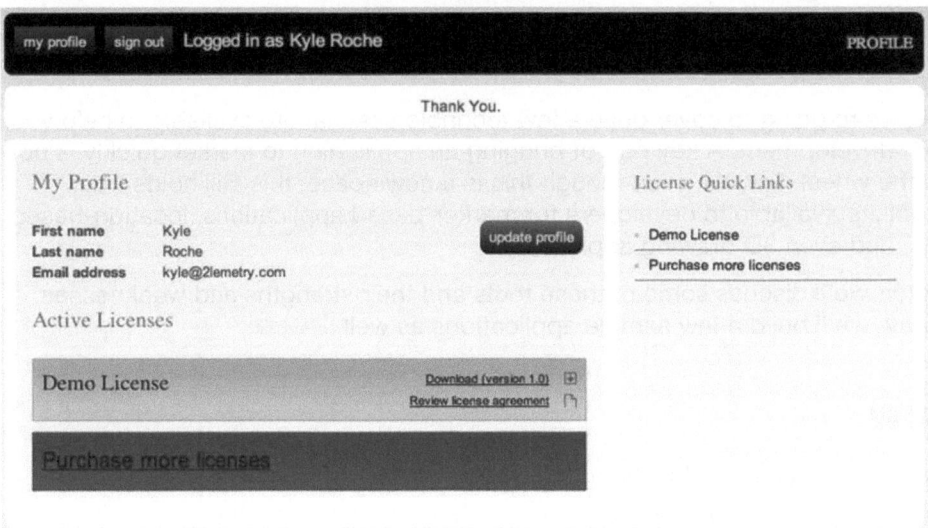

Figure 9–1. *Go to the Powered by String download to get the Demo version.*

Download the latest version of the SDK. On your local machine, unzip the archive and find the **OGL Tutorial** directory. Open the Xcode project and run it on a physical device. Open the Marker1.png file on your computer screen. After the application launches, direct the camera so the marker comes into focus. Figure 9–2 shows the result.

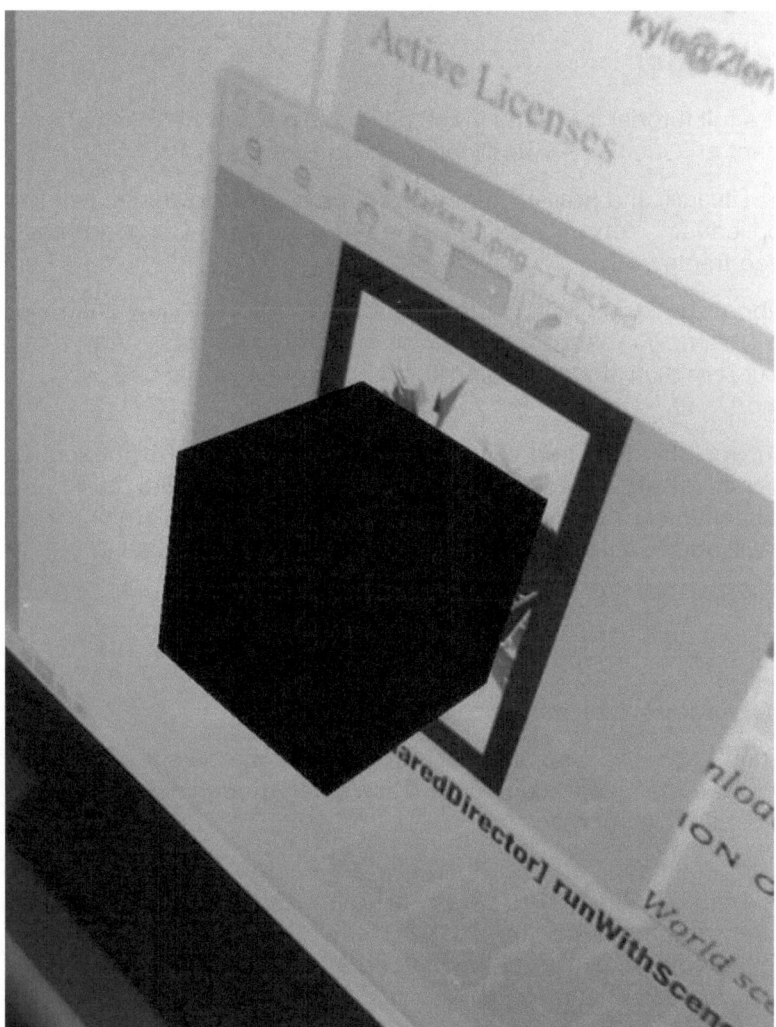

Figure 9–2. *View the marker in the String SDK sample application.*

This application is something we'll dive into more in Chapter 10, so you don't have to worry too much about the contents at the moment. However, if this is your first marker-based AR application, this might be pretty interesting. With just a few lines of code, String was able to load and capture the marker from our camera's view.

String's Basic Workflow

Again, we'll be looking at a full tutorial for String in the next chapter, but here's the basic steps required to implement an OpenGL AR application using String's SDK.

First, you need to add the **Libraries** and **Headers** folders from the source download (where you found the sample application). You will also need the AVFoundation, CoreGraphics, CoreMedia, and CoreVideo frameworks.

One of the great things about the String SDK is that you can add it to any view controller (or even another class). You simply create an instance of the StringOGL class and implement the StringOGLDelegate protocol. This protocol only requires that you implement a render method.

Before you initialize string, you should set up your framebuffer, renderbuffer, projection matrix, viewport, and other initial states as you normally would in an OpenGL application. Most of this is taken care of you in the OpenGL ES Game template provided by Xcode. The code you will add to initialize String will look something like Listing 9–1.

Listing 9–1. *String Sample Initialization Code*

```
stringOGL = [[StringOGL alloc] initWithDelegate: self context: myEAGLContext
frameBuffer: myFrameBuffer leftHanded: NO];
[stringOGL setProjectionMatrix: myProjectionMatrix viewport: myViewport
orientation: [self interfaceOrientation] reorientIPhoneSplash: NO];
```

String recommends you don't allow your application to rotate. In some of our sample applications, we actually follow that same recommendation, even though not every toolkit requires or recommends this approach.

Markers are required for String. In comparison, String has the least restrictive requirements for markers. Markers should be included in your main bundle as PNG files. Surprisingly, the smaller they are, the better they work. This has more to do with the loading time of the toolkit than the resolution of the marker, as you might expect. After you include your PNG files, you can load them, as shown in Listing 9–2.

Listing 9–2. *Load String Markers*

```
myMarkerID = [stringOGL loadImageMarker: @"MyMarker" ofType: @"png"];
```

String performs very well with high contrast (near black on near white) markers and doesn't require a high level of detail. Also, String can track countless markers at a time in the paid versions of the toolkit. The drawback with the marker-recognition algorithms from String is the lack of ability to track a partial marker. If it is at all obstructed or moves from the view, String loses the marker entirely. Also, String's object ratio is set on a percentage scale from the marker. For example, String considers that all markers have a diagonal length of one unit. So, if you'd like your marker's diagonal to have a length of five, you need to multiply the tracked position by five before projecting your image. These settings can be applied to normal OpenGL transforms.

As I mentioned, there is only one required delegate method in the protocol. You need to implement the render method in your class. The suggested format for this method is shown in Listing 9–3.

Listing 9–3. *Suggested Format for render Method*

```
- (void)render
{
// Read data for markers that were detected this frame
const int maxMarkerCount = 10;
struct MarkerInfoMatrixBased markerInfo[10];
!
int markerCount = [stringOGL getMarkerInfoMatrixBased: markerInfo
maxMarkerCount: maxMarkerCount];
// Iterate through detected markers
for (int i = 0; i < markerCount; i++)
{
// Draw appropriate content for this image marker
}
}
```

Not much code is expected to get the framework to function. You simply track the markers, then iterate through the marker information. If you are using a license that tracks more than one marker, you might have different actions for each marker. You can tell which marker is being tracked using the markerInfo class.

Each marker has a specific color, imageID, and uniqueInstanceID. The uniqueInstanceID is helpful if you have multiple markers that are identical. They can be tracked separately using this property.

Extra Functionality

String also provides some easy wrappers for useful functions you might need in your AR application. In some cases, like in our facial-recognition examples later in this book, we need direct access to the frame buffer. String actually "owns" the screen buffer delegate, so we need to request each frame from String using the getCurrentVideoBuffer method. The method is shown in Listing 9–4.

Listing 9–4. *Get the Current Frame Buffer*

```
- (void)getCurrentVideoBuffer: (unsigned *)buffer viewToVideoTextureTransform:
(float *)viewToVideoTextureTransform;
```

This method retrieves the current video texture and a matrix to transform coordinates from view space to texture space for OpenGL. We don't actually require all that information for our other examples. If you decide you do want to track markers and analyze the frame buffer, you should call this method on each frame because the video stream is double buffered.

The second useful function is String's helpful method to provide snapshots of the screen buffer. This would be useful for e-mailing pictures of your application or posting them to Facebook, etc. Listing 9–5 shows this simple method.

Listing 9–5. *Take a Snapshot of the Frame Buffer*

```
- (void)takeSnapshotAndPause;
```

This method is set up almost like an asynchronous callback method. You need to wait before you call the `resume` method until the `handleSnapshot` method (which you'll also need to implement) has completed.

Unity Integration

Unity 3D isn't something we're covering in this book, but Apress has many titles available on the subject. Unity is a super-powerful 3D gaming engine that has native integration with String. If you're interested in Unity, you can build an AR application with zero lines of code right from their starter projects.

Advanced Shaders and OpenGL Features

If you want to see an example of what you can build with String, visit their showcase on their web site or download the sample application from the App Store.

String works very well with more advanced shaders and lighting effects. It handles the loading of the objects quickly and has a near-instant response to the marker's presentation.

Figure 9–3 shows a screenshot from a demo application built using String. It loads a 3D lamp from a marker and allows the user to turn the light on and off using Open GL ES shading and lighting effects.

Figure 9–3. *The demo String application loads a 3D lamp that can be turned off and on.*

This demo project extends the Cube sample (notice the second tab in Figure 9–3) and renders a different object for the Lantern tab. The source will be in the supplemental materials for this book on GitHub and available from the Source Code/Download area of the Apress web site (www.apress.com).

Qualcomm SDK

Qualcomm released an AR SDK late summer of 2011, just before the launch of iOS 5. The Qualcomm SDK is very different from the Powered by String SDK, which is one of the reasons I chose to cover these two frameworks.

Visit Qualcomm's web site, https://ar.qualcomm.at, and sign up for a free account. After you have signed up, you can switch from the **Android** to the **iOS** tab, as shown in Figure 9–4, and download the QCAR SDK for Mac.

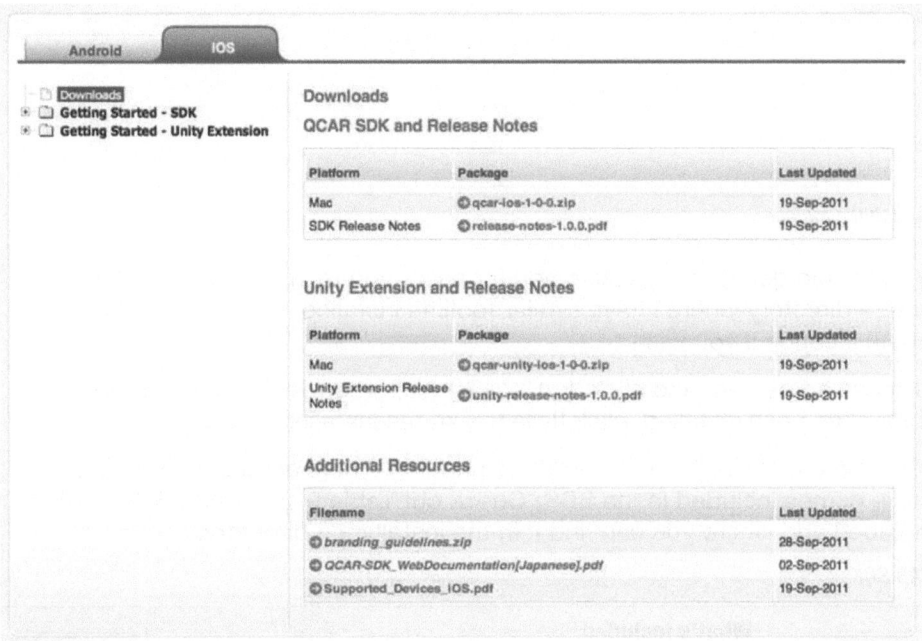

Figure 9–4. *Download the QCAR SDK.*

Unlike String, which is a static library and a set of files, QCAR actually provides an installer to keep the library separate from your code. This allows for you to more easily upgrade the SDK as changes are introduced.

> **NOTE:** You might have to upgrade Java before the installer will launch.

Unzip the archive and launch the installer. You will see a screen like the one shown in Figure 9–5.

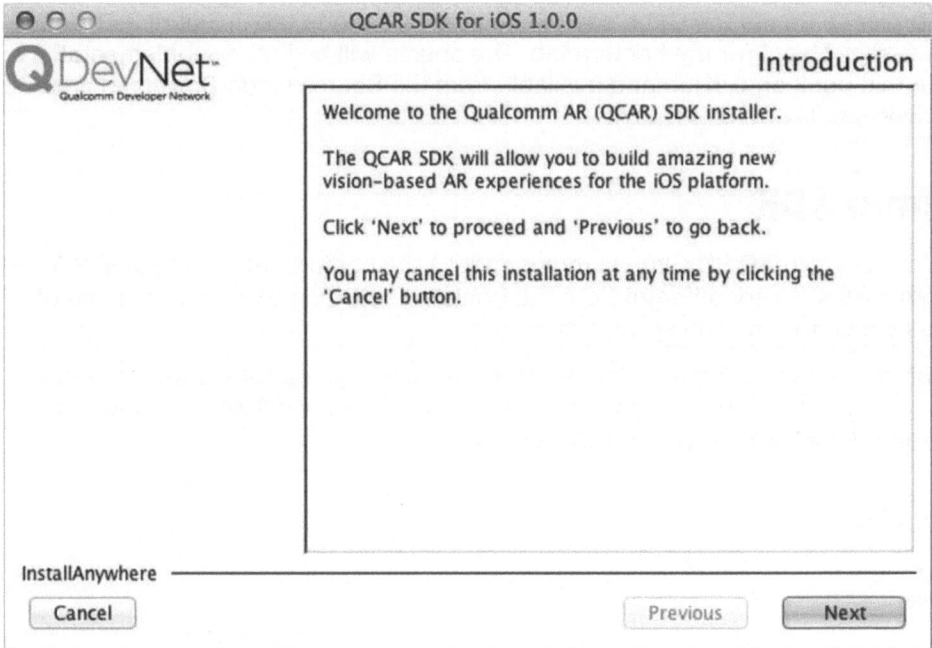

Figure 9–5. *Launch the installer.*

Click **Next**. You should get a dialog asking you for a location to install the toolkit. I've moved mine to a directory where I have similar toolkits installed, but you can choose to keep the default location if you wish.

Accept the license agreement and click **Next**. Click **Install** when you're ready to proceed. When the library has been installed, click **Done** to exit the installer.

The directory structure of the library is worth mentioning. There are a decent amount of very impressive demos included in the SDK. Check out Table 9–2 for more information on what's included and where you can find it in the installation directory.

Table 9–2. *QCAR SDK*

Path	What's Included
build/	Qualcomm augmented reality SDK
build/include	Commented header files
build/lib	Static link libraries
samples/	Sample applications
samples/Dominoes	Amazing sample that demos virtual buttons, sound, and touch screen interaction

Path	What's Included
samples/ImageTargets	Tracks two image targets
samples/FrameMarkers	Tracks multiple markers
samples/MultiTargets	Tracks a multitarget
samples/VirtualButtons	Shows virtual button interactions
assets/	Additional assets for the SDK
readme.txt	Starter document

Let's start with the Dominoes application. There's quite a bit of code and math behind this application, but it demonstrates all the functionality of the framework. Launch the project in Xcode and run it on a physical device.

Make sure you either print or bring up on the screen the stones.jpg file from the **Media** subdirectory of the project. This is the marker for the application. Put the marker in the view of the camera. It will ask you to drag your finger around the screen slowly. As you do so, it builds out a set of dominoes.

This is the amazing part. You can use the menu to enable a virtual button where you can flick over the dominoes in a mixed-reality space (your finger is in view of the camera while it is projecting the augmented scene).

The running project is shown in Figure 9–6.

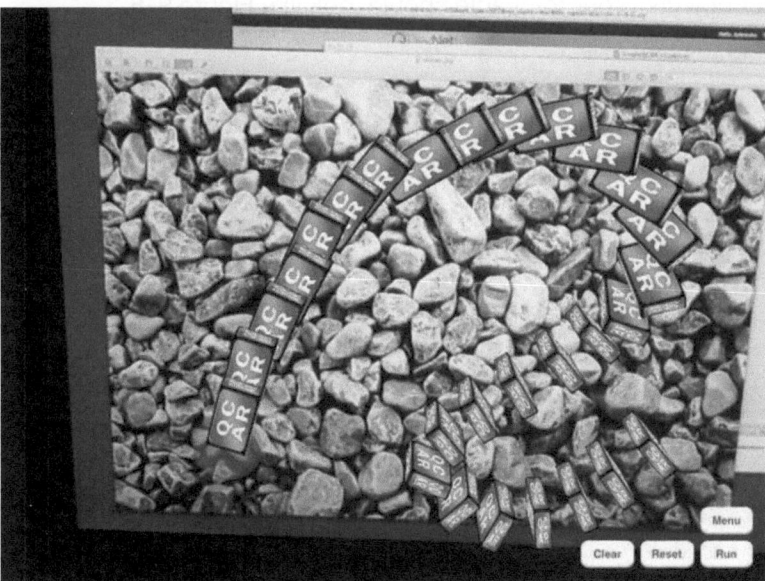

Figure 9–6. *Run the Dominoes demo.*

You can see the green dot under domino #1 on the left. That's the virtual button. If your user strikes that with his finger, the SDK will register that and handle the event. The event in this case, is to start the dominos falling in order.

That's a pretty amazing Hello World application, isn't it? Let's build something not so impressive from scratch so you can get used to the SDK.

Building Our Own QCAR Demo

Before we can start building from scratch, let's create the marker for our application. Click on the **My Trackables** link from the Qualcomm site. Create a new project by clicking the **New Project** link. I'm naming my project Apress.

You'll be taken to a screen that resembles Figure 9–7.

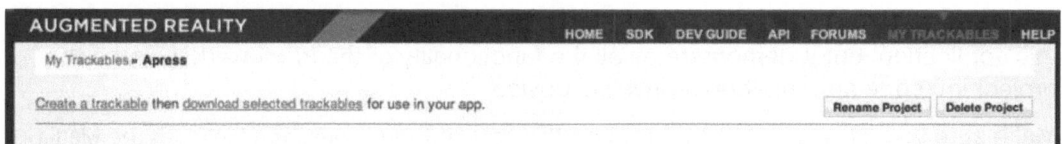

Figure 9–7. *Use the New Project link to create a new project.*

Click on the **Create a trackable** link. Name the trackable ApressTrackable and set the type to the single image type. Set the width to 100.

It's important to note that the width does not correspond to the marker's width nor does the marker get resized to this width. In the AR space around the marker, the 3D objects you'll load into the scene have a relative size to the marker. Setting this to 100 sets the initial comparison for other objects. Your trackable should look like Figure 9–8.

Create Trackable

Trackable Name:
ApressTrackable

Select Trackable Type:

Trackable Scene Size:
Enter the desired width of your trackable. The trackable's height will be calculated automatically when you upload your image.

Width: 100

⊙ Create Trackable

Figure 9–8. *We've created a new trackable.*

Now, Qualcomm expects a very different marker than String. Qualcomm prefers a high-resolution, high-detail marker to increase the number of points that it can track. The marker must have a large number of small details. Something like the river rock example that came with the tutorials would be best.

Just to compare the images, I randomly searched Google Images for "Free high resolution wallpaper" and found what I thought were fairly high-detailed images.

I ran a few of these through the Qualcomm trackable test. My results were typically something like Figure 9–9.

Figure 9–9. *The new trackable failed!*

If you want to come up with your own image, keep experimenting. Make sure you find an image that has detail throughout most of the space. I reloaded the image called `stones.jpg`. It can be found in the **Media** subdirectory of the Dominos sample application. The results were much better, as you can see from Figure 9–10.

Figure 9–10. *The next trackable was a success!*

Save the trackable, by clicking the **Back** button, and you'll be returned the **My Trackables** page again. You'll now have a new image in your list of trackables. Click on the image, and you'll be taken to a screen where you can select the trackable and download it for use in our application. The screen will look something like Figure 9–11.

Figure 9–11. *Download the trackable.*

Download the trackable using the link on the top of the selection window. Make sure you choose the SDK download and not the Unity version. The archive contains the following two files:

- `config.xml`
- `qcar-resources.dat`

Creating the Xcode Project

Create a new project in Xcode. Use the Single View application template. Name the project Ch9. Make sure you use Automatic Reference Counting. My settings are shown in Figure 9–12.

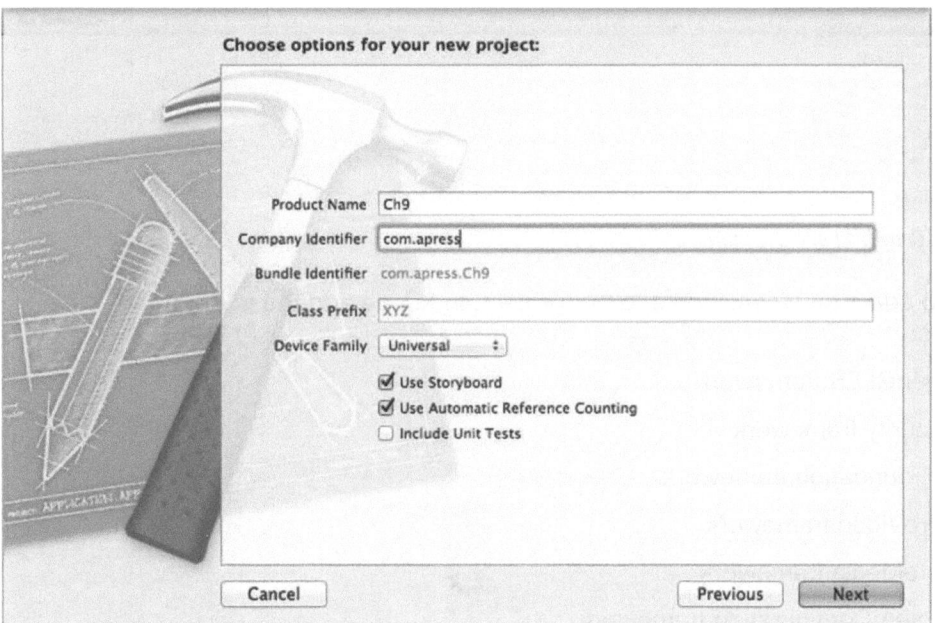

Figure 9–12. *Set up the project settings.*

Open Finder. Navigate to the location where you installed the QCAR SDK. There is a subdirectory called **build**. Open that directory in Finder. Copy the contents of this directory (lib and include folders) to the project's directory.

Open the **Build Settings** tab in your Xcode project settings page. Update the Header Paths to include **$(SRCROOT)/Ch9/include**. Now, open Finder to the project's directory. Drag and drop the **lib** directory into the Xcode project. Make sure you don't select to copy the resources (because they already exist).

From the book's source repository on GitHub or Apress (from the Source Code/Download area at www.apress.com) copy GLProgram.h and GLProgram.m to the project. Jeff LaMarche originally wrote these files. They've been adapted for iOS 5 automatic reference counting.

Copy Cube.h from the source repository also. This file, written by Qualcomm, is used to test OpenGL ES drawing.

Finally, copy the SimpleLightShader.vsh and SimpleLightShader.fsh files to the project. Open the **Build Phases** tab and make sure both of these files are copied as bundle resources as shown in Figure 9–13.

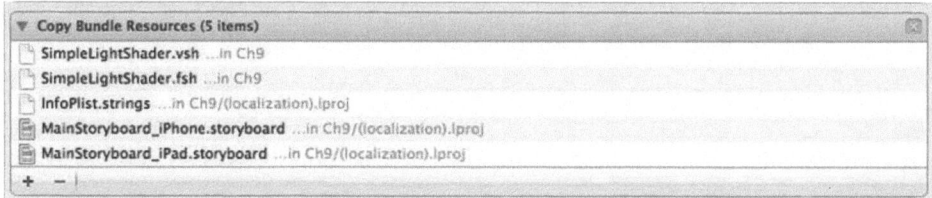

Figure 9–13. *Copy the bundle resources.*

We need to add a few frameworks to our project. In Xcode add the following frameworks:

- OpenGLES.framework

- Security.framework

- AVFoundation.framework

- CoreVideo.framework

- CoreMedia.framework

- SystemConfiguration.framework

- QuartzCore.framework

Okay, now we're ready to add back our marker files. Copy the two files you downloaded from the Qualcomm site to the project.

As we saw with String, it's typically recommended to restrict dynamic reorientation of the device in augmented reality applications, especially those that are using third-party SDKs. Open the project's **Summary** tab and make sure that the application is only enabled for **Landscape Right** orientation.

EAGLView

Create a new class that subclasses `UIView`. Name it `EAGLView`. Open `EAGLView.h` in Xcode, and import the headers shown in Listing 9–6.

Listing 9–6. *import Statements*

```
#import <OpenGLES/EAGL.h>
#import <OpenGLES/ES1/gl.h>
#import <OpenGLES/ES1/glext.h>
#import <OpenGLES/ES2/gl.h>
#import <OpenGLES/ES2/glext.h>
#import <QCAR/Tool.h>
#import <QCAR/UIGLViewProtocol.h>
#import "GLProgram.h"
```

Just below the `import` statements, set up an enumeration to track what state the application is current running. Copy the code from Listing 9–7.

Listing 9–7. *Status Enumeration*

```
typedef enum _status {
    APPSTATUS_UNINITED,
    APPSTATUS_INIT_APP,
    APPSTATUS_INIT_QCAR,
    APPSTATUS_INIT_APP_AR,
    APPSTATUS_INIT_TRACKER,
    APPSTATUS_INITED,
    APPSTATUS_CAMERA_STOPPED,
    APPSTATUS_CAMERA_RUNNING,
    APPSTATUS_ERROR
} status;
```

Before we update the implementation block, rename EAGLView.m to EAGLView.mm. Qualcomm's SDK is C++ based, and we'll need that extension to access the C++ classes.

Update the interface block, as shown in Listing 9–8.

Listing 9–8. *EAGLView Interface*

```
@interface EAGLView : UIView <UIGLViewProtocol> {
    EAGLContext *context;
    GLint framebufferWidth;
    GLint framebufferHeight;

    GLuint defaultFramebuffer;
    GLuint colorRenderbuffer;
    GLuint depthRenderbuffer;

    QCAR::Matrix44F projectionMatrix;
    CGRect screenRect;
    int QCARFlags;
    status appStatus;
    GLProgram *shader;
    GLint shaderPositionAttribute, shaderNormalAttribute, shaderModelViewMatrixUniform,
shaderProjectionMatrixUniform, shaderColorUniform;
}
@end
```

Here, we first set up an instance variable for our OpenGL context. We then set up some variables for width and height of our frame buffer, and our default buffer handles. Next, we set up the projection matrix to multiply our 3D coordinates. This is the line that required the name change to .mm. You can swap it back if you want to experiment. It'll give you a build error.

Finally, we hold some variables for our screen size, QCAR flags, and the status of the application (from our enumeration).

Declare the methods from Listing 9–9 in the header.

Listing 9–9. *New Method Declarations*

```
- (void)renderFrameQCAR;
- (void)onCreate;
- (void)onDestroy;
- (void)onResume;
- (void)onPause;
```

The first method will be used render the frames called by the QCAR SDK. The view controller will call the others when the state of the application changes.

Switch over to EAGLView.mm in Xcode, and add the import statements from Listing 9–10.

Listing 9–10. *New import Statements*

```
#import <QuartzCore/QuartzCore.h>
#import <QCAR/QCAR.h>
#import <QCAR/CameraDevice.h>
#import <QCAR/Tracker.h>
#import <QCAR/VideoBackgroundConfig.h>
#import <QCAR/Renderer.h>
#import <QCAR/Tool.h>
#import <QCAR/Trackable.h>

#import "Cube.h"
```

We're going to need pretty much everything the SDK has to offer. So, that means lots of import statements here. You can already see the difference in ease of use and time required between Qualcomm and String. It's worth the effort though if you need the more advanced tracking capabilities of the QCAR SDK.

Add the following block of Private method declarations from Listing 9–11 to the class.

Listing 9–11. *Private Methods*

```
@interface EAGLView (PrivateMethods)
- (void)setFramebuffer;
- (BOOL)presentFramebuffer;
- (void)createFramebuffer;
- (void)deleteFramebuffer;
- (void)updateApplicationStatus:(status)newStatus;
- (void)bumpAppStatus;
- (void)initApplication;
- (void)initQCAR;
- (void)initApplicationAR;
- (void)loadTracker;
- (void)startCamera;
- (void)stopCamera;
- (void)configureVideoBackground;
- (void)initRendering;
@end
```

Add the static method from Listing 9–12 to the implementation. This method is required by OpenGL to draw on the layer.

Listing 9–12. *layerClass Static Method*

```
+ (Class)layerClass
{
    return [CAEAGLLayer class];
}
```

We're going to load this class from our storyboard's view controller NIB file. So, we're going to have to implement the initWithCoder method. Copy the method from Listing 9–13.

Listing 9–13. *initWithCoder*

```
- (id)initWithCoder:(NSCoder*)coder
{
    self = [super initWithCoder:coder];

        if (self) {
        NSLog(@"Initialising EAGLView");
        CAEAGLLayer *eaglLayer = (CAEAGLLayer *)self.layer;

        eaglLayer.opaque = TRUE;
        eaglLayer.drawableProperties = [NSDictionary dictionaryWithObjectsAndKeys:
                                        [NSNumber numberWithBool:FALSE],
kEAGLDrawablePropertyRetainedBacking,
                                        kEAGLColorFormatRGBA8,
kEAGLDrawablePropertyColorFormat,
                                        nil];

        context = [[EAGLContext alloc] initWithAPI:kEAGLRenderingAPIOpenGLES2];
        QCARFlags = QCAR::GL_20;

        NSLog(@"QCAR OpenGL flag: %d", QCARFlags);

        if (!context) {
            NSLog(@"Failed to create ES context");
        }
    }

    return self;
}
```

The key difference between this code and the code we would typically see from the OpenGL ES template or another OpenGL application is the QCAR flags. We are setting them up here so the SDK knows what to expect.

Copy the method from Listing 9–14 to the implementation.

Listing 9–14. *createFrameBuffer Method*

```
- (void)createFramebuffer
{
    if (context && !defaultFramebuffer) {
        [EAGLContext setCurrentContext:context];

        // Create default framebuffer object
        glGenFramebuffers(1, &defaultFramebuffer);
        glBindFramebuffer(GL_FRAMEBUFFER, defaultFramebuffer);

        // Create colour render buffer and allocate backing store
        glGenRenderbuffers(1, &colorRenderbuffer);
        glBindRenderbuffer(GL_RENDERBUFFER, colorRenderbuffer);

        // Allocate the renderbuffer's storage (shared with the drawable object)
        [context renderbufferStorage:GL_RENDERBUFFER fromDrawable:(CAEAGLLayer
*)self.layer];
        glGetRenderbufferParameteriv(GL_RENDERBUFFER, GL_RENDERBUFFER_WIDTH,
&framebufferWidth);
```

```
        glGetRenderbufferParameteriv(GL_RENDERBUFFER, GL_RENDERBUFFER_HEIGHT,
&framebufferHeight);

        // Create the depth render buffer and allocate storage
        glGenRenderbuffers(1, &depthRenderbuffer);
        glBindRenderbuffer(GL_RENDERBUFFER, depthRenderbuffer);
        glRenderbufferStorage(GL_RENDERBUFFER, GL_DEPTH_COMPONENT16, framebufferWidth,
framebufferHeight);

        // Attach colour and depth render buffers to the frame buffer
        glFramebufferRenderbuffer(GL_FRAMEBUFFER, GL_COLOR_ATTACHMENT0, GL_RENDERBUFFER,
colorRenderbuffer);
        glFramebufferRenderbuffer(GL_FRAMEBUFFER, GL_DEPTH_ATTACHMENT, GL_RENDERBUFFER,
depthRenderbuffer);

        // Leave the colour render buffer bound so future rendering operations will act
on it
        glBindRenderbuffer(GL_RENDERBUFFER, colorRenderbuffer);

        if (glCheckFramebufferStatus(GL_FRAMEBUFFER) != GL_FRAMEBUFFER_COMPLETE) {
            NSLog(@"Failed to make complete framebuffer object %x",
glCheckFramebufferStatus(GL_FRAMEBUFFER));
        }
    }
}
```

This method, and some of the following methods are taken from the OpenGL templates.
The method we copied from Listing 9–14 sets up the frame buffer to make it possible for
OpenGL to begin drawing on the layer.

We're going to also need the tear down method for the frame buffer. The method from
Listing 9–15 releases memory when the frame buffer no longer requires it.

Listing 9–15. *deleteFrameBuffer Method*

```
- (void)deleteFramebuffer
{
    if (context) {
        [EAGLContext setCurrentContext:context];
        if (defaultFramebuffer) {
            glDeleteFramebuffers(1, &defaultFramebuffer);
            defaultFramebuffer = 0;
        }

        if (colorRenderbuffer) {
            glDeleteRenderbuffers(1, &colorRenderbuffer);
            colorRenderbuffer = 0;
        }

        if (depthRenderbuffer) {
            glDeleteRenderbuffers(1, &depthRenderbuffer);
            depthRenderbuffer = 0;
        }
    }
}
```

Copy the method from Listing 9–16. This method sets up the defaultFramebuffer
instance variable we declared earlier.

Listing 9–16. *setFrameBuffer*

```
- (void)setFramebuffer
{
    if (context) {
        [EAGLContext setCurrentContext:context];

        if (!defaultFramebuffer) {
            // Perform on the main thread to ensure safe memory allocation for
            // the shared buffer. Block until the operation is complete to
            // prevent simultaneous access to the OpenGL context
            [self performSelectorOnMainThread:@selector(createFramebuffer)
withObject:self waitUntilDone:YES];
        }
        glBindFramebuffer(GL_FRAMEBUFFER, defaultFramebuffer);

    }
}
```

We are almost done with the boring stuff. Copy the methods from Listing 9–17 to the implementation.

Listing 9–17. *presentFramebuffer and layoutSubviews Methods*

```
- (BOOL)presentFramebuffer
{
    BOOL success = FALSE;

    if (context) {
        [EAGLContext setCurrentContext:context];

        glBindRenderbuffer(GL_RENDERBUFFER, colorRenderbuffer);

        success = [context presentRenderbuffer:GL_RENDERBUFFER];
    }

    return success;
}

- (void)layoutSubviews
{
    [self deleteFramebuffer];
}
```

The first method we just copied holds the colorRenderbuffer context for our class. The second method is called if subviews of our EAGLView were changed and the view is redrawn. When that occurs, we want to release memory used by the current image.

When we were setting up the interface file, we discussed that this class will most likely be called from an external view controller. The next set of events is for that view controller. Copy the methods from Listing 9–18.

Listing 9–18. *External Methods for the ViewController*

```
- (void)onCreate
{
    NSLog(@"EAGLView onCreate()");
    appStatus = APPSTATUS_UNINITED;
```

```
        [self updateApplicationStatus:APPSTATUS_INIT_APP];
}


- (void)onDestroy
{
    NSLog(@"EAGLView onDestroy()");

    // Deinitialise QCAR SDK
    QCAR::deinit();
}


- (void)onResume
{
    NSLog(@"EAGLView onResume()");
    // QCAR-specific resume operation
    QCAR::onResume();

    if (APPSTATUS_CAMERA_STOPPED == appStatus) {
        [self updateApplicationStatus:APPSTATUS_CAMERA_RUNNING];
    }
}


- (void)onPause
{
    NSLog(@"EAGLView onPause()");
    // QCAR-specific pause operation
    QCAR::onPause();

    if (APPSTATUS_CAMERA_RUNNING == appStatus) {
        [self updateApplicationStatus:APPSTATUS_CAMERA_STOPPED];
    }
}
```

Each of these methods will be called at different times during the application's life cycle.
None of them are very detailed. Each changes the status to a particular value in the
enumeration and either pauses, starts, or resumes the QCAR SDK operations.

Now, when the application changes status, we're going to have to handle that as well.
Copy the method from Listing 9–19 to handle the application's change of status.

Listing 9–19. *Handle Status Updates*

```
- (void)updateApplicationStatus:(status)newStatus
{
    if (newStatus != appStatus && APPSTATUS_ERROR != appStatus) {
        appStatus = newStatus;

        switch (appStatus) {
            case APPSTATUS_INIT_APP:
                [self initApplication];
                [self updateApplicationStatus:APPSTATUS_INIT_QCAR];
                break;

            case APPSTATUS_INIT_QCAR:
                [self performSelectorInBackground:@selector(initQCAR) withObject:nil];
```

```
                    break;

            case APPSTATUS_INIT_APP_AR:
                [self initApplicationAR];
                [self updateApplicationStatus:APPSTATUS_INIT_TRACKER];
                break;

            case APPSTATUS_INIT_TRACKER:
                [self performSelectorInBackground:@selector(loadTracker)
withObject:nil];
                break;

            case APPSTATUS_INITED:
                QCAR::setHint(QCAR::HINT_IMAGE_TARGET_MULTI_FRAME_ENABLED, 1);
                QCAR::setHint(QCAR::HINT_IMAGE_TARGET_MILLISECONDS_PER_MULTI_FRAME, 25);
                [self updateApplicationStatus:APPSTATUS_CAMERA_RUNNING];
                break;

            case APPSTATUS_CAMERA_RUNNING:
                [self startCamera];
                break;

            case APPSTATUS_CAMERA_STOPPED:
                [self stopCamera];
                break;

            default:
                NSLog(@"updateApplicationStatus: invalid app status");
                break;
        }
    }

    if (APPSTATUS_ERROR == appStatus) {
        UIAlertView* alert = [[UIAlertView alloc] initWithTitle:@"Error"
message:@"Application initialisation failed." delegate:self cancelButtonTitle:@"OK"
otherButtonTitles:nil];

        [alert show];
    }
}
```

Take special note of the lines that are in bold. The first line calls a background thread to initialize QCAR. The second loads the marker image in the background. We haven't implemented either of those methods yet. Let's do that next.

Copy the two methods from Listing 9–20.

Listing 9–20. *Load the Marker (or Trackable)*

```
- (void)bumpAppStatus
{
    [self updateApplicationStatus:(status)(appStatus + 1)];
}

- (void)loadTracker
{
    int nPercentComplete = 0;
```

```
    // Background thread must have its own autorelease pool
    // Load the tracker data
    do {
        nPercentComplete = QCAR::Tracker::getInstance().load();
    } while (0 <= nPercentComplete && 100 > nPercentComplete);

    if (0 > nPercentComplete) {
        appStatus = APPSTATUS_ERROR;
    }

    // Continue execution on the main thread
    [self performSelectorOnMainThread:@selector(bumpAppStatus) withObject:nil
waitUntilDone:NO];

}
```

These methods load the marker. When the marker is loaded, we move the application status to the next item in the enumeration as shown by the line in bold. The other selector that we referenced, but hadn't implemented, was the initialization method for QCAR. Let's add the three initialization methods for the whole class at one time. Copy the methods from Listing 9–21 to the implementation.

Listing 9–21. *Various init Methods*

```
- (void)initApplication
{
    screenRect = [[UIScreen mainScreen] bounds];

    NSLog(@"Screen rect %@",screenRect);

    QCAR::onSurfaceCreated();
    QCAR::onSurfaceChanged(screenRect.size.height, screenRect.size.width);
}

- (void)initQCAR
{
    QCAR::setInitParameters(QCARFlags);

    int nPercentComplete = 0;

    do {
        nPercentComplete = QCAR::init();
    } while (0 <= nPercentComplete && 100 > nPercentComplete);

    NSLog(@"QCAR::init percent: %d", nPercentComplete);

    if (0 > nPercentComplete) {
        appStatus = APPSTATUS_ERROR;
    }

    [self performSelectorOnMainThread:@selector(bumpAppStatus) withObject:nil
waitUntilDone:NO];
}

- (void)initApplicationAR
{
    [self initRendering];
}
```

The first method grabs the size of the screen and creates the surface for QCAR and resizes it to match the screen dimensions. It notifies the SDK after this is complete (onSurfaceCreated).

Next, we initialize the Qualcomm SDK. This will be performed on a background thread. After it's complete, we again move the status enumeration along.

The last method we just implemented initializes the rendering. This is the main init for the AR portion of the application.

We need two methods that will be called from the pause and resume routines to start and stop the camera. They are in Listing 9–22.

Listing 9–22. *Start and Stop the Camera View*

```
- (void)startCamera
{
    NSLog(@"Start Camera!");
    // Initialise the camera
    if (QCAR::CameraDevice::getInstance().init()) {
        // Configure video background
        [self configureVideoBackground];

        // Select the default mode
        if
(QCAR::CameraDevice::getInstance().selectVideoMode(QCAR::CameraDevice::MODE_DEFAULT)) {
            // Start camera capturing
            if (QCAR::CameraDevice::getInstance().start()) {
                // Start the tracker
                QCAR::Tracker::getInstance().start();

                // Cache the projection matrix
                const QCAR::CameraCalibration& cameraCalibration =
QCAR::Tracker::getInstance().getCameraCalibration();
                projectionMatrix = QCAR::Tool::getProjectionGL(cameraCalibration, 2.0f,
2000.0f);
                [self onResume];
            }
        }
    }
}

- (void)stopCamera
{
    QCAR::Tracker::getInstance().stop();
    QCAR::CameraDevice::getInstance().stop();
    QCAR::CameraDevice::getInstance().deinit();
}
```

These are all C++ functions from the QCAR library. The structure is very similar to how we handle things in Objective-C or using an OpenGL Texture for video, but the methods are specific to the SDK.

We're almost ready to test the application. This was quite a lot of code without being able to test anything.

Let's configure the video as the background of our layer. Copy the method from Listing 9–23.

Listing 9–23. *Configure the Video As the Background Image*

```
- (void)configureVideoBackground
{
    // Get the default video mode
    QCAR::CameraDevice& cameraDevice = QCAR::CameraDevice::getInstance();
    QCAR::VideoMode videoMode =
cameraDevice.getVideoMode(QCAR::CameraDevice::MODE_DEFAULT);

    // Configure the video background
    QCAR::VideoBackgroundConfig config;
    config.mEnabled = true;
    config.mSynchronous = true;
    config.mPosition.data[0] = 0.0f;
    config.mPosition.data[1] = 0.0f;

    // Compare aspect ratios of video and screen. If they are different
    // we use the full screen size while maintaining the video's aspect
    // ratio, which naturally entails some cropping of the video.
    // Note: screenRect is portrait but videoMode is always landscape,
    // which is why "width" and "height" appear to be reversed.
    float arVideo = (float)videoMode.mWidth / (float)videoMode.mHeight;
    float arScreen = screenRect.size.height / screenRect.size.width;

    if (arVideo > arScreen)
    {
        // Video mode is wider than the screen. We'll crop the left and right edges of
the video
        config.mSize.data[0] = (int)screenRect.size.width * arVideo;
        config.mSize.data[1] = (int)screenRect.size.width;
    }
    else
    {
        // Video mode is taller than the screen. We'll crop the top and bottom edges of
the video.
        // Also used when aspect ratios match (no cropping).
        config.mSize.data[0] = (int)screenRect.size.height;
        config.mSize.data[1] = (int)screenRect.size.height / arVideo;
    }

    // Set the config
    QCAR::Renderer::getInstance().setVideoBackgroundConfig(config);
}
```

This method was copied directly from one of the samples. Qualcomm is setting the video to match the screen, then drawing what the camera sees as our background.

Let's load up the shaders for light settings in OpenGL. Copy the method from Listing 9–24.

Listing 9–24. *Load the Test Shaders*

```
-(void)loadShaders {
    // Loading shaders for light only
```

```
    shader = [[GLProgram alloc] initWithVertexShaderFilename:@"SimpleLightShader"
fragmentShaderFilename:@"SimpleLightShader"];
    [shader addAttribute:@"a_position"];
    [shader addAttribute:@"a_texCoord"];
    [shader addAttribute:@"a_normal"];

    if (![shader link])
    {
        // Compilation failed
        NSLog(@"light shader link failed");
        NSString *progLog = [shader programLog];
        NSLog(@"Program Log: %@", progLog);
        NSString *fragLog = [shader fragmentShaderLog];
        NSLog(@"Frag Log: %@", fragLog);
        NSString *vertLog = [shader vertexShaderLog];
        NSLog(@"Vert Log: %@", vertLog);
        shader = nil;
    } else {
        NSLog(@"Light Shader compiled successfuly!");
    }

    shaderPositionAttribute = [shader attributeIndex:@"a_position"];
    shaderNormalAttribute   = [shader attributeIndex:@"a_normal"];
    shaderColorUniform = [shader uniformIndex:@"a_color"];
    shaderModelViewMatrixUniform = [shader uniformIndex:@"modelViewMatrix"];
    shaderProjectionMatrixUniform = [shader uniformIndex:@"projectionMatrix"];
}
```

We have two more tasks left before we can wire up the EAGLView class in place of our applications UIView. We need to initialize the OpenGL rendering and then render the frames. You can find these two methods in Listing 9–25.

Listing 9–25. *Initialize OpenGL Rendering and Render Frames*

```
- (void)initRendering
{
    // Define the clear colour
    glClearColor(0.0f, 0.0f, 0.0f, QCAR::requiresAlpha() ? 0.0f : 1.0f);

    [self loadShaders];
}

- (void)renderFrameQCAR
{
    [self setFramebuffer];

    // Clear colour and depth buffers
    glClear(GL_COLOR_BUFFER_BIT | GL_DEPTH_BUFFER_BIT);

    QCAR::State state = QCAR::Renderer::getInstance().begin();

    glEnable(GL_DEPTH_TEST);
    glEnable(GL_CULL_FACE);

    for (int i = 0; i < state.getNumActiveTrackables(); ++i) {
        // Get the trackable
        const QCAR::Trackable* trackable = state.getActiveTrackable(i);
```

```
        QCAR::Matrix44F modelViewMatrix = QCAR::Tool::convertPose2GLMatrix(trackable-
>getPose());

        [shader use];

        float Sash_Kd [] = {0.589414,0.042139,0.042139};
        // Set the sampler texture unit to 0
        glUniformMatrix4fv(shaderProjectionMatrixUniform, 1, 0,
&projectionMatrix.data[0]);
        glUniformMatrix4fv(shaderModelViewMatrixUniform, 1, 0,
&modelViewMatrix.data[0]);
        glUniform3fv(shaderColorUniform, 1, Sash_Kd);


        glVertexAttribPointer(shaderPositionAttribute, 3, GL_FLOAT, GL_FALSE, 0, (const
GLvoid*)&cubeVertices[0]);
        glVertexAttribPointer(shaderNormalAttribute, 3, GL_FLOAT, GL_FALSE, 0, (const
GLvoid*)&cubeNormals[0]);

        glEnableVertexAttribArray(shaderPositionAttribute);
        glEnableVertexAttribArray(shaderNormalAttribute);

        glDrawElements(GL_TRIANGLES, NUM_CUBE_INDEX, GL_UNSIGNED_SHORT, (const
GLvoid*)&cubeIndices[0]);
    }

    glDisable(GL_DEPTH_TEST);
    glDisable(GL_CULL_FACE);

    QCAR::Renderer::getInstance().end();
    [self presentFramebuffer];

}
```

The first method loads the shaders and defines a clear color for us to reference in the layer. After OpenGL rendering has been initialized, we can draw the QCAR frame.

In this method, we are iterating over the array of trackables that were found, much like we did in the String SDK, and we're rendering the cube in the 3D space just above the trackable. You can replace this code block with any OpenGL rendering routine.

Redirecting the UIView

Change the name of ViewController.m to ViewController.mm. We did this same thing with our EAGLView class earlier. We are going to require access to the C++ functions of the Qualcomm SDK, so this name is required for the compiler.

Open ViewController.mm. Import the EAGLView.h header. Update the viewDidLoad method, as shown in Listing 9–26.

Listing 9–26. *New viewDidLoad*

```
- (void)viewDidLoad
{
    [super viewDidLoad];
```

```
    EAGLView * eaglview = (EAGLView*) self.view;
    [eaglview onCreate];
    // Do any additional setup after loading the view, typically from a nib.
}
```

We create a new instance of the EAGLView and alert the class that it was created. Update the viewWillAppear and viewWillDisappear methods, as shown in Listing 9–27.

Listing 9–27. *New viewWillAppear and viewWillDisappear*

```
- (void)viewWillAppear:(BOOL)animated
{
    [super viewWillAppear:animated];
    EAGLView * eaglview = (EAGLView*) self.view;
    [eaglview onResume];
}

- (void)viewWillDisappear:(BOOL)animated
{
    [super viewWillDisappear:animated];
    EAGLView * eaglview = (EAGLView*) self.view;
    [eaglview onPause];
}
```

Phew! We made it. Okay, we need a few more things to make sure our class is actually used. Open either (or both) of the storyboards and update the class of the UIView in the background to EAGLView, as shown in Figure 9–14.

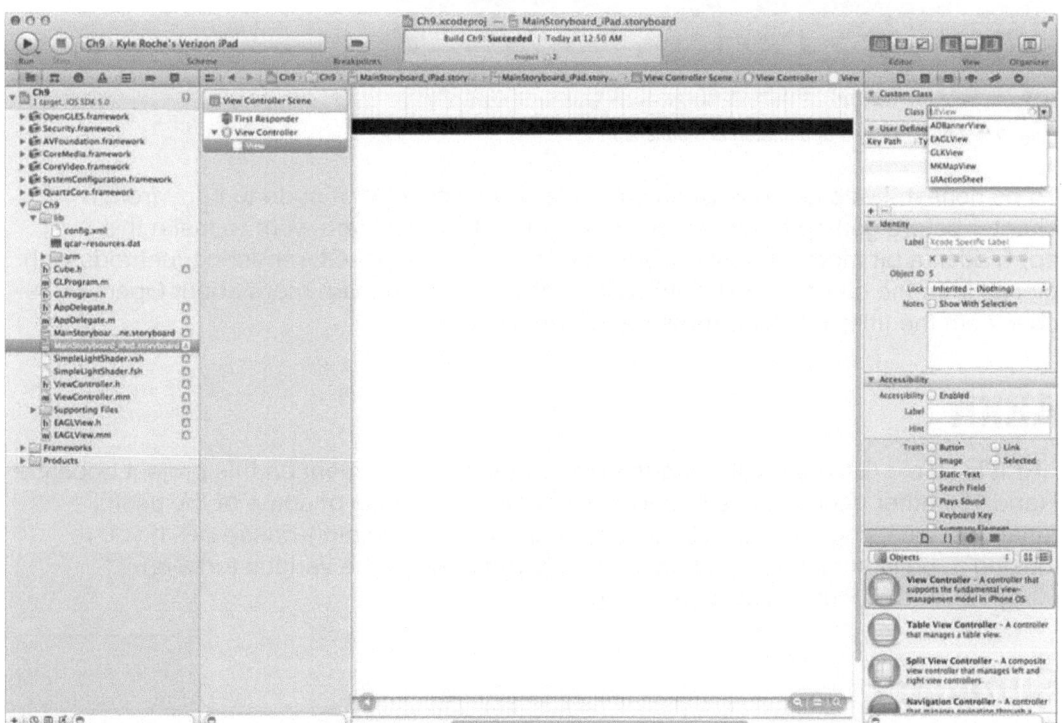

Figure 9–14. *Update the class of the UIView to EAGLView.*

Okay, you may run the project now. Don't forget to print the marker or bring it up on your screen. If you just loaded the configuration files from the book's source code repository, you can find the marker in the Qualcomm downloaded directory under /Samples/Dominos/media.

The application should launch in a single view showing a full-screen camera. Point the camera to the marker and you'll see something similar to Figure 9–15.

Figure 9–15. *The demo application is a success!*

To be honest, I was nervous when I ran this. That was a lot of code to copy from a chapter before getting to test anything. Congratulations! If you want to make this application a bit more interesting, you can replace the OpenGL rendering methods with pieces from the other sample applications. If you want to learn more about OpenGL, check out the titles on from Apress (www.apress.com).

ARKit

ARKit is an old GitHub project started by Zac White. I only mention this project because I (and 100 other people) have forked the repository because of some of the useful functions. I'm using some pieces of it in Chapter 11 for location-based AR. If you're looking to build something from scratch, browse through the various forks on www.github.com. Plus, social code = fun.

Summary

There are lots of other SDKs and toolkits that I didn't mention. This is mostly because they are so well documented already. Metaio, for example, has tons of sample projects and documentation available on the Internet already. String was launched in summer of 2011, but still doesn't have documentation on their web site (at the time of this writing). Qualcomm released their SDK just before the launch of iOS 5. They have some documentation on their developer portal and have some amazing samples in the SDK, but it's just getting out there.

I hope you learned something new in this chapter about helper libraries that are available to cut your application development time. In Chapter 10, we'll build another marker-based AR application using String. You'll have a good comparison between two great toolkits and their very different implementation styles.

Building a Marker-Based AR Application with OpenGL ES

In Chapter 9, we learned about a few different SDKs that are available for iOS developers building augmented reality applications. In this chapter, we'll start with one of those SDKs, the String SDK for iOS, and build a marker-based augmented reality application.

Augmented reality markers are physical identifiers that instruct the application on how to orient and scale in response to the physical world. For example, in Chapter 1, I showed a sample of how the United States Postal Service uses markers to orient and scale a shipping container. You can do the same in your applications.

The advantage to using markers in your application is that you can add value to things that already exist in the physical world. For example, consider you have a customer with a paper-based periodical who operates on a low budget. Using one of the existing advertisements or logos, you can bring a 3D advertisement to life. Aside from adding value, it offers a chance for the customer to further monetize his advertising clients.

Advertising is a great use case for marker-based augmented reality. We'll expand on this use case with a real-life example.

Building a Marker

Markers have a few characteristics that ensure the applications using them perform correctly. First, an AR marker should have only one correct orientation. You should clearly be able to differentiate whether the marker is upside down or sideways. Square markers aren't effective because the application will have no way to determine its proper orientation. Second, an AR marker should be constructed from a high-contrast, unique image. Use black and white, or any colors that are distinguishable from each other in low-light environments. In most cases, if you're printing the markers, you should be aware of glare and reflective surfaces.

Our Marker

For this example, I've included the marker in our GitHub repository. All the code from this chapter is available at https://github.com/kyleroche/Professional_iOS_AugmentedReality. The source code is also available from the Source Code/Download area of the Apress web site at www.apress.com.

We'll be using the book's cover as our AR marker. Assuming there have been no changes to the image during the printing process, this should make testing slightly easier because you won't have to print anything.

To project the 3D model, we're going to use OpenGL ES (OpenGL for Embedded Systems). Xcode has an OpenGL Gaming template available right out of the box. However, for educational purposes, let's build this app from the ground up. Before we get started, let's go over the basic features of OpenGL.

OpenGL ES

OpenGL ES is a low-level, lightweight API for advanced embedded of graphics using well-defined subset profiles of OpenGL. It provides a low-level API between software applications and hardware or software graphics engines.

There are many advantages to using OpenGL ES as a developer:

- *Industry standard and royalty free:* Anyone can download the OpenGL ES specification and implement and ship products based on OpenGL ES.

- *Small footprint and low power consumption:* The embedded space varies on processing capabilities. OpenGL ES accommodates these differences by requiring a minimum footprint with minimum data storage.

- *Extensible and evolving:* OpenGL's extension mechanism functions in OpenGL ES, so you can add new hardware profiles as they become available.

- *Easy to use and well documented:* OpenGL is the foundation for OpenGL ES. There are numerous training materials available on the web and in published form.

Neither this book, nor this chapter, will make you an expert on OpenGL ES. However, we will make notes of the features we use to build out this application, and I'll reference some materials you can access if you want to learn more about 3D programming on iOS.

Creating the Project

Open Xcode and start a new project. Use the Single View Application to get some of the default setup for the project. Make sure you select **Universal** as your **Device Family**. You can leave **Automatic Reference Counting** enabled.

Adding the String SDK

Unzip the download from String to a directory on your local machine. From the Libraries folder, copy libStringOGL*.a to your Xcode project. From the Headers folder, copy StringOGL.h and TrackerOutput.h to your Xcode project. This is all we need from the String SDK. Let's move on to adding the project dependencies, and then we'll circle back on how to use the String SDK.

Project Dependencies

We need to add a few frameworks to our Xcode project to make sure the String SDK has the resources it needs. Click your project name in the Xcode navigator. Switch to the **Build Phases** tab and add the QuartzCore, OpenGLES, AVFoundation, CoreGraphics, CoreMedia, and CoreVideo frameworks to the section called **Link Binary with Libraries**.

Switch from the **Build Phases** tab to the **Build Settings** tab. Find the configuration key called **Other Linker Flags**. Enter -lstdc++ as the value. Refer to Figure 10–1 for the setup we've completed thus far.

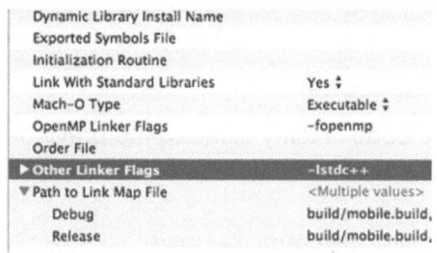

Figure 10–1. *We've set up the Frameworks and Linker Flags correctly.*

EAGLView

In previous versions of Xcode, the OpenGL templates included the EAGLView template. Xcode 4.2, along with iOS 5, introduced a new OpenGL Gaming template and removed the previous OpenGL application template. This new template no longer provides the EAGLView files we had in previous versions. So, we are left to create these ourselves. Automatic Reference Counting was not available in the iOS 4.3 templates. We will add that to our project as well.

Create a new Objective-C class in your Xcode project. Name the class EAGLView. Make it a subclass of NSObject for now. We will change this in a moment.

Open EAGLView.h in Xcode and remove the existing import statements. Add the new import statements from Listing 10–1.

Listing 10–1. *import Statements*

```
#import <UIKit/UIKit.h>
#import <OpenGLES/ES1/gl.h>
#import <OpenGLES/ES1/glext.h>
#import <OpenGLES/ES2/gl.h>
#import <OpenGLES/ES2/glext.h>
@class EAGLContext;
```

Next, change the interface declaration so that EAGLView extends UIView and not NSObject. We are going to declare a few properties related to the frame buffer we'll be using to render our 3D object. Update the EAGLView.h class to look like the code found in Listing 10–2.

Listing 10–2. *Updated @interface for EAGLView*

```
@interface EAGLView : UIView {
    GLint framebufferWidth;
    GLint framebufferHeight;

    GLuint defaultFramebuffer, colorRenderbuffer;
    GLuint depthRenderbuffer;
}

@property (nonatomic, retain) EAGLContext *context;
@property (nonatomic, readonly) GLuint defaultFramebuffer;
@property (nonatomic, readonly) GLint framebufferWidth;
@property (nonatomic, readonly) GLint framebufferHeight;

- (void)setFrameBuffer;
```

Most of this code is fairly close to the previous iOS 4.3 templates. We trimmed it down a bit for simplicity. Switch over to EAGLView.m and add the import statements from Listing 10–3.

Listing 10–3. *Import the QuartzCore Library*

```
#import <QuartzCore/QuartzCore.h>
```

Next, we need to declare a few private methods for our class. Just below the import statements and above the implementation block, add the code from Listing 10–4.

Listing 10–4. *Private Methods*

```
@interface EAGLView (PrivateMethods)
- (void)createFramebuffer;
- (void)deleteFramebuffer;
@end
```

We'll implement these methods shortly. First, let's set up the basics of our class. We need to synthesize the properties we added to the interface. Inside the implementation block of EAGLView.m, add the code from Listing 10–5.

Listing 10–5. *Synthesize the Properties*

```
@synthesize context;
@synthesize framebufferWidth;
@synthesize framebufferHeight;
@synthesize defaultFramebuffer;
```

The CAEGLLayer class is what supports the drawing for OpenGL content in iOS applications. Because we are using OpenGL for rendering our 3D objects, we need a reference to the CAEGLLayer class. Create the static method found in Listing 10–6, just after the synthesize statements.

Listing 10–6. *layerClass Method Required for OpenGL Apps*

```
+ (Class)layerClass {
    return [CAEAGLLayer class];
}
```

Before we set up our layer's associated view, we have to change the rendering attributes that we want to use. The drawableProperties property lets you configure the color format for the rendering surface and the content. We will set this property's value in our init method. Copy the method from Listing 10–7 to the implementation.

Listing 10–7. *initWithCoder Method*

```
- (id)initWithCoder:(NSCoder*)coder
{
    self = [super initWithCoder:coder];
        if (self) {
        CAEAGLLayer *eaglLayer = (CAEAGLLayer *)self.layer;

        eaglLayer.opaque = TRUE;
        eaglLayer.drawableProperties = [NSDictionary dictionaryWithObjectsAndKeys:
                                        [NSNumber numberWithBool:FALSE],
kEAGLDrawablePropertyRetainedBacking,
                                        kEAGLColorFormatRGBA8,
kEAGLDrawablePropertyColorFormat,
                                        nil];
    }

    return self;
}
```

The code in bold is where we set up our drawableProperties for this rendering. For more information on OpenGL color and formatting options, refer to *Pro OpenGL ES for iOS* (Apress), which can be found at www.apress.com/mobile/ios/9781430238409.

Because the rendering surface is presented to the user using Core Animation, any effects or animations you apply affect the 3D content that will be rendered to the user. Apple's documentation recommends the following best practices:

- Set the layer's opaque attribute to TRUE.
- Set the layer's bounds to match the dimensions of the display.
- Make sure the layer is not transformed.

- Avoid drawing other layers on top of the CAEGLLayer object. Other, non-OpenGL content, might negatively affect performance.

- When drawing landscape content on a portrait display, you should rotate the content yourself rather than using the CAEGLLayer transform.

Now that we understand some of the basic principles and best practices, let's create our OpenGL layer. We declared a few methods in our interface file. Add the code from Listing 10–8 to the implementation.

Listing 10–8. *setContext Method*

```
- (void)setContext:(EAGLContext *)newContext
{
    if (context != newContext) {
        [self deleteFramebuffer];

        context = newContext;

        [EAGLContext setCurrentContext:nil];
    }
}
```

This method will be called from our viewDidLoad method in the parent UIViewController. We'll be using this to set up our OpenGL context before we set our frame buffers. Copy the code from Listing 10–9 to set up the frame buffer.

Listing 10–9. *createFrameBuffer Method*

```
- (void)createFramebuffer
{
    if (context && !defaultFramebuffer) {
        [EAGLContext setCurrentContext:context];

        // 1
        if ([self respondsToSelector:@selector(setContentScaleFactor:)])
        {
        float screenScale = [UIScreen mainScreen].scale;

        self.contentScaleFactor = screenScale;
        }

        // 2
        glGenFramebuffers(1, &defaultFramebuffer);
        glBindFramebuffer(GL_FRAMEBUFFER, defaultFramebuffer);

        // 3
        glGenRenderbuffers(1, &colorRenderbuffer);
        glBindRenderbuffer(GL_RENDERBUFFER, colorRenderbuffer);
        [context renderbufferStorage:GL_RENDERBUFFER fromDrawable:(CAEAGLLayer
*)self.layer];
        glGetRenderbufferParameteriv(GL_RENDERBUFFER, GL_RENDERBUFFER_WIDTH,
&framebufferWidth);
        glGetRenderbufferParameteriv(GL_RENDERBUFFER, GL_RENDERBUFFER_HEIGHT,
&framebufferHeight);
```

```
        glFramebufferRenderbuffer(GL_FRAMEBUFFER, GL_COLOR_ATTACHMENT0, GL_RENDERBUFFER,
colorRenderbuffer);

        // 4
        glGenRenderbuffers(1, &depthRenderbuffer);
        glBindRenderbuffer(GL_RENDERBUFFER, depthRenderbuffer);
                glRenderbufferStorage(GL_RENDERBUFFER, GL_DEPTH_COMPONENT16,
framebufferWidth, framebufferHeight);

        glFramebufferRenderbuffer(GL_FRAMEBUFFER, GL_DEPTH_ATTACHMENT, GL_RENDERBUFFER,
depthRenderbuffer);

        if (glCheckFramebufferStatus(GL_FRAMEBUFFER) != GL_FRAMEBUFFER_COMPLETE)
            NSLog(@"Failed to make complete framebuffer object %x",
glCheckFramebufferStatus(GL_FRAMEBUFFER));
        }
}
```

This method is a bit more complex. Look for the comments in bold, and we'll step through each section. The comment marked "1" handles scaling for our OpenGL layer. We are basically setting it to match the scale of the screen. Section "2" creates the default Framebuffer object. Section "3" creates a color buffer as well as allocates the buffer storage for the context. The last section, section "4", creates the depth buffer and attaches it.

For marker-based augmented reality applications, most of this code will be the same. You can usually simply swap out your marker image and some of the matrices in your rendering layer.

We've already created the method to handle creating our frame buffer. We need to set up some methods to clean up the objects as well. Add the code from Listing 10–10 to the implementation.

Listing 10–10. *deleteFramebuffer (and dealloc) Methods*

```
- (void)deleteFramebuffer
{
    if (context) {
        [EAGLContext setCurrentContext:context];

        if (defaultFramebuffer) {
            glDeleteFramebuffers(1, &defaultFramebuffer);
            defaultFramebuffer = 0;
        }

        if (colorRenderbuffer) {
            glDeleteRenderbuffers(1, &colorRenderbuffer);
            colorRenderbuffer = 0;
        }
    }
}
- (void)dealloc
{
    [self deleteFramebuffer];
}
```

These wrappers check the context to determine which type of buffer should be removed, and then it removes that particular buffer. We also added a call to this method from dealloc. Finally, we need a method that binds our frame buffer to the view. Copy the code from Listing 10–11.

Listing 10–11. *setFramebuffer Method*

```
- (void)setFramebuffer
{
    if (context) {
        [EAGLContext setCurrentContext:context];

        if (!defaultFramebuffer)
            [self createFramebuffer];

        glBindFramebuffer(GL_FRAMEBUFFER, defaultFramebuffer);

        glViewport(0, 0, framebufferWidth, framebufferHeight);
    }
}
```

The last two lines of this method are the only ones of which you need to take note. The first binds our frame buffer to our layer. The second sets up the positioning of the layer, starting at the top left of the screen (0,0) and expanding the width/height of the defined frame buffers.

This is all we need to change in our EAGLView class. Let's make sure our views utilize our new class.

For each of our storyboards, **MainStoryboard_iPhone.storyboard** and **MainStoryboard_iPad.storyboard**, we need to set our **View** to the custom class, **EAGLView**. See Figure 10–2 for a detailed illustration of how this should look.

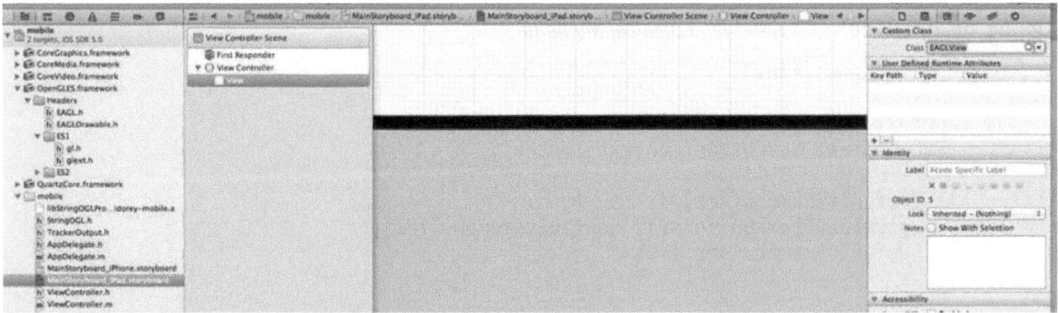

Figure 10–2. *Set the view to our EAGLView class.*

In the navigator, on the left, I've selected the storyboard. Then expanded the **View Controller** and selected its default **View**. From the **Identity Inspector** tab on the right, we've selected our new EAGLView class for this **View**. Make sure you repeat this process for both storyboards.

Now that we know our view is set up correctly, let's make the necessary changes.

Creating the AR ViewController

Open ViewController.h in Xcode. First, we need to import the required headers to set up our view. Listing 10–12 shows the import statements that are required for this class.

Listing 10–12. *import Statements for ViewController*

```
#import "StringOGL.h"
#import <OpenGLES/EAGL.h>
#import <OpenGLES/ES1/gl.h>
#import <OpenGLES/ES1/glext.h>
#import <OpenGLES/ES2/gl.h>
#import <OpenGLES/ES2/glext.h>
```

Next, we have to nominate ViewController as a StringOGLDelegate class. While we do this, let's also define our instance variables. Copy the code from Listing 10–13 to the interface block.

Listing 10–13. *Instance Variables*

```
@interface ViewController : UIViewController <StringOGLDelegate> {
    EAGLContext *context;
    StringOGL *stringOGL;
    float projectionMatrix[16];
    BOOL animating;
}
```

Next, define the methods shown in Listing 10–14.

Listing 10–14. *Instance Methods*

```
- (void)startAnimation;
- (void)stopAnimation;
```

I'll explain these methods and what they do when we implement them later in this chapter. Switch over to ViewController.m. The first method we need to add creates a standard projection matrix for our 3D object. This method is about as basic of a projection matrix as possible. It's modeled slightly after the glFrustum specification. glFrustum describes a perspective matrix that produces a perspective projection. This is done by multiplying the current matrix by the glFrustum matrix and then replacing the current matrix with the resulting matrix. Add the code from Listing 10–15, just before the didReceiveMemoryWarning method.

Listing 10–15. *Create the Projection Matrix*

```
- (void)createProjectionMatrix: (float *)matrix verticalFOV: (float)verticalFOV
aspectRatio: (float)aspectRatio nearClip: (float)nearClip farClip: (float)farClip
{
        memset(matrix, 0, sizeof(*matrix) * 16);

        float tan = tanf(verticalFOV * M_PI / 360.f);

        matrix[0] = 1.f / (tan * aspectRatio);
        matrix[5] = 1.f / tan;
        matrix[10] = (farClip + nearClip) / (nearClip - farClip);
        matrix[11] = -1.f;
        matrix[14] = (2.f * farClip * nearClip) / (nearClip - farClip);
}
```

I'll refer you again to the Apress publication on OpenGL programming for iOS (*Pro OpenGL ES for iOS*) for more detail into what exactly is going on with this method. However, as you read through this method, keep in mind that depth buffer precision is affected by the values of nearClip and farClip. As the ratio of farClip to nearClip increases, the depth buffer will be less distinguishable between surfaces that are near each other in the view. nearClip can never be set to zero because the multiplier approaches infinity as nearClip approaches zero.

We defined two methods in our header that we'll complete next. However, before we move on, import the EAGLView header to ViewController.h. Then, add the code from Listing 10–16 to the ViewController.

Listing 10–16. *Animation Start and Stop Methods*

```
- (void)startAnimation
{
    if (!animating) {
        [stringOGL resume];
        animating = TRUE;
    }
}

- (void)stopAnimation
{
    if (animating) {
        [stringOGL pause];
        animating = FALSE;
    }
}
```

There is only one required method for a class that implements the StringOGLDelegate protocol. That is the render method. This method handles the actions that the String SDK will take after it recognizes a potential marker. Add the method from Listing 10–17 to the ViewController.

Listing 10–17. *Render the 3D Objects*

```
- (void)render
{
    [(EAGLView *)self.view setFramebuffer];

    static const GLfloat squareVertices[] = {
        -0.33f, -0.33f,
        0.33f, -0.33f,
        -0.33f,  0.33f,
        0.33f,  0.33f,
    };

    static const GLubyte squareColors[] = {
        255, 255,   0, 255,
        0,   255, 255, 255,
        0,     0,   0,   0,
        255,   0, 255, 255,
    };

    const int maxMarkerCount = 10;
```

```
        struct MarkerInfoMatrixBased markerInfo[10];

        int markerCount = [stringOGL getMarkerInfoMatrixBased: markerInfo
maxMarkerCount: maxMarkerCount];
    for (int i = 0; i < markerCount; i++)
    {
        glMatrixMode(GL_PROJECTION);
        glLoadMatrixf(projectionMatrix);

        glMatrixMode(GL_MODELVIEW);
        glLoadIdentity();
        glMultMatrixf(markerInfo[i].transform);

        glVertexPointer(2, GL_FLOAT, 0, squareVertices);
        glEnableClientState(GL_VERTEX_ARRAY);
        glColorPointer(4, GL_UNSIGNED_BYTE, 0, squareColors);
        glEnableClientState(GL_COLOR_ARRAY);

        glDrawArrays(GL_TRIANGLE_STRIP, 0, 4);

    }
}
```

The method has a few purposes. First, we set up the vertices of our rendering location, as well as the color. Next, we set a limit of how many markers the String SDK will recognize. We have set this to 10. We create a `struct` to contact the `MarkerInfo` as it gets recognized, and then we loop through the results of the `getMarkerInfoMatrixBased` method. This method will use any of the image files we have loaded in our project and will attempt to recognize them in our camera view.

In the loop, we have our standard OpenGL code. This example prints out a standard OpenGL cube, like we saw back in the iOS 4.3 templates. Before we update our viewDidLoad method, change the class so it renders only in portrait mode. Update the shouldAutorotateToInterfaceOrientation method as shown in Listing 10–18.

Listing 10–18. *Allow for Only Portrait Orientation*

```
return (interfaceOrientation == UIInterfaceOrientationPortrait);
```

We're almost done. But, before we test the application we need to update the viewDidLoad method. Update the method with the code in Listing 10–19.

Listing 10–19. *Updated viewDidLoad*

```
- (void)viewDidLoad
{
    [super viewDidLoad];
    animating = NO;

    EAGLContext *aContext = [[EAGLContext alloc]
initWithAPI:kEAGLRenderingAPIOpenGLES1];

    if (!aContext)
        NSLog(@"Failed to create ES context");
    else if (![EAGLContext setCurrentContext:aContext])
        NSLog(@"Failed to set ES context current");
```

```
    context = aContext;

    EAGLView *eaglView = (EAGLView *)self.view;

    [(EAGLView *)self.view setContext:context];
    [(EAGLView *)self.view setFrameBuffer];

    int viewport[4] = {0, 0, eaglView.framebufferWidth, eaglView.framebufferHeight};
    viewport[1] = (eaglView.framebufferHeight - viewport[3]) / 2;

    glViewport(viewport[0], viewport[1], viewport[2], viewport[3]);

    float aspectRatio = viewport[2] / (float)viewport[3];

    [self createProjectionMatrix: projectionMatrix verticalFOV: 47.22f aspectRatio:
aspectRatio nearClip: 0.1f farClip: 100.f];

    // Initialize String
    stringOGL = [[StringOGL alloc] initWithDelegate: self context: aContext
frameBuffer:[eaglView defaultFramebuffer] leftHanded: NO];

    [stringOGL setProjectionMatrix:projectionMatrix viewport:viewport orientation:[self
interfaceOrientation] reorientIPhoneSplash:YES];

    // Load image markers
    [stringOGL loadImageMarker: @"bookcover" ofType: @"png"];

}
```

The first half of this method sets up our OpenGL context using the methods we've already created in this chapter. The bold lines of code are specific to the String SDK. First, we initialize String with self as the delegate and crate the appropriate frame buffer. Next, we set up the projection matrix. Finally, we load up the markers. If you have multiple markers, you can add them all here.

Our final code update is with the viewWillAppear and viewWillDisappear methods. Update them as shown in Listing 10–20.

Listing 10–20. *Start and Stop the Animation*

```
- (void)viewWillAppear:(BOOL)animated
{
    [self startAnimation];

    [super viewWillAppear:animated];
}

- (void)viewWillDisappear:(BOOL)animated
{
    [self stopAnimation];

    [super viewWillDisappear:animated];
}
```

String will not actually start until the first resume method is called. If you remember, we referenced this method in our startAnimation wrapper. That's why we're placing this in our viewWillAppear method.

Run the project on a physical device. Because we built this as a universal program, it should run fine on an iPad or iPhone device. Make sure you point your camera at the book or the image on your screen. You will see something similar to Figure 10–3.

Figure 10–3. *View our AR marker application in action.*

Summary

In Chapter 9, we discussed a few of the toolkits available on the market for developers building augmented reality applications. In most cases, reinventing the wheel around object recognition isn't the best use of your resources. The value proposition with these toolkits is to handle the foundational work and let you concentrate on the business layer or functionality in the app.

In this chapter, we started with a single view application and built up a marker-based augmented reality application powered by String's AR SDK. We barely scratched the surface on OpenGL and 3D modeling, but we learned enough to set the stage for more complex applications.

In Chapter 11, we'll be switching gears to social media and building an augmented reality application to render social data based on geographical coordinates.

Summary

Building a Social AR Application

In Chapter 10, we discussed marker-based augmented reality applications using the String SDK. Location-based AR applications have been available longer than marker-based AR applications due to the processing power required on a handheld device to recognize markers.

In this chapter, we'll take a more traditional look at AR applications, and build something closer to the original apps that started the revolution on the AppStore and Android Market.

We are going to build a GPS-enabled AR application to find nearby Facebook places.

Getting Set Up

First, we need to make sure we are set up for developing an application around Facebook's Open Graph. There are a few steps to this process. Basically, they are:

- Create a Facebook application
- Clone the Facebook iOS SDK GitHub repository
- Enable single sign-on for the application

Creating a Facebook Application

Creating an application for Facebook gives the API and your users context for permissions and data. Without an application, there would be no bounds for what you are retrieving via the Open Graph API. The Facebook application allows your users to decide what type of access they will give to your application.

Visit https://developers.facebook.com/apps. If you have worked with the Facebook APIs in the past, you should be all set up to create a new Facebook application. In the top right of the Developer's Dashboard there is a button labeled **Create New App**. Click this button and follow the instructions to set up your application. I've named my application *kyleroche*. When you're set up, you should see something like Figure 11–1 on your app's Dashboard.

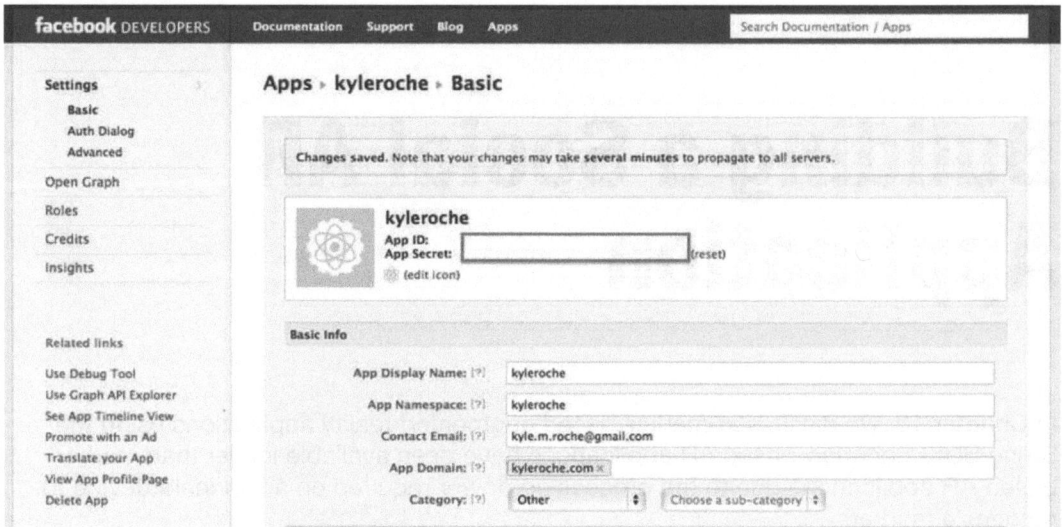

Figure 11–1. *Set up the Facebook application.*

Take note of your **App ID** and **App Secret**. You will need your **App ID** when you set up your Xcode project.

Cloning the Facebook iOS SDK

Using your browser, visit https://github.com/facebook/facebook-ios-sdk to download the latest version of the Facebook iOS SDK. Clone the repository to your local machine. If you're interested, you can run through some of the sample application. Open the Xcode project located in the sample subdirectory. Open DemoAppViewController.m in Xcode, and locate the section of code shown in Listing 11–1.

Listing 11–1. *Set Your Facebook App ID*

```
// Your Facebook APP Id must be set before running this example
// See http://www.facebook.com/developers/createapp.php
// Also, your application must bind to the fb[app_id]:// URL
// scheme (substitute [app_id] for your real Facebook app id).
static NSString* kAppId = nil;
```

Make sure you change nil to your Facebook App ID. There is one more step you need to complete to test the demo application provided with the SDK. Open your application's .plist file and find the entry for URL Schemes. Item 0, of that array, needs a value of fb[*your app id*] to run properly. When authenticating from a native iOS application, Facebook validates the local app's authenticity by using a URL Scheme. In iOS, URL Schemes are used to launch other native applications in context. The prefix (now your app ID) is used to uniquely identify the application. For example, if my app ID was 123456 I would set my URL Scheme to fb123456, and after authentication, Facebook would verify that the native app binds to the URL Scheme fb123456://[action].

At this point, the application won't function unless you have the Facebook application installed on the same device.

Vocabulary Lesson

So far in this book, we've built application examples for marker-based augmented reality and gaming scenarios for augmented reality. We haven't yet discussed some of the differences with location-based AR. In this section, we'll discuss a few new terms we'll be using in this application.

Azimuth

Azimuth is a word from the Arabic language. Its literal translation is "direction." Azimuth is an angular measurement used in spherical coordinate systems, such as is found in geospacial calculations. The azimuth is the angle between the projected vector and a reference vector on a well-defined reference plane. For example, consider a location-based application in which there is a point of interest. If we would like to know which direction we need to face to be pointing toward this point of interest, we might calculate the azimuth of that point from the North Pole. We would draw (figuratively) a perpendicular plane from our current position to the North Pole, and a second perpendicular plane from the point of interest through to sea level (or an equal plane under our position). The angle between the two planes is the azimuth.

As they say, "a picture is worth a thousand words." See Figure 11–2 for a more detailed explanation.

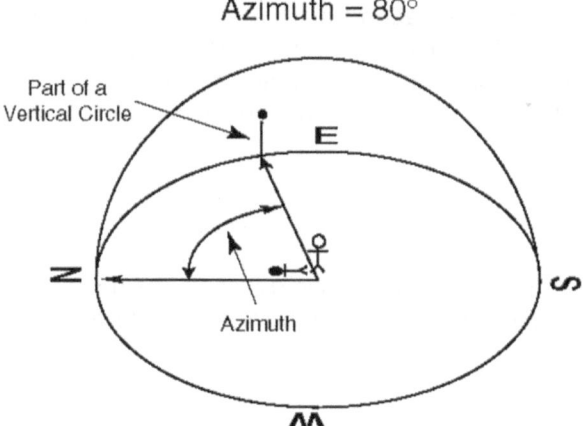

Figure 11–2. *Calculate the azimuth. Azimuth of the point and the North Pole is 80 degrees.*

In the example application we'll be building, we'll discuss the formula used to calculate the azimuth from our viewpoint to a viewpoint at another GPS coordinate. However, if you just can't wait that long, here's an example: if we are standing at latitude φ_1, longitude zero and we want to find the azimuth from our viewpoint to Point 2 at latitude φ_2, longitude L (positive eastward), the formula is shown in Figure 11–3.

$$\Lambda \;=\; (1-e^2)\frac{\tan\phi_2}{\tan\phi_1} \;+\; e^2\sqrt{\frac{1+(1-e^2)(\tan\phi_2)^2}{1+(1-e^2)(\tan\phi_1)^2}}$$

Figure 11–3. *Here is a formula example to find the azimuth.*

Corrected Heading

We've actually discussed this concept already in the book. I'm not sure there's a standard term for this, but remember back to our magnetometer discussion in Chapter 4 where we discussed orientation changes. Consider an iPhone in portrait view with a heading of north. If you lay the iPhone on its side, and it is now in landscape right mode (for example), you are still facing north, but the iPhone's heading might mistakenly think you have changed your heading to west.

When the orientation changes in an AR application (especially one built around location-based information), you must take care to adjust your heading accordingly.

Building the Application

Let's get started. Open Xcode and create a project called Ch11 using the **Empty Application** template. This template builds a simple application using a single window.

Credits

There are a lot of works on github.com, stackoverflow.com, Apple's developer forums, and other various online communities that discuss location-based AR. There are toolkits like ARKit (https://github.com/zac/iphonearkit), which has almost 100 different forked variations from contributors. The work in this chapter is based on some of those variations. So, I would like to credit Zac White and Niels Hansen, specifically, for providing a starting point upon which we could build.

Required Frameworks

We are building a location-based application. As you might have guessed, we need to add the CoreLocation Framework to the project. Make sure you have that included before you move ahead.

Adding the Facebook iOS SDK

When we downloaded the SDK earlier, there was an example application provided. Because we are now starting with a clean application, we need to add the SDK back to this project.

Open the archived SDK directory in Finder. Drag the src directory from the SDK to your Xcode project. Make sure you select the option to copy resources to the project's directory. We will get back to this later in the chapter.

And, We're Off!

Okay, enough setup. Let's get coding. Create a Group in your Xcode project called ARController. We'll separate the AR-specific code here so you can reuse it in your own projects later.

Create a new class in the ARController Group called ARController.m. Make sure this class subclasses NSObject and not UIViewController. Open ARController.h in Xcode. Update the interface as shown in Listing 11–2.

Listing 11–2. *Updated ARController.h*

```objectivec
#import <Foundation/Foundation.h>
#import <CoreLocation/CoreLocation.h>
#import <UIKit/UIKit.h>

@interface ARController : NSObject <UIAccelerometerDelegate, CLLocationManagerDelegate>
{

}

@property (nonatomic, retain) UIViewController *rootViewController;
@property (nonatomic, retain) UIImagePickerController *pickerController;
@property (nonatomic, retain) UIView *hudView;
@property (nonatomic, retain) CLLocationManager *locationManager;
@property (nonatomic, retain) UIAccelerometer *accelerometer;

- (id)initWithViewController:(UIViewController *)viewController;
- (void)presentModalARControllerAnimated:(BOOL)animated;

@end
```

We are setting up some properties here for later use. I'll explain each of these in detail in the implementation file. Switch over to ARController.m and add the code from Listing 11–3.

Listing 11–3. *ARController.m*

```objectivec
#import "ARController.h"

@implementation ARController
@synthesize rootViewController = _rootViewController;
@synthesize pickerController = _pickerController;
```

```
@synthesize hudView = _hudView;
@synthesize locationManager = _locationManager;
@synthesize accelerometer = _accelerometer;

- (id)initWithViewController:(UIViewController *)viewController {
    self.rootViewController = viewController;
    CGRect screenBounds = [[UIScreen mainScreen] bounds];
    self.hudView = [[UIView alloc] initWithFrame:screenBounds];
    self.rootViewController.view = self.hudView;

    self.pickerController = [[[UIImagePickerController alloc] init] autorelease];
        self.pickerController.sourceType = UIImagePickerControllerSourceTypeCamera;
        self.pickerController.cameraViewTransform = CGAffineTransformScale(
self.pickerController.cameraViewTransform, 1.13f,  1.13f);

        self.pickerController.showsCameraControls = NO;
        self.pickerController.navigationBarHidden = YES;
        self.pickerController.cameraOverlayView = _hudView;

        self.locationManager = [[CLLocationManager alloc] init];
        self.locationManager.headingFilter = kCLHeadingFilterNone;
        self.locationManager.desiredAccuracy = kCLLocationAccuracyBest;
        self.locationManager.delegate = self;
        [self.locationManager startUpdatingHeading];
        [self.locationManager startUpdatingLocation];

        _accelerometer = [UIAccelerometer sharedAccelerometer];
        _accelerometer.updateInterval = 0.25;
        _accelerometer.delegate = self;


    [[NSNotificationCenter defaultCenter] addObserver:self
selector:@selector(deviceOrientationDidChange:)
name:UIDeviceOrientationDidChangeNotification object:nil];
    [[UIDevice currentDevice] beginGeneratingDeviceOrientationNotifications];

    return self;
}

- (void)presentModalARControllerAnimated:(BOOL)animated {
    [self.rootViewController presentModalViewController:[self pickerController]
animated:animated];
    _hudView.frame = _pickerController.view.bounds;
}

- (void)deviceOrientationDidChange:(NSNotification *)notification {

}

@end
```

Let's step through this section, before we get too far ahead. First, we need to synthesize the properties we defined in our implementation file. We have three methods so far in this class. First, the initWithViewController method is used to add a UIImagePicker (much like we did in Chapter 7) to the view, and then overlay it with a new type of HUD layer.

We then set up our location manager and accelerometer and start our update services. This will look very similar to the code we created in Chapter 4 when we were experimenting with iOS sensor programming. By itself, this class isn't all that useful. Let's start building some new classes that leverage what we have so far.

Create a new file in your Xcode project called RootViewController that subclasses the UIViewController template. Make sure you uncheck the **With XIB for user interface** option. Open RootViewController.h in Xcode and make the changes reflected in Listing 11–4.

Listing 11–4. *Updated RootViewController.h*

```
#import <UIKit/UIKit.h>
@class ARController;

@interface RootViewController : UIViewController {
}

@property (nonatomic, retain) ARController *arController;
@end
```

We referenced our ARController class and set up a new property of the same type. Switch to RootViewController.m in Xcode. Update the class as shown in Listing 11–5.

Listing 11–5. *Updated RootViewController.m*

```
#import "RootViewController.h"
#import "ARController.h"

@implementation RootViewController
@synthesize arController = _arController;

- (id)initWithNibName:(NSString *)nibNameOrNil bundle:(NSBundle *)nibBundleOrNil
{
    self = [super initWithNibName:nibNameOrNil bundle:nibBundleOrNil];
    if (self) {
        // Custom initialization
    }
    return self;
}

- (void)didReceiveMemoryWarning
{
    // Releases the view if it doesn't have a superview.
    [super didReceiveMemoryWarning];

    // Release any cached data, images, etc that aren't in use.
}

#pragma mark - View lifecycle

// Implement loadView to create a view hierarchy programmatically, without using a nib.
- (void)loadView
{
    _arController = [[ARController alloc] initWithViewController:self];
}

- (void)viewDidAppear:(BOOL)animated {
```

```
            [super viewDidAppear:animated];
            [self.arController presentModalARControllerAnimated:NO];
}

- (void)viewWillAppear:(BOOL)animated {
        [super viewWillAppear:animated];
}

/*
// Implement viewDidLoad to do additional setup after loading the view, typically from a
nib.
- (void)viewDidLoad
{
    [super viewDidLoad];
}
*/

- (void)viewDidUnload
{
    [super viewDidUnload];
    // Release any retained subviews of the main view.
    // e.g. self.myOutlet = nil;
}

-
(BOOL)shouldAutorotateToInterfaceOrientation:(UIInterfaceOrientation)interfaceOrientatio
n
{
    // Return YES for supported orientations
        return YES;
}

@end
```

We made a few small changes here. In the viewDidAppear method, we present our modal AR controller. This allows us to reuse the code we are building in other applications without re-creating the base UIViewControllers. In the loadView method, we allocate our new arController instance with the UIImagePickerController and HUD layer.

We have one more step before we have our base project set up with a UIImagePicker (camera view) under our user interface. Open AppDelegate.h in Xcode. Update the header file as shown in Listing 11–6.

Listing 11–6. *Updated AppDelegate.h*

```
#import <UIKit/UIKit.h>

@class RootViewController;
@interface AppDelegate : UIResponder <UIApplicationDelegate> {

}

@property (strong, nonatomic) UIWindow *window;
@property (nonatomic, retain) RootViewController *rootViewController;
@end
```

Open AppDelegate.m in Xcode. We will be overriding our
didFinishLaunchingWithOptions method so that we can add our RootViewController to
the view stack. Update AppDelegate.m with the changes reflected in Listing 11–7.

Listing 11–7. *Updated AppDelegate.m*

```objc
#import "AppDelegate.h"
#import "RootViewController.h"

@implementation AppDelegate

@synthesize window = _window;
@synthesize rootViewController = _rootViewController;

- (void)dealloc
{
    [_window release];
    [super dealloc];
}

- (BOOL)application:(UIApplication *)application
didFinishLaunchingWithOptions:(NSDictionary *)launchOptions
{
    self.window = [[[UIWindow alloc] initWithFrame:[[UIScreen mainScreen] bounds]]
autorelease];
    // Override point for customization after application launch.
    _rootViewController = [[RootViewController alloc] init];
    [_window addSubview:_rootViewController.view];

    self.window.backgroundColor = [UIColor clearColor];
    [self.window makeKeyAndVisible];
    return YES;
}
```

Again, this is nothing we haven't seen before. We imported our new RootViewController
class, synthesized the variable, and then added it as a subview to our UIWindow.

Run the application on a physical device that allows for Core Location (iPhone or iPad).
Since we're using the camera, we won't be able to debug using the simulator. You
should be prompted by the location manager, as shown in Figure 11–4, to allow your
current location to be shared with the application.

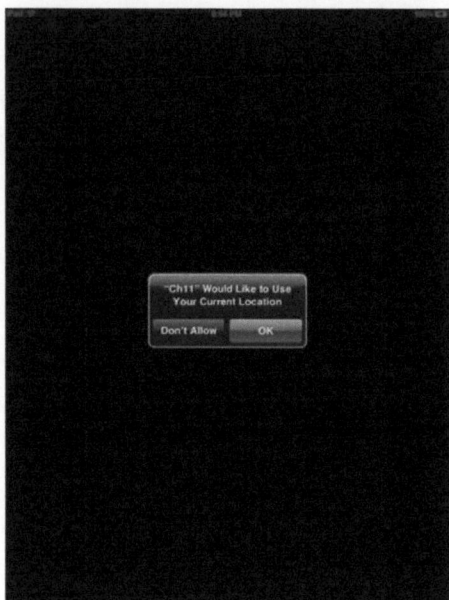

Figure 11–4. *Allow location sharing through location manager permissions.*

After you accept the message, you will be taken to a full-screen camera view, as shown in Figure 11–5. Hopefully, you'll have better scenery.

Figure 11–5. *Giving permission for location sharing will bring up the camera view.*

Listening for Sensor Updates

We have updates for heading and location enabled, but we aren't doing anything with these yet. Nor are we responding to change in the orientation of the device. In Chapter 7, we discussed the conversion from radians to degrees, and how this is necessary when calculating angles on the screen. Let's set up some convenience methods for this purpose. Open Ch11_Prefix.pch and add the code from Listing 11–8.

Listing 11–8. *Degrees to Radians and Back Again*

```
#define degreesToRadians(x) (M_PI * (x) / 180.0)
#define radiansToDegrees(x) ((x) * 180.0/M_PI)
```

Now that we have that out of the way, we need to define a few more variables. Open ARController.h and add the variables from Listing 11–9.

Listing 11–9. *Updated ARController.h*

```
@property (nonatomic) UIDeviceOrientation deviceOrientation;
@property (nonatomic) double range;
```

Switch to ARController.m and synthesize the variables as shown in Listing 11–10.

Listing 11–10. *Synthesize the Properties*

```
@synthesize deviceOrientation = _deviceOrientation;
@synthesize range = _range;
```

We now have a place to store the current device orientation and the range of view. The range variable will be used to store the angle of the view subtended by the screen. An example of calculating a subtended angle is shown in Figure 11–6. At point A, the tree subtends an angle of 25 degrees. We will be calculating an acceptable view by subtending the full width of the screen, assuming an approximate 15-degree view window.

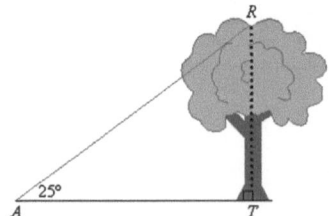

Figure 11–6. *Calculate the acceptable view with a subtended angle.*

In ARController.m, update the deviceOrientationDidChange method with the code shown in Listing 11–11.

Listing 11–11. *New deviceOrientationDidChange Method*

```
- (void)deviceOrientationDidChange:(NSNotification *)notification {
    UIDeviceOrientation orientation = [[UIDevice currentDevice] orientation];
    UIApplication *app = [UIApplication sharedApplication];

    if ( orientation != UIDeviceOrientationUnknown &&
         orientation != UIDeviceOrientationFaceUp &&
         orientation != UIDeviceOrientationFaceDown) {

            CGAffineTransform transform =
CGAffineTransformMakeRotation(degreesToRadians(0));
            CGRect bounds = [[UIScreen mainScreen] bounds];
            [app setStatusBarHidden:YES];
            [app setStatusBarOrientation:UIInterfaceOrientationPortrait animated:
NO];

            if (orientation == UIDeviceOrientationLandscapeLeft) {
                transform                    =
CGAffineTransformMakeRotation(degreesToRadians(90));
                    bounds.size.width  = [[UIScreen mainScreen] bounds].size.height;
                    bounds.size.height = [[UIScreen mainScreen] bounds].size.width;
```

```
                                      [app
setStatusBarOrientation:UIInterfaceOrientationLandscapeRight animated: NO];

                } else if (orientation == UIDeviceOrientationLandscapeRight) {
                                transform                              =
CGAffineTransformMakeRotation(degreesToRadians(-90));
                                bounds.size.width  = [[UIScreen mainScreen] bounds].size.height;
                                bounds.size.height = [[UIScreen mainScreen] bounds].size.width;
                                [app setStatusBarOrientation:UIInterfaceOrientationLandscapeLeft
animated: NO];

                } else if (orientation == UIDeviceOrientationPortraitUpsideDown) {
                                transform =
CGAffineTransformMakeRotation(degreesToRadians(180));
                                [app
setStatusBarOrientation:UIInterfaceOrientationPortraitUpsideDown animated: NO];

                }
                _hudView.transform = transform;
                _hudView.bounds = bounds;
                _range = _hudView.bounds.size.width / 12;

        }
        _deviceOrientation = orientation;
}
```

Let's step through this code from the top. First, we declare a few variables to reference more of the global application. We set up a reference to the device's orientation, as well as our sharedApplication singleton.

We next use the conversion methods defined in our prefix file to swap from degrees to radians, and transform the screen for rotations not Face Up or Face Down (we are ignoring unknown orientations as well).

Finally, we add the transform to our HUD layer, and set the range of the screen. Remember, although the function for the range might look static, it will have a different numerator depending on orientation and device.

Return to ARController.h and set up a few more variables to manage our location updates and heading updates. Add the properties shown in Listing 11–12.

Listing 11–12. *Properties for Heading and Location*

```
@property (nonatomic, retain) CLLocation *deviceLocation;
@property (nonatomic, retain) CLHeading *deviceHeading;
```

Synthesize the properties as shown in Listing 11–13.

Listing 11–13. *Synthesize the Properties*

```
@synthesize deviceHeading = _deviceHeading;
@synthesize deviceLocation = _deviceLocation;
```

We'll use these variables later in the example.

Storing Coordinates

We are pretty close to having everything we need to store the location, range of view of the screen, and heading of our device. However, we haven't defined a place to store the coordinates of our points of interest. This section is modified, but based on work by Alasdair Allan, who based his work on Zac White's ARKit.

Create a new class called ARCoordinate that subclasses NSObject. Open the header file, and add the code from Listing 11–14.

Listing 11–14. *ARCoordinate.h*

```
#import <Foundation/Foundation.h>

@interface ARCoordinate : NSObject {

}

@property (nonatomic, retain) NSString *name;
@property (nonatomic, retain) NSString *place;
@property (nonatomic) double distance;
@property (nonatomic) double inclination;
@property (nonatomic) double azimuth;

- (id)initWithRadialDistance:(double)distance inclination:(double)inclination
azimuth:(double)azimuth;
@end
```

We will eventually be pulling the Facebook places of some of our social network. We will overlay the coordinate with the name of the person and the name of the Facebook place. The other properties store the distance, inclination, and azimuth of the place we are tracking.

The method we defined will be used to create a new coordinate instance with the specified properties.

Switch to ARCoordinate.m and let's finish the implementation of this class. Add the code from Listing 11–15 to ARCoordinate.m.

Listing 11–15. *ARCoordinate.m*

```
#import "ARCoordinate.h"

@implementation ARCoordinate

@synthesize name = _name;
@synthesize place = _place;
@synthesize distance = _distance;
@synthesize inclination = _inclination;
@synthesize azimuth = _azimuth;

- (id)initWithRadialDistance:(double)distance inclination:(double)inclination
azimuth:(double)azimuth {
    if (self = [super init]) {
        _distance = distance;
```

```
        _inclination = inclination;
        _azimuth = azimuth;
    }
    return self;
}
- (void)dealloc {
    [_name release];
    _name = nil;
    [_place release];
    _place = nil;
}

@end
```

There shouldn't be anything surprising here. We are simply setting up our class to retrieve and store the properties of the coordinate. We need another class, which will subclass ARCoordinate, to add the location information.

Create a new class called ARGeoCoordinate. Open the new class in Xcode, and add the code shown in Listing 11–16.

Listing 11–16. *ARGeoCoordinate.h*

```
#import <Foundation/Foundation.h>
#import <CoreLocation/CoreLocation.h>
#import "ARCoordinate.h"

@interface ARGeoCoordinate : ARCoordinate {

}

@property (nonatomic, retain) CLLocation *geoLocation;

- (id)initWithCoordinate:(CLLocation *)location name:(NSString *)name place:(NSString
*)place;
- (id)initWithCoordinateAndOrigin:(CLLocation *)location name:(NSString *)name
place:(NSString *)place origin:(CLLocation *)origin;
- (float)angleFromCoordinate:(CLLocationCoordinate2D)first
second:(CLLocationCoordinate2D)second;
- (void)calibrateUsingOrigin:(CLLocation *)origin;
@end
```

We start by importing the CoreLocation Framework and the ARCoordinate class we just created. We then change the parent class from NSObject to ARCoordinate.

Finally, we declare a property to hold the CLLocation of the point of interest and define a few methods, which we'll discuss in a bit. Switch over to ARGeoCoordinate.m and add the code from Listing 11–17.

Listing 11–17. *ARGeoCoordinate.m*

```
#import "ARGeoCoordinate.h"

@implementation ARGeoCoordinate
@synthesize geoLocation = _geoLocation;
```

```objc
- (id)initWithCoordinate:(CLLocation *)location name:(NSString *)name place:(NSString
*)place {
    if (self = [super init]) {
        self.geoLocation = location;
        // Properties of base class
        self.name = name;
        self.place = place;
    }
    return self;
}

- (id)initWithCoordinateAndOrigin:(CLLocation *)location name:(NSString *)name
place:(NSString *)place origin:(CLLocation *)origin {
    if (self = [super init]) {
        self.geoLocation = location;
        // Properties of base class
        self.name = name;
        self.place = place;
        [self calibrateUsingOrigin:origin];
    }
    return self;
}

- (float)angleFromCoordinate:(CLLocationCoordinate2D)first
second:(CLLocationCoordinate2D)second {
    float longDiff = second.longitude - first.longitude;
    float latDiff = second.latitude - second.latitude;
    float aprxAziumuth = (M_PI *.5f) - atan(latDiff / longDiff);

    if (longDiff > 0) {
        return aprxAziumuth;
    } else if (longDiff < 0) {
        return aprxAziumuth + M_PI;
    } else if (latDiff < 0) {
        return M_PI;
    }

    return 0.0f;
}

- (void)calibrateUsingOrigin:(CLLocation *)origin {
    double baseDistance = [origin distanceFromLocation:_geoLocation];
    self.distance = sqrt(pow([origin altitude] - [_geoLocation altitude], 2) +
pow(baseDistance, 2));
    float angle = sin(ABS([origin altitude] - [_geoLocation altitude]) / self.distance);

    if ([origin altitude] > [_geoLocation altitude]) {
        angle = -angle;
    }

    self.inclination = angle;
    self.azimuth = [self angleFromCoordinate:[origin coordinate] second:[_geoLocation
coordinate]];
}

@end
```

Let's take a break and review what we just added. First, we synthesize the properties we declared. Next, we create a method called initWithCoordinate. This takes in the name and place of the coordinate and sets the properties of the base class, ARCoordinate, so we can use them later in our visualization layer.

We then create a method called initWithCoordinateAndOrigin. This solves the same purpose as initWithCoordinate, but allows you to define an origin as well. The major difference is that this method calls a new internal method, which we will discuss next.

The calibrateUsingOrigin method takes the distance between the two points (your device and the point of interest) and calculates the raw distance, the angle (considering altitude changes), and the azimuth. These properties are set in the base class so we can reference them later in the example.

Finally, we create a method called angleFromCoordinate. This method calculates the distance of the angle between the two points.

Return to ARController.h and insert the code from Listing 11–18, right after the import statements.

Listing 11–18. *ARController.h*

```
@class ARCoordinate;
@class ARGeoCoordinate;
```

Next, declare a property for the ARCoordinate as shown in Listing 11–19.

Listing 11–19. *ARCoordinate Property*

```
@property (nonatomic, retain) ARCoordinate *coordinate;
```

Switch to ARController.m and synthesize the new property. Use the same underscore pattern for the private variable we've been using so far in this chapter. Adjust the initWithViewController method as shown in Listing 11–20. This code is at the bottom of the method.

Listing 11–20. *Updated initWithViewController Method*

```
......
_coordinate = [[ARCoordinate alloc] initWithRadialDistance:1.0 inclination:0 azimuth:0];
return self;
}
```

Add the following code from Listing 11–21 to the top of the ARController implementation file, just below the import statements.

Listing 11–21. *Imports and Private Method for ARController*

```
#import "ARCoordinate.h"
#import "ARGeoCoordinate.h"

@interface ARController (Private)
- (void)updateCurrentLocation:(CLLocation *)newLocation;
- (void)updateLocations;
- (void)updateCurrentCoordinate;
@end
```

In Listing 11–21, we are declaring a new private method that we'll use to update our location array. Also, we import the ARGeoCoordinate and ARCoordinate classes we created earlier. Add the methods from Listing 11–22 to the implementation file.

Listing 11–22. *Location and Heading Methods*

```
- (void)updateCurrentLocation:(CLLocation *)newLocation {
        self.deviceLocation = newLocation;

        for (ARGeoCoordinate *geoLocation in _coordinates ) {
                if ( [geoLocation isKindOfClass:[ARGeoCoordinate class]]) {
                        [geoLocation calibrateUsingOrigin:self.deviceLocation];
                }
        }

}

- (void)updateCurrentCoordinate {

        double adjustment = 0;
        if (_deviceOrientation == UIDeviceOrientationLandscapeLeft)
                adjustment = degreesToRadians(270);
        else if (_deviceOrientation == UIDeviceOrientationLandscapeRight)
                adjustment = degreesToRadians(90);
        else if (_deviceOrientation == UIDeviceOrientationPortraitUpsideDown)
                adjustment = degreesToRadians(180);

        _coordinate.azimuth =
    degreesToRadians(_deviceHeading.magneticHeading) - adjustment;

        [self updateLocations];
}

- (void)updateLocations {
        // we'll get to this one later
}
```

We'll explain these methods and what they do a bit later in the chapter. We used some variables that haven't been declared yet. Let's take care of that now. Switch over to ARController.h. Adjust the header as shown in Listing 11–23.

Listing 11–23. *Updated ARController.h*

```
#import <Foundation/Foundation.h>
#import <CoreLocation/CoreLocation.h>
#import <UIKit/UIKit.h>

@class ARCoordinate;
@class ARGeoCoordinate;

@interface ARController : NSObject <UIAccelerometerDelegate, CLLocationManagerDelegate>
{
        NSMutableArray *_coordinates;
}

@property (nonatomic, retain) UIViewController *rootViewController;
@property (nonatomic, retain) UIImagePickerController *pickerController;
@property (nonatomic, retain) UIView *hudView;
```

```
@property (nonatomic, retain) CLLocationManager *locationManager;
@property (nonatomic, retain) UIAccelerometer *accelerometer;

@property (nonatomic) UIDeviceOrientation deviceOrientation;
@property (nonatomic) double range;

@property (nonatomic, retain) CLLocation *deviceLocation;
@property (nonatomic, retain) CLHeading *deviceHeading;

@property (nonatomic, retain) ARCoordinate *coordinate;
@property (nonatomic) double viewAngle;

- (id)initWithViewController:(UIViewController *)viewController;
- (void)presentModalARControllerAnimated:(BOOL)animated;

- (void)addCoordinate:(ARCoordinate *)coordinate animated:(BOOL)animated;
- (void)removeCoordinate:(ARCoordinate *)coordinate animated:(BOOL)animated;

@end
```

The code in bold is new. Switch to `ARController.m` to synthesize the property and create our new methods. Add the code from Listing 11–24.

Listing 11–24. *Updated ARController.m*

```
// other synthesize statements
@synthesize viewAngle = _viewAngle;

// other methods
- (void)addCoordinate:(ARCoordinate *)coordinate animated:(BOOL)animated {
        [_coordinates addObject:coordinate];
}

- (void)removeCoordinate:(ARCoordinate *)coordinate animated:(BOOL)animated {
        [_coordinates removeObject:coordinate];
}
```

These are just method stubs for now. We will implement the functionality shortly. If you look at what we have so far, you'll notice that our updateLocations method still doesn't do anything. Before we can implement that method, we need to implement a UIView-based class to display the overlay on the ARView for each of our coordinates.

Create a new Objective-C class that extends UIView. Name the new class ARAnnotation. Open ARAnnotation.h and update it as shown in Listing 11–25.

Listing 11–25. *ARAnnotation.h*

```
#import <UIKit/UIKit.h>

@class ARCoordinate;
@interface ARAnnotation : UIView {

}

- (id)initWithCoordinate:(ARCoordinate *)coordinate;

@end
```

Switch over to ARAnnotation.m. Remove all the code in the file, and replace it with what is shown in Listing 11–26.

Listing 11–26. *ARAnnotation.m*

```objc
#import "ARAnnotation.h"
#import "ARCoordinate.h"

#define ANNOTATION_WIDTH 150
#define ANNOTATION_HEIGHT 100

@implementation ARAnnotation

- (id)initWithCoordinate:(ARCoordinate *)coordinate
{
    CGRect annotationFrame = CGRectMake(0, 0, ANNOTATION_WIDTH, ANNOTATION_HEIGHT);

    if (self = [super initWithFrame:annotationFrame]) {
        UILabel *nameLabel = [[UILabel alloc] initWithFrame:CGRectMake(0, 0,
ANNOTATION_WIDTH, 20.0)];
        nameLabel.backgroundColor = [UIColor whiteColor];
        nameLabel.textAlignment = UITextAlignmentCenter;
        nameLabel.text = coordinate.name;
        [nameLabel sizeToFit];
        [nameLabel setFrame:CGRectMake(0, 0, nameLabel.bounds.size.width + 8.0,
nameLabel.bounds.size.height + 8.0)];
        [self addSubview:nameLabel];

        UILabel *placeLabel = [[UILabel alloc] initWithFrame:CGRectMake(25, 0,
ANNOTATION_WIDTH, 20.0)];
        placeLabel.backgroundColor = [UIColor whiteColor];
        placeLabel.textAlignment = UITextAlignmentCenter;
        placeLabel.text = coordinate.place;
        [placeLabel sizeToFit];
        [placeLabel setFrame:CGRectMake(25, 0, placeLabel.bounds.size.width + 8.0,
placeLabel.bounds.size.height + 8.0)];
        [self addSubview:placeLabel];
    }
    return self;
}

@end
```

For the amount of code we just copied, there isn't that much going on here. We are simply creating two labels (one for name and one for place) and placing them in a rectangle that is 150 × 100 pixels. This will be created and placed on our HUD layer for each coordinate. Open ARCoordinate.h in Xcode, and add the code from Listing 11–27.

Listing 11–27. *Updates to ARCoordinate.h*

```objc
 // Declare the class
@class ARAnnotation;
// create this property
@property (nonatomic, retain) ARAnnotation *annotation;
```

In the implementation file, synthesize the property with a private instance variable, and make sure it's been released in the dealloc method.

Switch over to ARController.m. Import the ARAnnotation.h header. Adjust the addCoordinate method as shown in Listing 11–28.

Listing 11–28. *Updates to addCoordinate Method*

```
- (void)addCoordinate:(ARCoordinate *)coordinate animated:(BOOL)animated {
    ARAnnotation *annotation = [[ARAnnotation alloc] initWithCoordinate:coordinate];
    coordinate.annotation = annotation;
    [annotation release];

    [_coordinates addObject:coordinate];
}
```

The update creates a new instance of ARAnnotation for use with the coordinate. We have a few more methods to create before we can finish our updateLocations method. Copy the declarations from Listing 11–29 to the private interface block on the top of ARController.m.

Listing 11–29. *New Private Methods*

```
- (BOOL)viewportContainsCoordinate:(ARCoordinate *)coordinate;
- (double)deltaAzimuthForCoordinate:(ARCoordinate *)coordinate;
- (CGPoint)pointForCoordinate:(ARCoordinate *)coordinate;
- (BOOL)isNorthForCoordinate:(ARCoordinate *)coordinate;
```

Let's implement these one at a time and walk through what they accomplish. First, copy the method from Listing 11–30.

Listing 11–30. *viewportContainsCoordinate Method*

```
- (BOOL)viewportContainsCoordinate:(ARCoordinate *)coordinate {

        double deltaAzimuth = [self deltaAzimuthForCoordinate:coordinate];
        BOOL result    = NO;
        if (deltaAzimuth <= degreesToRadians(_range)) {
                result = YES;
        }

        return result;
}
```

This method checks the range we defined earlier (what the screen can see) and validates whether the passed-in coordinate is in the specified range. This method will help us ignore coordinates that are outside of our viewable screen. Next, copy the code from Listing 11–31.

Listing 11–31. *deltaAzimuthForCoordinate Method*

```
- (double)deltaAzimuthForCoordinate:(ARCoordinate *)coordinate {

        double currentAzimuth = _coordinate.azimuth;
        double pointAzimuth       = coordinate.azimuth;

        double deltaAzimith = ABS( pointAzimuth - currentAzimuth);

        if (currentAzimuth < degreesToRadians(_range) &&
                pointAzimuth > degreesToRadians(360-_range)) {
                deltaAzimith    = (currentAzimuth + ((M_PI * 2.0) - pointAzimuth));
```

```
        } else if (pointAzimuth < degreesToRadians(_range) &&
                        currentAzimuth > degreesToRadians(360-_range)) {
            deltaAzimith    = (pointAzimuth + ((M_PI * 2.0) - currentAzimuth));
        }
        return deltaAzimith;
}
```

This method calculates the difference between the azimuth of our location and the azimuth of the passed-in coordinate. This will help us find the point in the 360-degree view. We are also adjusting for both positive and negative degrees from north. Add the methods from Listing 11–32 to the implementation file.

Listing 11–32. *pointForCoordinate and isNorthForCoordinate Methods*

```
-(BOOL)isNorthForCoordinate:(ARCoordinate *)coordinate {

        BOOL isBetweenNorth = NO;
        double currentAzimuth = _coordinate.azimuth;
        double pointAzimuth     = coordinate.azimuth;

        if ( currentAzimuth < degreesToRadians(_range) &&
        pointAzimuth > degreesToRadians(360-_range) ) {
                isBetweenNorth = YES;
        } else if ( pointAzimuth < degreesToRadians(_range) &&
                currentAzimuth > degreesToRadians(360-_range)) {
                isBetweenNorth = YES;
        }
        return isBetweenNorth;
}


- (CGPoint)pointForCoordinate:(ARCoordinate *)coordinate {

        CGPoint point;
        CGRect viewBounds = _hudView.bounds;

        double currentAzimuth = _coordinate.azimuth;
        double pointAzimuth     = coordinate.azimuth;
        double pointInclination = coordinate.inclination;

        double deltaAzimuth = [self deltaAzimuthForCoordinate:coordinate];
        BOOL isBetweenNorth     = [self isNorthForCoordinate:coordinate];

        if ((pointAzimuth > currentAzimuth && !isBetweenNorth) ||
                (currentAzimuth > degreesToRadians(360-_range) &&
                 pointAzimuth < degreesToRadians(_range))) {

            // Right side of Azimuth
            point.x = (viewBounds.size.width / 2) + ((deltaAzimuth /
degreesToRadians(1)) * 12);
        } else {

            // Left side of Azimuth
            point.x = (viewBounds.size.width / 2) - ((deltaAzimuth /
degreesToRadians(1)) * 12);
        }
        point.y = (viewBounds.size.height / 2)
    + (radiansToDegrees(M_PI_2 + _viewAngle)  * 2.0)
    + ((pointInclination / degreesToRadians(1)) * 12);
```

```
        return point;
}
```

The first method, isNorthForCoordinate, follows the same pattern as when we checked the delta of the azimuth of our two coordinates. We are now doing the same thing between the coordinate and the north heading.

In the pointForCoordinate method, we are converting the ARCoordinate class to a CGPoint we can use in our view. We need to know if the coordinate difference in the azimuth values and whether the point is between north and us. We are returning this point so it can be updated in our view, which we'll do shortly.

Let's finish the updateLocations method in our ARController.m implementation. Update the method as shown in Listing 11–33.

Listing 11–33. *Updated updateLocations Method*

```
- (void)updateLocations {
        if ( !_coordinates || [_coordinates count] == 0 ) return;

        int totalDisplayed      = 0;

        for (ARCoordinate *item in _coordinates) {

                UIView *viewToDraw = item.annotation;

                if ([self viewportContainsCoordinate:item]) {

                        CGPoint point = [self pointForCoordinate:item];
                        float width     = viewToDraw.bounds.size.width;
                        float height = viewToDraw.bounds.size.height;

                        viewToDraw.frame = CGRectMake(point.x - width / 2.0, point.y -
(height / 2.0), width, height);

                        if ( !([viewToDraw superview]) ) {
                                [_hudView addSubview:viewToDraw];
                                [_hudView sendSubviewToBack:viewToDraw];
                        }
                        totalDisplayed++;

                } else {
                        [viewToDraw removeFromSuperview];
                }
        }
}
```

The new updateLocations method iterates over the _coordinates array, and adds the CGPoint objects from our pointForCoordinate method. The points are laid out on the screen if they are in the view's range, as verified by the viewportContainsCoordinate method.

We're almost there. Before we can test the app, we need to add the method handlers for the location and heading updates. Copy the methods from Listing 11–34 to the implementation file.

Listing 11–34. *Handle Location and Heading*

```
- (void)locationManager:(CLLocationManager *)manager didUpdateHeading:(CLHeading
*)newHeading {
        if (newHeading.headingAccuracy > 0) {
                _deviceHeading = newHeading;
                [self updateCurrentCoordinate];
        }
}

- (BOOL)locationManagerShouldDisplayHeadingCalibration:(CLLocationManager *)manager {
        return YES;
}

- (void)locationManager:(CLLocationManager *)manager didUpdateToLocation:(CLLocation
*)newLocation fromLocation:(CLLocation *)oldLocation {
        if (newLocation != oldLocation) {
                [self updateCurrentLocation:newLocation];
        }
}

- (void)locationManager:(CLLocationManager *)manager didFailWithError:(NSError *)error {
        [self.locationManager stopUpdatingLocation];
}
```

These methods should be fairly simple to follow. When we receive an updated heading, we update our current coordinate. When we receive a change in position, we update our location. If we receive an error, we stop the location manager updates.

Find the `initWithViewController` method in the `ARController.m` file. Add the code in Listing 11–35 to set some initial values for our properties.

Listing 11–35. *Set Initial Values*

```
_coordinates = [[NSMutableArray alloc] init];
_range = _hudView.bounds.size.width / 12;
_deviceLocation = [[CLLocation alloc] initWithLatitude:39.75 longitude:-104.86];
```

Switch over to RootViewController.m. Import the ARGeoCoordinate header. In the loadView method, add the code from Listing 11–36.

Listing 11–36. *Initialize with My Location*

```
_arController = [[ARController alloc] initWithViewController:self];

 ARGeoCoordinate *tempCoordinate;
CLLocation              *tempLocation;

tempLocation = [[CLLocation alloc] initWithLatitude:39.550051 longitude:-105.782067];
tempCoordinate = [[ARGeoCoordinate alloc] initWithCoordinate:tempLocation name:@"Kyle
Roche" place:@"Denver"];
[self.arController addCoordinate:tempCoordinate animated:NO];
```

We're finally ready to test this out. As with our other sample applications, you can't use the simulator for testing. On your physical device, you should see something similar to Figure 11–7.

Figure 11–7. *Here is what we have built so far.*

Adding Social Context

The application is starting to come along. We've already built the functionality to handle location and heading updates and display some tags on the screen. Currently, we have hard-coded a single location (for me) to debug the functionality. Let's add in the Facebook context and pull the locations for some of our Facebook friends.

If you didn't skip over that section in this chapter, you'll recall that the Facebook iOS SDK uses URL Schemes to manage the oAuth callback in its native apps. We have already copied the Facebook SDK to our project, so before we can use it we have to set up our URL Schemes in our .plist file.

In Xcode, find Ch11-Info.plist under the **Resources** Group.

1. Open the file and add a new row.

2. Set the Key to **URL Types**.

3. Expand the new group. Add a new subrow.

4. Name the Key **URL Schemes**.

5. Expand the new key. Set the value of Item 0 to fb[**appID**], where **appID** is your Facebook APP ID.

We already tested this process in the Facebook demo app that was downloaded with the SDK.

Open RootViewController.h. Update the interface file as shown in Listing 11–37.

Listing 11–37. *Add Facebook Connect to RootViewController*

```
#import <UIKit/UIKit.h>
#import "FBConnect.h"

@class ARController;

@interface RootViewController : UIViewController <FBRequestDelegate, FBDialogDelegate,
FBSessionDelegate> {
    NSArray *_permissions;
}

@property (nonatomic, retain) Facebook *facebook;
@property (nonatomic, retain) ARController *arController;

@end
```

The permissions array is actually not necessary. We could localize that to the login method, but I'm following the code in the demo application and documentation so you can more easily move this to future applications.

Check your project to make sure it builds correctly. After the import statement, you'll get a compiler error if you didn't include your Facebook SDK correctly.

Switch over to RootViewController.m. Add the code from Listing 11–38, just after your last synthesize statement. Obviously, replace this with your own App ID.

Listing 11–38. *Create Variable for FB App ID*

```
@synthesize facebook = _facebook;
static NSString* kAppId = @"your app id";
```

At the end of the loadView method, add the code from Listing 11–39.

Listing 11–39. *Launch Facebook oAuth Dialog*

```
_permissions = [[NSArray arrayWithObjects:@"read_stream", @"publish_stream",
@"offline_access", @"friends_checkins", nil] retain];
_facebook = [[Facebook alloc] initWithAppId:kAppId andDelegate:self];
[_facebook authorize:_permissions];
```

There are three basic steps to authenticating to Facebook, as you can see. First, you set up the list of permissions your application will require. Second, you init the facebook class with the App ID and the delegate (in this case, we use self). Next, you use the authorize instance method to launch the oAuth dialog in a web browser. Remember, Facebook then calls your application back using the URL Scheme we set up earlier.

Facebook's platform is built around the Graph API. It provides a simple and consistent mechanism to retrieve and update information about the social graph of the user. The drawback for us, however, is that we need to query a cross-section of data. Namely, we need a subset of our friends and their last known check-in location. This is too complex for the standard Graph API. So, we will be querying the Graph API through a more advanced medium called FQL (Facebook Query Language). FQL exposes the data in the Graph API through a SQL-like interface.

To demonstrate both a Graph API call and an FQL call, we will be pulling our friends list from the standard Graph API, then using FQL calls to pull the last check-in location for each friend. Let's get started.

Graph for Friends

Open RootViewController.m. Because this is where we set our GPS coordinate in our example, it makes sense to extend this class to query the Facebook locations.

Facebook's iOS SDK uses a delegate protocol, which we've already added to RootViewController.h, to handle the results of API calls. Before we make a call to the Graph API, we need to create the delegate methods. Add the code from Listing 11–40 to RootViewController.m.

Listing 11–40. *Facebook Request Delegate Methods*

```
/**
 * Called when the Facebook API request has returned a response. This callback
 * gives you access to the raw response. It's called before
 * (void)request:(FBRequest *)request didLoad:(id)result,
 * which is passed the parsed response object.
 */
- (void)request:(FBRequest *)request didReceiveResponse:(NSURLResponse *)response {
  NSLog(@"received response");
}

/**
 * Called when a request returns and its response has been parsed into
 * an object. The resulting object may be a dictionary, an array, a string,
 * or a number, depending on the format of the API response. If you need access
 * to the raw response, use:
 *
 * (void)request:(FBRequest *)request
 *     didReceiveResponse:(NSURLResponse *)response
 */
- (void)request:(FBRequest *)request didLoad:(id)result {
    NSLog(@"RESULT: %@", result);
};

/**
 * Called when an error prevents the Facebook API request from completing
 * successfully.
 */
- (void)request:(FBRequest *)request didFailWithError:(NSError *)error {
    NSLog(@"ERROR: %@", [error localizedDescription]);
};
```

These methods are copied straight from the example application that came with the SDK. They handle the three events that can happen after a call out to Facebook. The response is received, the response is loaded, and the response was an error. For now, let's log the results.

The callback delegate from authentication requires some methods as well. Add the methods from Listing 11–41 to RootViewController.m.

Listing 11–41. *Facebook Auth Delegate Methods*

```
- (void)fbDidLogin {
    NSLog(@"LOGGED IN");
}

-(void)fbDidNotLogin:(BOOL)cancelled {
    NSLog(@"did not login");
}

- (void)fbDidLogout {
    NSLog(@"LOGOUT");
}
```

Open AppDelegate.m in Xcode. Add the method shown in Listing 11–42.

Listing 11–42. *Handle the URLScheme Sent from oAuth Dialog*

```
- (BOOL)application:(UIApplication *)application handleOpenURL:(NSURL *)url {
    return [[_rootViewController facebook] handleOpenURL:url];
}
```

So, we have everything we need to respond to queries, URL Schemes, and authentication requests. Let's launch the authentication dialog. The first time you access the application, you will see something similar to Figure 11–8. On subsequent authentication attempts, you'll see something more like Figure 11–9. Watch your console during this process. You should see notes where the authentication callbacks were made.

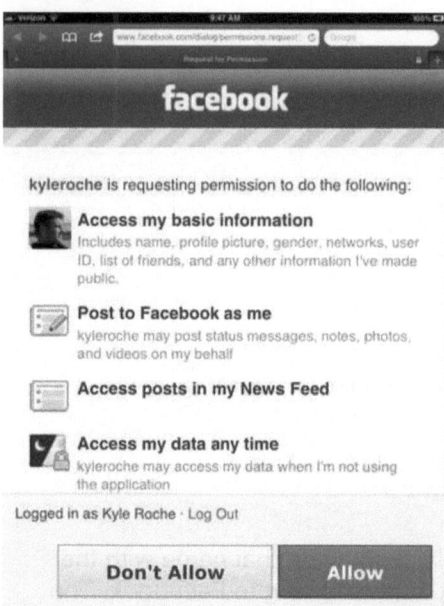

Figure 11–8. *The initial authentication dialog launches.*

As you can see, the app has not yet been authorized for the permissions we have requested (the NSArray we passed to the authorize method). You only need to do this on the first login for the application.

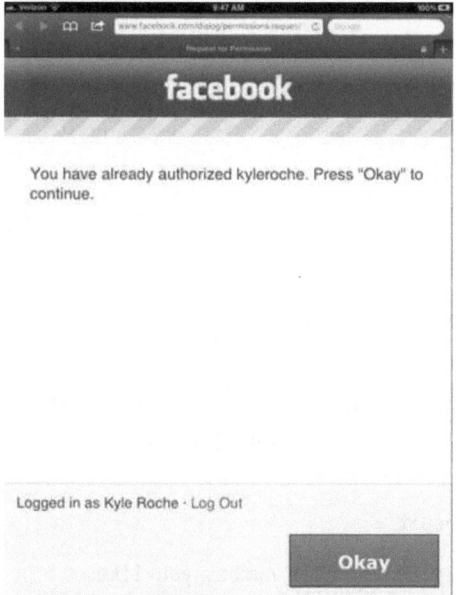

Figure 11–9. *Subsequent login attempts bring up a different dialog.*

There are ways to avoid this pop-up message entirely (on subsequent logins, that is). If you persist the access token that is returned from the oAuth callback, you can pass that to the authorize method to get a refreshed token. But, this will work fine for our purposes.

In RootViewController.h, add two private FBRequest variables called _friendsRequest and _checkinRequest. On the callback, Facebook sends a reference to the FBRequest object that created the call. This is the only way we can differentiate between the Graph API calls for which we are parsing the response.

Open RootViewController.m in Xcode. Let's make a call to the Graph API and view the results in the console. Update the fbDidLogin method as shown in Listing 11–43.

Listing 11–43. *Updated fbDidLogin Method*

```
- (void)fbDidLogin {
    NSLog(@"LOGGED IN");
    _friendsRequest = [_facebook requestWithGraphPath:@"me/friends" andDelegate:self];
}
```

This call makes a request to the Graph API using a predefined path. We are using the me keyword, which represents the current user. The friends route returns a JSON representation of our friends list. You will notice that this call is now referencing the private _friendsRequest FBRequest object we created.

If you run the application again, you should see something similar to Listing 11–44 in your console.

Listing 11–44. *Results from me/friends (Names and IDs Have Been Changed)*

```
2011-10-08 10:14:55.281 Ch11[1302:707] RESULT: {
    data =      (
                {
            id = 12345;
            name = "Bob Smith";
        },
                {
            id = 12345;
            name = "Bob Smith";
        },
                {
            id = 12345;
            name = "Bob Smith";
        },
```

Let's stick with the first ten that are returned, and load up their last check-in in the AR view. Update the Facebook query delegate method as shown in Listing 11–45.

Listing 11–45. *Updated didLoad Method*

```
- (void)request:(FBRequest *)request didLoad:(id)result {
    if (request == _friendsRequest) {
        for (int i = 0; i < 1; i++) { // change this to whatever number you like
            [_facebook requestWithGraphPath:[NSString stringWithFormat:@"%@/checkins",
[[[result objectForKey:@"data"] objectAtIndex:i] objectForKey:@"id"]] andDelegate:self];
        }
    } else {
        NSLog(@"RESULT: %@", [[result objectForKey:@"data"] objectAtIndex:1]);
    }
};
```

Let's take a moment to walk through this code block. We are checking to see that the referenced FBRequest object is our _friendsRequest object. If it is, we set up a for loop (change i < # if you want to expand this further) to create a second call to the Graph API to pull the user's check-ins. We are logging the result of that call.

An example response is shown in Listing 11–46. (Again, the names are changed.)

Listing 11–46. *Example JSON Response*

```
2011-10-08 10:49:01.573 Ch11[1523:707] RESULT: {
    application =       {
        id = 350685531728;
        name = "Facebook for Android";
    };
    comments =       {
        data =          (
                {
                "created_time" = "2011-10-03T21:43:16+0000";
                from =          {
                    id = 345435;
                    name = "Bob Smith";
                };
                id = "42_4";
```

```
                message = "Can't wait to hear all about the new assignment.";
            },
                        {
                "created_time" = "2011-10-04T01:33:16+0000";
                from =                    {
                    id = 345345;
                    name = "Dustin Smith";
                };
                id = "602267025184_841815";
                message = "Maybe do this one faster?";
            }
        );
    };
    "created_time" = "2011-10-03T19:52:47+0000";
    from =      {
        id = 34534435;
        name = "Jason Smith";
    };
    id = 602267025184;
    likes =      {
        data =          (
                    {
                id = 09870928;
                name = "Bob Barbin";
            }
        );
    };
    message = "Starting the next project. Should be fun!";
    place =       {
        id = 110506962309835;
        location =            {
            city = "Palo Alto";
            country = "United States";
            latitude = "37.41761460129";
            longitude = "-122.15007660582";
            state = CA;
            street = "1601 S California Ave";
            zip = 94304;
        };
        name = "Facebook HQ";
    };
};
}
```

Lucky that we have a check-in related to Facebook. That makes it at least appear relevant. If you analyze the structure of the data, you can see that there is an element called place that contains most of what we will need to send a new GPS coordinate to our ARView. Let's attach the check-in message to the annotation instead of names, so we can use some of the real data.

Adjust the didLoad delegate method as shown in Listing 11–47.

Listing 11–47. *Updated didLoad Method*

```
- (void)request:(FBRequest *)request didLoad:(id)result {
    if (request == _friendsRequest) {
        for (int i = 0; i < 10; i++) {
```

```
                    [_facebook requestWithGraphPath:[NSString stringWithFormat:@"%@/checkins",
[[[result objectForKey:@"data"] objectAtIndex:i] objectForKey:@"id"]] andDelegate:self];
            }
    } else {
        if ([[result objectForKey:@"data"] count] > 0) {
            NSString *placeName = [[[[result objectForKey:@"data"] objectAtIndex:0]
objectForKey:@"place"] objectForKey:@"name"];
            NSString *placeLat = [[[[[result objectForKey:@"data"] objectAtIndex:0]
objectForKey:@"place"] objectForKey:@"location"] objectForKey:@"latitude"];
            NSString *placeLong = [[[[[result objectForKey:@"data"] objectAtIndex:0]
objectForKey:@"place"] objectForKey:@"location"] objectForKey:@"longitude"];
            NSString *checkinMessage = [[[result objectForKey:@"data"] objectAtIndex:0]
objectForKey:@"message"];

            ARGeoCoordinate *tempCoordinate;
            CLLocation        *tempLocation;

            tempLocation = [[CLLocation alloc] initWithLatitude:[placeLat floatValue]
longitude:[placeLong floatValue]];
            tempCoordinate = [[ARGeoCoordinate alloc] initWithCoordinate:tempLocation
name:checkinMessage place:placeName];
            [self.arController addCoordinate:tempCoordinate animated:NO];
            [tempLocation release];
        }
    }
```

The new code sets up a few new temp variables to store the values from the JSON response. The temp variables are passed to the addCoordinate method so that they will appear in our AR view. JSON parsing is fairly simple, once it has been converted to an NSDictionary, as we have here. You simply follow the path down the structure using the objectForKey method.

Run the application again. If most of your friends are checking in to places that are geographically close together, you might need to adjust how many places are shown in the view at one time. The example from our console is shown in AR view in Figure 11–10.

Figure 11–10. *Facebook HQ displays as a Facebook place.*

We could probably dress this up a bit and add some interactivity. How about we add a UIButton that launches a Facebook sharing dialog?

Open ARAnnotation.m. Adjust the top of the class as shown in Listing 11–48.

Listing 11–48. *Updated ARAnnotation*

```
#import "ARAnnotation.h"
#import "ARCoordinate.h"
#import "AppDelegate.h"
#import "RootViewController.h"
#import "FBConnect.h"

#define ANNOTATION_WIDTH 150
#define ANNOTATION_HEIGHT 200

@implementation ARAnnotation
static NSString* kAppId = @"your app id";
```

We need to import the RootViewController as well as the AppDelegate. This is because the RootViewController has the reference to our Facebook class and will be acting as the delegate for our sharing dialog.

Add the method from Listing 11–49 to the class.

Listing 11–49. *shareButtonClicked Method*

```
- (IBAction)shareButtonClicked:(id)sender {
    AppDelegate *_appDelegate = (AppDelegate *)[[UIApplication sharedApplication]
delegate];
    RootViewController *_rootViewController = _appDelegate.rootViewController;
```

```
NSMutableDictionary* params = [NSMutableDictionary dictionaryWithObjectsAndKeys:
                               kAppId, @"app_id",
                               @"http://amzn.com/1430239123", @"link",
                               @"http://bit.ly/qILSZh", @"picture",
                               @"Facebook Places AR App", @"name",
                               @"Sharing information on a Facebook Place",
@"caption",
                               @"Look, All my Facebook places are in Augmented
Reality view.", @"description",
                               @"Buy the book",  @"message",
                               nil];

    [_rootViewController.facebook dialog:@"feed"
           andParams:params
         andDelegate:_rootViewController];
}
```

This method will be called from the UIButton outlet we're about to add to the pop-up. It finds a reference to the RootViewController instance the application is running, and then it creates an NSMutableDictionary with the POST parameters required for our call to the Facebook API. We then call the dialog method from the facebook property of our RootViewController. This will launch a dialog prompting us to add a comment as we share the post.

Update the initWithCoordinate method as shown in Listing 11–50.

Listing 11–50. *Updates to initWithCoordinate*

```
- (id)initWithCoordinate:(ARCoordinate *)coordinate
{
    CGRect annotationFrame = CGRectMake(0, 0, ANNOTATION_WIDTH, ANNOTATION_HEIGHT);

    if (self = [super initWithFrame:annotationFrame]) {
        UIButton *shareButton = [UIButton buttonWithType:UIButtonTypeCustom];
        [shareButton setFrame:CGRectMake(0, 0, 32, 32)];
        [shareButton setBackgroundImage:[UIImage imageNamed:@"Facebook-Places.png"]
forState:UIControlStateNormal];
        [shareButton addTarget:self action:@selector(shareButtonClicked:)
forControlEvents:UIControlEventTouchUpInside];
        [self addSubview:shareButton];

        UILabel *nameLabel = [[UILabel alloc] initWithFrame:CGRectMake(40, 0,
ANNOTATION_WIDTH, 20.0)];

        nameLabel.backgroundColor = [UIColor clearColor];
        nameLabel.textAlignment = UITextAlignmentCenter;
        nameLabel.text = coordinate.name;
        [nameLabel sizeToFit];
        [nameLabel setFrame:CGRectMake(40, 0, nameLabel.bounds.size.width + 8.0,
nameLabel.bounds.size.height + 8.0)];
        [self addSubview:nameLabel];

        UILabel *placeLabel = [[UILabel alloc] initWithFrame:CGRectMake(40, 0,
ANNOTATION_WIDTH, 20.0)];
        placeLabel.backgroundColor = [UIColor clearColor];
        placeLabel.textAlignment = UITextAlignmentCenter;
```

```
        placeLabel.text = coordinate.place;
        [placeLabel sizeToFit];
        [placeLabel setFrame:CGRectMake(40, 25, placeLabel.bounds.size.width + 8.0,
placeLabel.bounds.size.height + 8.0)];
        [self addSubview:placeLabel];

        [self setBackgroundColor:[UIColor clearColor]];
    }
    return self;
}
```

We moved the existing outlets to the right by 40 pixels to make room for our UIButton. I'm using an image found on Google Image Search. Any image with the same name will work for this demonstration. We also set the background color of our labels to clear, and wired the UIControlEventTouchUpInside of the UIButton to our shareButtonClicked method.

Remember, we set the delegate for the sharing dialog to RootViewController, so we need to make a quick update to that class as well.

Open RootViewController.m and add the method from Listing 11–51.

Listing 11–51. *dialogDidComplete Method from FBDialogDelegate Protocol*

```
- (void)dialogDidComplete:(FBDialog *)dialog {
    NSLog(@"publish successful");
}
```

This method is a delegate method for the FBDialogDelegate protocol. It will be called after the dialog completes and closes. Run the app. First, you'll see a slightly updated interface. I found the same check-in in my AR view to provide some side-by-side comparison. See the illustration in Figure 11–11.

Figure 11–11. *We've updated Facebook HQ as a Facebook place.*

You can see that our font now has a clear background and we have made room for a
UIButton to the left of our labels. If you click the button, a sharing dialog will launch, as
illustrated in Figure 11–12.

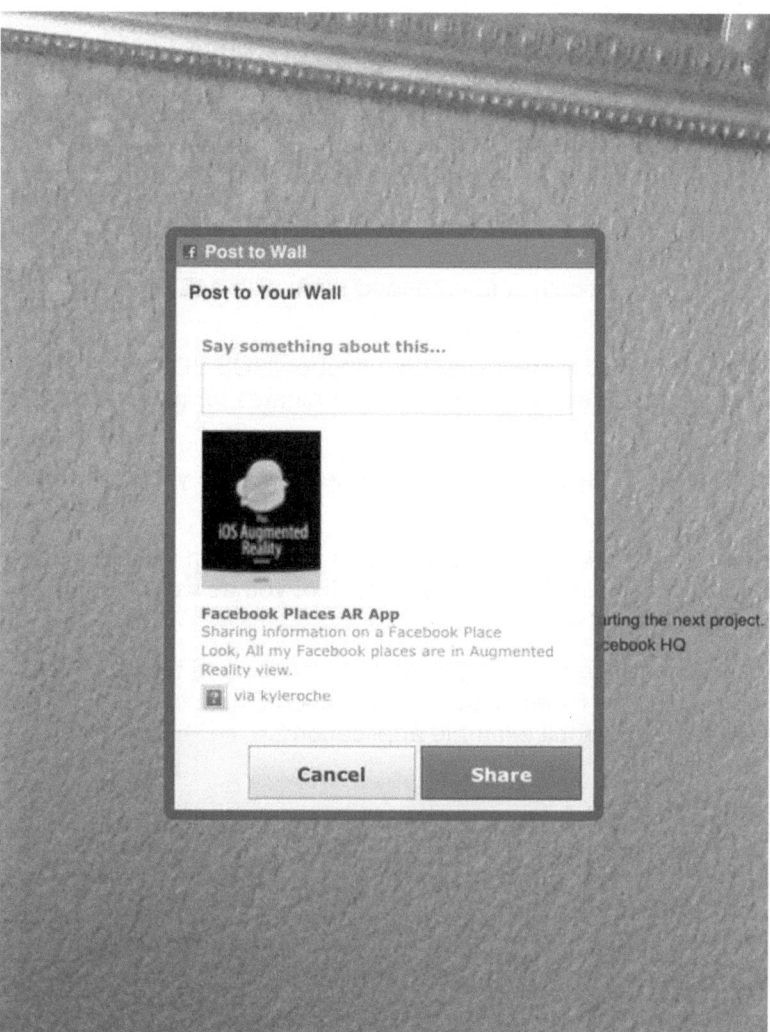

Figure 11–12. *Launch the sharing dialog.*

You can add a comment to the post or just share it, as shown. After you add it to your wall, you will see it on your timeline, as shown in Figure 11–13.

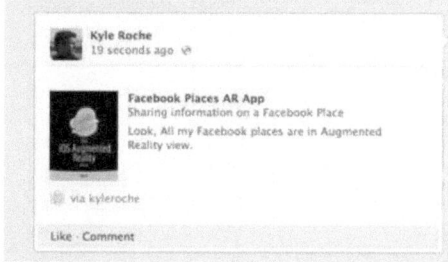

Figure 11–13. *We've posted the sharing dialog to our timeline.*

Summary

Congratulations! That was a very complicated example. We built on some existing open source projects, namely ARKit, and extended them into a fully functional social AR application. Thanks to the work from Zac, Neil, and Alasdair, we had a good starting point for our application setup.

We extended the setup to handle custom application view and annotations. We changed their appearance programmatically and extended them with a UIButton to handle interactivity.

After we connected our example to Facebook using the Facebook iOS SDK, we were able to use the Graph API to pull our friends list and add coordinates for their most recent check-ins.

We added a button to the AR view on each check-in with a template, so you know how to share posts back to the user's wall.

This chapter was a lot of fun. I look forward to extending this example on GitHub in the future. I hope to see GitHub forks with improvements from all of you as well. Adding social context to AR has endless possibilities.

In Chapter 12, we're going to discuss facial-recognition approaches and technologies. We'll look at three ways of recognizing faces in an AR application. Then, in Chapter 13, we'll pick an approach and turn it into a full example application.

Facial-Recognition Techniques

One of the more impressive demonstrations of augmented reality application programming centers around facial recognition. From security applications that can recognize a friendly person vs. a known threat, to social applications that scan the crowd for your Facebook friends, to retail applications that allow you to try on sunglasses or different hairstyles, facial AR is amazing.

Traditionally, the challenge with facial-recognition programming is the amount of resources required by the machine to process the images in real time. This, naturally, makes it very difficult to target mobile devices. This is why we see most facial-recognition algorithms running through a browser or installable program.

This has changed with iOS and the newer versions of mobile devices. The iPad 2 has more than enough processing power to handle the more intensive CPU requirements of facial-recognition applications.

In this chapter, we're going to discuss some of the newer approaches to facial recognition in a mobile iOS environment.

Choices for Facial Recognition

There are many ways to add facial recognition capabilities to your application. We are going to cover three of those. The first approach has been around the longest and has the most amount of information available on the subject. This approach is called Open Computer Vision, or OpenCV.

OpenCV

OpenCV was originally authored by Intel and was released around 2006 into the open source community. It has gained corporate support from Willow Garden and is still in active development at the time of this writing.

OpenCV's original code base was C, which allowed for easy portability to most platforms. There are ports for everything from C# to Java. And, of course, there's a port for iOS.

OpenCV is the most complicated and advanced of the topics we'll cover in this chapter. Because of its age and foundation in C, it has the least amount of "developer friendliness." However, the advantage over the other approaches is the extensive examples and tutorials available on the web. At the time of this writing, I couldn't find an example of either of the other approaches online.

iOS 5 CIDetector Class

iOS 5 introduced a new set of classes under the CoreImage framework for facial detection. We will use the CIDetector and CIFeature classes to pinpoint a face in the live camera view.

The CIDetector class shipped as part of iOS 5. This class finds features in images using a set of predefined detectors. iOS 5 has a single detector defined for facial recognition. Presumably, this class is structured for expansion to other common object maps in the future.

There aren't many options available when setting up a detector, as we'll discuss. Basically, you can set your type (CIDetectorTypeFace is the only type available at this time) and you can set your accuracy (high or low).

I will mention, however, that the speed of using CIDetector is significantly faster than OpenCV.

Face.com

Consider this the "third-party API approach." With the availability of an Internet connection increasing so rapidly, we're able to explore options what were never before possible. Platforms such as face.com offer a free REST API for processing facial detection in images.

I'm going to introduce the API and some of the features in this chapter, and we'll take this approach a step further in Chapter 13 and build a fully functional application.

Using the OpenCV Approach

Let's get started with an OpenCV example. Before we can create the Xcode project, we need to download and install the library. Point your browser to http://www.eosgarden.com/en/opensource/opencv-ios/download/. This is a compiled distribution of OpenCV built for iOS. Its source can be found at https://github.com/macmade/OpenCV-iOS, should you be interested in rebuilding the binary.

For this example, we'll be using the precompiled distribution from eosgarden for iPad. Download the files labeled **iPad**. Navigate to the downloaded directory in Finder and open the archive. We're going to build right on top of this distribution for the example.

Let's first examine the file structure of the download. If you expand the main subdirectories of the downloaded project, you'll see something similar to Figure 12–1.

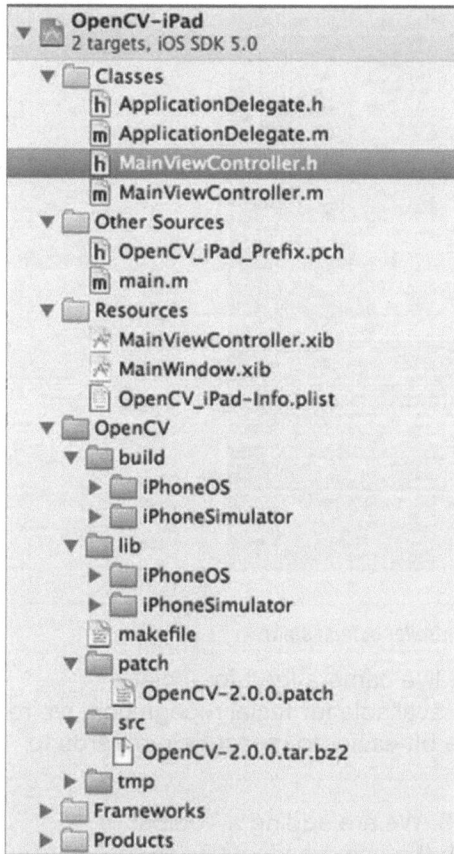

Figure 12–1. *Download and expand the directories of the OpenCV-iPad example application.*

The main files to take note of are under the **OpenCV** directory. If you were to download and build your own distribution, you would only have the files under the **src** and **patch** directories. The **lib** and **bin** directories are precompiled distributions for both the iOS simulator and the iOS physical device family.

Capturing the Image for Testing

Open `MainViewController.xib` in interface builder. There isn't much going on with this file so far. If you launch the application, it would simply display the title and link labels shown in Figure 12–2.

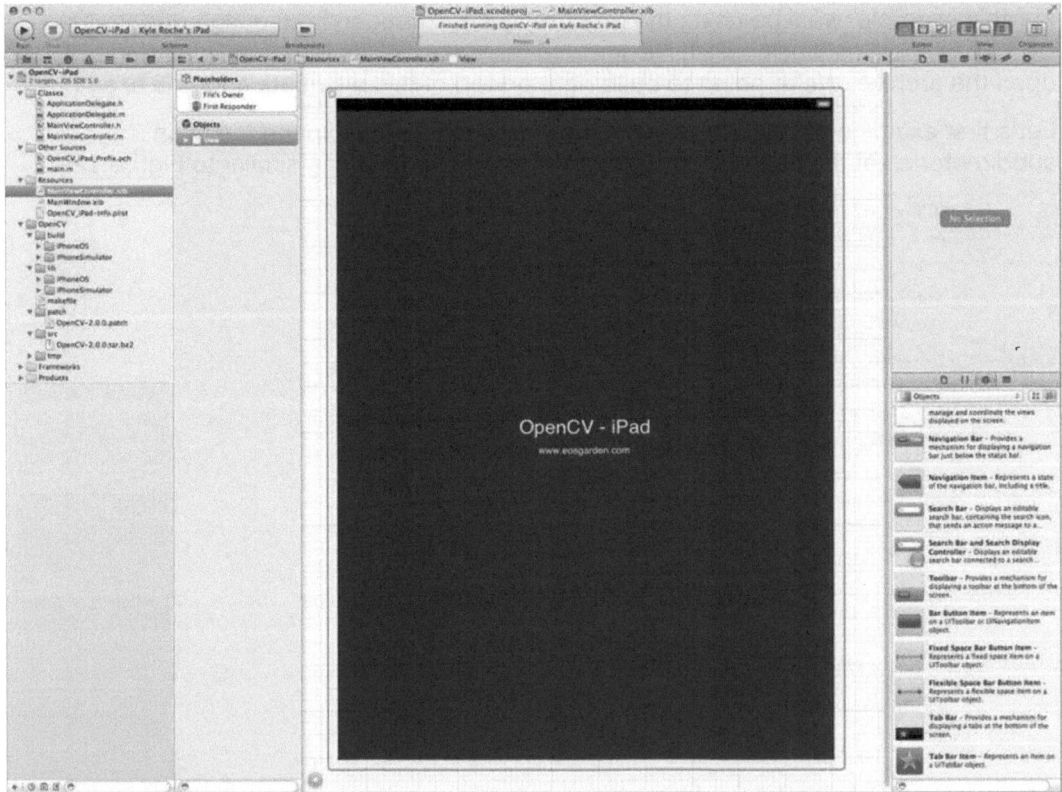

Figure 12–2. *Launching the application displays the MainViewController default state.*

In Chapter 13, we're going to discuss analyzing the live camera feed for facial recognition. To introduce some of the technologies available for facial recognition, we're going to use static camera images to make things a bit easier to measure in regards to performance and ease of use.

Adjust MainViewController as shown in Figure 12–3. We are adding a Toolbar, a UIImageView, a UILabel, and a Bar Button Item (with the camera identifier) to the view.

Create a property called toolbar for the UIToolbar in MainViewController.h. Also, link an IBAction method called cameraButtonClicked to the Bar Button Item. In addition, the UIImageView is linked to a property called cameraView, and the Timer Label (in the bottom right) is linked to a property called timerLabel. I created the UIImageView with dimensions of 600 × 800 to match the iPad camera's aspect ratio, so we don't have to rescale the images to display them. In Chapter 13, we'll discuss scaling the camera view on the fly to display the raw camera feed in the correct aspect ratio.

Figure 12-3. *Adjust the MainViewController layout.*

While you still have MainViewController.h open in Xcode, declare a
UIImagePickerController ivar called _imagePicker. In addition, nominate the class as a
UINavigationControllerDelegate, UIImagePickerControllerDelegate,
UIPopoverControllerDelegate, and a UIActionSheetDelegate.

Lastly, create an ivar called _imagePopover of the UIPopoverController class. We will
use this to hold the pop-ups for the photo library or saved photo applications.

Your new MainViewController.h should read like Listing 12-1.

Listing 12-1. *New MainViewController.h*

```
#import <UIKit/UIKit.h>
@interface MainViewController : UIViewController <UINavigationControllerDelegate,
UIImagePickerControllerDelegate, UIActionSheetDelegate, UIPopoverControllerDelegate> {
    UIImagePickerController *_imagePicker;
    UIPopoverController *_imagePopover;
}

@property (retain, nonatomic) IBOutlet UIImageView *cameraView;
@property (retain, nonatomic) IBOutlet UILabel *timerLabel;
@property (retain, nonatomic) IBOutlet UIToolbar *toolbar;
- (IBAction)cameraButtonClicked:(id)sender;
@end
```

Switch over to MainViewController.m. If you linked the IBOutlets using interface builder,
you won't have to add any synthesize or release statements to the implementation. You
should release _imagePicker in your implementation's dealloc method, either way.

> **NOTE:** This class contains two methods derived from
> https://github.com/macmade/facedetect. The source on GitHub and from Apress
> (www.apress.com) has the appropriate license text in the headers.

Find the viewDidLoad method and update it, as shown in Listing 12–2.

Listing 12–2. *New viewDidLoad in MainViewController.h*

```
- (void)viewDidLoad
{
    [super viewDidLoad];
    // Do any additional setup after loading the view from its nib.
    _imagePicker = [[UIImagePickerController alloc] init];
    _imagePicker.delegate = self;
}
```

We need to make sure that our UIImagePickerController is allocated before we attempt to present it in a modal view, or we will end up with an error caused by displaying a nil ViewController. Next, we simply set the delegate to self so we can handle the didFinishPickingImage delegate method in our class.

Locate the cameraButtonClicked method that interface builder declared for us. Add the code shown in Listing 12–3.

Listing 12–3. *Updated cameraButtonClicked Method*

```
- (IBAction)cameraButtonClicked:(id)sender {
    UIActionSheet *_sheet = [[UIActionSheet alloc] initWithTitle:@"Choose Source"
delegate:self cancelButtonTitle:@"Cancel" destructiveButtonTitle:nil
otherButtonTitles:@"Camera", @"Library", @"Photo Album", nil];
    [_sheet showInView:self.view];
    [_sheet release];
}
```

This method simply forwards control to a UIActionSheet. We will handle the user's choice in the UIActionSheet's delegate methods. Let's implement that next. Add the method shown in Listing 12–4 to the implementation.

Listing 12–4. *UIActionSheet Delegate Methods*

```
- (void)actionSheet:(UIActionSheet *)actionSheet
clickedButtonAtIndex:(NSInteger)buttonIndex {
    if (buttonIndex == 0) {
        _imagePicker.sourceType = UIImagePickerControllerSourceTypeCamera;
        [self presentModalViewController:_imagePicker animated:YES];
        return;
    } else if (buttonIndex == 1) {
        _imagePicker.sourceType = UIImagePickerControllerSourceTypePhotoLibrary;
    } else {
        _imagePicker.sourceType = UIImagePickerControllerSourceTypeSavedPhotosAlbum;
    }
// only for iPad
    _imagePopover = [[UIPopoverController alloc]
initWithContentViewController:_imagePicker];
    _imagePopover.delegate = self;
```

```
        [_imagePopover presentPopoverFromRect:toolbar.frame
                                     inView:self.view
                    permittedArrowDirections:UIPopoverArrowDirectionAny
                                   animated:YES];
        [_imagePicker release];
}
```

This method presents the three different source choices for the UIImagePickerController. We could simply show the camera by default, but if you would like to test this application on the simulator, you'll need the option to change the source type to the photo library or photo album application.

Remember, this is an iPad application. The iPad requires that UIImagePickerControllers are displayed in UIPopoverControllers, not ModalViewControllers. This differs from the iPhone or iPod touch, so if you are not testing on an iPad, make sure you launch all the UIImagePickerControllers in a modal dialog and not a UIPopoverController.

After the user selects and image, the UIImagePickerController class (as you probably remember from Chapter 6) calls its didFinishPickingImage delegate method. We will handle that method with the code from Listing 12–5.

Listing 12–5. *UIImagePickerController Delegate Method*

```
- (void)imagePickerController:(UIImagePickerController *)picker
didFinishPickingImage:(UIImage *)image editingInfo:(NSDictionary *)editingInfo {
    [self dismissModalViewControllerAnimated:YES];
    cameraView.image = image;
}
```

Your application should be at a point where it can be tested on either the simulator or on a physical device. Run the application. Click on the camera button in the toolbar, and you'll be presented with a UIActionSheet, as shown in Figure 12–4.

If you are running on the simulator, be sure to choose either **Library** or **Photo Album**. You will see a pop-up similar to Figure 12–5. If you choose the **Camera** view, you'll see the camera display in full screen.

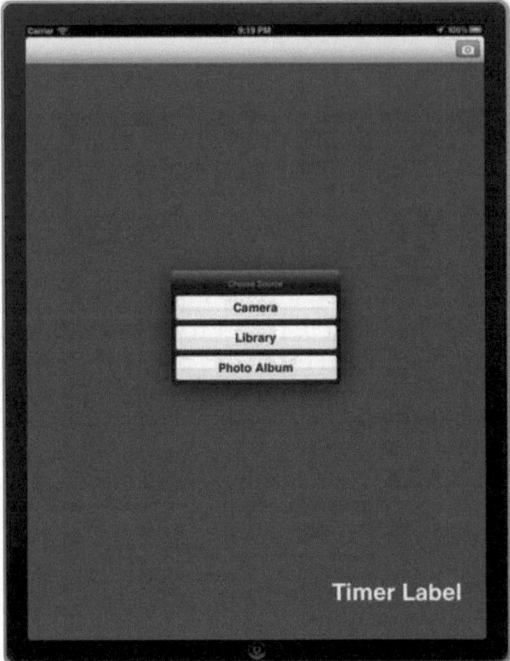

Figure 12–4. *Pick the camera source from the UIActionSheet.*

Figure 12–5. *UIPopoverController displays UIImagePickerController on the iPad.*

Haar Cascades

Before we can do anything with OpenCV, we need to add a few Haar cascades to our project. Haar cascades are a set of organized classifier cascades or digital image features used for object recognition. The name originates from Haar wavelets, which were used in the first facial-detection system.

Before Haar wavelets, image recognition analyzed the intensity of each pixel's RGB values, which took a considerable amount of time and computing resources. A Haar cascade is used to analyze adjacent rectangular regions of a detection window and to sum up the pixel intensity of these regions so they can be compared to each other, instead of comparing pixel by pixel. This approach was documented by Viola and Jones in the 2001 publication "Rapid Object Detection using Boosted Cascade of Simple Features," Accepted Conference on Computer Vision and Pattern Recognition 2001.[1]

The math behind the algorithm is well documented if you'd like to research this subject further. We will be using the supplied Haar cascades that came with the source distribution of OpenCV. You can find the distribution on `http://opencv.willowgarage.com/wiki/`. If you'd rather not download yet another version of OpenCV (this is the original, to be accurate), you can just copy the files from this book's example code on GitHub or from the Source Code/Download area of the Apress web site (`www.apress.com`).

Find the directory of cascades you'll be using, and drag and drop them into your Xcode project. Make sure you select the option to copy resources as needed.

> **NOTE:** If you compiled your own distribution of OpenCV for iOS 5, you can skip this next section. Add your compiled library to the project, and you should be all set.

Switch over to `MainViewController.m`. Just after the `import` statements, add the code from Listing 12–6.

Listing 12–6. *Private Methods*

```
@interface MainViewController (Private)
- (IplImage *)createIplImage:(UIImage *)image;
- (void)openCVFaceDetect;
@end
```

We're simply declaring a few private methods that we'll be using to analyze the image. Let's implement these methods now, then we'll walk through them step by step.

---

[1] You can find the entire paper at `http://research.microsoft.com/en-us/um/people/viola/Pubs/Detect/violaJones_CVPR2001.pdf`.

First, add the method from Listing 12–7 to the implementation. As I mentioned earlier, these next two utility methods are from the eosgarden sample project. They won't work on iOS 5 as distributed, but we'll fix that in a moment.

Listing 12–7. *createIplImage Method*

```
- ( IplImage * )createIplImage: ( UIImage * )image
{
    CGImageRef      imageRef;
    CGColorSpaceRef colorSpaceRef;
    CGContextRef    context;
    IplImage       * iplImage;
    IplImage       * returnImage;

    imageRef      = image.CGImage;
    colorSpaceRef = CGColorSpaceCreateDeviceRGB();
    iplImage      = cvCreateImage( cvSize( image.size.width, image.size.height ),
IPL_DEPTH_8U, 4 );
    context       = CGBitmapContextCreate
    (
     iplImage->imageData,
     iplImage->width,
     iplImage->height,
     iplImage->depth,
     iplImage->widthStep,
     colorSpaceRef,
     kCGImageAlphaPremultipliedLast | kCGBitmapByteOrderDefault
     );

    CGContextDrawImage( context, CGRectMake( 0, 0, image.size.width, image.size.height
), imageRef );
    CGContextRelease( context );
    CGColorSpaceRelease( colorSpaceRef );

    returnImage = cvCreateImage( cvGetSize( iplImage ), IPL_DEPTH_8U, 3 );

    cvCvtColor( iplImage, returnImage, CV_RGBA2BGR );
    cvReleaseImage( &iplImage );

    return returnImage;
}
```

When we get the selected image back from either the camera or the library, we're storing it in a UIImageView. OpenCV can't use the UIImage format, so we need to convert the image to something it can process. OpenCV uses a format called IplImage, which is part of the Intel Image Processing Library. For this demonstration, there isn't much more we need to know. Helper functions, like the one from eosgarden, are available in many formats on the Internet.

Our conversion method, which will be called from within the OpenCV processing block, takes the UIImage and draws a new IplImage with the same representation. The dimensions and colors will be close enough for us to still use x,y coordinates to overlay a translucent square around any detected faces.

Next, copy the method from Listing 12–8 to the implementation.

Listing 12–8. *openCVFaceDetect Method*

```
- ( void )openCVFaceDetect
{
    NSInteger                 i;
    NSUInteger                scale;
    NSAutoreleasePool       * pool;
    IplImage                * image;
    IplImage                * smallImage;
    NSString                * xmlPath;
    CvHaarClassifierCascade * cascade;
    CvMemStorage            * storage;
    CvSeq                   * faces;
    UIAlertView             * alert;
    CGImageRef                imageRef;
    CGColorSpaceRef           colorSpaceRef;
    CGContextRef              context;
    CvRect                    rect;
    CGRect                    faceRect;

    pool  = [ [ NSAutoreleasePool alloc ] init ];
    scale = 2;

    cvSetErrMode( CV_ErrModeParent );

    xmlPath    = [ [ NSBundle mainBundle ] pathForResource:
@"haarcascade_frontalface_default" ofType: @"xml" ];
    image      = [ self createIplImage: cameraView.image ];
    smallImage = cvCreateImage( cvSize( image->width / scale, image->height / scale ),
IPL_DEPTH_8U, 3 );

    cvPyrDown( image, smallImage, CV_GAUSSIAN_5x5 );

    cascade = ( CvHaarClassifierCascade * )cvLoad( [ xmlPath cStringUsingEncoding:
NSASCIIStringEncoding ], NULL, NULL, NULL );
    storage = cvCreateMemStorage( 0 );
    faces   = cvHaarDetectObjects( smallImage, cascade, storage, ( float )1.2, 2,
CV_HAAR_DO_CANNY_PRUNING, cvSize( 20, 20 ) );

    cvReleaseImage( &smallImage );

    imageRef      = cameraView.image.CGImage;
    colorSpaceRef = CGColorSpaceCreateDeviceRGB();
    context       = CGBitmapContextCreate
    (
     NULL,
     cameraView.image.size.width,
     cameraView.image.size.height,
     8,
     cameraView.image.size.width * 4,
     colorSpaceRef,
     kCGImageAlphaPremultipliedLast | kCGBitmapByteOrderDefault
    );

    CGContextDrawImage
    (
     context,
```

```
        CGRectMake( 0, 0, cameraView.image.size.width, cameraView.image.size.height ),
        imageRef
        );

    CGContextSetLineWidth( context, 1 );
    CGContextSetRGBStrokeColor( context, ( CGFloat )0, ( CGFloat )0, ( CGFloat )0, (
CGFloat )0.5 );
    CGContextSetRGBFillColor( context, ( CGFloat )1, ( CGFloat )1, ( CGFloat )1, (
CGFloat )0.5 );

    if( faces->total == 0 )
    {
        alert = [ [ UIAlertView alloc ] initWithTitle: @"No faces" message: @"No faces
were detected in the picture. Please try with another one." delegate: NULL
cancelButtonTitle: @"OK" otherButtonTitles: nil ];

        [ alert show ];
        [ alert release ];
    }
    else
    {
        for( i = 0; i < faces->total; i++ )
        {
            rect     = *( CvRect * )cvGetSeqElem( faces, i );
            faceRect = CGContextConvertRectToDeviceSpace( context, CGRectMake( rect.x *
scale, rect.y * scale, rect.width * scale, rect.height * scale ) );

            CGContextFillRect( context, faceRect );
            CGContextStrokeRect( context, faceRect );
        }

        cameraView.image = [ UIImage imageWithCGImage: CGBitmapContextCreateImage(
context ) ];
    }

    CGContextRelease( context );
    CGColorSpaceRelease( colorSpaceRef );
    cvReleaseMemStorage( &storage );
    cvReleaseHaarClassifierCascade( &cascade );
    cvReleaseImage( &smallImage );

    [pool release];
}
```

Let's step through this for a moment. First, we set up an NSAutoReleasePool to handle memory allocation and release during the processing of the image. We load our Haar cascade from the file path and set up some basic information for the detector such as size, width, and scale.

After we convert the UIImage to an IplImage using our new helper method, we use the cvHaarDetectObjects function to detect the faces in the picture. From there, we have a few paths the method can take. First, if we don't find any faces, we fire a UIAlertView to notify the user to select a new image. If we do find faces, we iterate over them and overlay a translucent square on the image.

There are a few interesting methods here that you might recognize if you dove any deeper into cocos2D earlier in this book. The notion of DeviceSpace and WorldSpace are common in game programming. Sometimes, you are working in pixels on an image, which might differ from CGPoints or percentages in other systems. These C-based conversion functions make it easy to switch between special systems.

Okay, we have both of our processing methods in place. We need to call them after we obtain the UIImage from the library or camera. Find the didFinishPickingImage delegate method and add the line from Listing 12–9 at the end of the routine.

Listing 12–9. *Call the OpenCV Routine*

```
[self openCVFaceDetect];
```

You should be ready to test the routine. Launch the application on the simulator or on a physical device. I'm choosing the **Library** option for my image. After I select the image, something unexpected happens: my console shows the output from Listing 12–10.

Listing 12–10. *Not Great Output*

```
Detected an attempt to call a symbol in system libraries that is not present on the
iPhone:
strtod$UNIX2003 called from function _ZL10icv_strtodP13CvFileStoragePcPS1_ in image
OpenCV-iPad.
```

Luckily, we know what causes this situation. In most available OpenCV distributions, there isn't an appropriate build for the architecture of our devices and simulators. We used a static library for this example that needs to be updated. Let's update that and try again.

OpenCV has a lot of great open source build scripts. The version I have used the most was contributed by Yoshimasa Niwa (https://github.com/niw). We'll be following this recommendation to fix our sample project. Download the OpenCV source for 2.2.0 from this URL: http://sourceforge.net/projects/opencvlibrary/files/opencv-unix/2.2/OpenCV-2.2.0.tar.bz2/download.

> **NOTE:** There may be new versions of OpenCV available. This routine should still work without issue. If you can't find 2.2.0, try to use a newer version.

Open the command line utility on your Mac. Navigate to the directory where you downloaded the archive. Run the command from Listing 12–11.

Listing 12–11. *Extract OpenCV*

```
Kyle-Roches-MacBook-Pro-2:Downloads kyleroche$ tar xjvf OpenCV-2.2.0.tar.bz2
x OpenCV-2.2.0/.DS_Store
x OpenCV-2.2.0/3rdparty/CMakeLists.txt
x OpenCV-2.2.0/3rdparty/ilmimf/LICENSE
x OpenCV-2.2.0/3rdparty/ilmimf/README
….. on and on and on…..
```

Now that we've extracted the library, we need to apply a quick patch to make sure we can build this for iOS. Download the patch files from https://github.com/niw/iphone_opencv_test. To make things easier, I downloaded the whole GitHub repository and moved my OpenCV distribution to that directory. Run the commands shown in Listing 12–12.

Listing 12–12. *Patch OpenCV*

```
Kyle-Roches-MacBook-Pro-2:OpenCV-2.2.0 kyleroche$ patch -p1 < ../OpenCV-2.2.0.patch
patching file CMakeLists.txt
patching file modules/CMakeLists.txt
```

> **NOTE:** We are going to need cmake for this next section. If you don't have that installed, you can get it from Macports or Homebrew. If you do have to install cmake, you might want to start it and go get some coffee. It takes quite a while.

Now that we have a patched version of OpenCV, we can rebuild it for our current architecture. Run the commands shown in Listing 12–13.

Listing 12–13. *Build OpenCV Static Library for the Simulator*

```
Kyle-Roches-MacBook-Pro-2:build_simulator kyleroche $ export IPHONEOS_VERSION_MIN="4.0"
Kyle-Roches-MacBook-Pro-2:build_simulator kyleroche$ ../opencv_cmake.sh Simulator
../OpenCV-2.2.0
Kyle-Roches-MacBook-Pro-2:build_simulator kyleroche$ make -j 4
Kyle-Roches-MacBook-Pro-2:build_simulator kyleroche$ make install
```

You can repeat the same process to build OpenCV for the device. Use `Device` instead of `Simulator` as your argument to `opencv_cmake.sh` (shown in bold in Listing 12–13).

Okay, we should have a new build directory to replace the one that isn't working in our current project. Open Xcode and delete the **OpenCV** directory from your project. Add the newly built directory including the targets for the `Simulator` and `Device` (if you plan on testing on a device).

> **NOTE:** If you're testing on the simulator, you'll need to add the Accelerate framework to your project. This wasn't included in the sample project.

Let's try to run this project again. Either use your camera or select a file from the library. You should see something similar to Figure 12–6.

Figure 12–6. *OpenCV is now working on the iPad simulator.*

We found Elvis in the picture from the photo library.

OpenCV Review

OpenCV turned out to not be that user friendly. Although well documented, the more prominent examples aren't ready for iOS 5 and they aren't compiled for current architectures. The power of OpenCV is tremendous, but it takes quite a bit of work to get things going. As an exercise, use the UILabel to measure the time it takes OpenCV to analyze the image. You can compare the results for each of the next two approaches.

Using the CIDetector Class Approach

The CIDetector class is new to iOS 5. At the release of iOS 5, only one detector was available, and that is for facial recognition. Let's take a look at the difference between using the native class and using OpenCV.

To keep the comparisons as close to fair as possible, let's use the same application and add a few methods to analyze the face using CIDetector instead of OpenCV.

Open the OpenCV-iPad project again, and add the CoreImage framework to the project. We will need this to access the CIDetector classes. Open MainViewController.h and update it, as shown in Listing 12–14.

Listing 12–14. *Updated MainViewController.h*

```
#import <UIKit/UIKit.h>
#import <CoreImage/CoreImage.h>

#define DETECT_IMAGE_MAX_SIZE   1024

@interface MainViewController : UIViewController <UINavigationControllerDelegate,
UIImagePickerControllerDelegate, UIActionSheetDelegate, UIPopoverControllerDelegate> {
    UIImagePickerController *_imagePicker;
    UIPopoverController *_imagePopover;
}

@property (nonatomic, retain) CIDetector *detector;
@property (retain, nonatomic) IBOutlet UIImageView *cameraView;
@property (retain, nonatomic) IBOutlet UILabel *timerLabel;
@property (retain, nonatomic) IBOutlet UIToolbar *toolbar;
- (IBAction)cameraButtonClicked:(id)sender;
@end
```

We're going to need a property of the CIDetector type to analyze the image. Switch over
to MainViewController.m and synthesize the new detector property. Next, add the
declaration from Listing 12–15 to the Private block, just under the import statements.

Listing 12–15. *Private Method Declaration for CIDetectorFaceDetect*

```
-(void) CIDetectorFaceDetect {
    NSLog(@"CI Face Detect started");
    NSArray *arr = [self.detector featuresInImage:[CIImage
imageWithCGImage:[cameraView.image CGImage]]];
    NSLog(@"Set up Array");
    if([arr count]>0){
        for(int i=0;i<[arr count];i++){
            NSLog(@"%d Face found!",i + 1);
            CIFaceFeature * feature = [arr objectAtIndex:i];
            if(feature.hasLeftEyePosition){
                NSLog(@"Left eye position: (%f,
%f)",feature.leftEyePosition.x,feature.leftEyePosition.y);
            }
            if(feature.hasRightEyePosition){
                NSLog(@"Right eye position: (%f,
%f)",feature.rightEyePosition.x,feature.rightEyePosition.y);
            }
            if(feature.hasMouthPosition){
                NSLog(@"Mouth position: (%f,
%f)",feature.mouthPosition.x,feature.mouthPosition.y);
            }

        }
    } else {
        NSLog(@"Nothing detected");
    }
}
```

Make sure you synthesize and release the property in the implementation. Finally, we
need to update the didFinishPickingImage delegate method, as shown in Listing 12–16.

Listing 12–16. *Updated didFinishPickingImage*

```
- (void)imagePickerController:(UIImagePickerController *)picker
didFinishPickingImage:(UIImage *)image editingInfo:(NSDictionary *)editingInfo {
    [self dismissModalViewControllerAnimated:YES];
    cameraView.image = image;

    //[self openCVFaceDetect];
    [self CIDetectorFaceDetect];
}
```

And, that's it. Very different than OpenCV, especially if you're an Objective-C coder who's not that fond of a ton of C code in your projects. This is pretty easy to follow. We call the featuresInImage instance method of the CIDetector class to analyze the UIImage. There is no need to convert the image to IplImage format, as we had to do with OpenCV. CIDetector can analyze the image in the native UIImage format.

Run the project on the simulator or on your physical device. Watch the console and you should see something similar to Figure 12–7.

```
All Output ⬍

GNU gdb 6.3.50-20050815 (Apple version gdb-1708) (Mon Aug  8 20:32:45 UTC 2011)
Copyright 2004 Free Software Foundation, Inc.
GDB is free software, covered by the GNU General Public License, and you are
welcome to change it and/or distribute copies of it under certain conditions.
Type "show copying" to see the conditions.
There is absolutely no warranty for GDB.  Type "show warranty" for details.
This GDB was configured as "x86_64-apple-darwin".sharedlibrary apply-load-rules all
Attaching to process 25008.
[Switching to process 25008 thread 0x13313]
[Switching to process 25008 thread 0x10103]
2011-10-22 11:21:27.791 OpenCV-iPad[25008:10103] CI Face Detect started
2011-10-22 11:21:28.001 OpenCV-iPad[25008:10103] Set up Array
2011-10-22 11:21:28.002 OpenCV-iPad[25008:10103] 1 Face found!
2011-10-22 11:21:28.002 OpenCV-iPad[25008:10103] Left eye position: (183.000000, 341.000000)
2011-10-22 11:21:28.003 OpenCV-iPad[25008:10103] Right eye position: (244.000000, 330.000000)
2011-10-22 11:21:28.003 OpenCV-iPad[25008:10103] Mouth position: (202.000000, 266.000000)
```

Figure 12–7. *CIDetector is working on the iPad simulator.*

You can extend this example to redraw a box around the image, if you want. You can tell a bit about the x,y coordinates if you compare it to the photo of Elvis I'm using for testing. You can see that the left eye is located at 183,341 and the right eye position is 244,330. It is important to realize that the image is mirrored. So, the right eye, on our right side when looking at the simulator, is to the right and a bit lower than the eye on our left when looking at the simulator. Given the angle of Elvis' face, this looks fairly accurate.

CIDetector returns a CIFaceFeature object, which has some properties we've logged in the console. Hopefully, we'll see this class extended over time to add new features, such as mood detection and more.

CIDetector Review

With less than 15 lines of actual code (discounting logging code) we were able to analyze a photo for faces. There was no need to add third-party libraries or build any static libraries manually. It simply worked with iOS 5.

Plus, if you were to attach this to a live camera view, you'd be able to see that it can keep up with the speed of the camera buffer. As an exercise, if you did this after OpenCV, use the timerLabel to compare performance between the two approaches we've discussed so far.

Using the Face.com API Approach

In the previous examples, we benefited from the speed and power of native processing. However, we either sacrificed ease of setup or lack of information about the recognized facial object.

Wouldn't it be nice to have an easy way to detect not only the face, but also its mood and any other useful information that can be derived from the photo?

Face.com uses a REST API to accomplish just that. The disadvantage, for us mobile developers, is the need to always have a connection to the Internet. But, these days, that might not be that big of a drawback.

Faces.detect API Call

This API call, from face.com, returns tags for detected faces in one or more photos, with geometric information of the tag, eyes, nose, and mouth, as well as various attributes such as gender, is wearing glasses, and is smiling.

Photos can also be uploaded directly in the API request. A request that uploads a photo must be formed as a MIME multipart message sent using POST data. Each argument, including the raw image data, should be specified as a separate chunk of form data.

Following are a few things to note when using the face.com API:

- All coordinates are provided in percent values to support any photo scale. Photo height and width (vs. tag height/width) are provided in pixels. Yaw, roll, and pitch are provided on the –90° to 90° scale.

- The maximum width or height of a photo is 900 pixels. You may POST or send links to higher-size photos, but those will be resized internally to improve performance.

■ Every tag we return contains a set of attributes. The most important of them is the face attribute. It contains the confidence level of that tag being a face. As shown in the developer tools demo, I recommend using tags with confidence greater than 50 percent. Tags with lower confidence might also be a face, but have a higher probability to be false-positive detection.

To compare the facial-recognition algorithms, we'll extend our example with a method that calls the face.com API. We'll be taking a look at this approach in Chapter 13 in more detail.

Adding Face.com Support to Our Sample

Open OpenCV-iPad in Xcode again. Copy the following files from either the GitHub repository or the Source Code/Download area of the Apress web site (www.apress.com). Alternatively, you can download them yourself from http://allseeing-i.com/ASIHTTPRequest. We'll talk more about this library in Chapter 13. For now, just copy these files into your project.

■ ASIHTTPRequestConfig.h

■ ASIHTTPRequestDelegate.h

■ ASIProgressDelegate.h

■ ASICacheDelegate.h

■ ASIHTTPRequest.h

■ ASIHTTPRequest.m

■ ASIDataCompressor.h

■ ASIDataCompressor.m

■ ASIDataDecompressor.h

■ ASIDataDecompressor.m

■ ASIFormDataRequest.h

■ ASIInputStream.h

■ ASIInputStream.m

■ ASIFormDataRequest.m

■ ASINetworkQueue.h

■ ASINetworkQueue.m

■ ASIDownloadCache.h

■ ASIDownloadCache.m

■ ASIAuthenticationDialog.h

■ ASIAuthenticationDialog.m

■   Reachability.h (in the External/Reachability folder)

■   Reachability.m (in the External/Reachability folder)

In addition, you need to add the CFNetwork, SystemConfiguration, MobileCoreServices, and the libz.dylib frameworks to the project. Make sure your project builds without errors before you move forward.

Face.com API Key

Open your browser to http://www.face.com. In the top right-hand corner, there should be a link called **Developers**. Follow that link, then click the gigantic **Get Started** image in the middle of the page. The sign-up process for face.com is fairly noninvasive. It only requires you to provide your name, e-mail, and a password. If you're feeling more generous, give them the rest of the information. Either way, prove you're human by completing the CAPTCHA and click **Signup**. Follow the instructions in your confirmation e-mail to verify your account.

Go to the **API Keys** tab after you're logged in. Create a new application. It doesn't matter what you name the application. I've used iOS AR Demo for my application name. You will see a page similar to Figure 12–8.

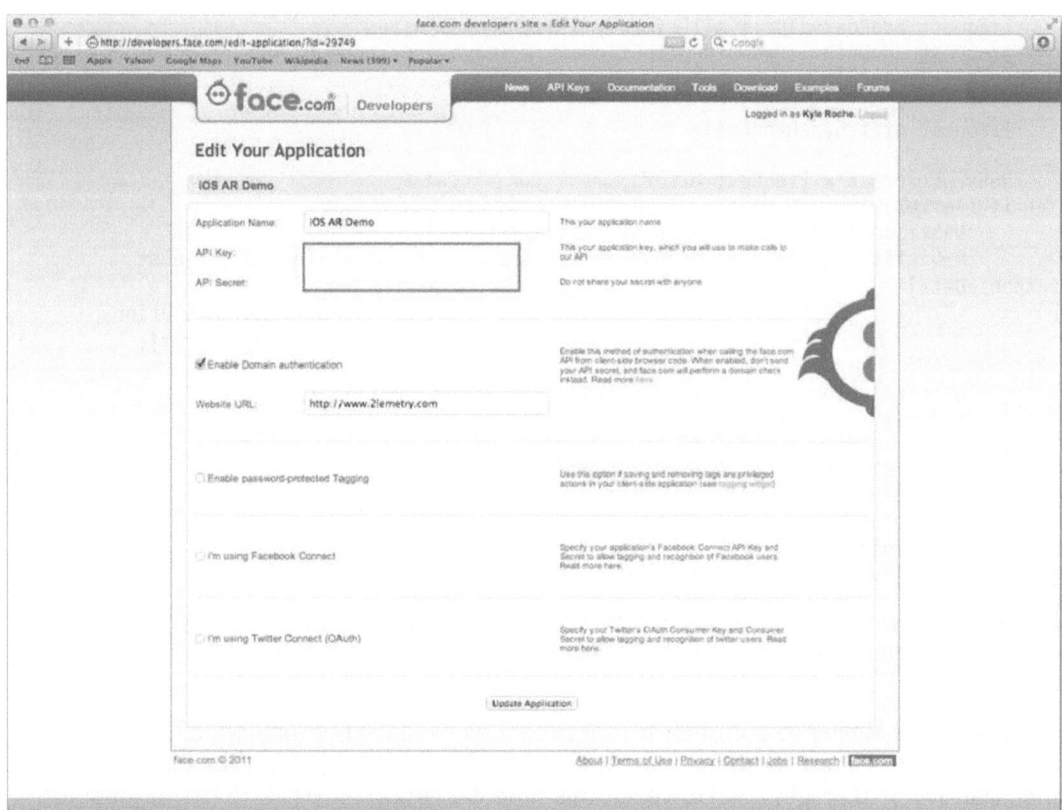

Figure 12–8. *Set up your face.com application.*

There are two settings here you will need when we start building the application. They are the **API Key** and the **API Secret**.

Adding the Face.com Callout

Open `MainViewController.h` in Xcode. Import `ASIFormDataRequest.h` in your header. Switch over to `MainViewController.m`. Declare a new private method called `FaceDotComFaceDetect` in the private block, just after the `import` statements.

Add the method from Listing 12–17.

Listing 12–17. *FaceDotComFaceDetect Method*

```
- (void)FaceDotComFaceDetect {
    NSAutoreleasePool * pool = [[NSAutoreleasePool alloc] init];
    NSData * imageData = UIImageJPEGRepresentation(cameraView.image, 90);

    NSURL * url = [NSURL URLWithString:@"http://api.face.com/faces/detect.json"];

    ASIFormDataRequest *request = [ASIFormDataRequest requestWithURL:url];
    [request addPostValue:@"" forKey:@"api_key"];
    [request addPostValue:@"" forKey:@"api_secret"];
```

```
    [request addPostValue:@"all" forKey:@"attributes"];
    [request addData:imageData withFileName:@"image.jpg" andContentType:@"image/jpeg"
forKey:@"filename"];

    [request startSynchronous];

    NSError *error = [request error];
    if (!error) {
        NSString *response = [request responseString];
        NSDictionary *feed = [NSJSONSerialization JSONObjectWithData:[request
responseData]

                                                    options:kNilOptions
                                                      error:&error];

        NSLog(@"RETURN: %@", [feed allKeys]);
        NSLog(@"%@",response);
    } else {
        NSLog(@"An error occured %d",[error code]);
    }

    [pool drain];
}
```

Before we step through this, make sure you substitute the real values for your face.com credentials in the code shown in bold. We'll talk more about the second bolded section in a moment.

The method is similar to our other two approaches to facial recognition. First, we set up an NSAutoreleasePool for memory management. Once again, we get the UIImage from the cameraView UIImageView. However, this time we set up an HTTP POST request for the face.com API. We add the raw JPEG representation data to the POST body as a null parameter.

Next, we analyze our response to make sure it didn't throw an exception. If there's no error, we move on to serialize the JSON response and convert it into an NSDictionary.

Then, we simply print the response to the console. Update the didFinishPickingImage method one last time to comment out our previous approaches and call our new method. The updated method should read like Listing 12–18.

Listing 12–18. *Updated didFinishPickingImage*

```
- (void)imagePickerController:(UIImagePickerController *)picker
didFinishPickingImage:(UIImage *)image editingInfo:(NSDictionary *)editingInfo {
    [self dismissModalViewControllerAnimated:YES];
    cameraView.image = image;

    //[self openCVFaceDetect];
    //[self CIDetectorFaceDetect];
    [self FaceDotComFaceDetect];
}
```

Before we run the application, let's discuss the second section of bolded code from Listing 12–17. iOS 5 introduced native JSON support for framework objects. You use the new NSJSONSerialization class to convert JSON to Foundation objects and convert Foundation objects to JSON.

An object that may be converted to JSON must have the following properties:

- The top-level object is an NSArray or NSDictionary.

- All objects are instances of NSString, NSNumber, NSArray, NSDictionary, or NSNull.

- All dictionary keys are instances of NSString.

- Numbers are not NaN or infinity.

Okay, run the project. I'm going to select the same Elvis image again to keep things consistent. The console output from the new request is shown in Listing 12–19.

Listing 12–19. *Console Output from face.com Request*

```
2011-10-22 14:41:08.392 OpenCV-iPad[25731:10103] RETURN: (
    status,
    photos,
    usage
)
2011-10-22 14:41:08.393 OpenCV-iPad[25731:10103]
{
    "photos":[
        {
            "url":"http:\/\/face.com\/images\/ph\/f1a498f5c46aab132f4a1d980297698f.jpg",
            "pid":"F@daa96ea9dcce39470a09ea5648c87356_cd31b28498224cf9ccb39f9194569af8",
            "width":380,
            "height":481,
            "tags":[
                {
"tid":"TEMP_F@daa96ea9dcce39470a09ea5648c87356_cd31b28498224cf9ccb39f9194569af8_53.68_35
.55_0_0",
                    "recognizable":true,
                    "threshold":null,
                    "uids":[
                    ],
                    "gid":null,
                    "label":"",
                    "confirmed":false,
                    "manual":false,
                    "tagger_id":null,
                    "width":32.11,
                    "height":25.36,
                    "center":{
                        "x":53.68,
                        "y":35.55
                    },
                    "eye_left":{
                        "x":48.95,
                        "y":27.54
                    },
                    "eye_right":{
                        "x":63.83,
                        "y":32.24
                    },
                    "mouth_left":{
```

```
                                "x":45.09,
                                "y":39.27
                            },
                            "mouth_center":{
                                "x":49.54,
                                "y":41.74
                            },
                            "mouth_right":{
                                "x":56.75,
                                "y":42.99
                            },
                            "nose":{
                                "x":50.21,
                                "y":37.12
                            },
                            "ear_left":null,
                            "ear_right":null,
                            "chin":null,
                            "yaw":-14.78,
                            "roll":21.81,
                            "pitch":-7.49,
                            "attributes":{
                                "glasses":{
                                    "value":"false",
                                    "confidence":88
                                },
                                "smiling":{
                                    "value":"true",
                                    "confidence":83
                                },
                                "face":{
                                    "value":"true",
                                    "confidence":92
                                },
                                "gender":{
                                    "value":"male",
                                    "confidence":33
                                },
                                "mood":{
                                    "value":"happy",
                                    "confidence":76
                                },
                                "lips":{
                                    "value":"parted",
                                    "confidence":92
                                }
                            }
                        }
                    }
                ]
            }
        ],
        "status":"success",
        "usage":{
            "used":1,
            "remaining":4999,
            "limit":5000,
            "reset_time_text":"Sat, 22 Oct 2011 21:41:07 +0000",
```

```
        "reset_time":1319319667
    }
}
```

Other than the 33 percent confidence that Elvis is a male, the results are similar to what we've seen before. There are a few things to notice in the difference in the data structure. Face.com uses percentages for x,y instead of pixels. Also, the y coordinate starts from the top of the screen instead of the bottom.

Spend some time analyzing the details in the return from face.com. Face.com detects the mood of the user as well as some identifiable features like whether they are wearing glasses and whether their lips are parted. There are tons of applications that could benefit from this level of detail. Hopefully, we'll see that in the CIDetector classes someday.

Measuring Performance

These are all somewhat different methods, but let's compare their speed for reference. Create a new class in your project called CodeTimestamps.m that subclasses NSObject. Update the header so it reflects the code from Listing 12–20.

It might be easier to copy these files right from the project in GitHub or from Apress (www.apress.com). The appropriate headers and copyright statements are in the code repository for the book.

Listing 12–20. *CodeTimestamps.h*

```
#import <Foundation/Foundation.h>

// Comment out this line to disable timestamp logging.
#define USE_TIMESTAMPS 1

// How often timing data is output to the logs.
#define kLogTimeInterval 10.0

// Macro to give us an efficient one-time function call.
// The token trickiness is from here:
// http://bit.ly/fQ6Glh
#define TokenPasteInternal(x,y) x ## y
#define TokenPaste(x,y) TokenPasteInternal(x,y)
#define UniqueTokenMacro TokenPaste(unique,__LINE__)
#define OneTimeCall(x) \
{ static BOOL UniqueTokenMacro = NO; \
if (!UniqueTokenMacro) {x; UniqueTokenMacro = YES; }}

// Speed performance-tuning functions & macros.
void LogTimeStampInMethod(const char *fnName, int lineNum);
void LogTimestampChunkInMethod(const char *fnName, int lineNum, BOOL isStart, BOOL
isEnd);
void printAllLogs();
#ifdef USE_TIMESTAMPS

#define LogTimestamp LogTimeStampInMethod(__FUNCTION__, __LINE__)
```

```
#define LogTimestampStartChunk LogTimestampChunkInMethod(__FUNCTION__, __LINE__, YES,
NO)
#define LogTimestampMidChunk LogTimestampChunkInMethod(__FUNCTION__, __LINE__, NO, NO)
#define LogTimestampEndChunk LogTimestampChunkInMethod(__FUNCTION__, __LINE__, NO, YES)

#else

#define LogTimestamp
#define LogTimestampStartChunk
#define LogTimestampMidChunk
#define LogTimestampEndChunk

#endif

#ifndef PrintName
#define PrintName NSLog(@"%s", __FUNCTION__)
#endif
```

Open CodeTimestamps.m in Xcode, and add the code from Listing 12–21.

Listing 12–21. *CodeTimestamps.m*

```objc
#import "CodeTimestamps.h"

#import <mach/mach.h>
#import <mach/mach_time.h>

#define kNumSlowestChunks 5
#define kNumMidPoints 5

static NSMutableArray *chunkData = nil;

@class ChunkTimeInterval;

@interface LogHelper : NSObject {
@private
    NSTimer *logTimer;
    NSMutableArray *pendingLines;
    NSMutableArray *slowestChunks;
}

+ (LogHelper *)sharedInstance;

- (void)startLoggingTimer;
- (void)printOutTimingData:(NSTimer *)timer;
- (void)addLogString:(NSString *)newString;

- (void)maybeAddTimeIntervalAsSlowest:(ChunkTimeInterval *)timeInterval;
- (void)logSlowestChunks;

- (void)consolidateTimeIntervals:(NSMutableArray *)timeIntervals;

@end

@interface ChunkStamp : NSObject {
@public
    const char *fnName;
    int lineNum;
```

```
    uint64_t timestamp;
    NSThread *thread;
    BOOL isStart;
    BOOL isEnd;
}

- (NSComparisonResult)compare:(id)other;

@end

void printAllLogs() {
        [[LogHelper sharedInstance] printOutTimingData:nil];
}

uint64_t NanosecondsFromTimeInterval(uint64_t timeInterval) {
    static struct mach_timebase_info timebase_info;
    OneTimeCall(mach_timebase_info(&timebase_info));
    timeInterval *= timebase_info.numer;
    timeInterval /= timebase_info.denom;
    return timeInterval;
}

// This function needs to be _fast_ to minimize interfering with
// timing data.  So we don't actually NSLog during it, using LogHelper.
void LogTimeStampInMethod(const char *fnName, int lineNum) {
    OneTimeCall([[LogHelper sharedInstance] startLoggingTimer]);
    static uint64_t lastTimestamp = 0;
    uint64_t thisTimestamp = mach_absolute_time();
    NSString *logStr = nil;
    if (lastTimestamp == 0) {
        logStr = [NSString stringWithFormat:@"* %s:%4d", fnName, lineNum];
    } else {
        uint64_t elapsed = NanosecondsFromTimeInterval(thisTimestamp - lastTimestamp);
        logStr = [NSString stringWithFormat:@"* %s:%4d - %9llu nsec since last
timestamp",
                    fnName, lineNum, elapsed];
    }
    [[LogHelper sharedInstance] addLogString:logStr];
    lastTimestamp = thisTimestamp;
}

void InitChunkData() {
    if (chunkData) return;
    chunkData = [NSMutableArray new];
}

void LogTimestampChunkInMethod(const char *fnName, int lineNum, BOOL isStart, BOOL
isEnd) {
    OneTimeCall(InitChunkData());
    OneTimeCall([[LogHelper sharedInstance] startLoggingTimer]);
    ChunkStamp *stamp = [[ChunkStamp new] autorelease];
    stamp->fnName = fnName;
    stamp->lineNum = lineNum;
    stamp->timestamp = mach_absolute_time();
    stamp->thread = [NSThread currentThread];
    stamp->isStart = isStart;
    stamp->isEnd = isEnd;
```

```objc
    @synchronized(chunkData) {
        [chunkData addObject:stamp];
    }
}

@interface ChunkTimeInterval : NSObject {
@public
    NSString *intervalName;  // strong
    uint64_t nanoSecsElapsed;
}
- (id)initFromStamp:(ChunkStamp *)stamp1 toStamp:(ChunkStamp *)stamp2;
@end

@implementation ChunkTimeInterval
- (id)initFromStamp:(ChunkStamp *)stamp1 toStamp:(ChunkStamp *)stamp2 {
    if (![super init]) return nil;
    intervalName = [[NSString stringWithFormat:@"%s:%d - %s:%d",
                    stamp1->fnName, stamp1->lineNum, stamp2->fnName, stamp2->lineNum]
retain];
    nanoSecsElapsed = NanosecondsFromTimeInterval(stamp2->timestamp - stamp1-
>timestamp);
    return self;
}
- (void)dealloc {
    [intervalName release];
    [super dealloc];
}
- (NSString *)description {
    return [NSString stringWithFormat:@"<%@ %p> %@ %llu", [self class], self,
intervalName, nanoSecsElapsed];
}
@end



@implementation LogHelper

+ (LogHelper *)sharedInstance {
    static LogHelper *instance = nil;
    if (instance == nil) instance = [LogHelper new];
    return instance;
}

- (id)init {
    if (![super init]) return nil;
    pendingLines = [NSMutableArray new];
    slowestChunks = [NSMutableArray new];
    return self;
}

- (void)startLoggingTimer {
    if (logTimer) return;
    logTimer = [NSTimer scheduledTimerWithTimeInterval:kLogTimeInterval
                                        target:self
                                        selector:@selector(printOutTimingData:)
                                        userInfo:nil
                                         repeats:YES];
```

```objc
}
- (void)printOutTimingData:(NSTimer *)timer {
    BOOL didLogAnything = NO;

    // Handle pending lines.
    if ([pendingLines count]) {
        NSLog(@"==== Start non-chunk timestamp data (from \"LogTimestamp\") ====");
        for (NSString *logString in pendingLines) {
            NSLog(@"%@", logString);
        }
        [pendingLines removeAllObjects];
        didLogAnything = YES;
    }

    // Handle chunk data.
    if ([chunkData count]) {
        NSLog(@"==== Start chunk timestamp data (from
\"LogTimestamp{Start,Mid,End}Chunk\") ====");
        @synchronized(chunkData) {
            [chunkData sortUsingSelector:@selector(compare:)];
            NSThread *thread = nil;
            NSMutableArray *timeIntervals = [NSMutableArray array];
            uint64_t totalNanoSecsThisChunk;
            uint64_t totalNanoSecsThisThread;
            int numRunsThisThread;
            BOOL thisThreadHadChunks = NO;
            BOOL midChunk = NO;
            ChunkStamp *lastStamp = nil;
            NSString *chunkName = nil;
            for (ChunkStamp *chunkStamp in chunkData) {
                if (chunkStamp->thread != thread) {
                    if (thisThreadHadChunks) {
                        NSLog(@"++ Chunk = %@, avg time = %.4fs", chunkName,
                                (float)totalNanoSecsThisThread / numRunsThisThread / 1e9);
                    }

                    thread = chunkStamp->thread;
                    NSLog(@"--- Data for thread %p ---", thread);
                    [timeIntervals removeAllObjects];
                    midChunk = NO;
                    thisThreadHadChunks = NO;
                    totalNanoSecsThisChunk = 0;
                    totalNanoSecsThisThread = 0;
                    numRunsThisThread = 0;
                }
                if (chunkStamp->isStart) {
                    if (midChunk) {
                        NSLog(@"ERROR: LogTimestampStartChunk hit twice without a
LogTimestampEndChunk between them.");
                    }
                    midChunk = YES;
                    thisThreadHadChunks = YES;
                    chunkName = [NSString stringWithFormat:@"%s:%d", chunkStamp->fnName,
chunkStamp->lineNum];
                } else if (midChunk) {
                    ChunkTimeInterval *timeInterval = [[[ChunkTimeInterval alloc]
initFromStamp:lastStamp toStamp:chunkStamp] autorelease];
```

```
                        [timeIntervals addObject:timeInterval];
                        totalNanoSecsThisChunk += timeInterval->nanoSecsElapsed;
                        if (chunkStamp->isEnd) {
                            totalNanoSecsThisThread += totalNanoSecsThisChunk;
                            numRunsThisThread++;
                            chunkName = [NSString stringWithFormat:@"%@ - %s:%d", chunkName,
chunkStamp->fnName, chunkStamp->lineNum];
                            NSLog(@"+ Chunk = %@, time = %.4fs", chunkName,
(float)totalNanoSecsThisChunk/1e9);

                            [self consolidateTimeIntervals:timeIntervals];
                            for (int i = 0; i < [timeIntervals count] && i < kNumMidPoints;
++i) {
                                ChunkTimeInterval *timeInterval = [timeIntervals
objectAtIndex:i];

                                int percentTime = (int)round(100.0 * (float)timeInterval-
>nanoSecsElapsed / totalNanoSecsThisChunk);
                                NSLog(@"    %2d%% in %@", percentTime, timeInterval-
>intervalName);
                            }

                            ChunkTimeInterval *totalInterval = [[ChunkTimeInterval new]
autorelease];
                            totalInterval->intervalName = [chunkName retain];
                            totalInterval->nanoSecsElapsed = totalNanoSecsThisChunk;
                            [self maybeAddTimeIntervalAsSlowest:totalInterval];

                            [timeIntervals removeAllObjects];
                            totalNanoSecsThisChunk = 0;
                            midChunk = NO;
                        }
                    }
                    lastStamp = chunkStamp;
                }
                if (thisThreadHadChunks) {
                    NSLog(@"++ Chunk = %@, avg time = %d nsec", chunkName,
                            totalNanoSecsThisThread / numRunsThisThread);
                }
                [chunkData removeAllObjects];
            }
            didLogAnything = YES;
        }
        if (didLogAnything) {
            [self logSlowestChunks];
            NSLog(@"==== End timestamp data ====");
        }
}

- (void)addLogString:(NSString *)newString {
    [pendingLines addObject:newString];
}

- (void)maybeAddTimeIntervalAsSlowest:(ChunkTimeInterval *)timeInterval {
    if ([slowestChunks count] < kNumSlowestChunks ||
        ((ChunkTimeInterval *)[slowestChunks lastObject])->nanoSecsElapsed <
timeInterval->nanoSecsElapsed) {
        [slowestChunks addObject:timeInterval];
```

```
        NSSortDescriptor *sortByTime = [[[NSSortDescriptor alloc]
initWithKey:@"nanoSecsElapsed" ascending:NO] autorelease];
        [slowestChunks sortUsingDescriptors:[NSArray arrayWithObject:sortByTime]];
        if ([slowestChunks count] > kNumSlowestChunks) [slowestChunks removeLastObject];
    }
}

- (void)logSlowestChunks {
    if ([slowestChunks count] == 0) return;
    NSLog(@"==== Slowest chunks so far ====");
    for (ChunkTimeInterval *timeInterval in slowestChunks) {
        NSLog(@"# Chunk = %@, time = %.4fs", timeInterval->intervalName,
(float)timeInterval->nanoSecsElapsed/1e9);
    }
}

- (void)consolidateTimeIntervals:(NSMutableArray *)timeIntervals {
    NSSortDescriptor *sortByName = [[[NSSortDescriptor alloc]
initWithKey:@"intervalName" ascending:YES] autorelease];
    [timeIntervals sortUsingDescriptors:[NSArray arrayWithObject:sortByName]];

    NSMutableArray *consolidatedIntervals = [NSMutableArray array];
    NSString *lastName = nil;
    ChunkTimeInterval *thisInterval = nil;
    for (ChunkTimeInterval *timeInterval in timeIntervals) {
        if ([lastName isEqualToString:timeInterval->intervalName]) {
            thisInterval->nanoSecsElapsed += timeInterval->nanoSecsElapsed;
        } else {
            thisInterval = [[ChunkTimeInterval new] autorelease];
            thisInterval->intervalName = [timeInterval->intervalName retain];
            thisInterval->nanoSecsElapsed = timeInterval->nanoSecsElapsed;
            [consolidatedIntervals addObject:thisInterval];
        }
        lastName = timeInterval->intervalName;
    }
    [timeIntervals removeAllObjects];
    [timeIntervals addObjectsFromArray:consolidatedIntervals];

    NSSortDescriptor *sortByTime = [[[NSSortDescriptor alloc]
initWithKey:@"nanoSecsElapsed" ascending:NO] autorelease];
    [timeIntervals sortUsingDescriptors:[NSArray arrayWithObject:sortByTime]];
}

@end

@implementation ChunkStamp

- (NSComparisonResult)compare:(id)other {
    ChunkStamp *otherStamp = (ChunkStamp *)other;
    if (thread != otherStamp->thread) {
        return (thread < otherStamp->thread ? NSOrderedAscending : NSOrderedDescending);
    }
    if (strcmp(fnName, otherStamp->fnName) != 0) {
        return (strcmp(fnName, otherStamp->fnName) < 0 ? NSOrderedAscending :
NSOrderedDescending);
    }
    if (timestamp == otherStamp->timestamp) return NSOrderedSame;
```

```
     return (timestamp < otherStamp->timestamp ? NSOrderedAscending :
NSOrderedDescending);
}
```

```
@end
```

This code is part of the open source moriarty library from Pulse. You can read more about it on their web site (www.pulse.me). Basically, you insert function calls to the LogTimestamp macro at the beginning and the end of the methods you'd like to measure. It measures the time to the nanosecond, so you can record exactly how long each method in your project is taking.

Return to `MainViewController.m` and import the new class we just created. At the top and bottom of each of our facial-recognition methods, add the code from Listing 12–22.

Listing 12–22. *LogTimestamp Macro*

```
LogTimestamp;
```

Update the `didFinishPickingImage` method, as shown in Listing 12–23.

Listing 12–23. *Updated didFinishPickingImage Method*

```
- (void)imagePickerController:(UIImagePickerController *)picker
didFinishPickingImage:(UIImage *)image editingInfo:(NSDictionary *)editingInfo {
    [self dismissModalViewControllerAnimated:YES];
    cameraView.image = image;

    [self openCVFaceDetect];
    //[self CIDetectorFaceDetect];
    //[self FaceDotComFaceDetect];
}
```

Run the project. You should see output similar to Listing 12–24 in your console. It does take a few seconds to print the output, so be patient.

Listing 12–24. *Console Output*

```
2011-10-22 15:12:27.753 OpenCV-iPad[26058:10103] ==== Start non-chunk timestamp data
(from "LogTimestamp") ====
2011-10-22 15:12:27.754 OpenCV-iPad[26058:10103] * -[MainViewController
openCVFaceDetect]:  76
2011-10-22 15:12:27.754 OpenCV-iPad[26058:10103] * -[MainViewController
openCVFaceDetect]: 163 -  664215125 nsec since last timestamp
2011-10-22 15:12:27.755 OpenCV-iPad[26058:10103] ==== End timestamp data ====
```

It appears that it took 61231366 nanoseconds to process the image using OpenCV. Repeat the process for the other approaches. My results show that CIDetector took about 29 percent of the time of OpenCV. Plus, if you add some measurements to the applications launch time, you'll notice that OpenCV takes drastically more time than the other approaches to start up.

CIDetector only took 18 percent of the time of face.com. This, of course, is understandably due to the network callout and huge response returned and parsed using the native JSON serialization classes.

Comparing OpenCV and face.com is interesting. OpenCV, which again takes full seconds longer on application startup, was about 35 percent faster than the full face.com transaction. In subsecond timing, that's nearly indistinguishable to the user.

Summary

We learned a lot in this chapter. There are some paint points involved in the older approaches to facial recognition, like OpenCV. These libraries have been around for years and are missing some of the ease we take for granted in native Objective-C functions and macros. However, they are powerful libraries and have paved the way for the innovations we demonstrated in the newer approaches to facial recognition.

We talked about the new iOS 5 CIDetector class and its ability to analyze the native UIImage object for facial patterns without the need to load Haar cascades or train the library with samples.

Finally, we covered a non-native approach using a free REST API that has the capability of analyzing raw JPEG data. This approach also helped us introduce the native JSON parsing that is new to iOS 5.

All of these approaches had their advantages and disadvantages. We took a quick look at the speed performance of the transactions using an iPad 2 and found that the new iOS 5 CIDetector classes outperform both the other approaches significantly. It is important to note that face.com does require a full network callout and response and almost kept up with the native approaches. Also, if you're using a cross-platform application or you have additional capabilities on a web API, the face.com approach might lend itself to your needs better than a fully native approach.

In Chapter 13, we'll take a deeper look at the face.com approach. We'll analyze the screen buffer and send a request to face.com every few seconds. We'll use cocos2D to overlay some information on the screen about the response.

Building a Facial Recognition AR App

In Chapter 12, we introduced a few ways to bring facial and object recognition to your applications. Some of the approaches are more difficult than others. In this chapter, we are going to pick one of those approaches and build out a fully functional AR application using facial recognition and some of the other technologies we've already discussed in the book.

The Application's Purpose

Thinking of a specific purpose for this application was a bit difficult. I wasn't trying to solve a really practical problem as much as trying to demonstrate some of the key concepts that we've learned in this book so far.

Having said that, the premise of this application is customer service. Admittedly, it's a bit overblown, but it will be fun nonetheless. For this project, picture an iPad mounted above a table in a restaurant or in the common area of a pub. We are going to analyze the mood of the person in the iPad's camera and alert customer service if we find his/her mood to be angry.

As a side note, we're going to build this application based on what we've learned so far in the book. Unfortunately, the approaches we've learned up to this point aren't going to work as we hope they will. I want to warn you of this ahead of time. When the app looks broken halfway through the chapter, that's on purpose. It's not something you did wrong! We will fix it and learn a bit about OpenGL and its dislike for threading along the way.

Technology Used

At first, we'll just overlay some information about the user on the screen. This will be good practice for building a more complex HUD layer in cocos2D. We'll extend this application to actually send an SMS (Short Message Service) to the customer service representative and report the incident.

The core piece of technology we'll be using is the face.com REST API. As we discussed in Chapter 12, the face.com API takes a JPEG image over a REST request and returns the x,y coordinates of the recognized face, as well as information about the person's mood, glasses, and mouth position. It's a very useful and quick API.

Getting Set Up

Let's get the technology we need for the example application lined up. There are three main sign up processes you'll have to endure to get to the fun stuff.

Face.com

Open your browser to www.face.com. In the top right-hand corner, there should be a link called **Developers**. Follow that link, then click the gigantic **Get Started** image in the middle of the page. The sign-up process for face.com is fairly noninvasive. It only requires you to provide your name, e-mail, and a password. If you're feeling more generous, give them the rest of the information. Either way, prove you're human by completing the CAPTCHA and click **Signup**. Follow the instructions in your confirmation e-mail to verify your account.

Go to the **API Keys** tab after you're logged in. Create a new application by clicking the link that says **Click here to set up a new application**. It doesn't matter what you name the application. I've used iOS AR Demo for my application name. You will see a page similar to Figure 13–1.

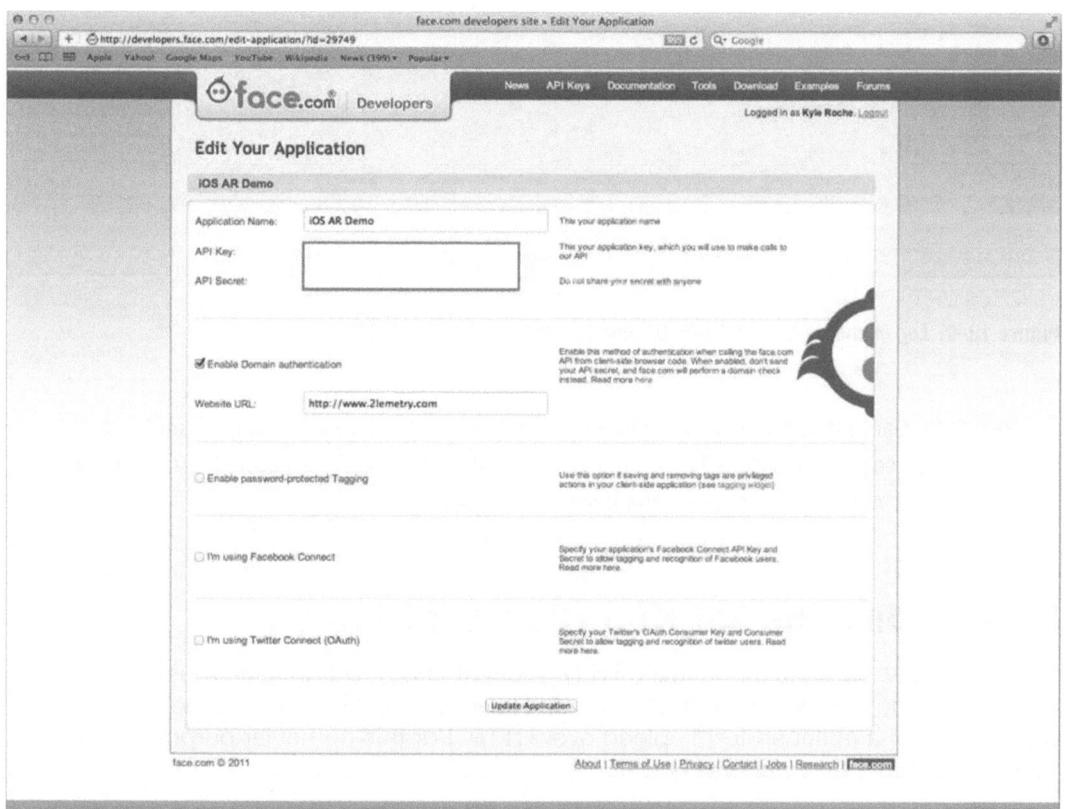

Figure 13–1. *Complete the face.com application page.*

There are two settings here you will need when we start building the application. They are the API Key and the API Secret. That's it for face.com for now.

cocos2D

If you don't already have cocos2D visit `www.cocos2d-iphone.org/download` to download the latest stable build of cocos2D for iPhone, which at the time of this writing is 1.0.1. We covered installing cocos2D in Xcode 4.2 back in Chapter 7, so if you're the type that skips chapters you should flip back there now.

Setting Up Our Twilio Account

Twilio is a cloud communications platform that provides support for SMS, Voice, and even VOIP communications. This is an easy sign-up process as well. Visit `www.twilio.com/try-twilio` to set up your free trial.

After you have your account set up, log in and you will see something like Figure 13–2 on the top of your Dashboard page.

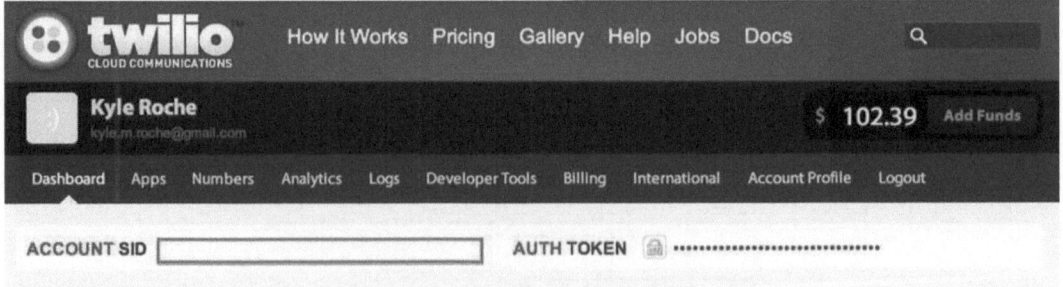

Figure 13–2. *Log in and go to your Twilio Dashboard page.*

> **NOTE:** Similar to face.com's credentials, you'll need to remember your Account SID and your Auth Token so you can access Twilio's API in our demo application. Your Account SID is useless without your Auth Token. So, never share the Auth Token!

Downloading the ASI-HTTP-Request Library

There are a few libraries for handling HTTP requests from iOS. In face, most of the features can be simply written from scratch. However, we'll be sending the raw image data as part of a multipart form upload over HTTP. For this particular purpose, there is a third-party library that works very well.

ASI-HTTP-Request is an open source library available on GitHub at pokeb/asi-http-request. I've forked the version I'm using for this example to kyleroche/asi-http-request in case you have any issues with a newer version. Store this somewhere on your local machine.

JSON-Framework

We are also going to need some help parsing JSON (JavaScript Object Notation) messages, as that is the preferred output of the face.com API (and works great for Twilio as well). Similar to ASI-HTTP-Request, there is an open source project on GitHub at stig/json-framework that I've forked to kyleroche/json-framework for reference. Store this somewhere on your local machine.

Project Structure

Let's create our project. Open Xcode and create a new project using the cocso2D template, as shown in Figure 13–3.

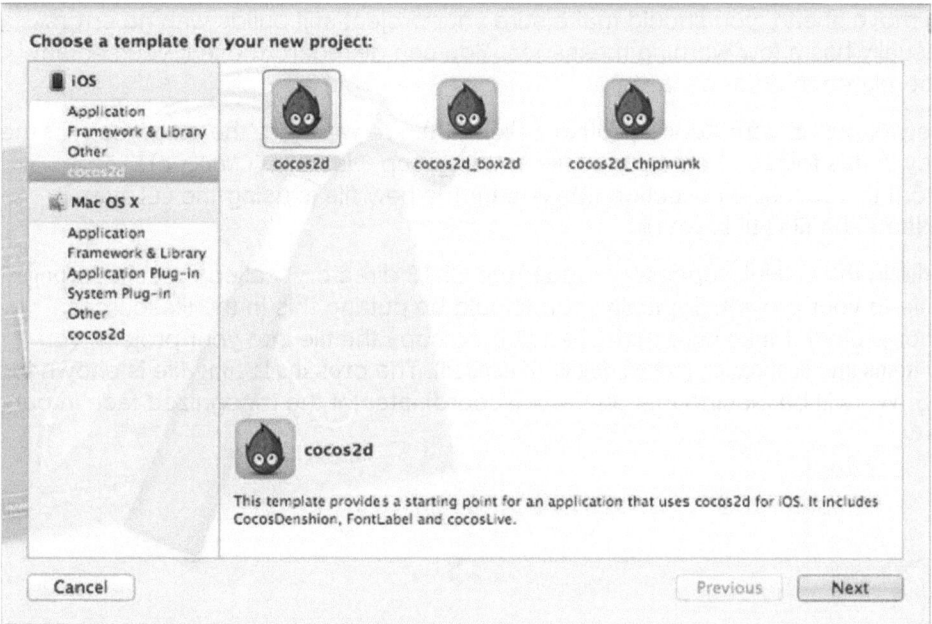

Figure 13–3. *Create a new cocos2D project.*

Name the project **Ch13**. If you need to reference the working source code, it is available from https://github.com/kyleroche/Professional_iOS_AugmentedReality or from www.apress.com.

First, let's make sure we have all the references we need to run this application. Add the frameworks and libraries shown in Figure 13–4.

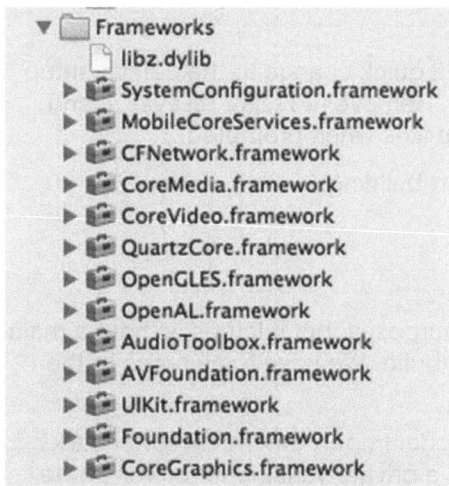

Figure 13–4. *Add the required frameworks.*

Before you move ahead, you should make sure your project still builds with no errors. cocos2D usually has a few warning messages. You can disregard those if you see any (that are not related to code we write).

Create a new Group in your Xcode project called **HUD**. We will store the resources for the HUD overlay in this folder. Create a new file in this group. Use the CCNode class template from the cocos2D collection. Make sure the new file is using the CCLayer subclass. Name the file HUDLayer.m.

There is a file in the GitHub repository (under the Ch13 directory) called crosshair.png. Copy this file to your project. Typically, you should be putting this in the Resources folder of your project. Make sure that when you do copy the file into your project, you select **Copy items into destination group's folder (if needed)**. The crosshair.png file is shown in Figure 13–5. We will be placing this on the x,y coordinates of the recognized face in our camera view.

Figure 13–5. *Copy the crosshair.png (for face overlay) to your project.*

Next, we need to create a class to hold the logic for our facial recognition routines. Let's call this class FaceDetectionLayer. Create another class using the CCNode template and make sure it also is a subclass of CCLayer. This file should be named FaceDetectionLayer.m.

Now, because I'm a clean freak, I'm going to make a quick change to the default setup and remove some more files we aren't going to use. Remove HelloWorldLayer.h and HelloWorldLayer.m. You can permanently delete the files when prompted.

Open FaceDetectionLayer.h in Xcode, and let's start building.

Setting Up the Main Scene

Removing HelloWorldLayer was great for cleanup purposes, but it left us without a main scene in our project. At this point, the project won't build. We have a reference to the HelloWorldLayer scene in our AppDelegate.

You should have FaceDetectionLayer.h open in Xcode. Import the HUDLayer.h header so we can reference that later in the project. Create a private variable to reference the HUD layer class called _hud. Also, declare a static method to return the scene object and create a new method called initWithHUD like we did in the example from Chapter 7.

Your new FaceDetectionLayer.h file should look like Listing 13–1.

Listing 13–1. *Updated FaceDetectionLayer.h*

```
#import <Foundation/Foundation.h>
#import "cocos2d.h"
#import "HUDLayer.h"

@interface FaceDetectionLayer : CCLayer {
    HUDLayer *_hud;
}

+ (CCScene *)scene;
- (id)initWithHUD:(HUDLayer *)hud;

@end
```

Switch to FaceDetectionLayer.m. Add the method from Listing 13–2.

Listing 13–2. *Static Scene Method*

```
+ (CCScene *)scene {
    CCScene *scene = [CCScene node];

    HUDLayer *hud = [HUDLayer node];
    [scene addChild:hud z:1];

    FaceDetectionLayer *layer = [[[FaceDetectionLayer alloc] initWithHUD:hud]
autorelease];
    [scene addChild:layer];

    return scene;
}
```

This method should look familiar (unless you skipped Chapter 7). We are creating a new scene for cocos2D. Then, we create an additional instance of the HUDLayer with a z index greater than our main scene. This will allow for us to easily overlay the camera view (which will handle face detection) with some useful graphics like the crosshair PNG file or textual information about the target's mood (happy, sad, neutral).

Finally, we call the initWithHUD method. Speaking of which, we need to add that code as well. Add the method from Listing 13–3, just after the static scene method.

Listing 13–3. *initWithHUD Method*

```
- (id)initWithHUD:(HUDLayer *)hud {
    if (self = [super init]) {
        _hud = hud;
    }
    return self;
}
```

This method simply takes the place of the default init method the cocos2D template provides. We are creating our own layer with the HUD instance instead of the base layer on its own.

There is one last item to add to FaceDetectionLayer.m. It's the dealloc method. Add the method from Listing 13–4 to the base of the implementation file.

Listing 13–4. *dealloc Method*

```
- (void)dealloc {
    [super dealloc];
}
```

If you try to build the project now, you should still receive an error. It'll be some sort of mach-o-link error about the reference to HelloWorldLayer in your AppDelegate class. Open AppDelegate.m in Xcode and change the HelloWorldLayer import statement to now import FaceDetectionLayer.h.

Find the code in Listing 13–5 and replace it with the code in Listing 13–6.

Listing 13–5. *Find This . . .*

```
// Run the intro Scene
 [[CCDirector sharedDirector] runWithScene: [HelloWorldLayer scene]];
```

Listing 13–6. *Replace with This . . .*

```
// Run the intro Scene
 [[CCDirector sharedDirector] runWithScene: [FaceDetectionLayer scene]];
```

Your project should be building with no errors at this point. There is still absolutely no functionality here, but we are at least ready to start moving forward.

I should point out that some of what we just added isn't actually going to be needed in the end application. This is the point in the project where a typical application might start off. We have a CCNode class that has a static method for returning our main theme. However, we need to do things a bit differently in this example. When we end up removing some of the code we just added later on, this will make more sense.

Enabling the Camera

I'm sure you're waiting to see the camera view, so let's get to it. Open AppDelegate.h in Xcode. Import the AVFoundation header and the FaceDetectionLayer header. Next, nominate the AppDelegate as an AVCaptureVideoDataOutputSampleBufferDelegate.

We also need to declare a private AVCaptureSession variable called _session and create a void method called setupCaptureSession that will be used to store the preferences for our capture session.

Your modified AppDelegate.h file should look like Listing 13–7.

Listing 13–7. *AppDelegate.h After Updates*

```
#import <UIKit/UIKit.h>
#import <AVFoundation/AVFoundation.h>
#import "FaceDetectionLayer.h"

@class RootViewController;

@interface AppDelegate : NSObject <UIApplicationDelegate,
AVCaptureVideoDataOutputSampleBufferDelegate> {
    UIWindow          *window;
    RootViewController *viewController;
```

```
        AVCaptureSession *_session;
}

@property (nonatomic, retain) UIWindow *window;
- (void)setupCaptureSession;

@end
```

Switch over to AppDelegate.m. You can now remove the reference to
FaceDetectionLayer, as we have it on our header file. Find the section of code shown in
Listing 13–8. Replace it with the code shown in Listing 13–9.

Listing 13–8. *Find This . . .*

```
EAGLView *glView = [EAGLView viewWithFrame:[window bounds]
                 pixelFormat:kEAGLColorFormatRGB565 // kEAGLColorFormatRGBA8
        depthFormat:0                               // GL_DEPTH_COMPONENT16_OES
        ];
```

Listing 13–9. *Replace with This . . .*

```
EAGLView *glView = [EAGLView viewWithFrame:[window bounds]
                 pixelFormat: kEAGLColorFormatRGBA8 // kEAGLColorFormatRGBA8
        depthFormat:0                               // GL_DEPTH_COMPONENT16_OES
        ];
```

We discussed this briefly in Chapter 7 as well. We need to change the default
pixelFormat if we want to overlay our application layers on the camera instead of a
static background class.

I'm going to add a small utility method here to make debugging easier. If you're testing
this in a crowd somewhere or have plenty of test subjects to which to point your iPad
camera, you can skip this step. Otherwise, the lone wolf coder might benefit from using
the front-facing camera for this example. Add the code from Listing 13–10 above the
dealloc method.

Listing 13–10. *Check for Front-Facing Camera*

```
-(AVCaptureDevice *)frontFacingCameraIfAvailable
{
    NSArray *videoDevices = [AVCaptureDevice devicesWithMediaType:AVMediaTypeVideo];
    AVCaptureDevice *captureDevice = nil;
    for (AVCaptureDevice *device in videoDevices)
    {
        if (device.position == AVCaptureDevicePositionFront)
        {
            captureDevice = device;
            break;
        }
    }

    if ( ! captureDevice)
    {
        captureDevice = [AVCaptureDevice defaultDeviceWithMediaType:AVMediaTypeVideo];
    }

    return captureDevice;
```

}

This method simply checks for the front-facing camera and returns a reference to it, if it exists. If it does not exist, it returns the rear-facing camera. We will use this method when setting the capture device.

In the header file, we declared a method called setupCaptureSession. Let's create that now. Add the method from Listing 13–11 just below the frontFacingCameraIfAvailable method we just added.

Listing 13–11. *Set Up the CaptureSession*

```
- (void)setupCaptureSession
{
    NSError *error = nil;

    // Create the session.
    _session = [[AVCaptureSession alloc] init];

    // Configure the session to produce lower resolution video frames, if your
    // processing algorithm can cope. We'll specify medium quality for the
    // chosen device.
    _session.sessionPreset = AVCaptureSessionPresetMedium;

    // Find a suitable AVCaptureDevice.
    AVCaptureDevice *device = [self frontFacingCameraIfAvailable];/*[AVCaptureDevice

defaultDeviceWithMediaType:AVMediaTypeVideo];*/

    // Create a device input with the device and add it to the session.
    AVCaptureDeviceInput *input = [AVCaptureDeviceInput deviceInputWithDevice:device
                                                                        error:&error];
    if (!input) {
        // Handling the error appropriately.
    }
    [_session addInput:input];

    // Create a VideoDataOutput and add it to the session.
    AVCaptureVideoDataOutput *output = [[AVCaptureVideoDataOutput alloc] init];
    [_session addOutput:output];

    // Configure your output.
    dispatch_queue_t queue = dispatch_queue_create("chapter13", NULL);
    [output setSampleBufferDelegate:self queue:queue];
    dispatch_release(queue);

    // Specify the pixel format.
    output.videoSettings =
    [NSDictionary dictionaryWithObject:
     [NSNumber numberWithInt:kCVPixelFormatType_32BGRA]
                               forKey:(id)kCVPixelBufferPixelFormatTypeKey];


    // If you wish to cap the frame rate to a known value, such as 15 fps, set
    // minFrameDuration.

    //output.minFrameDuration = CMTimeMake(1, 15);
```

```
    // Start the session running to start the flow of data.
    [_session startRunning];
}
```

Some of this code is straight from the Apple developer's documentation. Let's walk through it from the top. After we set up a placeholder for any unforeseen errors, we create a new instance of AVCaptureSession. As we discussed in Chapter 6, this class is used for capturing video frames from the camera. It's a bit more flexible than displaying the UIImagePicker to the user.

Next, we use the utility method we created earlier to detect whether there is a front-facing camera available. If you don't have one, or you actually are testing this app in a crowd, I left the default option in the code comments for you to use. Using our camera device, we set up the AVCaptureDeviceInput object and add the input to our AVCaptureSession.

We are also going to use the video output in this example. So, we next allocate a new AVCaptureVideoDataOutput object and add that to our AVCaptureSession.

This next step is new for us. We need to set up a dispatch_queue_t ivar to hold our queued up video frames. We aren't discussing GCD (Grand Central Dispatch) in this example, but it would be interesting to extend this chapter to use GCD instead of the normal dispatch_queue_t ivar we have set up.

Finally, we set the pixelFormat of our AVCaptureVideoDataOutput instance, and then we can finally start the capture session.

So, I think we're caught up. Find the last line of the applicationDidFinishLaunching method and add the code from Listing 3-12.

Listing 13–12. *Call Our New Method*

```
[self setupCaptureSession];
```

If you run the application now, you'll just see the black screen. This is because our background was never set to transparent. Find the line of code shown in Listing 13–13. It's located in the middle of the applicationDidFinishLaunching method.

Listing 13–13. *Find This Section . . .*

```
// make the View Controller a child of the main window
 [window addSubview: viewController.view];
```

After that line, we're going to set our view to be transparent so we can see the camera view underneath. Before we can do that, declare a private variable called _cameraView of type UIView in the AppDelegate.h file. Actually, while you're there, also add an instance of UIImageView called _imageView. Then, switch back to AppDelegate.m and add the code from Listing 13–14 just below where you located Listing 13–13.

Listing 13–14. *Set View to Be Transparent*

```
// Set view to be transparent.
    [CCDirector sharedDirector].openGLView.backgroundColor = [UIColor clearColor];
    [CCDirector sharedDirector].openGLView.opaque = NO;
```

```
glClearColor(0.0, 0.0, 0.0, 0.0);

// Prepare the overlay view and add it to the window.
_cameraView = [[UIView alloc] initWithFrame:[[UIScreen mainScreen] bounds]];
_cameraView.opaque = NO;
_cameraView.backgroundColor = [UIColor clearColor];

[window addSubview:_cameraView];

_imageView = [[UIImageView alloc] initWithFrame:[[UIScreen mainScreen] bounds]];
[_cameraView addSubview:_imageView];

[window bringSubviewToFront:viewController.view];
```

We start out by setting the backgroundColor and opaque attribute of the sharedDirector from our singleton CCDirector class so that both settings are transparent to the screen.

Go ahead and run the project as it stands. When we approached a cocos2D project like this using the UIImagePickerViewController, we used the same steps and we were able to start building on layers above the camera view. However, as you'll notice when you run the application, we are still getting a full black screen. This is because (as you'll remember from Chapter 6) there are two steps involved with utilizing the AVCaptureSession: We queue up the images from the buffer, but we also need to actually do something with those images.

To access images from the buffer, we can use the delegate method called didOutputSampleBuffer from the AVCaptureVideoDataOutputSampleBufferDelegate class. This method allows us to pull images from the buffer as they are captured.

Before we introduce the delegate method, switch over to AppDelegate.h again and declare a BOOL flag called _settingImage so we can keep track of when we are in the middle of this process. Add the utility method from Listing 13–15 to your implementation file.

Listing 13–15. *setImageToView Method*

```
-(void)setImageToView:(UIImage*)image {
    _imageView.image = image;
    _settingImage = NO;
}
```

*There isn't a lot to this method. It simply sets the UIImageView to the image sent to the method. Let's link this up to the delegate method that receives the buffered images. Add the methods from Listing 13–16 just below the setImageToView method. Facial recognition:camera:**Listing 13–16.** Methods for Pulling the Image off the Buffer*

```
- (UIImage *) imageFromSampleBuffer:(CMSampleBufferRef) sampleBuffer
{
    // Get a CMSampleBuffer's Core Video image buffer for the media data
    CVImageBufferRef imageBuffer = CMSampleBufferGetImageBuffer(sampleBuffer);
    // Lock the base address of the pixel buffer
    CVPixelBufferLockBaseAddress(imageBuffer, 0);

    // Get the number of bytes per row for the pixel buffer
    void *baseAddress = CVPixelBufferGetBaseAddress(imageBuffer);

    // Get the number of bytes per row for the pixel buffer
    size_t bytesPerRow = CVPixelBufferGetBytesPerRow(imageBuffer);
```

```objc
    // Get the pixel buffer width and height
    size_t width = CVPixelBufferGetWidth(imageBuffer);
    size_t height = CVPixelBufferGetHeight(imageBuffer);

    // Create a device-dependent RGB color space
    CGColorSpaceRef colorSpace = CGColorSpaceCreateDeviceRGB();

    // Create a bitmap graphics context with the sample buffer data
    CGContextRef context = CGBitmapContextCreate(baseAddress, width, height, 8,
                                        bytesPerRow, colorSpace,
kCGBitmapByteOrder32Little | kCGImageAlphaPremultipliedFirst);
    // Create a Quartz image from the pixel data in the bitmap graphics context
    CGImageRef quartzImage = CGBitmapContextCreateImage(context);
    // Unlock the pixel buffer
    CVPixelBufferUnlockBaseAddress(imageBuffer,0);

    // Free up the context and color space
    CGContextRelease(context);
    CGColorSpaceRelease(colorSpace);

    // Create an image object from the Quartz image
    UIImage *image = [UIImage imageWithCGImage:quartzImage];

    // Release the Quartz image
    CGImageRelease(quartzImage);

    return (image);
}

- (void)captureOutput:(AVCaptureOutput *)captureOutput
didOutputSampleBuffer:(CMSampleBufferRef)sampleBuffer
fromConnection:(AVCaptureConnection *)connection
{
    UIImage *image = [self imageFromSampleBuffer:sampleBuffer];

    if(_settingImage == NO){
        _settingImage = YES;
        [NSThread detachNewThreadSelector:@selector(setImageToView:) toTarget:self
withObject:image];
    }
}
```

The first method we copied is, again, straight from the Apple developer documentation. This method returns a UIImage object from the CMSampleBufferRef buffer. We call that from the first line in our didOutputSampleBuffer delegate method. Next, in the didOutputSampleBuffer method, we check to see whether we are already in the process of setting an image for our UIImageView. If we aren't, we detach a new thread for the setImageToView utility method we created earlier.

Run the project again. The video is showing, but not quite in the way we would expect. My screen is shown in Figure 13–6.

Figure 13–6. *We're sideways!* ☹

Use the digital overlay from the cocos2D template for reference. For this example (although it will rotate when we're finished) I'm testing in Landscape Right mode for all the screen shots.

Okay, so we need to reorient things by 90 degrees and keep the image from stretching. Add the utility method from Listing 13–17 to AppDelegate.m. Make sure you put this above the setImageToView method or you will get a warning message when you try to compile the project.

Listing 13–17. *rotateImage Utility Method*

```
-(UIImage *) rotateImage:(UIImage*)image orientation:(UIImageOrientation) orient {
    CGImageRef imgRef = image.CGImage;
    CGAffineTransform transform = CGAffineTransformIdentity;
    //UIImageOrientation orient = image.imageOrientation;
    CGFloat scaleRatio = 1;
    CGFloat width = image.size.width;
    CGFloat height = image.size.height;
    CGSize imageSize = image.size;
    CGRect bounds = CGRectMake(0, 0, width, height);
    CGFloat boundHeight;

    switch(orient) {
        case UIImageOrientationUp:
            transform = CGAffineTransformIdentity;
            break;
        case UIImageOrientationUpMirrored:
            transform = CGAffineTransformMakeTranslation(imageSize.width, 0.0);
            transform = CGAffineTransformScale(transform, -1.0, 1.0);
            break;
        case UIImageOrientationDown:
```

```
                transform = CGAffineTransformMakeTranslation(imageSize.width,
imageSize.height);
                transform = CGAffineTransformRotate(transform, M_PI);
                break;
        case UIImageOrientationDownMirrored:
            transform = CGAffineTransformMakeTranslation(0.0, imageSize.height);
            transform = CGAffineTransformScale(transform, 1.0, -1.0);
            break;
        case UIImageOrientationLeftMirrored:
            boundHeight = bounds.size.height;
            bounds.size.height = bounds.size.width;
            bounds.size.width = boundHeight;
                transform = CGAffineTransformMakeTranslation(imageSize.height,
imageSize.height);
            transform = CGAffineTransformScale(transform, -1.0, 1.0);
            transform = CGAffineTransformRotate(transform, 3.0 * M_PI / 2.0);
            break;
        case UIImageOrientationLeft:
            boundHeight = bounds.size.height;
            bounds.size.height = bounds.size.width;
            bounds.size.width = boundHeight;
            transform = CGAffineTransformMakeTranslation(0.0, imageSize.width);
            transform = CGAffineTransformRotate(transform, 3.0 * M_PI / 2.0);
            break;
        case UIImageOrientationRightMirrored:
            boundHeight = bounds.size.height;
            bounds.size.height = bounds.size.width;
            bounds.size.width = boundHeight;
            transform = CGAffineTransformMakeScale(-1.0, 1.0);
            transform = CGAffineTransformRotate(transform, M_PI / 2.0);
            break;
        case UIImageOrientationRight:
            boundHeight = bounds.size.height;
            bounds.size.height = bounds.size.width;
            bounds.size.width = boundHeight;
            transform = CGAffineTransformMakeTranslation(imageSize.height, 0.0);
            transform = CGAffineTransformRotate(transform, M_PI / 2.0);
            break;
        default:
            [NSException raise:NSInternalInconsistencyException format:@"Invalid image
orientation"];
    }
    UIGraphicsBeginImageContext(bounds.size);
    CGContextRef context = UIGraphicsGetCurrentContext();
    if (orient == UIImageOrientationRight || orient == UIImageOrientationLeft) {
        CGContextScaleCTM(context, -scaleRatio, scaleRatio);
        CGContextTranslateCTM(context, -height, 0);
    } else {
        CGContextScaleCTM(context, scaleRatio, -scaleRatio);
        CGContextTranslateCTM(context, 0, -height);
    }
    CGContextConcatCTM(context, transform);
    CGContextDrawImage(UIGraphicsGetCurrentContext(), CGRectMake(0, 0, width, height),
imgRef);
    UIImage *imageCopy = UIGraphicsGetImageFromCurrentImageContext();
    UIGraphicsEndImageContext();
```

```
        return imageCopy;
}
```

We saw pieces of this method back in Chapter 7. Basically, we are checking the device's rotation, then reorienting and rescaling the image accordingly. Adjust the setImageToView method as shown in Listing 13–18.

Listing 13–18. *Updated setImageToView Method*

```
-(void)setImageToView:(UIImage*)image {
    UIImage * capturedImage = [self rotateImage:image
orientation:UIImageOrientationLeftMirrored ];
    _imageView.image = capturedImage;
    _settingImage = NO;
}
```

Instead of just setting the UIImage, this method gets passed. We are first rotating it properly using the utility method we just created. Then we set the returned (and adjusted) UIImage back to the caller.

Run the project again. You will see much better results. The screenshot of my iPad is shown in Figure 13–7.

Figure 13–7. *We're NOT sideways!* ☺

So, the world is right side up again. Next, what do we do with this image now that we have captured it and oriented it correctly? Remember, the goal here is to send the image from the camera buffer to face.com and get back the coordinates of any faces found in the picture.

We have to decide on an approach to this feature. There are a number of ways to tackle it, each with its own set of advantages and drawbacks. First, let's review the face.com

API and required parameters so we can make a decision on how we want to handle sending the image.

Face.com API

The face.com API is a surprisingly straightforward REST API that takes a multipart form upload with the raw data of the image you want to analyze in the body of the request.

We're going to be using only one call from the face.com API. The `faces.detect` call returns tags for detected faces in one or more photos, with geometric information of the tag, eyes, nose, and mouth, as well as various attributes such as gender, is wearing glasses, and is smiling.

The usage notes on the call (from the online documentation) include the following:

- All coordinates are provided in percent values to support any photo scale. Photo height and width (vs. tag height/width) are provided in pixels. Yaw, roll, and pitch are provided on the –90 degrees to 90 degrees scale.

- The maximum width or height of a photo is 900 pixels. You may POST or send links to higher-size photos, but those will be resized internally to improve performance.

- Every tag returned contains a set of attributes. The most important of them is the face attribute. It contains the confidence level of that tag being a face. Yada, yada, don't use tags with less than 50 percent confidence.

- Face detection is a prerequisite step in adding training-set data for a user to the recognition index. (We won't be doing this.)

The API is also rate limited. At the time of this writing, the limit was 5,000 requests per minute from the same application. So, I think we'll be fine for this example.

The REST URL for this call is `http://api.face.com/faces/detect.[format]`. For us, we will be setting the format equal to JSON. The input parameters for the POST request are described in Table 13–1.

Table 13–1. *Parameters for faces.detect Call*

Required?	Name	Description
Yes	api_key	Your face.com API Key
Yes	api_secret	Your face.com API Secret
Yes	urls	A comma-separated list of JPG photos
No	[no name]	Raw image data from photo (replaces need for urls param)

Required?	Name	Description
No	detector	Sets the face detector mode: Normal or Aggressive. Aggressive mode may find more faces, but is slower
No	attributes	All, none, or a list of comma-separated attributes
No	format	"json" or "xml" (we'll use json)
No	callback	JavaScript method to wrap a json-formatted response (JSONP support)
No	callback_url	Async callback URL

If you look through the parameter list, this call actually turns out to be fairly simple. Our options are to upload the image somewhere and send a reference URL so face.com can fetch it and analyze it, or we can post the raw image data directly in the POST request. Without actually testing this theory, I'd imagine that uploading it somewhere else, then having face.com download it and analyze it is far less efficient than uploading it directly in the POST request. So, let's go that route.

Now that we have an approach, let's figure out timing. We already have the UIImage object, which we could convert to JPEG and attach to the POST request as it comes in, but that could easily lead to requests running on top of themselves and a bunch of unnecessary CPU time. I'm going to recommend we use an NSTimer to grab the screen image periodically; then send it on a background thread to face.com for analyzing. When it's returned, we'll draw on the HUD layer to provide information on the attributes found, and we'll fade into the background until the next request is sent.

Using the ASI-HTTP-Request Library

We're going to need that library we downloaded earlier in the chapter before we can move too much further ahead. Find the downloaded archive we stored earlier. Copy the following files to your project. Because I like my project structure nice and clean, I created another Group called ASI to store these files.

- ASIHTTPRequestConfig.h
- ASIHTTPRequestDelegate.h
- ASIProgressDelegate.h
- ASICacheDelegate.h
- ASIHTTPRequest.h
- ASIHTTPRequest.m
- ASIDataCompressor.h
- ASIDataCompressor.m

- ASIDataDecompressor.h

- ASIDataDecompressor.m

- ASIFormDataRequest.h

- ASIInputStream.h

- ASIInputStream.m

- ASIFormDataRequest.m

- ASINetworkQueue.h

- ASINetworkQueue.m

- ASIDownloadCache.h

- ASIDownloadCache.m

- ASIAuthenticationDialog.h

- ASIAuthenticationDialog.m

- Reachability.h (in the External/Reachability folder)

- Reachability.m (in the External/Reachability folder)

The library also requires a few references, but since I was thinking ahead, we added them earlier in the chapter.

Let's take a step back for a moment and think about the best placement for the HTTP POST request. Remember, cocos2D applications, like any other iOS application, are built on view hierarchies. We have stacked two of our own scenes on top of the OpenGL view and camera layer. Take a look at Figure 13–8 for reference. (This is a logical model, not an exact representation of the classes.)

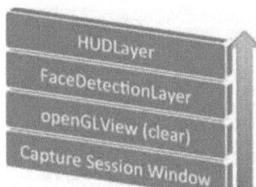

Figure 13–8. *The logical hierarchy of our scene shows the stacked views.*

The POST request to face.com will be executed on a separate thread. Because of this, we will want the return code to be parsed at a layer that can interact with the HUD layer. The HUD layer is where we will be actually creating the images and text that will overlay the interface, so we will have methods exposed to handle those actions.

It looks like the best candidate to handle our POST request would be the FaceDetectionLayer. If we can handle the POST request there, we don't have to traverse two layers from our AppDelegate.

Let's create the method to send the POST request and NSLog the response. Then, we'll create our NSTimer and finish by parsing our JSON response.

Creating the POST Request Method

Open FaceDetectionLayer.m in Xcode. Import the ASIFormDataRequest.h and AppDelegate.h headers. Declare a private BOOL called _sendingRequest to keep track of when a POST request is in process and create a void method called facialRecognitionRequest that takes a UIImage as a parameter. Your updated FaceDetectionLayer.h file should look like Listing 13–19.

Listing 13–19. *Updated FaceDetectionLayer.h*

```
#import <Foundation/Foundation.h>
#import "cocos2d.h"
#import "HUDLayer.h"
#import "ASIFormDataRequest.h"
#import "AppDelegate.h"

@interface FaceDetectionLayer : CCLayer {
    HUDLayer * _hud;
    BOOL _sendingRequest;
}

+ (CCScene *)scene;
- (id)initWithHUD:(HUDLayer *)hud;
- (void)facialRecognitionRequest:(UIImage *)image;
@end
```

Switch over to FaceDetectionLayer.m. Create the method as shown in Listing 13–20.

Listing 13–20. *facialRecognitionRequest Method*

```
- (void)facialRecognitionRequest:(UIImage *)image {
    NSLog(@"Image width = %f height = %f",image.size.width, image.size.height);

    if (!_sendingRequest) {
        _sendingRequest = YES;

        NSAutoreleasePool * pool = [[NSAutoreleasePool alloc] init];

        NSData * imageData = UIImageJPEGRepresentation(image, 90);

        NSURL * url = [NSURL URLWithString:@"http://api.face.com/faces/detect.json"];

        ASIFormDataRequest *request = [ASIFormDataRequest requestWithURL:url];
        [request addPostValue:@"your face.com api_key" forKey:@"api_key"];
        [request addPostValue:@"your face.com api_secret" forKey:@"api_secret"];
        [request addData:imageData withFileName:@"image.jpg"
andContentType:@"image/jpeg" forKey:@"filename"];

        [request startSynchronous];

        NSError *error = [request error];
        if (!error) {
            NSString *response = [request responseString];

            NSLog(@"Response: %@",response);
        } else {
```

```
        NSLog(@"Error: %d",[error code]);
    }

    _sendingRequest = NO;

    [pool drain];
  }
}
```

Starting at the top of this method, we are first checking to see if another call is in progress, by referencing the _sendingRequest BOOL. If there isn't a current call in progress, we set the flag to YES to prevent any other calls (on separate threads) to collide with this transaction.

Next, we allocate an NSAutoreleasePool. The NSAutoreleasePool class (from the Apple developer documentation) is used to support cocoa's reference-counted memory management system. An autorelease pool stores objects that are sent a release message when the pool itself is drained.

In a reference-counted environment (as opposed to one that uses garbage collection), an NSAutoreleasePool object contains objects that have received an autorelease message and, when drained, it sends a release message to each of those objects. Thus, sending autorelease instead of release to an object extends the lifetime of that object at least until the pool itself is drained (it may be longer if the object is subsequently retained). An object can be put into the same pool several times, in which case it receives a release message for each time it was put into the pool.

After we have our NSAutoreleasePool in place, we create an NSData object to hold the raw image data from the JPEG image. We set up our NSURL REST target for face.com, our HTTP POST values (one of which is the raw image data) and we start a synchronous call to face.com.

We'll add the JSON parsing logic a little later. For now, we are just logging the output.

To send the POST request from FaceDetectionLayer, we're going to need to reference that class from our AppDelegate. If you do that now, we will be creating cyclical dependencies between the two headers. This is easy to fix, as our solution isn't all that complicated yet. Move the import AppDelegate.h statement from FaceDetectionLayer.h to FaceDetectionLayer.m and we won't experience this issue. If you run into a compiler error that starts with expected specifier-qualifier-list before… you still have the cyclical reference somewhere else in the project.

Let's create the NSTimer and the process to send the UIImage object from our AppDelegate to the FaceDetectionLayer, so we're ready for the POST request.

Creating the NSTimer

Open AppDelegate.h in Xcode. Create a private variable of type FaceDetectionLayer called _layer, and another private variable of type NSTimer called _timer. The changes we made to the header are shown in Listing 13–21.

Listing 13–21. *Changes to AppDelegate.h*

```
@interface AppDelegate : NSObject <UIApplicationDelegate,
AVCaptureVideoDataOutputSampleBufferDelegate> {
    …

    FaceDetectionLayer *_layer;
    NSTimer *_timer;
}

…
```

Switch over to AppDelegate.m. Find the line shown in Listing 13–22.

Listing 13–22. *Find This Line in AppDelegate.m . . .*

```
[[CCDirector sharedDirector] runWithScene: [FaceDetectionLayer scene]];
```

This line used the CCDirector singleton to launch a default FaceDetectionLayer scene. We have a static method in FaceDetectionLayer that we are using to create our scene. That method launches the scene with the HUDLayer. To keep from managing too many instances or creating another set of singleton classes, we're going to move some of our functionality from the static scene method to our AppDelegate.

Replace the line from Listing 13–22 with the code from Listing 13–23.

Listing 13–23. *Launch the FaceDetectionLayer in a Different Way*

```
CCScene *scene = [CCScene node];
HUDLayer *hud = [HUDLayer node];
[scene addChild:hud z:1];
_layer = [[[FaceDetectionLayer alloc] initWithHUD:hud] autorelease];
 [scene addChild:_layer];

 [[CCDirector sharedDirector] runWithScene: scene];
```

This code was taken from our static scene method in the FaceDetectionLayer class. If you run the application now, it should look just about the same. You will see the camera view, oriented correctly, taking up the full screen.

Add the method from Listing 13–24 to AppDelegate.m.

Listing 13–24. *Add the Background Method*

```
-(void)backgroundRequest:(UIImage * ) image{
    NSAutoreleasePool * pool = [[NSAutoreleasePool alloc] init];

    UIInterfaceOrientation orient =  [UIApplication
sharedApplication].statusBarOrientation;
    UIImage * rotatedImage = image;
    switch (orient) {
        case UIInterfaceOrientationPortrait:
            NSLog(@"Device orientation portrait");
            break;
        case UIInterfaceOrientationPortraitUpsideDown:
            NSLog(@"Device orientation portrait upside down");
            break;
        case UIInterfaceOrientationLandscapeLeft:
```

```
        rotatedImage = [self rotateImage:image orientation:
UIImageOrientationRight];
            NSLog(@"Device orientation landscape left");
            break;
        case UIInterfaceOrientationLandscapeRight:
            rotatedImage = [self rotateImage:image orientation: UIImageOrientationLeft];
            NSLog(@"Device orientation landscape right");
            break;
    };

    [_layer facialRecognitionRequest:rotatedImage];

    [pool drain];
}
```

This method will be the caller for the facialRecognitionRequest method we created earlier in our FaceDetectionLayer class. We are, again, using an NSAutoReleasePool to manage the automatic release of objects from memory. Next, we check the orientation of the device. Again, I'm using Landscape Right for all my testing, but this method should suffice to reorient the image properly for other orientations. Basically, we have to do this so that we send face.com the image right side up. If we send the image in sideways or upside down, face.com won't be able to recognize the faces in the picture.

When we're done rotating the image, we send the updated image object to the FaceDetectionLayer's facialRecognitionRequest method. Okay, let's create the timer callback, and then we'll create our NSTimer. The callback will be the event that is fired each time the timer expires (I didn't mean for that to rhyme, it's just the way it is). This should be a simple method. We simply need to call our new backgroundRequest method every few seconds on a new thread. Copy the method from Listing 13–25 just above the backgroundRequest method.

Listing 13–25. *Timer Callback Method*

```
-(void) timerCallback {
    [NSThread detachNewThreadSelector:@selector(backgroundRequest:) toTarget:self
withObject:_imageView.image];
}
```

We are simply detaching a new thread to run the backgroundRequest method and assigning the delegate to self.

So, the last step to this process is to start the timer. In the last line of the applicationDidFinishLaunching method, we start our AVCaptureSession. Just before that line, add the code from Listing 13–26.

Listing 13–26. *Start a Five-Second Timer*

```
_timer = [NSTimer scheduledTimerWithTimeInterval:5.0 target:self
selector:@selector(timerCallback) userInfo:nil repeats:YES];
```

The code in bold shows you where to reset the timing in between executions. If you are running a very slow Internet connection, you might need to increase this setting.

If you run this project now, and let it run for a few seconds, you should see something like Figure 13–9 in your debug console.

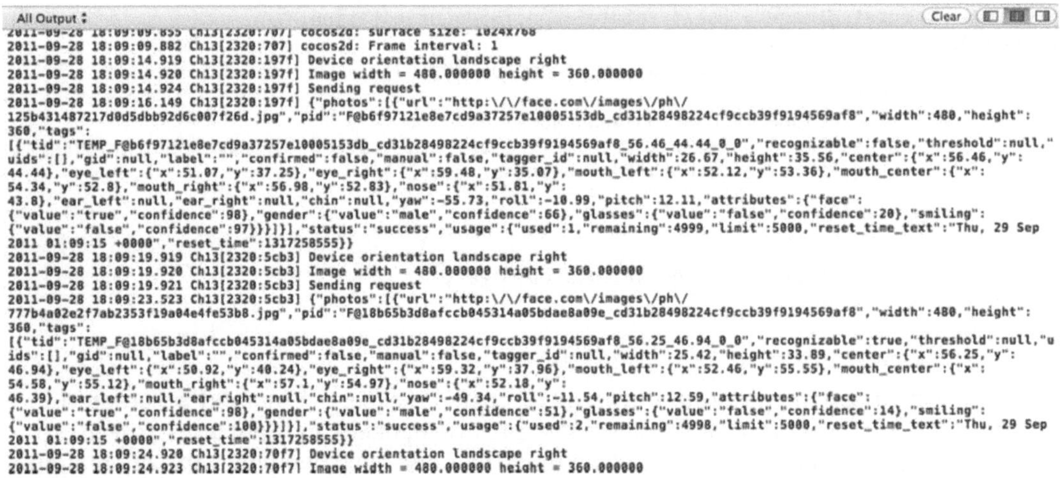

All Output ⁝   Clear ▢ ■ ▢
2011-09-28 18:09:09.855 Ch13[2320:707] cocos2d: Surface size: 1024x768
2011-09-28 18:09:09.882 Ch13[2320:707] cocos2d: Frame interval: 1
2011-09-28 18:09:14.919 Ch13[2320:197f] Device orientation landscape right
2011-09-28 18:09:14.920 Ch13[2320:197f] Image width = 480.000000 height = 360.000000
2011-09-28 18:09:14.924 Ch13[2320:197f] Sending request
2011-09-28 18:09:16.149 Ch13[2320:197f] {"photos":[{"url":"http:\/\/face.com\/images\/ph\/
125b431487217d0d5dbb92d6c007f26d.jpg","pid":"F@b6f97121e8e7cd9a37257e10005153db_cd31b28498224cf9ccb39f9194569af8","width":480,"height":
360,"tags":
[{"tid":"TEMP_F@b6f97121e8e7cd9a37257e10005153db_cd31b28498224cf9ccb39f9194569af8_56.46_44.44_0_0","recognizable":false,"threshold":null,"
uids":[],"gid":null,"label":"","confirmed":false,"manual":false,"tagger_id":null,"width":26.67,"height":35.56,"center":{"x":56.46,"y":
44.44},"eye_left":{"x":51.07,"y":37.25},"eye_right":{"x":59.48,"y":35.07},"mouth_left":{"x":52.12,"y":53.36},"mouth_center":{"x":
54.34,"y":52.8},"mouth_right":{"x":56.98,"y":52.83},"nose":{"x":51.81,"y":
43.8},"ear_left":null,"ear_right":null,"chin":null,"yaw":-55.73,"roll":-10.99,"pitch":12.11,"attributes":{"face":
{"value":"true","confidence":98},"gender":{"value":"male","confidence":66},"glasses":{"value":"false","confidence":20},"smiling":
{"value":"false","confidence":97}}}]}],"status":"success","usage":{"used":1,"remaining":4999,"limit":5000,"reset_time_text":"Thu, 29 Sep
2011 01:09:15 +0000","reset_time":1317258555}}
2011-09-28 18:09:19.919 Ch13[2320:5cb3] Device orientation landscape right
2011-09-28 18:09:19.920 Ch13[2320:5cb3] Image width = 480.000000 height = 360.000000
2011-09-28 18:09:19.921 Ch13[2320:5cb3] Sending request
2011-09-28 18:09:23.523 Ch13[2320:5cb3] {"photos":[{"url":"http:\/\/face.com\/images\/ph\/
777b4a02e2f7ab2353f19a04e4fe53b8.jpg","pid":"F@18b65b3d8afccb045314a05bdae8a09e_cd31b28498224cf9ccb39f9194569af8","width":480,"height":
360,"tags":
[{"tid":"TEMP_F@18b65b3d8afccb045314a05bdae8a09e_cd31b28498224cf9ccb39f9194569af8_56.25_46.94_0_0","recognizable":true,"threshold":null,"u
ids":[],"gid":null,"label":"","confirmed":false,"manual":false,"tagger_id":null,"width":25.42,"height":33.89,"center":{"x":56.25,"y":
46.94},"eye_left":{"x":50.92,"y":40.24},"eye_right":{"x":59.32,"y":37.96},"mouth_left":{"x":52.46,"y":55.55},"mouth_center":{"x":
54.58,"y":55.12},"mouth_right":{"x":57.1,"y":54.97},"nose":{"x":52.18,"y":
46.39},"ear_left":null,"ear_right":null,"chin":null,"yaw":-49.34,"roll":-11.54,"pitch":12.59,"attributes":{"face":
{"value":"true","confidence":98},"gender":{"value":"male","confidence":51},"glasses":{"value":"false","confidence":14},"smiling":
{"value":"false","confidence":100}}}]}],"status":"success","usage":{"used":2,"remaining":4998,"limit":5000,"reset_time_text":"Thu, 29 Sep
2011 01:09:15 +0000","reset_time":1317258555}}
2011-09-28 18:09:24.920 Ch13[2320:70f7] Device orientation landscape right
2011-09-28 18:09:24.923 Ch13[2320:70f7] Image width = 480.000000 height = 360.000000

Figure 13–9. The output shows the looping execution of face.com request.

Parsing the Output

Next, we need to parse the output from face.com. To do this, we're going to use the JSON-Framework library we downloaded from GitHub earlier in the chapter.

Find the directory where you unzipped the downloaded files. There is a subdirectory called **Classes**. Open that directory. As with the ASI-HTTP-Request library, organization in Xcode is a bit of a preference. I created a **Group** in my Xcode project called **JSON**, but this is not necessary. Copy all the files from the **Classes** directory into the Xcode project. Make sure you check the option to **Copy items into destination group's folder (if needed)**.

Open FaceDetectionLayer.h in Xcode and import the SBJson.h header. Switch over to FaceDetectionLayer.m and find the lines of code shown in Listing 13–27.

Listing 13–27. *Find This Section…*

```
if (!error) {
        NSString *response = [request responseString];
```

After the code in Listing 13–27, we're going to be adding the logic to parse the JSON response. Before we get started, let's take another look at the response from face.com. The sample reply from my execution is shown in Listing 13–28.

Listing 13–28. *Sample Reply from face.com*

```
{
    "photos":[
        {
            "url":"http:\/\/face.com\/images\/ph\/90e76f377f93e949df78b552903a48b0.jpg",
            "pid":"F@6f518683514fac2eebe8d749b6121cc3_cd31b28498224cf9ccb39f9194569af8",
            "width":480,
            "height":360,
            "tags":[
                {
```

```
"tid":"TEMP_F@6f518683514fac2eebe8d749b6121cc3_cd31b28498224cf9ccb39f9194569af8_62.50_41
.11_0_0",
                "recognizable":true,
                "threshold":null,
                "uids":[
                ],
                "gid":null,
                "label":"",
                "confirmed":false,
                "manual":false,
                "tagger_id":null,
                "width":28.75,
                "height":38.33,
                "center":{
                    "x":62.5,
                    "y":41.11
                },
                "eye_left":{
                    "x":58.63,
                    "y":30.98
                },
                "eye_right":{
                    "x":71.52,
                    "y":33.14
                },
                "mouth_left":{
                    "x":58.34,
                    "y":49.64
                },
                "mouth_center":{
                    "x":64.25,
                    "y":51.62
                },
                "mouth_right":{
                    "x":69.34,
                    "y":50.91
                },
                "nose":{
                    "x":66.49,
                    "y":44.14
                },
                "ear_left":null,
                "ear_right":null,
                "chin":null,
                "yaw":26.25,
                "roll":7.16,
                "pitch":-1.99,
                "attributes":{
                    "glasses":{
                        "value":"false",
                        "confidence":16
                    },
                    "smiling":{
                        "value":"true",
```

```
                            "confidence":96
                        },
                        "face":{
                            "value":"true",
                            "confidence":87
                        },
                        "gender":{
                            "value":"male",
                            "confidence":46
                        },
                        "mood":{
                            "value":"happy",
                            "confidence":51
                        },
                        "lips":{
                            "value":"parted",
                            "confidence":98
                        }
                    }
                }
            ]
        }
    ],
    "status":"success",
    "usage":{
        "used":31,
        "remaining":4969,
        "limit":5000,
        "reset_time_text":"Thu, 29 Sep 2011 02:40:10 +0000",
        "reset_time":1317264010
    }
}
```

I highlighted a few sections that we will need to finish this example. Let's start with trying to capture the status value.

Parsing JSON is quite simple thanks to the SBJson library. Let's start by creating a new SBJsonParser object then creating an NSDictionary from the JSON string we got back from face.com. Add the code from Listing 13–29, just after the code you found back in Listing 13–27.

Listing 13–29. *Identifying the Keys in Your JSON Array*

```
SBJsonParser *jsonParser = [SBJsonParser new];
NSDictionary *feed = [jsonParser objectWithString:response error:nil];
NSLog(@"RETURN: %@", [feed allKeys]);
```

Since we can convert the JSON string to an NSDictionary, it is usually a good idea to validate that the keys you expect to find in the root of the NSDictionary match what the parser thinks is in the root of the dictionary. We do this with the allKeys attribute of NSDictionary. If you run the project again with this added, you will see something similar to Figure 13–10 in the console.

```
2011-09-28 19:40:10.240 Ch13[2353:5dc7] RETURN: (
    status,
    photos,
    usage
)
```

Figure 13–10. *The console shows the allKeys return value.*

You can see that the status element (the one we are searching for) is available right from the top level of the dictionary. Because this is a single element, we can simply grab the value for that key and log it to the console. Add the code from Listing 13–30 just after logging the allKeys output.

Listing 13–30. *Log the Status Messages*

```
if ([[feed valueForKey:@"status"] isEqualToString:@"success"]) {
        NSLog(@"face.com request = success");
}
```

If you run the project again, you will see the success message in the console. We will continue adding to the body of this if block and capture the x,y, width, and height of the recognized face.

Add the code from Listing 13–31 inside the success block.

Listing 13–31. *Find the Location of the Face in the Picture*

```
double xPosition = [[[[[photo objectForKey:@"tags"] objectAtIndex:0]
valueForKey:@"center"] valueForKey:@"x"] doubleValue];
double yPosition = [[[[[photo objectForKey:@"tags"] objectAtIndex:0]
valueForKey:@"center"] valueForKey:@"y"] doubleValue];
NSString *mood = [[[[[photo objectForKey:@"tags"] objectAtIndex:0]
objectForKey:@"attributes"] objectForKey:@"mood"] valueForKey:@"value"];
NSDictionary *photo = [[feed objectForKey:@"photos"] objectAtIndex:0];
```

So, these lines parse the remaining JSON elements to find the values that we had bolded in Listing 13–28. We will use them to build out our HUD layer next.

Constructing Our HUD Layer

The application on its own, to this point, is very cool if you're the developer. However, from a user's perspective, we can't really tell what's happening. We are about to change that by adding some feedback through the HUD layer we created in the first part of this chapter. Remember, the HUD layer is transparent, but sits on top of the rest of the stack of scenes. So, we can overlay everything at this level.

Remember back in the introduction to this chapter, I mentioned things won't go as expected. That section starts here. You can skim it over if you'd prefer, but it's a small detour; so, follow along with the code, if you're up to it.

Open HUDLayer.h and declare the method shown in Listing 13–32.

Listing 13–32. *Load the Crosshair and Mood Label*

```
- (void)loadCrosshair:(NSString *)mood x:(double)x y:(double)y;
```

Switch over to HUDLayer.m and implement the loadCrosshair method from Listing 13–33.

Listing 13–33. *Implement the loadCrosshair Method*

```
- (void)loadCrosshair:(NSString *)mood x:(double)x y:(double)y {
    CGSize size = [[CCDirector sharedDirector] winSize];

    CCLabelTTF *label = [CCLabelTTF labelWithString:@"test" fontName:@"Marker Felt"
fontSize:48];
    // position the label on the center of the screen
    label.position =  ccp( size.width /2 , size.height/2 );
    // add the label as a child to this Layer
    [self addChild: label];

    CCSprite *crosshair = [CCSprite spriteWithFile:@"crosshair.png"
rect:CGRectMake(0,0,390,390)];
    crosshair.position = ccp((size.width * (x/100)), (size.height * (1 - (y/100))));
    [self addChild:crosshair];
}
```

We use a few basic functions in this method to add the PNG file to the screen and set up a label to display the user's mood. The label object's position attribute is set using the ccp macro from cocos2D. This macro creates an anchor point for us to use when placing the images on the screen. We are setting the position of the anchor point to the center of the screen (half of the width, half of the height).

Next, we load a sprite from the PNG file and place that on the screen. Face.com, as part of its response, gives us the position (center) of the face that was recognized. It is expressed in percentages of the screen so that you don't have to recalculate the pixels if you are sending scaled-down images (as we are in this chapter). Since the percentages are whole numbers, we divide them by 100 and create an anchor point for the sprite at the same position where face.com recognized a face.

Switch over to FaceDetectionLayer.m and find the code from Listing 13–31 (parses the mood, x, and y of the face.com request). Add the code from Listing 13–34 just after those lines.

Listing 13–34. *Invoke the loadCrosshair Method*

```
[_hud loadCrosshair:mood x:xPosition y:yPosition];
```

We are going to call our new method using our HUD layer. If you think back to the diagram where we stacked our views, this should work just fine. Run the project. The result should look something like Figure 13–11.

Figure 13–11. *Wait, that's not right!*

The good news is that the image appears to have been placed in the right spot. The bad news is that you can't see the image. It seems like an opaque block on the screen.

This is due to how OpenGL handles threading. We detached a thread to handle the HTTP request, and OpenGL wants us to interact with the screen through the main thread. There are ways around threading with OpenGL, and there are plenty of articles on the topic. This is a basic example of the need for more organized threads in a cocos2D application. If you would like to learn more about OpenGL and threading, check out Mike Smithwick's *Pro OpenGL for iOS* book from Apress.

Let's fix this issue. As it turns out, we really don't need a HUD layer for this application. Since our base logic was in the AppDelegate, our FaceDetectionLayer is acting as our HUD layer. Let's move the drawing function down a level in the stack, and use our main thread to invoke the change in the label on the screen.

Instead of creating the label and the sprite on the fly, let's make a property so we can access it outside of the class. Also, we'll need a property to reference our RootViewController.

Adjust the FaceDetectionLayer.h file as shown in Listing 13–35. I commented out the lines we will no longer need.

Listing 13–35. *Changes to FaceDetectionLayer*

```
#import <Foundation/Foundation.h>
#import "cocos2d.h"
#import "HUDLayer.h"
#import "ASIFormDataRequest.h"
#import "SBJson.h"
```

```
@interface FaceDetectionLayer : CCLayer {
    //HUDLayer *_hud;
    BOOL _sendingRequest;

    CCSprite *crosshair;
}

@property (retain) UIViewController * root;
@property (retain) CCLabelTTF * label;

//+ (CCScene *)scene;
//- (id)initWithHUD:(HUDLayer *)hud;
- (void)facialRecognitionRequest:(UIImage *)image;
@end
```

Switch back to FaceDetectionLayer.m and synthesize the new properties as shown in Listing 13–36.

Listing 13–36. *Synthesize New Properties*

```
@synthesize root;
@synthesize label = _label;
```

Comment out the scene and initWithHUD methods as well. We won't be using those any longer. Create a new init method with the code from Listing 13–37.

Listing 13–37. *New init Method*

```
-(id) init {
    if(self = [super init]){
        CGSize size = [[CCDirector sharedDirector] winSize];

        crosshair = [CCSprite spriteWithFile:@"crosshair.png" ];
        crosshair.position = ccp((size.width * (50.0/100)), (size.height * (1 -
(50.0/100))));
        crosshair.opacity = 0;
        [self addChild:crosshair];

        _label = [CCLabelTTF labelWithString:@"" fontName:@"Marker Felt" fontSize:48];
        _label.position = ccp( size.width /2 , size.height/2 );
        [self addChild: _label];
    }
    return self;
}
```

We are simply moving some of our HUDLayer code to the init method of the FaceDetectionLayer. The only real difference in this code is that we are not setting the string of the label just yet. We will do that from our RootViewController in a moment.

Replace the line from Listing 13–38 with the code from Listing 13–39.

Listing 13–38. *Find This Line . . .*

```
[_hud loadCrosshair:mood x:xPosition y:yPosition];
```

Listing 13–39. *Replace with This . . .*

```
CGSize size = [[CCDirector sharedDirector] winSize];
crosshair.opacity = 255;
```

```
crosshair.position = ccp((size.width * (xPosition/100)), (size.height * (1 -
(yPosition/100))));
 [root performSelectorOnMainThread:@selector(updateMood:) withObject:mood
waitUntilDone:YES];
```

Instead of sending the request to the HUDLayer class, we are moving the sprite using the ccp macro and sending the update for the label back to the main thread. The updateMood function doesn't exist yet. We will create that next.

Open RootViewController.h. Import the FaceDetectionLayer.h header and add the property and method shown in Listing 13–40.

Listing 13–40. *Updated RootViewController*

```
#import <UIKit/UIKit.h>
#import "FaceDetectionLayer.h"

@interface RootViewController : UIViewController {

}
@property (retain) FaceDetectionLayer* fdLayer;
-(void)updateMood:(NSString*)mood;
@end
```

Switch over to RootViewController.m and synthesize the property we just created. Then create the method from Listing 13–41.

Listing 13–41. *updateMood Method*

```
-(void)updateMood:(NSString *) mood {
    [[[self fdLayer] label] setString:mood];
}
```

Open AppDelegate.m in Xcode. Update the applicationDidFinishLaunching method with the code from Listing 13–42.

Listing 13–42. *Updated applicationDidFinishLaunching Method*

```
...
// Removes the startup flicker
 [self removeStartupFlicker];
// Run the intro Scene
CCScene *scene = [CCScene node];
_layer =[[[FaceDetectionLayer alloc] init] autorelease];
[scene addChild:_layer];
viewController.fdLayer = _layer;
_layer.root = viewController;
 [[CCDirector sharedDirector] runWithScene: scene];

_timer = [NSTimer scheduledTimerWithTimeInterval:5.0 target:self
selector:@selector(timerCallback) userInfo:nil repeats:YES];
[self setupCaptureSession];
}
```

Instead of running the initWithHUD method, we are using our new init method to instantiate our FaceDetectionLayer. The other difference in this code snippet is that we are setting the viewController's (RootViewController) fdLayer property to our FaceDetectionLayer.

If you run the project as is, you should see the correct overlay and mood label on the screen after the request has been parsed. I got a bit of help from my kids for this part. The results are shown in Figure 13–12 through Figure 13–14.

Take note of the mood label change between expressions. Face.com did a great job recognizing the expression between each request. Our program correctly moved the PNG file to the x,y coordinates of the face, and now that we moved some logic back to the main thread, things are looking good.

Figure 13–12. *Aodhan is happy!*

Figure 13–13. *Avery is angry!*

Figure 13–14. *Avery is surprised!*

The last thing we are going to build into the application is SMS functionality to notify customer service if an angry or sad face has been detected.

Keep in mind that if you wanted to extend this for a practical purpose, there may be more than one person in the camera's view. The only adjustment you'd need to make is to create a loop over all the returned photos from face.com's JSON response. We are hard-coding `objectAtIndex:0` to only pick up the first face recognized. So, if you wanted to analyze a crowd, that adjustment would be required.

Adding a Twilio Callout

Twilio uses REST to initiate an outbound call or SMS. One of the reasons we are using SMS is because it only requires the REST callout. We don't have to host any code on a web server. Add the method from Listing 13–43 to the FaceDetectionLayer.m file.

Listing 13–43. *Send the SMS*

```
- (void)sendSMS {
    NSAutoreleasePool * pool = [[NSAutoreleasePool alloc] init];

    NSLog(@"Sending request");
    NSString *accountSid = @"Your Account SID Here";
    NSString *authToken = @"Your AuthToken Here";
    NSString *urlString = [NSString
stringWithFormat:@"https://%@:%@@api.twilio.com/2010-04-01/Accounts/%@/SMS/Messages",
accountSid, authToken, accountSid];

    NSURL *url = [NSURL URLWithString:urlString];

    ASIFormDataRequest *request = [ASIFormDataRequest requestWithURL:url];
    [request addPostValue:@"Your TO Number Here" forKey:@"To"];
    [request addPostValue:@"Angry Face Detected" forKey:@"Body"];
    [request addPostValue:@"Valid Twilio Number" forKey:@"From"];

    [request startSynchronous];

    NSError *error = [request error];
    if (!error) {
        NSString *response = [request responseString];
        NSLog(@"%@",response);
    } else {
        NSLog(@"An error occured %d; %@",[error code], [request responseString]);
    }

    [pool drain];
}
```

That was much simpler. Twilio has, as you've just seen, a VERY simple API to add quick value to your application. You can reference this new function from the facialRecognitionRequest method. Just wrap it in a quick check to match the mood with "angry" and you should be all set.

The SMS is shown in Figure 13–15.

Figure 13–15. *SMS was sent successfully.*

Summary

This chapter was a lot of fun. We started as we did in Chapter 7, and created a HUD layer. After some experimentation, we realized that wasn't necessary. By following the step-by-step process, we learned about threading with OpenGL (which is the foundation for cocos2D).

We extended our example to create an AVCaptureSession and send the UIImages to the face.com REST API. We used two different open source libraries to add functionality to our demo. ASI-HTTP-Request helped us wrap the REST callout in a short amount of code, and the SBJson library helped us parse the responses from face.com.

We used cocos2D to overlay a sprite on the target's face, and a label with the mood returned from face.com. Finally, we used Twilio's simple REST API to alert customer service over SMS that an angry face was detected.

Before using the facial recognition examples in your own applications, you should check your local privacy laws. In certain regions, capturing or storing facial patterns may be a privacy violation.

I hope you learned a lot during the examples in this book. Please review the supplemental materials at the end of the book for some more helpful topics. Feel free to contact me on twitter @kylemroche, and on GitHub if you have any questions or feedback on the demonstrations.

Index